Jeanne Cortiel, Christine Hanke, Jan Simon Hutta, Colin Milburn (eds.)
Practices of Speculation

Culture & Theory | Volume 202

Jeanne Cortiel is Professor of American Studies at Bayreuth University. Her research interests include American science fiction, post-apocalyptic film, and global catastrophic risk in fiction.

Christine Hanke is Chair of Digital and Audiovisual Media at Bayreuth University and conducts research in the fields of media resistance, postcolonial studies, and image theory.

Jan Simon Hutta is Assistant Professor in the Cultural Geography Research Group at Bayreuth University. His research focuses on formations of power, affect and citizenship in Brazil, sexual and transgender politics, urban governmentality, and relations of subjectivity, movement and space.

Colin Milburn is Gary Snyder Chair in Science and the Humanities and Professor of English, Science and Technology Studies, as well as Cinema and Digital Media at the University of California, Davis. His research focuses on the intersections of science, literature, and media technologies.

Jeanne Cortiel, Christine Hanke, Jan Simon Hutta, Colin Milburn (eds.)
Practices of Speculation
Modeling, Embodiment, Figuration

[transcript]

Bibliographic information published by the Deutsche Nationalbibliothek
The Deutsche Nationalbibliothek lists this publication in the Deutsche Nationalbibliografie; detailed bibliographic data are available in the Internet at http://dnb.d-nb.de

This work is licensed under the Creative Commons Attribution-NonCommercial-NoDerivatives 4.0 (BY-NC-ND) which means that the text may be used for non-commercial purposes, provided credit is given to the author. For details go to
http://creativecommons.org/licenses/by-nc-nd/4.0/
To create an adaptation, translation, or derivative of the original work and for commercial use, further permission is required and can be obtained by contacting rights@transcript-publishing.com
Creative Commons license terms for re-use do not apply to any content (such as graphs, figures, photos, excerpts, etc.) not original to the Open Access publication and further permission may be required from the rights holder. The obligation to research and clear permission lies solely with the party re-using the material.

© 2020 transcript Verlag, Bielefeld

Cover layout: Maria Arndt, Bielefeld
Cover illustration: Revanche / photocase.com
Typeset by Francisco Bragança, Bielefeld

Print-ISBN 978-3-8376-4751-8
PDF-ISBN 978-3-8394-4751-2
https://doi.org/10.14361/9783839447512

Contents

Practices of Speculation
An Introduction
Jeanne Cortiel, Christine Hanke, Jan Simon Hutta, and Colin Milburn 7

Chapter 1: Cultures of Speculation—Histories of Speculation
Susanne Lachenicht 31

Modeling: Speculating with Data

Chapter 2: The Working Planetologist
Speculative Worlds and the Practice of Climate Science
Katherine Buse 51

Chapter 3: The Rule of Productivity and the Fear of Transgression
Speculative Uncertainty in Digital Games
Felix Raczkowski 77

Chapter 4: Lagging Realities
Temporal Exploits and Mutant Speculations
Joseph Dumit 97

Embodiment: Speculating with Matter

Chapter 5: "La vie impossible"
Germfree Life in the Microbiome Era
Melissa Wills 119

Chapter 6: Spores of Speculation
Negotiating Mold as Contamination
Christoph Schemann 145

Chapter 7: Enacting Speculation
The Paradoxical Epistemology of Performance as Research
Wolf-Dieter Ernst and Jan Simon Hutta 167

Figuration: Speculating with Fiction

Chapter 8: Scale and Speculative Futures in
Russell Hoban's *Riddley Walker* and Kim Stanley Robinson's *2312*
Matthew Hannah and Sylvia Mayer 191

Chapter 9: The Lifecycle of Software Engineers
Geek Temporalities and Digital Labor
Jordan S. Carroll 209

Chapter 10: Uncertainty between Image and Text
in Ben Templesmith's *Singularity 7*
Interdisciplinary Perspectives on Narrative and Performance
Jeanne Cortiel and Christine Hanke 221

Chapter 11: This World Which Is Not One
Superhero Comics and Other Dimensions of Reference
Mark Jerng and Colin Milburn 243

List of Figures 275

Biographical Notes 277

Practices of Speculation
An Introduction

Jeanne Cortiel, Christine Hanke, Jan Simon Hutta, and Colin Milburn

May 2020. As we write this introduction, the COVID-19 pandemic has covered the world. Drastic political measures to contain the virus have followed, appearing already belated and inadequate even as they envision a future after the current crisis. With notable national and regional differences, the policies and practices implemented to deal with the spread of the virus act like magnifying glasses, illuminating the social and economic power relations of the Global North and Global South more clearly than ever before, while also highlighting the fissures and tensions where things may fall apart entirely. The most conspicuous of these breaking points include, for example, the insistent growth paradigm of neoliberal economics; the processes of transnationalization and re-bordering; the evolving role of spatial proximity for social networks and personal relationships, now articulated through the clumsy expression of "social distancing"; the preservation of civil liberties in the midst of massive data collection and surveillance; the relationship between science and politics; and the increasingly significant role of digital media and software platforms for civic participation and cultural belonging. Not least, the pandemic has reconfigured social, political, and ecological temporalities, provoking at the same time the invocation of past events, manifold scenarios of future developments, and calls for immediate action—often coexisting in different contexts. These responses endow the ongoing debate around climate change with a new sense of urgency, even while they tend to eclipse it. This is a moment of crisis writ large, and its heightened uncertainties force us to suspend any illusions of autonomy to fully face the vulnerabilities of ourselves and our life-supporting systems. The future has opened up in radically novel ways, and the speculative practices that give this volume its title become manifestly relevant.

As governments, health experts, companies, and investors struggle to gain control over a highly complex, already destructive situation, acts of speculation—particularly in the domains of economics and technoscience—are ubiquitous and proliferating. These speculations often take the form of colorful visualizations of data, for example, extrapolative maps and charts that appeal to the power of scientific evidence. But they also frequently latch onto apocalyptic, dystopian, and utopian narrative traditions, highlighting the need for an interdisciplinary response. Even before the current pandemic, interdisciplinary scholarship has amply shown how viruses and other contagious entities animate scientific, political, literary, and popular media discourses in a peculiarly speculative manner.[1] Today, engulfed in discrepant narratives of the pandemic, social media and television broadcasts abound with claims of "fake news" and conspiracy theories, even while reporting the risk assessments and predictive models of scientific, economic, and political authorities. Virologists and epidemiologists have become the leading experts of the day, making the basic operational modes of scientific knowledge more visible than ever. However, the speculative dimensions of their response to COVID-19 underscore the stark, inexorable force of uncertainty, even as we turn to science for certain answers. The current volume is grounded in this premise: as a field of practices oriented towards the future, speculation runs on non-knowledge and uncertainty to produce new knowledge. Yet even as it turns to the future, speculation is bound to existing knowledge and, as such, belongs as much to history as to any eventual world to come.

Therefore, the perturbation of linear time that we see so clearly played out in the COVID-19 pandemic is also central to speculation in general. The relationship between past, present, and future—the basic structure of collective histories and life narratives—emerges as radically unstable. Politicians, medical and scientific experts, and the press alike frame the pandemic's social realities—including the search for vaccines, treatments, and containment measures—in the language of 'not yet.' They couple the uncertainties of the current moment with a redemptive future, the contours of which tend to dissipate even as we imagine them. At the same time, researchers and reporters seek to document the course of the past, gathering anecdotes and data, visualizations and geographical mappings that meticulously trace the spread of the virus and its speed, the rates of infection and mortality, as well as the resilience of health care systems. Like the uncertain future, the past has not stopped assaulting the present. Squeezed between a radically contingent future and a past impossible to fix, the present has assumed the form of a speculative event.[2]

If the COVID-19 epidemic has unfolded through the speculative dimension of time, it has simultaneously revealed the workings of speculation on space. A health crisis that only weeks or days ago might have seemed far away suddenly presents itself as 'right here.' A tiny agent that implants itself in human bodies

---

1 For examples, see Treichler (1998); Mayer, R./Weingart (2004); Wald (2008); and Servitje/Vint (2016).

2 Here we are reminded of Deleuze and Guattari's conceptualization of an "aeonic time" that "continually divides that which transpires into an already-there that is at the same time not-yet-here, a simultaneous too-late and too-early" (Deleuze and Guattari [1980] 2003: 262).

is subsequently confronted with the spatial technologies of national borders. Visualizations of the virus's geographic distribution, distinguishing countries and states with graded shades of red and other alarming colorations, appear both as awkward tools for a comparative analysis and as instruments for a re-nationalizing strategy that corresponds with the massive tightening of border controls. Quotidien practices of translocality and mobility that have structured daily life in the Global North for decades, even while remaining cruelly foreclosed in many parts of the world, suddenly return as newly configured threats. Meanwhile, space has itself become speculatively temporalized. The asynchronous arrival of the disease in different places has provoked a discourse of differential 'stages' of disease progression, such that, for instance, "[Italy's] future is in the process of becoming America's present" (Jordheim et al. 2020). The 'here' is mirrored by an asynchronous 'there.' What the COVID-19 pandemic has revealed about the temporalities and spatialities of speculation is not new; nevertheless, it has become newly existential for all of us.

As indicated in the heterogeneous policies and discourses galvanized by COVID-19, the anticipation of the future and the circumscription of the as-yet unknown are core functions of contemporary knowledge production, facilitated by methods of segmentation and linearization, derivation and projection. The tools, techniques, and habits of speculation have become indispensable for thinking and acting within systems of advanced capitalism everywhere, anywhere, across the board. Aligned with instrumental knowledge and financial calculus, speculation has been complicit in the generation of profit. The nexus of knowledge production and profit generation in capitalism is further imbricated with state, corporate, and private interventions designed to make the future both imaginable and manageable. However, while speculation has nourished visions of eternal growth and profitable futures for the few, strategies and tactics developed to resist such visions have also relied on speculation. For example, in the COVID-19 pandemic, glimpses of different, alternative ways to inhabit the relation to past and future have also emerged. When several European states surprisingly interrupted harsh austerity politics, or when the U.S. government ordered firms to change their production to health-related equipment, or when calls to re-localize circuits of production and consumption grew louder, or when neighbors organized to assist the homeless and other vulnerable populations, the future began to mutate, opening different horizons, responding to practices hitherto often rejected as unrealistic, unviable, or 'socialist.'

A particularly strong case for a mode of speculating that escapes the mantra of growth and profit has been articulated in the manifesto *Rethinking the Apocalypse* (2020) by the North American indigenous collective Indigenous Action. Challenging hegemonic narratives of the disease that construct a linear story in which heroes of the Global North are called on to save 'the world,' the authors note,

> From religious tomes to fictionalized scientific entertainment, each imagined timeline constructed so predictably; beginning, middle, and ultimately, The End. [...] It's an apocalyptic that colonizes our imaginations and destroys our past and future simultaneously. It is a struggle to dominate human meaning and all existence. [...] This is the futurism of the colonizer, the capitalist. It is at once every future ever stolen by the plunderer, the warmonger and the rapist. [...] Apocalyptic idealization is a self-fulfilling prophecy. It is the linear world ending from within. (Indigenous Action 2020)

Against a linear sequence running from a definite past to a predictable future, the activists call for a folding of temporality, invoking ancestral prophecies enunciated in the midst of violence and exploitation: "Now. Then. Tomorrow. Yesterday." This powerful intervention into the rampant discourses around COVID-19 brings into relief another mode of speculating and, along with it, another set of speculative practices.

The uncertain commons collective, in their manifesto *Speculate This!* (2013), has provided a lucid rendition of such diverging modes of speculation. Taking clues from Nietzsche, Spinoza, Bataille, and Derrida, the authors propose a distinction between *firmative speculation* and *affirmative speculation*. Firmative speculation is about "turning uncertainty into (external, calculable, knowable) risk," whereas affirmative speculation leaves the future open, thriving on uncertainty, and it "progresses and lives by attending to what it does not know" (uncertain commons 2013: ch. 2). While the firmative mode predominates, casting futurity primarily in terms of technological progress, economic growth, and a prolongation of the status quo, the affirmative mode instead characterizes diverse efforts to invent alternatives, for example, in philosophy and the arts—especially in the domains of speculative fiction—but also in postcolonial and decolonial projects, environmental justice efforts, experiments in permaculture, antiracist worldmaking strategies, and all manner of activist agitations that insist another world is possible.[3]

Affirmative speculation, in this sense, is about habits and practices opening towards a future that is not only uncertain, but radically contingent: a future that is not turned into an extension of the present, but that bears the promise of genuine novelty and difference in relation to what can presently be known and predicted. Affirmative speculation, it seems, is what a radical politics of difference—radically postcapitalist and decolonial—needs, at least, to think that things could be otherwise.

---

3 See for example, Fisher/Ponniah (2003); McNally ([2002] 2006); Juris (2008); Bryant/Srnicek/Harman (2011); Otto (2012); Davis/Turpin (2015); Wilkie/Savransky/Rosengarten (2017); Bahng (2018); Jerng (2018); Milburn (2018); Streeby (2018); Chua/Fair (2019); Chang (2019); and Jue (2020).

Ambivalences, paradoxes, and indeterminacies remain, however, as already implied in the intellectual genealogy invoked by the uncertain commons. The two modes, while analytically useful, are inseparable regarding relations of knowledge production and politics. If imaginative, experimental, and performative practices of speculation have helped to animate insurgent movements from Haiti to the Arab Spring, Gezi protests in Turkey, or the Movement for Black Lives, it was also affirmative modes of speculation in relation to the unknown—hopes, dreams, and desires, as well as fears—that characterized colonial projects of exploration in early modernity. Likewise, the supposedly 'post-truth' situations propagated by Donald Trump, Jair Bolsonaro, and the Brexiteers cannot straightforwardly be captured in terms of a firmative mode of speculation that seeks to make uncertainties manageable—even though their affirmations of chaos and uncertainty clearly expose firmative orientations on other levels.[4] Whose purposes affirmative speculation serves and how it is interlaced with firmative processes thus remains an uncomfortable question.

Consider, for example, that firmative ways of speculating have acquired renewed relevance in activist strategies to counter 'alternative truth' and anti-science claims, such as those that run riot in the climate-change-denial movement. In her seminal theorization of situated knowledges, Donna Haraway formulated precisely this paradox of "how to have *simultaneously* an account of radical contingency for all knowledge claims and knowing subjects [...] *and* a no-nonsense commitment to faithful accounts of a 'real' world" (Haraway 1988: 579). With respect to the current situation of the COVID-19 pandemic—the moment when we write these words in our separate homes, in different countries, practicing prophylactic social distancing—the different national political strategies cannot in all cases be pinned down as instances of purely firmative or affirmative speculation. For example, some of these strategies enact a "precautionary principle," according to which it is precisely the lack of knowledge about the future that prompts preventive action. As Matthew Hannah, Jan Simon Hutta, and Christoph Schemann explain, "Many experts in the current crisis thus cite the limits of their own knowledge as a reason not for refraining from action but, on the contrary, for quarantine and the closing of borders" (Hannah/Hutta/Schemann 2020). Rather than making the endeavor to overcome uncertainty their prime objective and to close down an

---

4 Discussing Bolsonaro's government, Marcos Nobre (2019) has used the term "chaos as method" (cf. Meyer and Bustamente 2020). The calculated production of chaos and uncertainty, while seeming to affirm and promote contrarian beliefs, conspiracy theories, and other flights of speculative fancy, simultaneously aims to lock down the future, restore order, and return things to an imagined stability, remaking the future as an image of the past ("Make America great again," "Make Brazil great again," etc.).

uncertain future, these experts affirmatively posit their own irredeemable lack of knowledge as grounds for firmative recommendations.

Such simultaneity of different modes of speculation also shapes discussions about the legacies-to-be of the pandemic containment practices. On the one hand, firmative statements proliferate, ranging from stark warnings that the translocation of everyday life to online platforms will only fortify the neoliberal economy and enable increasingly comprehensive surveillance, to optimistic assurances that the widespread embrace of digital technologies and practices will ultimately improve social relations. On the other hand, some speculations have taken a more affirmative tack, welcoming the uncertainty that ensues from the fact that 'nobody knows' how we will come out of the crisis, imagining innovative possibilities for shifting power to the people and enhancing democratization (cf. Diez/Heisenberg 2020). But the "Amazonification of the planet" (Merchant 2020), a process that has been accelerating during the pandemic, depends as much on the interplay between closure and openness as does any utopian vision of a more egalitarian society to come after the pandemic. Much commentary has therefore combined firmative and affirmative (as well as anti-speculative) modes (cf. Strick 2020). It seems, then, we are situated in a historical moment when both modes are more interwoven than ever. Our aim, therefore, is not simply to pit the affirmative against the firmative, but rather to use this distinction as a heuristic for considering different ways of inhabiting the future-oriented present, a provocation for further enquiries into the material effects of speculation in specific contexts.

Since the eighteenth century, the profound transformation of scientific knowledge production in the context of industrialization has fundamentally shaped the development of the Global North: statistical and probabilistic thinking emerged hand in hand with mechanical objectivity, the projection of the Gaussian error curve onto social and natural phenomena, and the introduction of increasingly vast data practices into the arenas of science, politics, administrative governance, and civic life.[5] While these epistemic innovations have often seemed to disavow and exclude speculation, they nevertheless introduced new, data-driven modes of extrapolation, anticipation, and prediction into knowledge processes. Probabilistic theories and statistical methods came to permeate scientific knowledge, dissolving essentialist conceptions of law and causality while refurbishing notions of randomness and chance. The advent of quantum theory in the twentieth century likewise infused indeterminacy and uncertainty into the foundations of physics. These developments in the sciences, in parallel with the spreading tendrils of technological modernization and financial capitalism, created the conditions for a massive reorganization of epistemic fields and social orders around actuarial

---

5 See Porter (1986); Daston (1988); Hacking (1990); Desroisères ([1993] 1998); Daston/Galison (2007); and Link (1996, 2004a, 2004b, 2004c, 2004d).

logics, stochastic models, and risk assessments—that is, the emergence of risk society.⁶

In this context, since the late twentieth century, the operations of science, technology, medicine, and public health have become increasingly entwined with the speculative economies of the market, with all its attendant instruments of insurance, hedging, futures trading, and arbitrage, articulated in the grammar of forward-looking statements.⁷ On the flip side, in the realm of economics and economic behaviors, historical shifts in attitudes toward speculation and investment, as well as alternating positive and negative assessments and the scientification of finance markets, have evolved in concert with probabilistic and metrical ways of knowing (Stäheli [2007] 2013). The transformation of "investors into scientists bound to discover the hidden, objective laws of financial investments" (Preda 2005: 152) has resulted in characteristic speculative labor practices, for example, in stock exchanges and algorithmic finance markets (Zaloom 2004, 2005). At the same time, it has become clear how closely financial speculation in global capitalism has been linked to colonialism and its legacies, including exploitative, extractive methods of medical, environmental, and technological experimentation, debt-trap investment schemes, and the global shuffling of supply chain derivatives.⁸ Buoyed by such ventures and enterprises, financial markets—which are "not primarily concerned with the production of goods or with their distribution to clients but with the trading of financial instruments not designed for consumption" (Knorr Cetina/Preda 2005: 4)—thrive on their own promissory condition, their own subjunctivity. Conjured forth by the abstract models and theoretical conceits of economics, the performance of financial markets—indeed, the financialization of culture as such—relies deeply on imaginary visions of the future, in other words, speculative fictions.⁹

Speculative fictions—including the genres of utopian romance, scientific romance, extraordinary voyages, science fiction, science fantasy, weird tales, supernatural horror, fantasy, and alternate history—are devices for rendering two predominant types of speculation into narrative discourse: (1) extrapolation,

---

6 On risk society and its manifestations in technoscience, popular media, and environmental discourse, see Beck ([1986] 1992); Mayer, S./Weik von Mossner (2014); and Ghosh/Sarkar (2020). On the functions of uncertainty, indeterminacy, and risk in cultures of statistical knowledge production, see Hanke (2007, 2014); Bauer/Olsén (2009); Hannah (2010); and Jordan/Mitterhofer/Jørgensen (2018).

7 See Sunder Rajan (2006); Waldby/Mitchell (2006); Fortun (2008); Cooper (2008); Dumit (2012); Milburn (2015); and Patel (2017).

8 See Mitchell (2002); LiPuma/Lee (2004); Mignolo (2011); Bear/Birla/Puri (2015); Tilley (2011); Beisel/Boëte (2013); Peterson (2014); Chandler/Beisel (2017); and Mavhunga (2018).

9 See Callon (1998); Maeße/Sparsam (2007); Lütz (2007); MacKenzie/Muniesa/Siu (2008); Beckert (2016); Appadurai (2013); and Bear (2020).

which addresses the question, "What if this goes on?" based on what is "known to be known"[10]—whether in science or otherwise—and (2) a more open form of speculation that asks, "What if …?" without such constraints.[11] As cultural devices, speculative fictions have, since the origins of modern science, contributed to production of scientific knowledge and technical innovations.[12] At the same time, speculative fictions have helped to shape social imaginaries toward the possibility of radical change and political renovation—precisely by estranging the present from itself, remaking our world into the past of an altered future or the foil to a wholly alternative world.[13] As writers such as Judith Merril and Joanna Russ have famously suggested, speculative fictions are not constrained to particular forms or styles of speculation, for they can capaciously experiment with any number of speculative modalities.[14] For this reason, speculative fictions prove to be exquisite instruments for refracting the manifold practices of speculation that constitute the world today—the proliferating speculative markets, the forces of preemptive securitization, and the actuarial projections of pandemic pandemonium, as much as the longing for things to be otherwise.[15]

Considering how central speculation has become to all areas of our social, political, cultural, and personal existence, systematic exploration of the grammars, modes, and functions of speculation across these domains appears necessary. Such has been the motivation of this essay collection: to analyze speculation—whether in technoscience, finance, or fiction—as implemented by concrete practices, instantiated in particular forms of discourse, media apparatuses, techniques of application, and everyday activities.

Tracing the Practices of Speculation

Speculation ventures to create knowledge by conjecturing what may come, but it is not exclusively directed towards the future: societies speculate backwards and sideways as well as forwards and beyond. The aim of this book is to think about speculation in more expansive ways at a time when the anticipation of catastro-

---

10 This is Samuel Delany's phrase, according to Joanna Russ ([1971] 1972).
11 See Landon (2014); cf. Csicsery-Ronay (2008); Saler (2012).
12 For examples, see Penley (1997); Turney (1998); Hayles (1999); Doyle (2003); Kilgore (2003); Squire (2004); Willis (2006); Clarke (2008); Franklin ([1988] 2008); Milburn (2008, 2015); Wald (2008); Sharp (2018); and Rees/Morus (2019).
13 See Jameson (2005); cf. Freedman (2000); Sargent (2010); and Levitas (2013).
14 See Merril ([1966] 2017); Russ ([1971] 2017); cf. Cortiel (1999).
15 See Vint (2015); Carroll/McClanahan (2015); Haraway 2016; Higgins/O'Connell (2019); and Milburn (2020).

phe is the order of the day and an apocalyptic tone pervades public discourse on a global scale. Picking up the distinction between firmative and affirmative modes of speculation, this book proposes an approach that investigates the concrete ways in which these modes are enacted in practice, how they are sometimes differentially favored or mutually combined or rendered indistinguishable, as well as the entanglements and effects to which they give rise. While the essays collected here were written prior to COVID-19, at a moment when the image of global pandemic still resided in the 'there and then' instead of the 'here and now,' they bring into strong relief some of the speculative practices that have also shaped the current crisis.

This volume is the product of a long-standing cooperation between scholars at the University of Bayreuth and the University of California, Davis focusing on "cultures of speculation." The contributions, some of them coauthored across disciplines, examine an assortment of speculative practices from different angles, attending to the ways in which speculation opens new vantages and vistas, a spectral panoply of firmative and affirmative horizons.

Practices of Speculation represents an adventure in interdisciplinary collaboration, the outgrowth of our collective effort to rethink conceptualizations of speculation in and beyond our respective disciplines, across different academic cultures. Several of the chapters were written as methodological mashups by coauthors from different fields, but even the single-author chapters position themselves across fields and cultures of research. Moreover, the entire collection bears traces of the innumerable conversations we have had as a group of friends and colleagues working and thinking together for more than a decade.

To move towards a fuller sense of how speculation operates through situated practices, we have grouped the chapters into three sections: (1) Modeling: Speculating with Data; (2) Embodiment: Speculating with Matter; and (3) Figuration: Speculating with Fiction. These three kinds of speculative practices—all of which can exhibit firmative and affirmative modes—are not mutually exclusive, but they each have a distinctive manner of establishing relations between the known and the unknown.

Modeling uses data to develop descriptive or visual accounts of possible states of affairs. It thus draws on facticity to describe possible actualities. *Embodiment* concerns the ways in which specific materials, beings, and environments—for example, the subjects and objects of a scientific laboratory or a theater space—are mobilized to enact speculative processes and promissory visions, opening to futurity. *Figuration*, in turn, draws attention to practices of make-believe that speculate through the gathering and condensing of disparate signifying elements—whether images, words, scenes, or narratives. Each of these practices of speculation—modeling, embodiment, figuration—entails different processes of worldmaking, which we analyze from different disciplinary angles. The individual chapters provide paradigmatic glimpses of particular situated practices, but collectively, the book aspires to provoke discussion rather than provide an exhaustive survey.

While speculation has been endemic to the expansion of global capitalism, speculation as a practice of dealing with the unknown past, future, and present goes back deep into history—and this history shapes the contours and affordances of speculation today. The first chapter of this collection, Susanne Lachenicht's "Cultures of Speculation—Histories of Speculation," historicizes our approach to speculation by looking into early modern chronotopes and perspectives on speculation, how they evolved with the Renaissance and in the context of European voyages of exploration. Not only the development of probability and risk calculus but also literary genres such as travel narratives and utopian romances show how much the period between the fourteenth and the nineteenth centuries generated a broad range of speculative practices. Speculation in the early modern period was about futures that, while often representing extensions of the present, also enabled speculating on the past, on eternity and *untime*. Going back into these histories of speculation, Susanne Lachenicht discovers in them a *speculum* for today's practices of speculation. The diverse timescapes of the early modern period can help us to critically assess our own times, our own temporal orientations and modes of speculation, and to recall alternative conceptions for other times not yet here.

Modeling: Speculating with Data

Scientific speculation as we understand it today is rooted in numbers. Calculations, graphs, measurements, and quantified data feed the extrapolative thinking that yields predictive models in science and finance, as well as games both analog and digital. Exploring this field of speculation, the first section presents three case studies: one on the relationship between climate modeling in science and science fiction; one on manifestations of uncertainty in the model worlds of computer games; and one on the speculative affordances of 'lag' in high-frequency trading, online game economies, and other algorithmic recreations. All three contributions showcase approaches to speculation that play with calculated models. What they make clear is that models become tools of speculation through narrative and storytelling, above and beyond the raw calculus of quantifiable patterns.

Katherine Buse's "The Working Planetologist: Speculative Worlds and the Practice of Climate Science" examines journal articles, blog posts, textbooks, and lectures by climate scientists, uncovering a discourse around speculative fiction that not only refers to specific texts but also reflects upon the importance of science-fictional thinking for the technical work of modeling planetary systems.

Connecting the discursive and mathematical construction of worlds in climate modeling to the speculative fictions referenced by scientists, especially Frank Herbert's *Dune* (1965), the chapter characterizes a shared practice of climatological speculation in both science and fiction. The title of the chapter is adapted from Herbert's use of the phrase "the working planetologist" to describe *Dune*'s planetary ecologist, because this character enacts a kind of planetary consciousness that links science fiction with climate modeling. Climate scientists refer to science fiction pedagogically and methodologically to communicate the ideas of speculative climatology, suggesting that the comprehension of our own climate requires embedding it in a multiverse of imaginary otherworlds.

In "The Rule of Productivity and the Fear of Transgression: Speculative Uncertainty in Digital Games," Felix Raczkowski investigates how practices of speculation inscribe themselves into contemporary digital games while also arguing that games and play enable speculation through their inherent uncertainty. After a brief overview of the relationship between games, play, and uncertainty, the chapter analyzes two manifestations of uncertainty in digital games as well as the speculative strategies they foster in detail. On the one hand, ludic uncertainty serves the interest of game play in the context of online multiplayer games and simulations. On the other hand, uncertainty also appears as risk, and the fear of transgressive acts leads to various attempts to discipline the player base of online games. Raczkowski's chapter concludes that both productive and transgressive uncertainties are entrenched in speculative concerns about the future of digital games and games research.

Capitalist speculation dreams of reducing risks and obliterating waiting times, as the subsequent chapter reminds us. Yet it also depends on open futures and delays at both technical and social levels. In "Lagging Realities: Temporal Exploits and Mutant Speculations," Joseph Dumit studies shared speculative experiences of lag: what happens when lags are persistent, when they are encountered as things to which people must creatively adapt. How do they warp reality by warping time as lagged time—never lagged-time-in-general, but always specific forms of lag? Drawing on thick descriptions of financial speculation, first-person-shooter games, basketball, massively multiplayer online role-playing games, human simulation, and botting, the chapter follows where and how lag shows up, where it must be put into speech, and how it becomes a matter of concern, a material-semiotic actor that, once named into existence, has the potential to warp existence and time itself. Dumit's chapter finds that even as lag slows things down, it affords the potential for affirmative speculation, presenting unexpected opportunities and soliciting anticipatory practices that, by delaying a future, can produce new ways of speculating.

Embodiment: Speculating with Matter

Looking at material speculative practices, including experimentation in the sciences, social research, and performance art, highlights the role of embodiment and pushes against an overly limited notion of speculation as abstraction. Our case studies here delve into scientific practices involving germfree organisms and mold growth, as well as performance practices for an embodied epistemology of "performance as research." What these studies have in common is an interest in how speculation plays out in and through bodies—both human and nonhuman—and how materiality intersects with discourse, affects, and expectations in the formation of speculative alternatives to the known and the familiar.

Melissa Wills's "'La vie impossible': Germfree Life in the Microbiome Era" shows how narratives of life without microbes are being rewritten in the wake of twenty-first-century research into the human microbiome. Germfree life, whether animal or human, was long considered to be a technical achievement. Born and maintained within complex sterile chambers, germfree organisms were viewed as perfections of engineering and of modern medicine: healthy, long-lived, and free of microbial disease, they seemed to herald a future of radiant health for all. In the microbiome era, that assessment has changed profoundly. Examining a corpus of ten popular microbiome books, Wills shows how contemporary pop-science writers are actively rewriting the legacy and status of germfree animal research. Through a series of historical and rhetorical distortions, she argues, germfree bodies become sick, victims of the impulse to eradicate microbes and suffering the loss of their accustomed symbionts. Made into representatives of a catastrophic future to come, these bodies function as speculative interventions in a looming crisis of antibiotic-laced modernity, invoked as deterrents to the persistent dream of life beyond germs.

Social relations to the nonhuman that include endeavors of countering projected human impairment of health are also at the focus of another essay, which starts out from the observation that the fungi called "mold" are usually seen as contamination when encountered in and on buildings or food. Christoph Schemann's "Spores of Speculation: Negotiating Mold as Contamination" engages with some recurrent socio-material strategies through which such contamination is established and navigated, including the registers of visibility, ventilation, temporality, and disgust. Drawing on Karen Barad's (2007) notion of the "apparatus," the chapter shows that the activation of such processes of negotiation—as well as their alteration—can take shape only through specific practices of speculation. These include firmative practices that revolve around anticipated threats to human health and preemptive actions directed at securing an uncontaminated human future. Contrasting such a foreclosing mode of speculation with affirmative speculation, the essay goes on to examine practices such as urban exploration and dumpster diving that speculate *with*, rather than solely *about*, mold. Schemann argues that such a contingent and unprompted mode of speculating opens up future possibilities for prolific yet uncertain engagements with more-than-human materialities. It may also assist, he suggests, in reframing the category of contamination as a more nuanced and polyphonic form of collaborative encounters.

The speculative dimensions of performative knowledge production are at the center of Wolf-Dieter Ernst and Jan Simon Hutta's chapter, "Enacting Speculation: The Paradoxical Epistemology of Performance as Research." The authors point out that the generation of knowledge, despite the focus on how bodily contingency can be held at bay in Western traditions of science, necessarily depends on embodied and performative practices. While the sociology of knowledge and the feminist discussion of situated knowledges have by now made this much sufficiently clear, the essay enquires into the generative potential that resides in not only acknowledging bodily, performative, and speculative dimensions but also intensifying them. Such intensification, they argue, fosters the generation of new knowledge as well as ways of knowing otherwise. To develop this argument, the chapter relates the question of speculation to the discussions about "performance as research" (Kershaw 2008, 2009; Stutz 2008). Drawing on an interdisciplinary seminar that they conducted in collaboration with Matt Adams from the arts collective Blast Theory, Ernst and Hutta highlight the productive role of paradoxical constellations of facticity and fictionality, embodied specificity and boundlessness, as well as scientific inscription and practical performance. Amplifying rather than reducing such paradoxicality, they argue, prompts performing researchers to develop creative responses to unfolding events, potentially instigating new knowledge as well as new ways of knowing.

Figuration: Speculating with Fiction

As a word, a concept, figuration has traveled circuitous etymological routes, from its roots in the Latin *figura* to the German *Figur* and the English *figure*, to its usage in contemporary theoretical discourse. Two German-speaking scholars have been particularly influential in shaping the notion of figuration: the philologist Erich Auerbach and the sociologist Norbert Elias. Auerbach, in his 1938 essay "Figura," presents *figuration* as a way of reading the relationship between the Old Testament and the New Testament, in which the old prefigures and forecasts the new—a pattern of retroactive anticipation and prospective fulfillment that he traces across Western literature in his well-known book, *Mimesis* (Auerbach [1938] 2019; cf. Balke 2019). Similarly, Elias's concept of figuration in approaching society as a dynamic process—the basis of figurational sociology—suggests configurations, networks, or assemblages, influenced by the German word *Figur* (a character in a play) and drawing upon the etymological sense of figure as plastic form (Elias [1975] 1994). It is in this sense that figuration also refers to tropes and figures of speech, in which one thing points to another—in other words, in borrowed form. In English, figure is also a verb and a noun that refers to shapes and numbers as well as drawings and graphical images. Figuration is fraught with protean meaning—a projection or forecast of meaning as such.

In this section, we take a cue from Donna Haraway, who theorizes figuration by drawing from a range of contexts, including Auerbach's *Mimesis*. Haraway writes, "Figurations are performative images that can be inhabited. Verbal or visual, figurations can be condensed maps of contestable worlds" (Haraway 1997: 11). Figuration emerges as a mode of speculation that, grounded in both the *figural* (referring to individuated figures and configurations) and the *figurative* (spanning the range of visual and verbal expressions), spins a web of interdependent figures. Figuration characterizes speculative practices that draw inferential, conjectural, and anticipatory connections between one thing (a shape, a number, an actor, a cipher) and another (an object, an entity, a world, or whatever).

As a method of make-believe, speculation often plays out in the form of fiction, that is, imaginary and invented stories. On one level, all fictional texts are speculative in this sense (Merril [1966] 1971; Freedman 2000). Speculative fiction, however, deliberately envisions sociopolitical, economic, and cultural consequences of scientific and technological change, as well as other knowledge-making and world-building practices, including those that may not be possible in our own universe. The chapters in this section of the book focus on speculative fiction in different media, exploring questions of space and scale, temporality, uncertainty, and self-referentiality.

In "Scale and Speculative Futures in Russell Hoban's *Riddley Walker* and Kim Stanley Robinson's *2312*," Matthew Hannah and Sylvia Mayer discuss two science fiction novels that engage with contemporary key technologies: Russell Hoban's *Riddley Walker* (1980), which speculates about possible effects of nuclear technology, and Kim Stanley Robinson's *2312* (2012), which speculates about possible consequences of computational, biomedical, and geoengineering technologies. Hannah and Mayer focus on the spatiality of the future worlds presented by these novels and demonstrate how "scale" as a narrative strategy draws attention to the relevance of spatial and scalar structuring in fictional future worlds—and, by implication, in nonfictional worlds, as well. The re-scaled future worlds of *Riddley Walker* and *2312* shed light on the dynamics of the social constitution of both space and time and on the potential hazards of technological modernization.

Drawing on queer theory and fan studies, Jordan Carroll's "The Lifecycle of Software Engineers: Geek Temporalities and Digital Labor" argues that geeks share a common experience of time. Both fans and tech workers seem to lose track of all other schedules when they become immersed in labor or leisure—which, for geeks, blur together. While geeks have long been considered to be rebels or outsiders, geek temporalities actually prove to be more politically ambiguous. They allow tech workers to accommodate themselves to punishingly long hours, but they also push geeks to choose work and play over heterofamilial commitments, setting them at odds with temporal norms surrounding heterosexual maturity. Moreover, although geeks would seem to be ideal consumers, their excessive attachments to old media mean that they often resist capitalist narratives of progress. Geeks therefore frequently appear in fiction as archaic, childlike, or alien figures who are somehow out of synchronicity with normal people. Thus, geeks are often associated with characters in speculative fiction, including androids or artificial intelligences. They are capable of working like machines, but they operate on different timescales from most humans. Through a close reading of Ted Chiang's novella *The Lifecycle of Software Objects* (2010), this essay suggests that geek practices of speculation can present alternatives to chronormativity.

In "Uncertainty between Image and Text in Ben Templesmith's *Singularity 7*," Jeanne Cortiel and Christine Hanke focus on the relationship between images and text, and the ways in which the two work together in comics to create narrative. They point out that something more is also created in the interaction between the visual and the textual in comics—an effect perhaps best described as figuration. Seeing this interaction as figuration turns attention to speculation as integral to how comics engage in worldmaking beyond narrative. Based on a paradigmatic reading of a dystopian graphic novel, *Singularity 7* by Ben Templesmith (2004), the chapter attends to how comics as a medium speculate specifically in the tension between image and text, narrative and performance. Undertaking a dialogue between literary studies and media studies/image theory (*Bildwissenschaft*), Cortiel and Hanke explore the question of how the visual layers, box commentary and character speech work together (or across one another) to undermine the stabilizing tendencies of both story and visuals in comics. This interdisciplinary dialogue brings out the inherently paradoxical nature of speculation in comics and discusses how uncertainty shapes the interactions between image and text. *Singularity 7* is a comic that deliberately deploys the effects produced by the visuals and the ways in which images both propel and counteract the narrative flow. Images perform a medial presence by themselves that is in tension with the text layers. Addressing the questions raised by this highly self-referential comic, the authors investigate how *Singularity 7* specifically assembles images and text, but they also suggest how the uncertainty created in this performance of intermediality characterizes comics in general.

Approaching the speculative operations of comic books from another direction, Mark Jerng and Colin Milburn's chapter, "This World Which Is Not One: Superhero Comics and Other Dimensions of Reference," examines the practices of allusion, citation, and reference-making in superhero fictions. Noting that superhero comics always take place in an alternate reality from our own—and that the genre has cultivated the trope of the 'multiverse' or multiple universes to accommodate divergent, sometimes contradictory narratives—Jerng and Milburn show how references to historical events, works of art, or cultural clichés often seem to stabilize continuity and secure a consensus reality. Yet in superhero comics, such references also highlight discontinuities and perform a speculative ontology of difference, a worldview that affirms more worlds than one. The practices of reference in superhero comics reach out to occluded eras of the past, alternative histories of the present, and other worlds yet to come, assembling heterogeneous components through radical juxtapositions of image and text. But even at the moment of producing narrative cohesion and retroactive continuity—that is, at the moment of 'retcon'—superhero comics register the irreducible multiplicity of worlds and alternative frames of reference. As Jerng and Milburn remind us, superhero comics have long been self-aware and self-reflexive about such issues, suggesting the capacities of speculative media to grapple with the firmative and affirmative forces at play in our world and others.

These collected studies of diverse anticipations, projections, alterities, counterfactuals, simulations, and virtualities—spectral visions brought to life through acts of modeling, embodiment, and figuration—are situated in a particular historic moment. It is an era of urgent anticipation—like many others before. We are now urged to shelter in place, to ride out the pandemic storm—but tomorrow is another day. As they say, there's no time like the present. So, let us not dawdle any longer. We hereby release this book into an uncertain future, hoping that it will inspire reflections on past and future practices of speculation. Where things go from here, we can only imagine.

Acknowledgements

Many thanks to Laura Rosinger for her tremendous help with the copyediting of this book, as well as to Uli Beisel, Joe Dumit, Wolf-Dieter Ernst, Matt Hannah, Michael Hauhs, Mark Jerng, Susanne Lachenicht, and Sylvia Mayer for their detailed comments on earlier drafts of the chapters. The research collaboration represented in this book was supported over many years with contributions from the Bayreuth Institute for American Studies (BIFAS), the Emerging Field Kulturbegegnungen und transkulturelle Prozesse at the University of Bayreuth, the International Fellowship Program of the University of Bayreuth, the Bayreuth Academy of Advanced African Studies, the German Research Foundation (DFG), the Fritz Thyssen Stiftung, and the ModLab at the University of California, Davis. Thanks also to Laura Oehme, Jordan Carroll, Amanda Phillips, Susanne Lachenicht, Matt Hannah, and Sylvia Mayer for their help supporting our collaborative research in

Bayreuth and Davis from 2010–2020. We are grateful for the warm and inspiring space for speculation provided by the "Cultures of Speculation" group across the Atlantic and across disciplines.

References

Appadurai, Arjun (2013): *The Future as Cultural Fact: Essays on the Global Condition.* New York: Verso.

Auerbach, Erich ([1938] 2019): "Figura." In: Friedrich Balke/ Hanna Engelmeier (eds.): *Mimesis und Figura: Mit einer Neuausgabe des "Figura"-Aufsatzes von Erich Auerbach.* Paderborn: Wilhelm Fink, 121–188.

Bahng, Aimee (2018): *Migrant Futures: Decolonizing Speculation in Financial Times.* Durham, NC: Duke University Press.

Balke, Friedrich (2019): "Mimesis und Figura: Erich Auerbachs niederer Materialismus." In Friedrich Balke/Hanna Engelmeier (eds.): *Mimesis und Figura: Mit einer Neuausgabe des "Figura"-Aufsatzes von Erich Auerbach.* Paderborn: Wilhelm Fink, 13–88.

Barad, Karen (2007): *Meeting the Universe Halfway: Quantum Physics and the Entanglement of Matter and Meaning.* Durham, NC: Duke University Press.

Bauer, Susanne/Olsén, Jan (2009): "Observing the Others, Watching Oneself: Themes of Medical Surveillance in Society." In: *Surveillance and Society* 6, 116–127.

Bear, Laura/Birla, Ritu/Puri, Stine Simonsen (eds.) (2015): *Speculation: Futures and Capitalism in India* [special section]. In: *Comparative Studies of South Asia, Africa and the Middle East* 35, 387–485.

Bear, Laura (ed.) (2020): *Speculation: A Political Economy of Technologies of Imagination* [special issue]. In: *Economy and Society* 49, 1–186.

Beck, Ulrich ([1986] 1992): *Risk Society: Towards a New Modernity.* Mark Ritter (trans.). London: Sage.

Beckert, Jens (2016): *Imagined Futures: Fictional Expectations and Capitalist Dynamics.* Cambridge, MA: Harvard University Press.

Beisel, Uli/Boëte, Christophe (2013): "The Flying Public Health Tool: Genetically Modified Mosquitoes and Malaria Control." In: *Science as Culture* 22, 38–60.

Bryant, Levy/Srnicek, Nick/Harman, Graham (eds.) (2011): *The Speculative Turn: Continental Materialism and Realism.* Melbourne: re.press.

Callon, Michel (ed.) (1998): *The Laws of the Market.* Oxford: Blackwell.

Carroll, Hamilton/McClanahan, Annie (eds.) (2015): *Fictions of Speculation* [special issue]. In: *Journal of American Studies* 49: 655–859.

Chandler, Clare I. R./Beisel, Uli (2017): "The Anthropology of Malaria: Locating the Social." In: *Medical Anthropology* 36, 411–421.

Chang, Alenda Y. (2019): *Playing Nature: Ecology in Video Games*. Minneapolis: University of Minnesota Press.

Chua, Liana/Fair, Hannah (2019): "Anthropocene." In: Felix Stein/Sian Lazar/Matei Candea/Hildegard Diemberger/Joel Robbins/Andrew Sanchez/Rupert Stasch (eds.): *The Cambridge Encyclopedia of Anthropology* (https://www.anthroencyclopedia.com/entry/anthropocene).

Clarke, Bruce (2008): *Posthuman Metamorphosis: Narrative and Systems*. Fordham University Press.

Cooper, Melinda (2008): *Life as Surplus: Biotechnology and Capitalism in the Neoliberal Era*. Seattle: University of Washington Press.

Cortiel, Jeanne (1999): *Demand My Writing: Joanna Russ/Feminism/Science Fiction*. Liverpool: Liverpool University Press.

Csicsery-Ronay, Istvan, Jr. (2008): *The Seven Beauties of Science Fiction*. Middletown, CT: Wesleyan University Press.

Daston, Lorraine (1988): *Classical Probability in the Enlightenment*. Princeton, NJ: Princeton University Press.

Daston, Lorraine/Galison, Peter (2007): *Objectivity*. Cambridge, MA: MIT Press.

Davis, Heather/Turpin, Etienne (eds.) (2015): *Art in the Anthropocene: Encounters among Aesthetics, Politics, Environments and Epistemologies*. London: Open Humanities Press.

Deleuze, Gilles/Guattari, Félix ([1980] 2003): *A Thousand Plateaus: Capitalism and Schizophrenia*. Brian Massumi (trans.). London: Continuum.

Desrosières, Alain ([1993] 1998): *The Politics of Large Numbers: A History of Statistical Reasoning*. Cambridge, MA: Harvard University Press.

Diez, Georg/Heisenberg, Emanuel (2020): *Power to the People: Wie wir mit Technologie die Demokratie neu erfinden*. Berlin: Hanser.

Doyle, Richard (2003): *Wetwares: Experiments in Postvital Living*. Minneapolis: University of Minnesota Press.

Dumit, Joseph (2012): *Drugs for Life: How Pharmaceutical Companies Define Our Health*. Durham, NC: Duke University Press.

Elias, Norbert ([1975] 1994): "Introduction: A Theoretical Essay on Established and Outsider Relations." In: Norbert Elias/John L. Scotson: *The Established and the Outsiders: A Sociological Enquiry into Community Problems*. Second ed. London: Sage, xv–lii.

Fisher, William F./Ponniah, Thomas (eds.) (2003): *Another World Is Possible: Popular Alternatives to Globalization at the World Social Forum*. London: Zed Books.

Fortun, Michael (2008): *Promising Genomics: Iceland and deCODE Genetics in a World of Speculation*. Berkeley: University of California Press.

Franklin, H. Bruce ([1988] 2008): *War Stars: The Superweapon and the American Imagination*. Rev. and expanded ed. Amherst, MA: University of Massachusetts Press.

Freedman, Carl (2000): *Science Fiction and Critical Theory*. Hanover, NH: Wesleyan University Press.

Ghosh, Bishnupriya/Sarkar, Bhaskar (eds.) (2020): *The Routledge Companion to Media and Risk*. London: Routledge.

Hacking, Ian (1990): *The Taming of Chance*. Cambridge: Cambridge University Press.

Hanke, Christine (2007): *Zwischen Auflösung und Fixierung: Zur Konstitution von 'Rasse' und 'Geschlecht' in der physischen Anthropologie um 1900*. Bielefeld: transcript.

Hanke, Christine (2014): "Alles nur Programm? Überlegungen zum Unprogrammierten der Medien(wissenschaft)." In: Dieter Mersch/Joachim Paech (eds.): *Programm(e): Medienwissenschaftliche Symposien der DFG*. Berlin: Diaphanes, 269–297.

Hannah, Matthew G. (2010): *Dark Territory in the Information Age: Learning from the West German Census Controversies of the 1980s*. Farnham: Ashgate.

Hannah, Matthew G./Hutta, Jan Simon/Schemann, Christoph (2020): "Thinking through Covid-19 Responses with Foucault: An Initial Overview." *Antipode Online*, May 5 (https://antipodeonline.org/2020/05/05/thinking-through-covid-19-responses-with-foucault/).

Haraway, Donna J. (1988): "Situated Knowledges: The Science Question in Feminism and the Privilege of Partial Perspective." In: *Feminist Studies* 14, 575–599.

Haraway, Donna J. (1997): *Modest_Witness@Second_Millennium.FemaleMan©_Meets_OncoMouse™: Feminism and Technoscience*. New York: Routledge.

Haraway, Donna J. (2016): *Staying with the Trouble: Making Kin in the Chthulucene*. Durham, NC: Duke University Press.

Hayles, N Katherine (1999): *How We Became Posthuman: Virtual Bodies in Cybernetics, Literature, and Informatics*. Chicago: University of Chicago Press.

Higgins, David M./O'Connell, Hugh C. (eds.) (2019): *Speculative Finance/Speculative Fiction* [special issue]. In: *CR: The New Centennial Review* 19, 1–301.

Indigenous Action (2020): "Rethinking the Apocalypse. An Indigenous Anti-Futurist Manifesto," March 19 (http://www.indigenousaction.org/rethinking-the-apocalypse-an-indigenous-anti-futurist-manifesto/).

Jameson, Fredric (2005): *Archaeologies of the Future: The Desire Called Utopia and Other Science Fictions*. London: Verso.

Jerng, Mark C. (2018): *Racial Worldmaking: The Power of Popular Fiction*. New York: Fordham University Press.

Jordan, Silvia/Mitterhofer, Hermann/Jørgensen, Lene (2018): "The Interdiscursive Appeal of Risk Matrices: Collective Symbols, Flexibility Normalism and the Interplay of 'Risk' and 'Uncertainty'." In: *Accounting, Organizations and Society* 67, 34–55.

Jordheim, Helge/Lie, Anne Kveim/Ljungberg, Erik/Wigen, Einar (2020): "Epidemic Times." In: *Somatosphere*, April 2, http://somatosphere.net/2020/epidemic-times.html/.

Jue, Melody (2020): *Wild Blue Media: Thinking through Seawater*. Durham, NC: Duke University Press.

Juris, Jeffrey S. (2008): *Networking Futures: The Movements against Corporate Globalization*. Durham, NC: Duke University Press.

Kershaw, Baz (2008): "Performance as Research: Live Events and Documents." In: Tracy C. Davis (ed.): *The Cambridge Companion to Performance Studies*. Cambridge: Cambridge University Press, 23–45.

Kershaw, Baz (2009): "Performance Practice as Research: Perspectives from a Small Island." In: Shannon Rose Riley/Lynette Hunter (eds.): *Mapping Landscapes for Performance as Research: Scholarly Acts and Creative Cartographies*. London: Palgrave McMillan, 3–13.

Kilgore, De Witt Douglas (2003): *Astrofuturism: Science, Race, and Visions of Utopia in Space*. Philadelphia: University of Pennsylvania Press.

Knorr Cetina, Karin/Preda, Alex (eds.) (2005): *The Sociology of Financial Markets*. Oxford: Oxford University Press.

Landon, Brooks (2014): "Extrapolation and Speculation." In: Rob Latham (Ed.): *The Oxford Handbook of Science Fiction*. Oxford: Oxford University Press, 23–34.

Levitas, Ruth (2013): *Utopia as Method: The Imaginary Reconstitution of Society*. Houndmills: Palgrave Macmillan.

Link, Jürgen (1996): *Versuch über den Normalismus: Wie Normalität produziert wird*. Opladen: Westfälisches Dampfboot.

Link, Jürgen (2004a): "From the 'Power of the Norm' to 'Flexible Normalism': Considerations after Foucault." Mirko M. Hall (trans.). In: *Cultural Critique* 57, 14–32.

Link, Jürgen (2004b): "On the Contribution of Normalism to Modernity and Postmodernity." Mirko M. Hall (trans.). In: *Cultural Critique* 57, 33–46.

Link, Jürgen (2004c): "The Normalistic Subject and Its Curves: On the Symbolic Visualization of Orienteering Data." Mirko M. Hall (trans.). In: *Cultural Critique* 57, 47–67.

Link, Jürgen (2004d): "On the Temporal Quality of the Normalistic 'Fun and Thrill' Tape." Mirko M. Hall (trans.). In: *Cultural Critique* 57, 68–90.

LiPuma, Edward/Lee, Benjamin (2004): *Financial Derivatives and the Globalization of Risk*. Durham, NC: Duke University Press.

Lütz, Susanne (2017): "Finanzmärkte." In: Andreas Maurer (ed.): *Handbuch der Wirtschaftssoziologie*. Second ed. Wiesbaden: Springer, 385–413.

Maeße, Jens/Sparsam, Jan (2017): "Die Performativität der Wirtschaftswissenschaft." In: Andreas Maurer (ed.): *Handbuch der Wirtschaftssoziologie*. Second ed. Wiesbaden: Springer, 181–195.

Mavhunga, Clapperton Chakanetsa (2018): *The Mobile Workshop: The Tsetse Fly and African Knowledge Production.* Cambridge, MA: MIT Press.

Mayer, Ruth/Weingart, Brigitte (eds.) (2004): *Virus! Mutationen einer Metapher.* Bielefeld: transcript.

Mayer, Sylvia/Weik von Mossner, Alexa (eds.) (2014): *The Anticipation of Catastrophe: Environmental Risk in North American Literature and Culture.* Heidelberg: Universitätsverlag Winter.

McNally, David ([2002] 2006): *Another World Is Possible: Globalization and Anti-Capitalism.* Rev. expanded ed. Winnipeg: Arbeiter Ring.

Merchant, Briant (2020): "Coronavirus Is Speeding Up the Amazonification of the Planet." In: *OneZero*, March 19 (https://onezero.medium.com/coronavirus-is-speeding-up-the-amazonification-of-the-planet-21cb20d16372).

Merril, Judith ([1966] 2017): "What Do You Mean: Science? Fiction?" In: Rob Latham (ed.): *Science Fiction Criticism: An Anthology of Essential Writings.* London: Bloomsbury, 22–36.

Meyer, Emilio P.N./Bustamente, Thomas (2020): "Authoritarianism Without Emergency Powers: Brazil Under COVID-19." In: *Verfassungsblog on Matters Constitutional*, April 8 (https://verfassungsblog.de/authoritarianism-without-emergency-powers-brazil-under-covid-19).

Mignolo, Walter (2011): *The Darker Side of Western Modernity: Global Futures, Decolonial Options.* Durham, NC: Duke University Press.

Milburn, Colin (2008): *Nanovision: Engineering the Future.* Durham, NC: Duke University Press.

Milburn, Colin (2015): *Mondo Nano: Fun and Games in the World of Digital Matter.* Durham, NC: Duke University Press.

Milburn, Colin (2018): *Respawn: Gamers, Hackers, and Technogenic Life.* Durham, NC: Duke University Press.

Milburn, Colin (2020): "The Future at Stake: Modes of Speculation in *The Highest Frontier* and *Microbiology: An Evolving Science.*" In: Bruce Clarke (ed.): *Posthuman Biopolitics: The Science Fiction of Joan Slonczewski.* Cham: Palgrave Macmillan, 133–160.

Mitchell, Timothy (2002): *Rule of Experts: Egypt, Techno-Politics, Modernity.* Berkeley: University of California Press.

Nobre, Marcos (2019): "O Caos Como Método." In: *Piauí*, no. 151, April (https://piaui.folha.uol.com.br/materia/o-caos-como-metodo/).

Otto, Eric C (2012): *Green Speculations: Science Fiction and Transformative Environmentalism.* Columbus: Ohio State University Press.

Patel, Geeta (2017): *Risky Bodies and Techno-Intimacy: Reflections on Sexuality, Media, Science, Finance.* Seattle: University of Washington Press.

Penley, Constance (1997): *NASA/Trek: Popular Science and Sex in America.* London: Verso.

Peterson, Kristin (2014): *Speculative Markets: Drug Circuits and Derivative Life in Nigeria*. Durham, NC: Duke University Press.

Porter, Theodore M. (1986): *The Rise of Statistical Thinking, 1820–1900*. Princeton, NJ: Princeton University Press.

Preda, Alex (2005): "The Investor as a Cultural Figure of Global Capitalism." In: Karin Knorr Cetina/Alex Preda (eds.): *The Sociology of Financial Markets*. Oxford: Oxford University Press, 141–162.

Rees, Amanda/Morus, Iwan Rhys (eds.) (2019): *Presenting Futures Past: Science Fiction and the History of Science* [special issue]. In: *Osiris* 34.

Russ, Joanna (1972): "The Image of Women in Science Fiction." In: Rob Latham (ed.): *Science Fiction Criticism: An Anthology of Essential Writings*. London: Bloomsbury, 200–210.

Saler, Michael (2012): *As If: Modern Enchantment and the Literary Prehistory of Virtual Reality*. Oxford: Oxford University Press.

Sargent, Lyman Tower (2010): *Utopianism: A Very Short Introduction*. Oxford: Oxford University Press.

Servitje, Lorenzo/Vint, Sherryl (eds.): *The Walking Med: Zombies and the Medical Image*. University Park, PA: Penn State University Press, 2016.

Sharp, Patrick B. (2018): *Darwinian Feminism and Early Science Fiction: Angels, Amazons, and Women*. Cardiff: University of Wales Press.

Squier, Susan Merrill. (2004): *Liminal Lives: Imagining the Human at the Frontiers of Biomedicine*. Durham, NC: Duke University Press.

Stäheli, Urs (2013 [2007]): *Spectacular Speculation: Thrills, the Economy, and Popular Discourse*. Eric Savoth (trans.). Stanford, CA: Stanford University Press.

Strick, Simon (2020): "Digitally Drunk." In: *Zeitschrift für Medienwissenschaft: Gender-Blog*, March 28 (https://www.zfmedienwissenschaft.de/online/blog/digitally-drunk).

Streeby, Shelley (2018): *Imagining the Future of Climate Change: World-Making through Science Fiction and Activism*. Berkeley: University of California Press.

Stutz, Ulrike (2008): "Performative Forschung in der Kunstpädagogik am Beispiel von Szenen aus dem Seminar 'Erforschen performativer Rituale im Stadtraum.'" In: *Forum: Qualitative Social Research* 9(2) (http://dx.doi.org/10.17169/fqs-9.2.411).

Sunder Rajan, Kaushik (2006): *Biocapital: The Constitution of Postgenomic Life*. Durham, NC: Duke University Press.

Tilley, Helen (2011): *Africa as a Living Laboratory: Empire, Development, and the Problem of Scientific Knowledge, 1870–1950*. Chicago: Chicago University Press.

Treichler, Paula (1989): "AIDS, Homophobia, and Biomedical Discourse: An Epidemic of Signification." In: Douglas Crimp (ed.): *AIDS: Cultural Analysis/Cultural Activism*, Cambridge, MA: MIT Press, 31–70.

Turney, Jon (1998): *Frankenstein's Footsteps: Science, Genetics and Popular Culture*. New Haven: Yale University Press.

uncertain commons (2013): *Speculate This!* Durham, NC: Duke University Press

Vint, Sherryl (ed.) (2015): *The Futures Industry* [special issue]. In: *Paradoxa* 27, 7–282.

Wald, Priscilla (2008): *Contagious: Cultures, Carriers, and the Outbreak Narrative*. Durham, NC: Duke University Press.

Waldby, Cathy/Mitchell, Robert (2006): *Tissue Economies: Blood, Organs, and Cell Lines in Late Capitalism*. Durham, NC: Duke University Press.

Wilkie, Alex/Savransky, Martin/Rosengarten, Marsha (eds.) (2017): *Speculative Research: The Lure of Possible Futures*. London: Routledge.

Willis, Martin (2006): *Mesmerists, Monsters, and Machines: Science Fiction and the Cultures of Science in the Nineteenth Century*. Kent, OH: Kent State University Press.

Zaloom, Caitlin (2004): "Productive Life of Risk." In: *Cultural Anthropology* 19, 365–391.

Zaloom, Caitlin (2005) "The Discipline of Speculators." In: Aihwa Ong/Stephen J. Collier (eds.): *Global Assemblages: Technology, Politics, and Ethics as Anthropological Problems*. Malden, MA: Blackwell, 253–269.

Chapter 1: Cultures of Speculation—Histories of Speculation

Susanne Lachenicht

What is speculation? And since when have human societies developed *cultures of speculation*?

Cultures of speculation—the story goes—are inextricably linked to modernity, or, as Ulrich Beck suggests, the age of "simple modernity" (Beck 1994). For a couple of decades now, this "simple modernity" has been moving towards "reflexive modernity" or "risk society" (Beck [1986] 1992). If we follow this linear, teleological narrative, the early modern period conceived of as pre-modernity or the pre-industrialization period would have been the age that preceded modernity. Cultures of speculation, then, might have slowly started to develop with the Renaissance, the (European) expansion of empires, and the increasing exploitation of human beings, land, oceans, of resources of any kind with the rise of capitalism (Moore 2016; Levy 2012)—so, between the fourteenth and twentieth centuries (cf. uncertain commons 2013).

However, what is speculation? And what are cultures of speculation? More often than not, they have been depicted as prioritizing "trade in the future" (Haiven 2017: 4), putting "the future at the service of the present," and developing a set of practices that "converted the future from an enemy into an opportunity" (Bernstein 1996: 1). Modernity—according to some authors—was about bringing risk under control (Bernstein 1996: 11), about trading perils (pre-modern) for calculable risk (modern).

Some scholars claim that our so-called globalized society today "still largely privilege[s] a business-as-usual approach that reduces futures to matters of anticipation, calculation, management and pre-emption of risks and uncertainties in the present" (Wilkie/Savransky/Rosengarten 2017: 1). Others have gone further and have voiced serious doubts that we have any sense of the future at all, that we have ever been "modern" (Latour [1991] 1993), and that we have ever quit the immutable present—meaning that (we think) that nothing essentially new (can) occur(s) and/or that there is no development, a worldview that the historian Reinhart Koselleck associated with the pre-modern period (Koselleck [1979] 2004: 58; cf. uncertain commons 2013).

If cultures of speculation, as Wilkie, Savransky, and Rosengarten suggest, have mostly been about bringing *present* (especially financial) risks under control, then how old are cultures of speculation? Do they emerge with the Anthropocene (Crutzen/Stroemer 2000), that is, when humans started becoming a geological factor on earth, or with the Capitalocene (Moore 2015, 2016)? Many scholars hold that financialization, "the growing power of the so-called FIRE (finance, insurance and real estate) sector over the rest of capitalist economy" (Haiven 2017: 2), is one of the key elements of "risk society" today. Some call it "a global empire of speculative finance" (Haiven 2017: 2). However, societies and their economies have depended for thousands of years on historical forms of finance, whether in the context of agriculture, slave societies, or the Industrial Revolution. Lending, holding debt, and speculating on the return of credit are rather old in human history (Lapavitsas 2013; Ceccarelli 2016). According to some scholars, though, the seventeenth century brought about a major shift in risk assessment and calculation. Mathematicians such as Blaise Pascal and Pierre de Fermat developed a theory of probability. By 1725, mathematicians set out to calculate mortality and life expectancies, and by the mid-eighteenth century, insurance based on probability calculations was in place (Bernstein 1996: 57–96). Pre-probability calculation insurance had already been available from the mid-fourteenth century, mostly to cover maritime risks for commerce and trade in the Mediterranean, Northern, Western, and Near Eastern worlds. At the center of late medieval or early modern risk management with regard to commerce and trade, we find Venice and Florence (Ceccarelli 2016); from the sixteenth century onwards, Atlantic sea ports such as Bordeaux, Nantes, and London; and from the seventeenth century, Amsterdam and Hamburg (Zwierlein 2011: 27–29). With these insurance practices, speculation, that is, risk calculation was mostly about space: perils at sea, such as storms, pirates, shipwreck, or mutiny. Insurance was to cover uncertainty in a given space; it was less invested in a given time frame or with regard to more sophisticated notions of the future (Zwierlein 2011: 54–55). Has this changed? Or is this the immutable present? Historians hold that scale, which involves the temporal, societal, and spatial dimensions of the production and effects of speculation, changed dramatically over the last five hundred years, in particular with globalization taking off from the late-nineteenth century (Osterhammel/Petersson 2003). Cultures of speculation would then be closely related to processes of globalization.

The authors of *Speculate This!* suggest distinguishing between two distinct modes of speculation: firmative and affirmative (uncertain commons 2013). Firmative speculation is meant to "pin down, delimit, constrain, and enclose" the future, which thus becomes (more) predictable. Affirmative speculation is to refuse "the foreclosure of potentialities," it is about uncertainties, it is "to hold on to the spectrum of possibilities" (uncertain commons 2013: Prospects). We cannot clearly separate firmative and affirmative speculation. They form a tension field, they are in a dynamic and dialectic relationship with each other. Speculation about futures, then, would not only be about the probable, calculable, or plausible, but also about the possible and the impossible, "about futures that the present could never anticipate" (Wilkie/Savransky/Rosengarten 2017: 8).

Sophisticated methods to calculate risk developed during the Italian Renaissance. Cultures of speculation emerged with "business partnerships," "insurance contracts, or specialized markets for currency exchange and the trading of government bonds" (Ceccarelli 2016: 117–118). However, as early as the medieval period, speculation was also about testing, about the visible and the invisible, the knowable and the non-knowable, the certain and the uncertain. Different genres were used for speculation: philosophical and theological writings, travel literature, satire, utopian romances (starting with Thomas More's *Utopia* of 1516), and the visual arts.

In this chapter, I would like to zoom into the so-called pre-modern period, which, in a linear narrative, would have preceded modernity and Beck's "reflexive modernity." We are going to look into concepts of time and modes of speculation, into how different contexts and genres invited different forms of speculation. In this way, I would like to open up some "horizons of speculation" of the early modern period by using the latter as a *speculum* for today's cultures of speculation. I seek to test how much speculation in the early modern period might have been about speculating "about futures that are more than a mere extension of the present" (Wilkie/Savransky/Rosengarten 2017: 2), but also about speculating on the past (Landwehr 2016: 231–246), on eternity and untime.

'Discoveries,' Conquest, and Colonization

Despite centuries of human travel to foreign destinations, from the perspective of the so-called Atlantic World, uncertainties about the world allegedly increased with the rise and expansion of the Portuguese, Spanish, French, English, and Dutch empires, as well as the Ottoman, Safavid and Moghul empires from the 1400s onwards (Canny/Morgan 2011; Darwin 2017). Migrations (including the forced migrations of African slaves), the rise of plantation systems, the development of new and old economies, the Atlantic revolutions, nation-building and independence movements, and the accelerated exchange of knowledge and goods, brought about a higher degree of risk, financial risk in particular. Europeans back home, especially those who financed voyages of exploration and colonial ventures, would have perceived an increasing risk of failing enterprises, lost money, collapsed investments, and unfulfilled expectations. In this regard, the cultures of speculation were largely about bringing financial risk under control (Bernstein 1996; Zwierlein 2016).

Europeans struggled in their westward expansion with unknown sea currents, winds, storms, hurricanes, pirates and interlopers, as well as a variety of new climates, landscapes, resources, and cultures (Canny/Morgan 2011). Europeans, as Michel Foucault might have put it, moved "from the restrictive figures of similitude" to describing and classifying "difference and discontinuity" ([1966] 1970: 51).

Some of the earliest documents of the era of 'discoveries,' such as founding charters and royal privileges, illustrate the double-edged increase in risk and uncertainty. The 1492 *Privileges and Prerogatives Granted by Their Catholic Majesties to Christopher Columbus*, for example, makes clear that, in sailing west to unknown shores, Columbus was risking his and his shipmates' lives. But in case he should survive, Isabella of Castile and Ferdinand of Aragon granted Columbus the rights of an admiral, viceroy, and governor, which included the right to exploit any seas, lands, and peoples he might 'discover' or conquer. In the project of colonization, the taking over of all financial risks by a future proprietor or a merchants' company required major funds; the crown, in passing on those risks to merchant venturers, assured them of all the necessary rights to exploit the resources, human and non-human, of the colony to be founded. Taking risk, then, was about taking opportunities, about chancing *fortuna*; furthermore, calculating risk was not the least about the exploitation of unknown resources. One of the first English Letter Patents that King Henry VIII issued in 1496 for the Venetian Giovanni Caboto states: "upon their owne proper costs and charges, to seeke out, discover, and find whatsoever isles, countreys, regions or provinces of the heathen and infidels" ("Letters Patent to John Cabot" [1496] 1909: 46). In return, Caboto was allowed to "subdue, occupy and possesse all such townes, cities, castles and isles of them found, which they can subdue, occupy and possesse" and "be holden and bounder of all the fruits, profits, gaines, and commodities growing of such navigation" (46). Similar Letter Patents can be found for King Henry IV of France when, in 1603, he granted the Charter of Acadia to Pierre Du Gua de Monts, or again in England, in the first Virginia Charter of 1606 or the charters for Maryland (1632), the Carolinas (1663), and Pennsylvania (1681) (*Avalon Project*). These charters, however, simply further developed older, medieval patterns, established to grant major fiefs to dukes, counts and other vassals of the crown—especially when a given kingdom had acquired new lands during (and after) warfare. Members of the aristocracy and/or army officers received patents to exert royal control in newly acquired countries, to establish the prince's jurisdiction, armies, commerce, and trade. This required strict loyalty to the king. Furthermore, a certain percentage of the revenues coming out of a given fief or colony had to be left to the king, while the proprietor, lord lieutenant, or viceroy received monopolies for certain resources and goods. Peril, uncertainty, and risk entailed the right to conquest and exploitation. What was then new about European expansion—especially the one to the west?

I would argue that the expansion of European (and non-European) empires in the early modern period opened up 1) a larger plurality of time/space relationships, 2) a higher degree of uncertainties, 3) the scale of financial (and other) risks *and* opportunities, and 4) more varieties of firmative and affirmative speculation.

Time Regimes, Concepts of Time

Cultures of speculation are largely characterized by what notions of futurity they bring into play. Theorists of time (including historians) have often warned against purely linear concepts of time that organize time "along a modern arrow of progress" and have suggested to take varieties of concepts of time more seriously—including different futurities (Wilkie/Savransky/Rosengarten 2017: 4–5). However, speculation is not restricted to the future or similar timescapes. We can also speculate about the past, the immutable present, eternity, or untime. Furthermore, timescapes are context-related. To look into cultures of speculation—so-called modern or pre-modern ones—we thus need to inquire into contexts and time concepts.

With the Renaissance and the rise of the new sciences, concepts of time, timescapes, changed—or, to put it differently, the plurality of concepts of time increased (Brendecke/Fuchs/Koller 2007: 13). Many Renaissance theologians and philosophers started thinking and speculating on time. For instance, Petrarca (1304–1374) perceived humans as historical beings owning a past (*memoria*), a present (*ingenium*), and a future (*providentia*) (Keßler 2007: 34), even though the Latin suggests a rather different meaning of these three periods of time than our contemporary translation has it. However, not all humans had history, not all humans had a future.

During the so-called Age of Discovery, it became 'clear' for Christians/Europeans that they lived in present and civilized times, while non-Christian/non-European cultures—according to their degree of 'barbarism' and 'lack of civilization'—lived in the past (Fabian 2002: 75). This past, however, was different from European Antiquity (e.g. Thevet 1558: 54). According to many European authors, non-Europeans and Europeans did not share the same moment in history, nor did they share the same past. For André Thevet (1516–1590), a French Franciscan friar, explorer, and cosmographer who travelled to the Eastern Mediterranean and Brazil, Europeans lived in "modern times"; "savages," however, were closer "to man's origins, so to paradise" (Thevet 1558: 54, 87, 95). From Thevet's perspective, the "savages" lived in an immutable present (cf. Fabian's "allochrony" and "ethnographic present," 2002: 76) and had no history—at least, not prior to the arrival of Europeans (Thevet 1558: 84, 101–103, 106; cf. Labat 1722: 222, 317, 332). Only with conquest, colonization, and Christian missions, indigenous peoples of the Americas entered human history and thus progress; they turned into 'objects' that now had a past, present, and future (Fabian 2002: 78). By the Renaissance, we see time and civilization coming together. Civilization and the future, progress, develop into one timescape: "evolutionary time" (Fabian 2002: 17, 29). This timescape was closely related to the context of 'discoveries,' conquest, colonization, and the increasing exploitation of New World resources, human and non-human; it was a colonial concept that the colonized could not escape (cf. Hunt 2008: 94–96).

Only Europeans, as the present and modern people, were allegedly able to speculate on their own and other cultures' state of civilization. It was also up to Europeans to bring humanity closer to a Golden Age, a worldly one. The new sciences and new technologies, developed by Europeans, as many proponents of the Enlightenment claimed, could guide mankind back into a new Eden—on earth.

All of this sounds, indeed, like a pre-modern cultures of speculation narrative with the timescape *past—present—future* paving the way to modernity and its teleology about historical progress (Hunt 2008: 107). However, while the so-called European pre-modern period had "models of linear and measurable time" (Nagel/Wood 2005: 408), and while timescapes were developed that Newton and natural scientists would later call "absolute time," this was only one of a plurality of ways of organizing time and of being in time. Absolute time, then, was an invention, based on a metaphysical system important to the developing new sciences. It was also a highly contested timescape, criticized by empiricists such as David Hume and rationalists such as Gottfried Wilhelm Leibniz (Wilcox 1987: 17–18).

God's time regime (Gallois 2007: 243), however, embedded and integrated evolutionary time, models of linear and measurable time (Le Goff's famous "merchant's time" [1977] 1980), as much as absolute time—the biblical beginning of history and the end of mankind. Even if 'modern' timescapes such as evolutionary time and absolute time challenged this predominant timescape, God's time regime remained the most powerful far into the nineteenth century. Time was divided into this world and the hereafter: life, death, and eternity. Quite contrary to 'modern' visions of the future of mankind, which all seem to share great uncertainty about what the future might look like, Europeans of the early modern period could be sure about the end of history. The Bible seemed to be clear about the destiny of mankind. Humans would live through four ages (Babylon, Persia, the Greek, and the Roman), followed by the fifth age which would include the arrival of the Antichrist, the battle between good and evil, the very likely victory of Jesus Christ, the Last Judgement, and the end of days. While Christians could not be sure of the exact beginning of the fifth age, they knew, thanks to the revelations of St. John, what would await them (Gallois 2007: 244). Uncertainty reigned with regard to who would be among God's elect and who among the eternally condemned. Far into the nineteenth century (and for Christian believers up to the present day), speculating about the future of mankind seemed unnecessary, as God had provided for a teleological and orderly history of man (Gallois 2007: 33–35).

While mankind shared clear beginnings and a likely end of time, early modern Europeans, as many discourses from the fifteenth to the eighteenth centuries betray, could also be sure that they were in the hand of God, and if among the elect, guided by him—despite the many uncertainties about New World ventures. Zooming back into the late fifteenth century, we can see Isabella of Castile and Ferdinand of Aragon aware of the risks Columbus did run in sailing westwards; they hoped for the "assistance of God." Columbus, in his 1493 letter to Luis de Santángel, echoed the belief that he had been guided by God, who had granted him his successful voyage at sea (Mancall 2006: 209). Parallels can be drawn to Protestant Europe: in his New England Charter of 1620, King James I of England hoped that by establishing this colony he would "advance in Largement of Christian Religion, to the Glory of God Almighty," and he was sure that the colonizers would enjoy "God's assistance" and "God's divine blessing." Furthermore, James stated that the English, in colonizing that territory, "second and followe God's sacred Will, rendering reverend Thanks to his Divine Majestie for his gracious favour in laying open and revealing the same unto us" ("Charter of New England" [1620] 1909: 1830).

Surviving danger, calamities, peril depended on God's will, his pity, compassion, and grace—*and* on the growing abilities of man to calculate risk, to measure God's world, and to reign over his resources. In the long run, God's time regime was challenged, through humanism—which already by 1450 had produced "two canons" (Grafton 1992: 29)—the development of new sciences, and the radical Enlightenment. Paradigms changed with encounters with new worlds and, as Francis Bacon put it in his 1620 *Instauratio magna*, through new sciences being a result of the age of humanism and the 'discoveries' in the Atlantic World. New sciences, Bacon claimed, "could affect the course of nature in useful ways, knowledge about how to ward off disease, improve crops, extend the span of life, and enhance the general welfare" (Grafton 1992: 197).

It is important to state that the coexistence of overlapping or clashing temporalities (Nagel/Wood 2005: 404)—a plurality of temporalities as parallel, contextualized experiences coming together in *one moment*—was rather typical of the early modern period (Febvre [1942] 1982: 393–400). Despite the challenges of the developing new sciences and their *a priori* of measurable, linear, and—to some extent—absolute time, God's time regime was the one that embedded and integrated all other ones (from the emic, that is, the historical actors' perspectives). This is particularly true for the visual arts: what Alexander Nagel and Christopher S. Wood have dubbed "Renaissance anachronism" is rather typical far into the eighteenth and nineteenth centuries. Artefacts and monuments, especially if used in sacred/ritual events, were "embedded in history" even as their "spiritual meaning

[...] lifted the event out of the flow of history": "Visual artefacts collapsed past and present. They proposed an unmediated, present-tense, somatic encounter with the people and the things of the past" (Nagel/Wood 2005: 408).

While biblical narratives of the beginning and the end of the world—as much as the new sciences—strengthened linear and teleological temporalities, humans in the early modern period lived with plural concepts of time, allowing them specific forms of speculation. Like Einstein's later notions on the relativity of time, so-called pre-modern concepts or pluralities of time turn "modern western time"—"which describes itself as being rational, observational, chronological, universal, unambiguous, fixed, natural, constant"—into an "historical anomaly in human culture" (Gallois 2007: 221, 246–247). But how did the plurality of timescapes affect speculation in the early modern period?

Travel Narratives and Utopian Literatures

Travel narratives and utopian romances, which have often been defined as separate literary genres, exemplify the early modern period's cultures of speculation. More often than not, travel narratives cannot be clearly separated from fantastic, satirical, or utopian texts, and most of them come with firmative and affirmative elements. Travel narratives are as old as human history. Among the most famous are Marco Polo's of the late thirteenth century and John de Mandeville's of the later fourteenth century.

Printing made travel narratives (including so-called fantastic travels) widely available, especially in the sixteenth century and later. Next to printing, oral accounts and manuscripts continued to spread news about the wonders of the world (Mancall 2006: 4–7; Greenblatt 1991). In travel narratives, uncertainties play an eminent role, especially in stories where Europeans voyage to unknown shores. Many narratives from the Age of Discovery are based on logbooks and journals that explorers kept during their voyages, such as Columbus's logbook from 1492. The same holds for Amerigo Vespucci's *Mundus novus* of 1504, Jacques Cartier's travel account, published in Paris in 1545, and Captain John Smith's of the early 1600s—to name but a few. From these early European expansion travel narratives, we learn about things to be feared on these voyages. While most seamen, already in the 1400s, no longer believed in the terrifying edge of the abyss that should have awaited them if they had sailed too far west or east, sailing the Atlantic was nonetheless a terrifying thing. As Amerigo Vespucci writes in his 1504 *Mundus novus*:

> But what we suffered on that vast expanse of sea, what perils of shipwreck, what discomforts of the body we endured, with what anxiety of mind toiled, this I leave to the judgement of those who out of rich experience have well learned what it is

to seek the uncertain and to attempt discoveries even though ignorant. (Mancall 2006: 218)

Furthermore, as Columbus's logbook shows, his seamen were afraid of never finding any winds that would bring them back to Spain. They were afraid of their knowledge of the stars being untrustworthy. They were afraid of their maps being wrong about the actual islands in the Atlantic (Mancall 2006: 209–214).

Speculation about these unknown worlds and their uncertainties meant struggling to make the unknown better known, controllable. When describing new worlds from European eyes, travel narratives of the early modern period relied on older models in telling their stories, often models that had been in place since Antiquity. Furthermore, the 'new' could only be described through the already known, and the unknown was made known through comparisons, analogies, and classifications based on already existent knowledge (Pagden 1982: 1–4). Between the fifteenth and seventeenth centuries, Europeans drew upon a set of biblical (Old and New Testament) and mythological, that is, pagan images and paradigms. While (what we now call) the un- or supranatural was an element of everyday life even back in Europe, the further Europeans moved into unknown parts of the world, the more likely it became to meet monsters, pygmies, amazons, mermaids, giants, and other species as described, for example, by Pliny the Elder in his *Naturalis historia* (AD 77–79). Monstrous species inhabited the rim of the world. In one of his letters to Luis de Santángel (1493), Columbus seemed to be surprised to find no antique monsters in the West Indies (Mancall 2006: 212). Sailing westwards, then, must have been a rather 'calculable risk,' as many explorers thought they knew what and whom they would encounter. Had not Plato described Atlantis? Had not Seneca prophesized the 'discovery' of new worlds in his *Medea*? Cartographers and chroniclers in the sixteenth and early seventeenth centuries seem to have been well able to make the New World look old, for example, claiming that American Indians were descendants of some of the lost tribes of Israel. The 'discoveries' were, then, just "another classical revival" (Grafton 1992: 58, 149).

In the long run, though, describing new worlds through ancient texts proved to be a conundrum, a paradox. Drawing analogies, describing new worlds through ancient texts, images and concepts failed abysmally. Not only did the so-called New World upset much of what Europeans thought they knew about God and his world. The New World also required new concepts, and God's world had to be reconceptualized. Or, as Edmundo O'Gorman (1972) and Walter Mignolo (2005) have argued: helpless to grasp the New World with what they knew, Europeans 'invented' new worlds, first, according to their imaginary—concepts and paradigms—then through developing new, speculative categories based on Native American, African, and Asian knowledge (Mignolo 1992, 1995; Lachenicht 2019). The Age of Discovery changed the European canon of knowledge. It fostered encroachments on ancient texts, the Bible in particular. Certainties about God's world, this world, and the world hereafter came to be challenged. Affirmative speculation about the new, about the world to be, became common practice.

The Age of Discovery not only produced more travel narratives but also what has been dubbed a new genre: utopian literatures (Bruce 1999: ix–xi), which often open up as travel narratives. There has been much debate whether early modern utopias are about ideal or future societies, and how they relate to *real* space and time. While many early modern utopias are set up in yet to be 'discovered' space (Koselleck 1982: 2–3)—often Atlantic or Indian Ocean worlds—they have no temporal dimension, they are not about future societies (Bruce 1999: xiii). I would argue that utopias are—as (and together with) satires—the most speculative literary genre in the early modern period—while building on older biblical, ancient Greek and medieval models. Utopian literatures are speculative as 1) they always come as a mirror, a "distorted reflection" (Bruce 1999: xxiv) of the societies that produced them, and 2) they speculate at the same time about untime, about imagined worlds that *are not* and are not meant to be (cf. Marin 1973; Greenblatt 1980: 22). Many early modern utopias are dystopias, satires, and parodies at the same time. Some Renaissance and Baroque texts, such as Miguel de Cervantes's *Don Quixote* (1605/1615) or Rabelais's *Gargantua et Pantagruel* (1532–1564), have been classified as chivalric satires (Winter 1978); some, such as Cyrano de Bergerac's (1619–1655) *Les États et Empires de la Lune* (postum 1657) and *Les États et Empires du Soleil* (postum 1662) or Jonathan Swift's *Gulliver's Travels* (1726), have been described as satirical, fantastic travel narratives. Other narratives, such as Thomas More's *Utopia* (1516), Tommaso Campanella's *La città del sole* (1623), or Francis Bacon's *The New Atlantis* (1627), have been identified as real utopias, self-consciously depicting ideal societies. However, there is much doubt that the eponym of the utopian genre, Thomas More's *Utopia*, was meant to describe an ideal society (Bruce 1999: xvi–xviii). Rather, like Rabelais's work, it is as much a satire of More's own world as it is about alternative possibilities of his time (Bruce 1999: xix–xxvii).

Despite their originalities and specificities, utopian *and* fantastic narratives both critically (and often satirically) assess their own time and the possibilities arising from the 'discoveries' and the new sciences of the period. They are written from historical presentist perspectives (on presentism, see Lachenicht 2018: 5; Landwehr 2016: 28–39). They are not speculating on possible futures, but on untime and *Unorte* (spaces off) while reflecting the present (cf. Nakládalová 2013: 7). Most of these utopian narratives start in either the author's present or some past time. Voyagers set off to travel somewhere (often into Atlantic or Indian Ocean worlds) and end 'nowhere,' in an *Unort* where, more often than not, somebody narrates the history of the *Unort*. They play with the things yet to be discovered, with the unknown that the Age of Discovery had not discovered, yet. While they inscribe themselves (Lachenicht 2018: 6) into the historical period of the Age of Discovery, of the new sciences (*New Atlantis* in particular) and new technologies, they produce something new: novel imaginary worlds that are, however, not to be. As a fictional projection of the world that exists, they serve this world as a *speculum*— they are about self-recognition. They also make clear how much the world that exists is constructed and constantly performed, and how much it can be subject to change. Playing with the real and the unreal, with the ideal and the dystopian, they invite the reader "to talk about the possibilities of other, and perhaps better, worlds; and in so doing to acknowledge, perhaps, the shortcomings of our own" (Bruce 1999: xxvii).

Categorizing the New World

The process of European expansion between the 1400s and the twentieth century brought about contact, uncertainties, knowledge transfer, and (trans-)formation on a scale previously not known from a European perspective (e.g. MacKenzie 1990; Jardine/Secord/Spary 1995; Rice 2000; Parrish 2006). Historians of science claim that the process of European expansion, colonialism, empire building, and the development of new sciences (and their institutions) are inextricably linked— especially with the 'discovery' of the New World, i.e. the Americas (Barrera-Osorio 2006; Delbourgo/Dew 2008; Bleichmar et al. 2009).

European knowledge about the New World as it came to be institutionalized in the European Republic of Letters—its academies, royal societies, correspondence networks, universities, and media, including major collections of objects, maps, natural histories, encyclopedias, travel narratives, and dictionaries—was the result of Europeans speculating on the 'new' and how the 'new' fitted into God's creation. European cartographers, explorers, missionaries and scientists used the Bible as well as ancient Greek, Roman, Arabic, Muslim, Jewish, and other sources for the project of knowledge production about the New World. The exchange of knowledge about the New World was vast among Europeans (e.g. Bleichmar 2009; Jardine/Secord/Spary 1996; Boscani/Nicoli 2016). Counting and categorizing the world were based on practices of cultural mobility, transnational exchange, and knowledge formation and codification, which also involved—as more recent research in the history of science makes clear (Delbourgo/Dew 2008; Bleichmar 2009; Parrish 2006; Schiebinger 2004)—indigenous populations, African or Arabic slaves, pirates, maroons, and other groups so far/hitherto underrepresented in the master narratives of European expansion. Their presence left its traces in maps, encyclopedias, dictionaries, and travel narratives; Europeans used indigenous place names of mountains, rivers, and forests for plants, animals and people. Europeans also relied on indigenous knowledge with regard to the exploitation of nature's resources—be it with regard to pharmaceutical products or medicine, the growing and export of crops rich in carbohydrates, or the discovery and exploitation of precious metal mines.

Natural histories—that is, descriptions of the climate, landscape, flora, fauna, and people of the Americas—were popular in the early modern period. Between the sixteenth and eighteenth centuries, most natural histories use the *scala naturae*, the "Great Chain of Being," in which they integrate 'new' and uncertain knowledge: starting with climates and landscapes, the narratives then move on to minerals, plants, primitive forms of animals, and end with ethnographic descriptions of human beings. While the *scala naturae* remains largely intact, categories for minerals, plants, animals, and human beings changed dramatically between the sixteenth and late eighteenth century. New systems of categorization, new taxonomies developed. Obviously, Europeans saw the New World through their lenses, with the help of their cultural categories, as Christian Europeans, as colonizers, as heirs of Greek and Roman Antiquity. Yet, the knowledge they acquired about botany, zoology, ecology, architecture, landscapes, and other subjects came by way of contacts and exchange with indigenous people. As scholars have shown, European and indigenous American (and African) epistemic structures and practices did not match (e.g. Kidwell 2004). Translation was in many ways impossible when concepts and epistemes differed fundamentally. When Europeans wrote their descriptions of the landscapes, flora, and fauna of the New World, two or more knowledge systems had intersected. European knowledge about the New World thus comes across as "Third Space" (Bhabha 1994) knowledge; the constructed worlds we find in these natural histories did not exist as either indigenous or European worlds but rather as speculative *new worlds* at the intersection of different knowledge systems (Mignolo 1992).

Some scholars hold that while the basic structure of the natural histories remains relatively stable, the motives behind the production of natural histories changed fundamentally: from describing God's creation (e.g. Armstrong 2000), natural historians in the eighteenth became century more interested in using natural resources to improve the human condition, the economy, and the early modern state's prowess (e.g. Koerner 1999).

Speculating about the world and how God had made it was, at least up to the nineteenth century, about reconciling the old and the new, faith and reason. *Traditio et innovatio* was also about reconciling the past, present, and what we today would call the future. It was about God's *one* world, in its immutable present, its progress, *and* its eternity. Scientists or the so-called learned people of the later seventeenth and eighteenth centuries made attempts to rationalize biblical stories. Isaac La Peyrère (1596–1676) tried to conjoin faith and reason. However, beliefs developed that everything could be explained through new sciences, even Genesis and other biblical narratives, fostering the demotion and destruction of the authority of the Church and Bible. These beliefs produced new uncertainties with regard to the history and development of Man and led humans into unknown futures. Nonetheless, for much of the early modern period, the Bible and ancient texts remained authoritative even though the new sciences offered a competitive and challenging second powerful narrative to explain the world.

Conclusions

Today, in the age of Beck's "reflexive modernity," "discontinuities, irregularities, and volatilities seem to be proliferating rather than diminishing" and "global interdependence makes risk management increasingly complex" (Bernstein 1996: 329). 'Modernity' and 'reflexive modernity' seem to have traded the past 'certainties' about this world and the hereafter provided by the Bible and other ancient texts for the uncertainties of the future. Many political, economic, social, and cultural contexts make clear that we have further developed Enlightenment narratives about the possibilities of manufacturing or "engineering" the future (Milburn 2008), about molding less the future but some immutable present.

In comparison with the early modern period, Christian certainties that man will not fall any deeper than into God's hands are (mostly) absent from many contexts today, even if they survive in some domains, as much as ancient and pagan classical narratives persist, for example, in popular discourse about the uncertainties of new technologies, which often invokes Pandora's Box, humankind as Prometheus, or clichés about hubris. According to social psychologist Philip Macnaghten, these old narratives and myths have to be conceptualized

> not as antithetical to reason or science, which would be the Enlightenment fallacy, nor as reflective of primeval and universal structures (the Romantic fallacy), but rather as durable, historically-derived, collectively imagined and functional. [...] Myths, as paradigmatic stories, are interrogated as significant cultural resources that have the potential to enable discussion on the deep and challenging issues presented by technology. (Macnaghten 2012)

In comparison with the varieties and simultaneities of early modern timescapes, and also compared with non-European timescapes (Gallois 2007), we seem to face a period of flattened time (Hunt 2007: 107–108)—which might be one of the reasons behind trends towards firmative (and not towards affirmative) speculation. "Time is not a singular, natural and uncontested entity, but is viewed outside the discipline [of history] as both plural and as being constructed in varied manners in different cultures" (Gallois 2007: 242) and in different periods of time. Could the "pluralization of time" (Gallois 2007: 242) or a growing awareness of pluralities of time concepts in all cultures and periods in human history open up new horizons in speculation, in critically assessing our own times and in producing—through affirmative speculation—new possibilities and opportunities for the future beyond the immutable present? Many of the early modern utopias (whether they were meant to be utopias or not) have inspired modern social concepts, such as the equality of genders, social security and welfare, the omnipotence of science, or democratic cultures. To put it differently, cultures of speculation of the early modern period have shaped modern present times—for better or worse.

References

Armstrong, Patrick (2000): *The English Parson-Naturalist: A Companionship between Science and Religion*. Leominster: Gracewing.

The Avalon Project: Documents in History, Law, and Diplomacy. New Haven, CT: Yale Law School Lillian Goldman Law Library (https://avalon.law.yale.edu/).

Barrera-Osorio, Antonio (2006): *Experiencing Nature: The Spanish American Empire and the Early Scientific Revolution*. Austin: University of Texas Press.

Beck, Ulrich ([1986] 1992): *Risk Society: Towards a New Modernity*. Mark Ritter (trans.). London: Sage.

Beck, Ulrich (1994): "The Reinvention of Politics: Towards a Theory of Reflexive Modernity." In: Ulrich Beck/Anthony Giddens/Scott Lash (eds.): *Reflexive Modernization: Politics, Tradition, and Aesthetics in the Modern Social Order*. Cambridge: Polity Press, 1–55.

Bernstein, Peter L. (1996): *Against the Gods: The Remarkable Story of Risk*. New York: Wiley.

Bhabha, Homi K. (1994): *The Location of Culture*. London: Routledge.

Bleichmar, Daniela (2009): "A Visible and Useful Empire: Visual Culture and Colonial Natural History in the Eighteenth-Century Spanish World." In: Daniela Bleichmar/Paula De Vos/Kristin Huffine/Kevin Sheehan (eds.): *Science in the Spanish and Portuguese Empires, 1500–1800*. Stanford: Stanford University Press, 290–309.

Bleichmar, Daniela/De Vos, Paula/ Huffine, Kristin/ Sheehan, Kevin (eds.) (2009): *Science in the Spanish and Portuguese Empires, 1500–1800*. Stanford: Stanford University Press.

Boscani, Leoni Simona/Nicoli, Miriam (eds.) (2016): *La médiation des savoirs dans la Suisse du XVIIIe siècle: acteurs et pratiques*. Basel: Schwabe.

Brendecke, Arndt/Fuchs, Ralf-Peter/Koller, Edith (2007): "Die Autorität der Zeit." In: Arndt Brendecke/Ralf-Peter Fuchs/Edith Koller (eds.): *Die Autorität der Zeit in der Frühen Neuzeit*. Berlin: LIT, 9–22.

Bruce, Susan (1999): "Introduction." In: Susan Bruce (ed.): *Three Early Modern Utopias: Utopia, New Atlantis, and the Isle of Pines*. Oxford: Oxford University Press, ix–xlii.

Canny, Nicholas/Morgan, Philip D. (2011): "Introduction: The Making and Unmaking of an Atlantic World." In: Nicholas Canny/Philip D. Morgan (eds.): *The Oxford Handbook of the Atlantic World, 1450–1850*. Oxford/New York: Oxford University Press, 1–17.

Ceccarelli, Giovanni (2016): "Coping with Unknown Risks in Renaissance Florence: Insurers, Friars and Abacus Teachers." In: Cornel Zwierlein (ed.): *The Dark Side of Knowledge: Histories of Ignorance, 1400 to 1800*. Leiden: Brill, 117–138.

"The Charter of New England" ([1620] 1909). In: Francis Newton Thorpe (ed.): *The Federal and State Constitutions, Colonial Charters, and Other Organic Laws of the States, Territories, and Colonies Now or Heretofore Forming the United States of America*. Vol. 3. Washington, DC: Government Printing Office, 1827–1840.

Crutzen, Paul J./Stoermer, Eugene F. (2000): "The Anthropocene." In: *IGBP [International Geosphere-Biosphere Programme] Newsletter* 41, May, 17–18 (http://www.igbp.net/download/18.316f18321323470177580001401/1376383088452/NL41.pdf).

Darwin, John (2017): *Der imperiale Traum: Die Globalgeschichte großer Reiche 1400–2000*. Frankfurt a.M.: Campus.

Delbourgo, James/Dew, Nicholas (2008): "Introduction: The Far Side of the Ocean." In: James Delbourgo/Nicholas Dew (eds.): *Science and Empire in the Atlantic World*. London: Routledge, 1–28.

Fabian, Johannes (2002): *Time and the Other: How Anthropology Makes Its Object*. New York: Columbia University Press.

Febvre, Lucien ([1942] 1982): *The Problem of Unbelief in the Sixteenth Century: The Religion of Rabelais*. Cambridge, MA: Harvard University Press.

Foucault, Michel ([1966] 1970): *The Order of Things*. New York: Pantheon Books.

Gallois, William (2007): *Time, Religion and History*. London: Longman-Pearson.

Grafton, Anthony (1992): *New Worlds, Ancient Texts: The Power of Tradition and the Shock of Discovery*. Cambridge, MA: The Belknap Press.

Greenblatt, Stephen (1980): *Renaissance Self-Fashioning*. Chicago: Chicago University Press.

Greenblatt, Stephen (1991): *Marvelous Possessions: The Wonder of the New World*. Chicago: Chicago University Press.

Haiven, Max (2017): "Monsters of the Financialized Imagination." In: Nick Buxton/Deborah Eade (eds.): *State of Power 2017*. Amsterdam: Transnational Institute (https://www.tni.org/files/publication-downloads/stateofpower2017-monsters.pdf).

Hunt, Lynn (2008): *Measuring Time, Making History*. Budapest: Central European University Press.

Jardine, Nicholas/Secord, James A./Spary, Emma C. (eds.) (1996): *Cultures of Natural History*. Cambridge: Cambridge University Press.

Keßler, Eckhard (2007): "Zeitverständnisse in der Philosophie der Renaissance." In: Arndt Brendecke/Ralf-Peter Fuchs/Edith Koller (eds.): *Die Autorität der Zeit in der Frühen Neuzeit*. Berlin: LIT, 23–45.

Kidwell, Clara Sue (2004): "Native American Systems of Knowledge." In: Philip J. Deloria/Neal Salisbury (eds.): *A Companion to American Indian History*. Oxford: Wiley-Blackwell, 87–102.

Koerner, Lisbet (1999): *Linnaeus: Nature and Nation*. Harvard: Harvard University Press.

Koselleck, Reinhart (1982): "Die Verzeitlichung der Utopie." In: Wilhelm Voßkamp (ed.): *Utopieforschung: Interdisziplinäre Studien zur neuzeitlichen Utopie*. Vol. 3. Stuttgart: Metzler, 1–14.

Koselleck, Reinhart ([1979] 2004): *Futures Past: On the Semantics of Historical Time*. Keith Tribe (trans.). New York: Columbia University Press.

Labat, Jean-Baptiste (1722): *Nouveau voyage aux isles de l'Amérique*. Vol. 4. Paris: Guillaume Cavalier (http://gallica.bnf.fr/ark:/12148/bpt6k741041).

Lachenicht, Susanne (2018): "Learning from Past Displacements? The History of Migrations between Historical Specificity, Presentism and Fractured Continuities." In: *Humanities* 7(36), 1–11 (https://doi.org/10.3390/h7020036).

Lachenicht, Susanne (2019): "How the Americas Came to Be Known as 'the Americas': A Historical Approach to the Western Hemisphere." In: Volker Depkat/Britta Waldschmidt-Nelson (eds.): *Cultural Mobility and Knowledge Formation in the Americas*. Heidelberg: Winter, 13–29.

Landwehr, Achim (2016): *Die anwesende Abwesenheit der Vergangenheit: Essay zur Geschichtstheorie*. Frankfurt a.M.: S. Fischer.

Lapavitsas, Costas (2013): *Profiting Without Producing: How Finance Exploits Us All*. London: Verso.

Latour, Bruno ([1991] 1993): *We Have Never Been Modern*. Catherine Porter (trans.). Cambridge, MA: Harvard University Press.

Le Goff, Jacques ([1977] 1980): *Time, Work, and Culture in the Middle Ages*. Arthur Goldhammer (trans.). Chicago: Chicago University Press.

"Letters Patent to John Cabot" ([1496] 1909). In: Francis Newton Thorpe (ed.): *The Federal and State Constitutions, Colonial Charters, and Other Organic Laws of the States, Territories, and Colonies Now or Heretofore Forming the United States of America*. Vol. 1. Washington, DC: Government Printing Office, 45–47.

Levy, Jonathan (2012): *Freaks of Fortune: The Emerging World of Capitalism and Risk in America*. Cambridge, MA: Harvard University Press.

Mancall, Peter (2006): *Travel Narratives from the Age of Discovery: An Anthology*. Oxford: Oxford University Press.

Marin, Louis (1973): *Utopiques: Jeux d'espace*. Paris: Minuit.

MacKenzie, John (ed.) (1990): *Imperialism and the Natural World*. Manchester: Manchester University Press.
Macnaghten, Philip (2012): "Myth, Narrative and Ancient Wisdoms: The Role of Ancient Narratives for Conceptualizing the Dilemmas Posed by Advanced Science and Technology." Abstract for Conference "Risk—Effects and Affect: Technology and Narrative in the 21st Century," Bayreuth University (http://www.amerikanistik.uni-bayreuth.de/de/research/conference_2012/abstracts/Macnaghten/index.html).
Mignolo, Walter D. (1992): "The Darker Side of the Renaissance: Colonization and the Discontinuity of the Classical Tradition." In: *Renaissance Quarterly* 45, 808–828.
Mignolo, Walter D. (1995): *The Darker Side of the Renaissance: Literacy, Territoriality and Colonization*. Ann Arbor: University of Michigan Press.
Mignolo, Walter D. (2005): *The Idea of Latin America*. Oxford: Blackwell.
Milburn. Colin (2008): *Nanovision: Engineering the Future*. Durham, NC: Duke University Press.
Moore, Jason W. (2015): "Putting Nature to Work: Anthropocene, Capitalocene, and the Challenge of World-Ecology." In: Cecilia Wee/Janneke Schönenbach/Olof Arndt (eds.): *Supramarkt: A Micro-Toolkit for Disobedient Consumers, or How to Frack the Fatal Forces of the Capitalocene*. Gothenburg: Irene Books, 67–117.
Moore, Jason W. (2016): *Anthropocene or Capitalocene? Nature, History, and the Crisis of Capitalism*. Oakland: PM Press.
Nagel, Alexander/Wood, Christopher S. (2005): "Toward a New Model of Renaissance Anachronism." In: *The Art Bulletin* 87, 403–415.
Nakládalová, Iveta (2013): "Religion in Early Modern Utopia." In: Iveta Nakládalová (ed.): *Religion in Utopia: From More to the Enlightenment*. Sankt Augustin: Academia, 7–40.
O'Gorman, Edmundo (1972): *The Invention of America: An Inquiry into the Historical Nature of the New World and the Meaning of Its History*. Westport, CT: Greenwood Press.
Osterhammel, Jürgen/Petersson, Niels P. (2003): *Geschichte der Globalisierung: Dimensionen, Prozesse, Epochen*. München: C. H. Beck.
Pagden, Anthony (1982): *The Fall of Natural Man: The American Indian and the Origins of Comparative Ethnology*. Cambridge: Cambridge University Press.
Parrish, Susan Scott (2006): *American Curiosity: Cultures of Natural History in the Colonial British Atlantic World*. Chapel Hill: University of North Carolina Press.
Polo, Marco ([c. 1300] 1958): *The Travels of Marco Polo*. Ronald Latham (trans.). Harmondsworth: Penguin.
Rice, Tony (2000): *Voyages: Three Centuries of Natural History Exploration*. London: Museum of Natural History.

Schiebinger, Londa (2004): *Plants and Empire: Colonial Bioprospecting in the Atlantic World*. Cambridge: Cambridge University Press.

Thevet, André (1558): *Les Singularités de la France Antarctique*. Paris: Maurice de la Porte (http://gallica.bnf.fr/ark:/12148/bpt6k109516t).

uncertain commons (2013): *Speculate This!* Durham, NC: Duke University Press.

Wilcox, Donald J. (1987): *The Measure of Times Past: Pre-Newtonian Chronologies and the Rhetoric of Relative Time*. Chicago: University of Chicago Press.

Wilkie, Alex/Savransky, Martin/Rosengarten, Marsha (2017): "The Lure of Possible Futures: On Speculative Research." In: Alex Wilkie/Martin Savransky/Marsha Rosengarten (eds.): *Speculative Research: The Lure of Possible Futures*. London: Routledge, 1–18.

Winter, Michael (1978): *Compendium Utopiarum: Typologie und Bibliographie literarischer Utopien, Erster Teilband: Von der Antike bis zur deutschen Frühaufklärung*. Stuttgart: Metzler, 36–37.

Zwierlein, Cornel (2011): *Der gezähmte Prometheus: Feuer und Sicherheit zwischen Früher Neuzeit und Moderne*. Göttingen: Vandenhoeck & Ruprecht.

Zwierlein, Cornel (2016): "Introduction: Towards a History of Ignorance." In: Cornel Zwierlein (ed.): *The Dark Side of Knowledge: Histories of Ignorance, 1400 to 1800*. Leiden: Brill, 1–47.

Modeling: Speculating with Data

Chapter 2: The Working Planetologist
Speculative Worlds and the Practice of Climate Science

Katherine Buse

In a 2010 editorial in the journal *Nature*, the climate scientist and Executive Director of the International Geosphere–Biosphere Programme, Sybil Seitzinger, argues that scientists ought to be more centrally involved in international policy discussions about sustainable development. "In Frank Herbert's 1965 science-fiction classic *Dune*," she writes, "the number-one position on the planet is held not by a politician, but by a planetary ecologist" (Seitzinger 2010: 601). Seitzinger invokes Herbert's novel here to make a pointed comparison. In *Dune*, the inhabitants of the planet Arrakis are engaging in a long-term terraforming project that necessitates the oversight of a planetary ecologist. But here on Earth, we too have been making such changes, "altering, in profound and uncontrolled ways, key biological, physical and chemical processes of ecosystems." For Seitzinger, grappling responsibly with these processes requires a global, far-sighted perspective that she finds lacking in most Earth politicians. She advises that, while the governments of Earth have not yet considered appointing a planetary ecologist, "perhaps it is time to take the idea seriously."

And she is dead serious, both as a worried scientist and policy analyst, and also as a reader of *Dune*. Although she discusses the novel explicitly only in the first and last sentences of her editorial, Seitzinger does not invoke *Dune* merely to provide a bit of 'science communication' flavor to entertain *Nature*'s interdisciplinary readership. After all, the perspective she takes in the editorial is profoundly similar to Frank Herbert's vision in *Dune*: both pragmatic and theoretical, it subsumes socio-political concerns as components of a *planetary* ecological model.

What is striking about Seitzinger's claim about the "planetary ecologist" in *Dune* is not that she wants to see political systems that take a more ecological, more global, or longer-term view of the planet. Rather, it is that she believes that it is her own discipline that provides the best model for this political work. Seitzinger calls for a kind of leadership that "builds up a picture of Earth" as a complex system, to make sense of its points of resilience and vulnerability. To provide evidence for the special ability that scientists might have to keep track of a whole planet, Seitzinger refers to climate science. Beginning in the 1980s, climate modelers increasingly sought to couple standard atmospheric climate models with other ecological, geological and even social models. The complexity of such models dramatically increased in the early 2000s: Seitzinger highlights that, in addition to "the basics of the nitrogen cycle," climate models now included "elementary descriptions of social and economic systems." She uses this "explosion in our knowledge of Earth as a complex system" to demonstrate what she sees as shortcomings in the contemporary political landscape: the United Nations, in spite of "these advances," has failed to acknowledge that "Earth's restless and powerful social system operates within a complex and intricately linked ecological system." Noting that the UN has missed out on the insights provided from "advances" in Earth system modeling, Seitzinger implies that climate modeling may be necessary training for adequate world governance.

This editorial suggests that, because Earth system science is a capacious discipline that studies the entire planetary ecology, Earth system models afford a synthetic perspective that can encompass all scientific work about any Earth phenomenon.[1] Seitzinger calls for the inclusion of scientists "with a long view and an understanding of how Earth operates as a complex social–ecological system," and she later refers to scientists' grasp of the Earth system's "economic, political and social sub-systems." The editorial thus implies that scientists can model how Earth operates both socially *and* ecologically by embedding models of society into Earth system models, using the same methods that they have used to add complexity to climate models in the past. We live in an Earth system, Seitzinger suggests, and if scientists don't yet know how to couple full-blown economic models or models of political choice to an atmospheric general circulation model (GCM), they will achieve this unification soon enough.

This approach to a planetary system is strongly reminiscent of *Dune*. To Pardot Kynes, first planetary ecologist of Arrakis, "the planet was merely an expression of energy, a machine being driven by its sun" (Herbert [1965] 2010: 797). Kynes, whom Frank Herbert has claimed was the original intended protagonist of *Dune*, is also represented in the novel as the first off-worlder to truly see the potential of the planet. His perspective is rigidly top-down, subsuming social and political concerns to ecological ones. For example, he tells his son and successor as Imperial Planetologist that, "to the working planetologist, his most important tool is human beings" (440). But while it is important for the Fremen, the native inhabitants of Arrakis, to know they are working towards increasing the available water on the

---

[1] Although this is the rhetorical implication of Seitzinger's argument, it is to be taken metaphorically rather than literally: Earth system modeling has its own limitations, many of which stem from the difficulty of coupling different scales of data and simulation. For more about the rise of Earth system models and the challenges thereof, see Edwards (2010: 418–21). On the difficulties of multi-scale modeling, see Winsberg (2010).

planet, it is unimportant that they understand it in a way that goes beyond "semi-mystical" (444). Instead, "an act of disobedience [to their ecological aims] must be a sin and require religious penalties," as this is what will give the population the "bravery" to follow through on their multi-generational mission, even when none alive will witness the results (444). For Kynes, the entire political, social and ecological transformation he orchestrates on the planet is unified under a fundamental conception of the planet as an energy system.

However, as I will argue, it is not just Kynes (or even just Frank Herbert) who manifests this perspective on the relationship between a whole planet and what is found within that world. The world-building for which *Dune* is famous is characteristic of a wide swathe of planetary science fiction, all relying on the same basic operation. The operation relies on a sense of causal closure with the planetary scale as its object, looping questions about individual aspects of life or nature on that world back into the equation of the planet as a whole. In other words, the basic perspective that makes *Dune* iconic is that of a climate modeler. As in a climate model, the thing being explained is always the planet itself. Combined with her reference to *Dune*, Seitzinger's suggestion that a computational model of Earth's climate and biosphere might serve as a model for how to approach politics invokes this practice of world-building, which I call *speculative planetology*. This practice is common in speculative fiction and is emblematized by the Imperial Planetologists in *Dune*. But it is also, as Seitzinger reveals, a speculative practice for climate modelers, an important method for thinking holistically about worlds and what makes them work.

As we have just seen, this speculative practice is sometimes explicitly linked by planetary scientists to science fiction. In this chapter, I will trace the feedback relationship between the speculative world-building done by science fiction authors and the speculative world-building done by climate scientists. The practices of science fiction authors and of planetary scientists differ: one group is engaged in narration, while the other is engaged in simulation. However, it is also possible to observe narration and simulation acting upon one another, speculatively coevolving as part of an ongoing discourse about planets and their workings. For this reason, I am arguing for the existence of a shared practice of speculation that links these two activities: not two separate lines of development, but one speculative planetology that is negotiated across multiple domains.

One outcome of this analysis is that it forces a recontextualization of the oft-repeated idea that climate change is a kind of invisible monster only revealed by science, that it occurs at scales of space and time that dwarf human perception, forcing us to rely on models created by experts.[2] The idea that we depend on

---

2 For a scattering of examples, see Beck ([1986] 1992: 27); Heise (2008: 150–51, 206); Chakrabarty (2009: 221); and Clark (2015: 8, 140). For more critical discussions of scale and the Anthropocene, see Woods (2015) and Horton (2019).

scientific mediation to 'see' climate change (at least in a global sense) may be true, but this notion is often used to imply that climate modeling was developed apart from other ways of knowing—that it is an inhuman, computationally-sublime perspective, with little relationship to other domains of culture. To the contrary, I claim that the labor of Earthly self-understanding that revealed the climate crisis, and which continues to make sense of it, has been the collective work of scientists, artists, and members of the public. I call this "collective work" to draw attention to the fact that science is always bound up with other parts of culture, despite the efforts of science communicators to make the natural and the cultural seem easily separable.[3] I demonstrate this by drawing attention the active cultural participation of scientists themselves: their performance of, and participation in, science fiction fandom, and their efforts to engage the public by invoking science fiction tropes. However, as I will claim, the relationship goes much deeper than scientists' enjoyment of science fiction. After all, the central premise of climate modeling, that *things could be otherwise*, is also the central premise of science fiction.[4] This relationship is deepened by the role of science fiction in reworking, consolidating, speculating upon, and mutating existing science fact.

Among references to science fiction by climate scientists, Frank Herbert's *Dune* is a touchstone. I treat the novel as an ideal place to discuss the feedback relationship between science fiction and science: not only did *Dune* become an important cultural resource for climate modeling, but the novel itself draws from scientific sources in mid-twentieth century working ecology. In *Dune*, Frank Herbert repurposed many quotations from a short, popular science book, *Where There Is Life* (1962), by the ecologist Paul Sears. I show that when Herbert directly copied these passages from 1960s ecological science, he often simply altered the context from a regional to a planetary scale. And yet, by extrapolatively limning an entire planet out of these smaller-scale borrowings, Herbert is able to build the kind

---

3 Bruno Latour refers to this process as "purification" (Latour 1993: 10). Climate science—a discipline that has experienced an unusually high degree of political and ideological intervention—has every reason to participate in the work of purification, as attacks on the authority of climate scientists are very often attacks on their objectivity or on the clarity of the signals that they interpret from the natural world. The presumed capacity of natural things to 'speak for themselves,' and the presumed identity of the scientist as someone who straightforwardly communicates these matters of fact to the public, have become part of a battleground which climate scientists are often called upon to defend.

4 Fredric Jameson: "Its multiple mock futures serve the [...] function of transforming our own present into the determinate past of something yet to come" (Jameson 1982: 153). Darko Suvin: "At all events, the *possibility* of other strange, covariant coordinate systems and semantic fields is assumed" (Suvin 1979: 5). Or, more simply and echoing many others, James Gunn: "Science fiction, then, is the literature of change" (Gunn 2005: 10).

of simulated world that characterizes both planetary science fiction and climate models.

Indeed, the historical ties between climate modeling and science fiction go as far back as the very first implementation of the so-called standard model of planetary climate.[5] The ability to calculate a planet's surface temperature involves a few key insights. First, the atmosphere needs to be imagined as having layers. A climate model balances energy inputs and outputs—solar radiation on its way in and mainly infrared radiation on its way out—and this balance must be calculated from the top of the atmosphere, not from the Earth's crust. Second, equations for atmospheric convection must be used to describe how heat is transported around inside that envelope between the crust and the top of the atmosphere. When climate science was in its infancy, scientists regularly failed to incorporate each of these elements into a single model. The first person to manage this wasn't a meteorologist, and it wasn't done with respect to Earth. It was a 27-year-old Carl Sagan who, in 1962, applied a radiative-convective model to Venus in order to determine the structure and temperature of its lower atmosphere (Sagan 1962).

A year earlier, in 1961, Sagan had written an article on "The Planet Venus" in the journal *Science* that indicated the science-fictional thought processes behind his modeling of planetary temperature. Theorizing about Venus's greenhouse effect, he argued that the planet's carbon dioxide levels would explain recent temperature readings of 600 degrees Kelvin. Sagan opened the article with a quip about various speculative and fanciful scenarios that had previously been imagined for Venus's climate:

> The state of our knowledge of Venus is amply illustrated by the fact that the Carboniferous swamp, the wind-swept desert, the planetary oil field, and the global Seltzer ocean each have their serious proponents, and those planning eventual manned expeditions to Venus must be exceedingly perplexed over whether to send along a paleobotanist, a mineralogist, a petroleum geologist, or a deep-sea diver. (Sagan 1961: 849)

The article also included an imaginative illustration of Venus by the well-known science fiction magazine artist Chesley Bonestell (851). For Sagan, this image of Venus as a windswept "dust bowl" represented the only science-fictional scenario that still remained plausible: "temperatures are too high for the Carboniferous swamp, the planetary oil field, or the global Seltzer ocean, but, the desert [...] is

---

5   R.T. Pierrehumbert uses the term "standard model," adapted from physics, in his Tyndall lecture to the AGU (Pierrehumbert 2012: 11:30). It was this lecture that called my attention to Carl Sagan as the first to apply the standard model to a planet (23:50).

still roughly consistent with the data," he wrote in conclusion, adding that readers should "See Fig 1" [Bonestell's illustration] for reference (857).

Drawing attention to the history of wild theories about Venus, Sagan suggested the alignment of planetary science with the imaginative practices of science fiction. His own scientific work relied extensively on such practices: he was committed to thinking of distant planets as places, and to imagining what it would be like to inhabit them (Messeri 2016: 6). Furthermore, as complex as climate models have become over time, they remain bare-bones pictures of worlds. Sagan had no knowledge of Venus's actual surface temperature to trip himself up, and this situation necessitated using the standard model. Because the surface could not be seen through Venus's impenetrable shroud of clouds, Sagan was forced by circumstance to speculate upon it, and thus to recognize that the surface temperature depends on a balance between incoming and outgoing energy at the top of the atmosphere—that is, from outside the planet.[6] This emphasizes that the basic viewpoint of a climate modeler is a deeply estranged one, not the intuitive perspective of a citizen of Earth at all. An understanding of planetary climate—that is, the idea of climate as a planetary phenomenon—begins with looking at that planet from the outside, from space.[7]

Sagan was, of course, not alone. The planetary sciences, emerging around the same time as Frank Herbert's *Dune*, were already thinking in science-fictional terms about the other planets in our solar system, such as Mars and Venus. What has perhaps gone unrecognized are the ways that this mode of thinking about planets from a distance, as well as thinking of planets as energy systems, has become the backbone of a certain kind of speculative thinking about planetary climate and climate change in general, even on Earth and amongst scientists who are not compelled to it by distance from their planet of study. As evidence of the role of this speculative climate imaginary, I turn to examples of climate scientists who have written publicly about their interest in science fiction.

---

6 As Pierrehumbert (2012: 21:09) points out, even the equations that make up the convection part of the standard model were formulated several centuries earlier by astronomers seeking to measure the temperature of stars.

7 There are scientific theories of planetary climate that seem to approach climate from within the planet rather than outside of it, such as the Gaia hypothesis with its focus on the planet's biota. But even the Gaia hypothesis was originally formulated as an interplanetary thought experiment: James Lovelock (serving as a NASA astrobiologist at the time) claims to have first had the idea for Gaia when he considered how one might be able to tell from afar if a planet was inhabited by life (cf. Hitchcock/Lovelock 1967). For more about Lovelock's interactions with the space sciences, see Conway (2008).

"SFnal"

Notably, the *Bulletin of the American Meteorological Society*, the top-ranked journal in atmospheric science, has featured increasingly deep engagements with science fiction since the 1980s, from including science fiction texts in its book review section to publishing articles and even special issues discussing the utility of science fiction as a tool for climate science. In one such instance, climate physicist and Royal Society fellow Tim Palmer wrote an article titled, "Is Science Fiction a Genre for Communicating Scientific Research? A Case Study in Climate Prediction" (Palmer 2010a). His case study was a science fiction short story, "Sunrise," which he wrote and published as an online supplement in the same issue of *Bulletin of the American Meteorological Society* (Palmer 2010b). Palmer treats "Sunrise" as a kind of doubled thought experiment. Within the story, he speculates on the implications of climate models' low resolution with regard to regional change patterns. He allegorizes the problem on a recently climate-changed fantasy planet, Migosh, where scientists predict favorable new average values for weather but fail to anticipate extreme weather events, leaving the populace unprepared for a natural disaster (Palmer 2010b). In the essay accompanying the story, Palmer claims that the story tests a hypothesis: that when communicating scientific findings to decision makers, science fiction might "sometimes be a more effective genre for communication than conventional means" (Palmer 2010a: 1413).

In the essay, Palmer writes of his childhood experiences reading science fiction:

> I can still vividly recall Isaac Asimov's *Nightfall*, [which] describes a civilization's first encounter with darkness for thousands of years. [...] I started to wonder whether such an overwhelming existential crisis, in experiencing for the first time some dramatic and totally unforeseen natural phenomena, could be brought to bear in communicating my concerns about current uncertainties in the science of climate prediction? (Palmer 2010a: 1413)

For Palmer, and specifically in cases where what is at stake is helping policymakers understand the uncertainty behind predictions and the value of continued scientific research, science fiction can communicate about what one might call the "unknown unknowns" of climate prediction. In other words, what Palmer recognizes and values in science fiction is an aspect of his own work on chaos and predictability: the capacity of the nonhuman world to throw up the truly unanticipated, and the importance of maintaining a speculative attitude in order to appreciate what cannot be anticipated.[8]

Also in the *Bulletin of the American Meteorological Society*, Raymond T. Pierrehumbert, a lead author of the Third Assessment Report of the Intergovernmental Panel on Climate Change (IPCC), published a short article called "Science Fiction Atmospheres" (Stocker et al. 2001; Pierrehumbert 2005). In this piece, he considers various science fiction texts and wonders about the atmospheric physics of their worlds. Regarding *Dune*, he frets, "But how is the aquifer recharged if it never rains?" He then offers a speculative answer:

> My best guess is that Dune is a dying world, with slow leakage of water into an atmosphere that is becoming gradually warmer on account of the water vapor greenhouse effect. A word of warning to those Dune scientists to wish to re-engineer the climate to bring on rain and surface water: if they succeed, they will almost certainly precipitate a runaway greenhouse. If Dune is already in a habitable temperature range without much water vapor greenhouse effect, introducing an ocean is likely to be fatal. (Pierrehumbert 2005: 696)

In "Science Fiction Atmospheres," Pierrehumbert uses science fiction worlds as the occasion for showing off a climate modeler's mentality, which involves flexible inference about how atmospheric and terrestrial systems interact to produce the conditions on the planet. Does Arrakis have plate tectonics? If so, the lack of surface water will prevent weathering of rocks and lead to a build-up of carbon dioxide in the atmosphere. Is it possible to have an aquifer without also having a water-saturated atmosphere? No—although precipitation could evaporate before it reaches the ground. He playfully evaluates several science-fictional climates (as seen in *Dune*, Kim Stanley Robinson's Mars trilogy, and a few others) in this manner, adding, "Graduate students take note: This is good fodder for general exam questions!" (Pierrehumbert 2005: 696).

This last suggestion appears to be something Pierrehumbert has truly taken to heart, for he builds science fiction directly into his pedagogy. In several of the problems from his textbook *Principles of Planetary Climate* (2010), students are asked to read science fiction stories, such as Geoffrey Landis's "Ecopoesis" or Fritz Leiber's "A Bucket of Air," before attempting a solution. Other problems casual-

---

8 Palmer is not the only climate scientist to write a short story exploring a climate-related hypothesis and paired to a scholarly publication. NASA climatologist and Director of the Goddard Institute for Space Studies, Gavin A. Schmidt, coauthored the article "The Silurian Hypothesis: Would It Be Possible to Detect an Industrial Civilization in the Geological Record?" (Schmidt/Frank 2018). To accompany this piece, he published a science fiction story entitled "Under the Sun" (Schmidt 2018) about a scientist discovering that there had been an ancient industrial civilization in Earth's deep past.

ly describe science-fictional entities, as we see in the following exercise entitled "Springtime for Europa":

> Something is about to happen. Something wonderful. To promote life on Jupiter's moon Europa, which currently is composed of a liquid water ocean covered by a very thick water ice crust, the alien race which built Tycho Magnetic Anomaly 1 ignites thermonuclear fusion on Jupiter, heating Europa to the point that its icy crust melts, leaving it with a globally ocean covered surface having a temperature of 280K. Water vapor is the only source of atmosphere for this planet. Describe what the atmosphere would be like, and calculate T(p) for this atmosphere. Give a rough estimate of the depth (in km) of the layer containing most of the mass of the atmosphere. (Pierrehumbert 2010: 128)

The aliens referenced here are the same aliens who placed the obelisk in *2001: A Space Odyssey*, though the suggestion that "something wonderful" is about to happen on Europa is an allusion to the film's 1984 sequel, *2010: The Year We Made Contact*. Why does Pierrehumbert use this story as a way into the problem? In the first place, it is clear that he is a fan of science fiction and that he enjoys exhibiting his knowledge of the genre. This in itself is significant: in some disciplinary cultures, it is common for scientists to conceal their fandom, or to dismiss science fiction as something they used to read in their childhoods. The idea of science fiction somehow "infecting" or "planting a seed" in a scientist's mind might seem to threaten certain notions of scientific authority and rationality (Milburn 2010: 563). Considered in this light, the wide range of climate scientists who are willing to go 'on record' as science fiction enthusiasts of one kind or another speaks to a more pervasive disciplinary openness to the genre, even amongst those who are not actively blogging or giving talks about science fiction.

On the other hand, Pierrehumbert is also performing his interest in science fiction for heuristic purposes. He wants his students to think creatively about planetary atmospheres. He could have simply posed a series of equations about an atmosphere composed of water vapor, but by presenting a narrative context, he can instead ask students to "describe what the atmosphere would be like": a qualitative question. This recalls Lisa Messeri's point that for planetary scientists, thinking of planets as places that one "can imagine being on" is a crucial method that "potentially opens up new questions that can be asked about the planet" (Messeri 2016: 12). Asking what the atmosphere *would be like* invites the students to consider questions that are more experiential: not just what temperature and what depth, but also what weather, what kinds of clouds, what color the sky? Such open-ended speculations are part of the practice of world-building that science fiction authors have honed over more than a century of planetary science fiction.⁹

Pierrehumbert clearly aims to produce a kind of "cognitive estrangement" (Suvin 1979) for readers of his textbook. This aim is made evident in the workbook questions, but also in his concerns about generalizing climate knowledge. He remarks somewhat regretfully that "it is inevitable that any discussion of planetary climate will draw heavily" on our observations of Earth, which remains "our best-observed example of a planetary climate" (Pierrehumbert 2010: xi). Yet climate science's inheritance of Earthly terminology seems to be a source of consternation for Pierrehumbert:

> For example, if I sometimes refer to "the sun" or "solar radiation," it is to be thought of as referring to whatever star the planet under discussion is orbiting, and not necessarily Earth's Sun or even a star like it. In the same spirit, the term solar constant will be used to refer to the rate at which a planet receives energy from its star [...] regardless of what that star may be and where the planet may be located. (Pierrehumbert 2010: xii)

Noting that the standard vocabulary of climate science too often presumes our own solar system as a frame of reference, Pierrehumbert instead proposes more estranging terms, such as *stellar radiation* and *stellar constant*, to "help the reader get used to the idea that there are a lot of stars out there, with a lot of planets with a lot of climates" (xiii). The same work must be done in relation to other aspects of planetary climate, adapting terms from climate science but emphasizing their generality, their ability to detach themselves from the parochial Earthbound context in which they were developed:

> In a similar vein, "air" will mean whatever gas the atmosphere is composed of on the planet in question—after all, if you grew up there, you'd just call it "air." When I need to refer to the specific substances that make up our own atmosphere, it will be called "Earth air." (Pierrehumbert 2010: xiv)

---

9 World-building has for the most part been a science fiction practitioner's term of art, rather than a scholarly one, because the term is so difficult to delimit. However, many genre definitions of science fiction imply some degree of comparison between our own world and the world of the narrative. Delany ([1978] 2009) is of particular note for approaching the topic through language. On world-building as a collective transmedia practice, see Wolf (2012). On the practice of planetary world-building for science fiction authors, see Gillett (1996).

Earth air: just one flavor among many.[10] Pierrehumbert's comment that "[I]f you grew up there, you'd just call it 'air'" helps to get at one of the most significant moves that climate science shares with—or, as I am arguing, often explicitly borrows from—speculative fiction. In *Principles of Planetary Climate*, the science fictionality serves a purpose beyond that of enlivening an otherwise technical subject. It is a literal invitation to extrapolation, a mode that can be invoked in order to bridge between the known and the unknown. In a set of exercises about the boiling point of liquids, Pierrehumbert transitions from discussing water to the following: "Now, think of Glurg the Titanian, who would like to boil up liquid methane to make his tea. The surface pressure of Titan is about 2 bars (mostly nitrogen). How hot does his stove have to get?" (Pierrehumbert 2010: 124). Part of this pedagogy is not merely to teach the basics of thermodynamics, but to open up spaces for speculative thought about climatological concepts. Both the idea that "if you grew up there, you'd call it air" and the silly notion of "Glurg the Titanian" with his implausible thirst for methane tea invoke a science-fictional methodology that is part and parcel with what the textbook means to convey to the budding climate scientist.

Robert Grumbine, a climate modeler and oceanographer who works for the United States National Oceanic and Atmospheric Administration (NOAA), has written about this relationship between climate science and science fiction in a blog post entitled "Science Fiction and Science." After declaring himself a lifelong science fiction fan, he launches into an extended reflection on the relationship between the two fields. While he acknowledges that "Bad SF [...] can fuel some bad ideas about science," he suggests that, more importantly, science fiction shares with science a set of common assumptions about how "interesting" a place the universe is, about how "problems are (generally) solvable," how "the universe is (often) understandable," and how "science translated to technology can affect how you live (so think about the social effects sooner rather than later)" (Grumbine 2008). These are somewhat standard tropes of the "why science fiction?" discourse in popular culture—which makes sense, as Grumbine is clearly invested in science fiction as a genre. He consistently comments on blog and forum posts in which other scientists mention science fiction, often verifying or registering appreciation for a mention of a science fiction story or novel. For several years circa 2007, he also participated in the Usenet listserv *rec.arts.sf.science*, a discussion forum in which science-fictional scenarios—often world-building questions, resolving issues of scientific plausibility about a particular fictional world—are worked out

---

10 One might note, as Pierrehumbert does elsewhere, that Earth air itself has not been uniform across geological history: some of the most important questions in climate science are about past changes in Earth's atmospheric composition. For example, see Pierrehumbert (2010: 11–14).

by a community of lay fans, scientist-fans, and authors. For instance, Grumbine weighed in on a conversation about how long it would take for fast-growing Venusian sky-cities to exhaust the planet's sulphuric acid clouds by hydrogen mining—not long—and whether the climatic effect would be warming or cooling—definitely warming (Grumbine 2007).

However, Grumbine's reflections on why science fiction is important to him as a climate scientist, rather than as a scientist in general, are more specific, and could easily be taken to describe the same dynamics visible in Pierrehumbert's textbook:

> I do take advantage of a somewhat SFnal view of the universe in doing my research. That is, I'm trying to understand, say, the earth's climate. That's only one place with one particular set of conditions. What (the SF-fan in me asks) would it be like if the earth rotated much faster, more slowly, if the sun produced less UV (hence less ozone on earth, hence less greenhouse effect in the stratosphere, hence …?), if the earth were farther away/closer in, and so on. I can't say that it's resulted in any journal articles that I wouldn't have written anyhow, but it does make it easier for me to, say, read paleoclimate papers (the earth did rotate faster in the past, sea level has been much higher and lower than present, …). (Grumbine 2008)

"What (the SF-fan in me asks) would it be like?" This series of questions and concerns directly echo the sorts of questions performed by Pierrehumbert as a way of initiating students into the basics of planetary climate. Grumbine, like Pierrehumbert, refers to the idea that Earth is "only one place with one particular set of conditions," suggesting that there could be—and, as he notes, *has been*—any number of different Earths (or other planets) with different conditions.

In other words, the basic premise of science fiction—that things could be different—is also a basic premise of climate modeling. Is a set of observations about the likely climatic conditions on Gliese-581D science fiction or science? What about extrapolations regarding the atmosphere of Earth if its axial tilt were much greater? Much as they are perfectly reasonable topics for a climate science textbook, these questions are inevitably under the gravitational influence of a long history of speculative fiction, not only in terms of their content but in terms of method. This—Grumbine's "SFnal view of the universe"—is a method for thinking about planets that has been developed as a shared practice, a product of feedback between science and culture.

Dune Worlds

To provide more direct evidence of this feedback loop, I look to Frank Herbert's *Dune*, which is something of a touchstone for scientists interested in planetary climates. Both Pierrehumbert and Grumbine, for example, have written about it (Pierrehumbert 2005: 697; Grumbine 2008). But *Dune* also enjoys a more specific role as part of the field of planetary science—not just one imaginary planet among many, but a term of art that describes a *kind* of planet. As I will explore in the remainder of this chapter, *Dune*'s iconic status has to do with the way that it works as an imaginary system.

William Michael Connolley was a climate modeler at the British Antarctic Survey until 2007.[11] His climate science outreach blog, *Stoat*, was hosted for a time at the science communication hub *RealClimate*. Both *Stoat* and Connolley's personal blog are full of evidence of his status as a science fiction and fantasy reader. His posts abound with references, both oblique and explicit, to the work of Jack Vance, Samuel Delany, Ursula K. Le Guin, John Crowley and others. In a post entitled "Whats Wrong with the World" [sic], Connolley tasks himself with describing why he thinks future generations will resent the present generation. He lists several reasons, including the following:

> Waste and general "fatness." Not fat as in your body being overweight, though that is a small part of it. Water-fat, as in Dune. Fat as in all the rest: the fools who drive SUV's, who need ridiculous numbers of toys (who, after all, could possibly need a GPS watch? This one folds into "environment," too. (Connolley 2010)

Connolley's use of the phrase "Water-fat, as in Dune" indicates the extent to which fictional climates can come to be part of shared worlds and ways of knowing worlds. The idea of "water-fatness" in the novel evokes an understanding that off-worlders' bodies automatically carry a surplus of water that the native Arrakeen population and long-term immigrants do not. But it also indicates a sense that those off-worlders are soft, undisciplined, and ill-prepared for life on Arrakis. Using this phrase carries with it a whole world adapted to a shocking level of scarcity, indicating that Connolley imagines some future generation sneering at his own generation for their ignorance of what survival really means. Connolley's use of this term demonstrates how a fictional climate can become emblematic of a set of meanings, and that he may expect his own readership to recognize this set

---

11 After a series of controversies related to his role as a *Wikipedia* editor and as a *RealClimate* blogger, Connolley quit climate science and switched to electrical engineering, saying that he felt that science was no longer what would advance the climate conversation: political change was needed.

of meanings, signifying not only a dry climate but the ecological and social resonances of that climate.

It is not for nothing that the fictional climate of Arrakis can do this kind of cultural work. *Dune* has been hailed as "the first planetary ecology novel on a grand scale," and it certainly aims to convey a sense of system (Slonczewski/Levy 2003: 183). Each organism, each technology, each language, and each landscape in the text seems to have its own intricate and often diasporic natural history, evoking a planetary past that has been endlessly interlayered, obscured by cycles of mutation, adoption, or occlusion by other histories. These entangled elements are depicted not only in the novel's narration, but also in an extensive collection of appendices: a fictional scholarly apparatus including ecological histories, biographies of the central characters, a glossary, a map, and sociological tracts relating to the deep history of the planet and its inhabitants.[12]

Until this point, I have restricted my overview of planetary scientists and their interactions with science fiction to those who can be best described as climate modelers. And indeed, Pierrehumbert, Connolley and Grumbine have each posted online about their experiences reading *Dune*. But by comparison, *Dune*'s reach is even more unmistakable in the fields of astrobiology and planetary science focused outside of Earth.[13] As Stephen Dick and James Strick write in *The Living Universe*, their history of NASA astrobiology,

> American culture was influenced strongly in [the] direction [of believing life on Mars not to be impossible] by Frank Herbert's science fiction novel *Dune*, [which was] released in mass paperback just at the time of the Mariner 4 results from Mars and posit[ed] an entire complex culture exquisitely adapted to the conditions of a desert planet. (Dick/Strick 2004: 87)

Dick and Strick do not quite say this, but it seems clear that Norman Horowitz, head of the Biology Division at NASA's Jet Propulsion Laboratory at the time, was particularly influenced by *Dune*. Writing in *Science* about the worrisomely dry surface of Mars just one year after *Dune*'s publication, he offered hope for the possibility of life on the red planet by noting that "one of the most interesting drought-loving forms is the kangaroo rat" which can produce "all its water

---

12 Some aspects of Arrakis's ecosystems and their history are addressed only elliptically. For example, in a single sentence, the novel hints that the giant sandworms—huge beasts that swim in the desert sand like sea serpents—are not, in fact, indigenous to Arrakis. Instead, they are an invasive species, brought by some other people to Arrakis. This is never mentioned again in the novel and is only resolved two sequels later in *Children of Dune*.

13 For more about the relationship between climate modeling and planets other than Earth, see Weart (2019).

[...] metabolically" when fed on certain foods. "I am not suggesting that Mars is inhabited by kangaroo rats and that the first life-detection device on Mars should be a mousetrap," he quipped, but he nonetheless felt the kangaroo rat could serve as an example of "what evolution can accomplish" (Horowitz 1966: 790). And yet there appears to be more to this choice of example than he lets on: as every *Dune* fan reading Horowitz's piece no doubt noticed, the "kangaroo mouse," close relative to the kangaroo rat, is the specific animal after whom the protagonist, Paul "Muad'Dib," is supposed to be named. In the novel, when Paul asks to be named after a mouse he had seen, the Fremen receive it as a hopeful omen. Their leader says that "Muad'Dib," their word for the kangaroo mouse, "is wise in the ways of the desert. Muad'Dib creates his own water. Muad'Dib hides from the sun and travels in the cool night. [...] Muad'Dib we call 'instructor-of-boys.' That is a powerful base on which to build your life, Paul-Muad'Dib" (Herbert [1965] 2010: 497). Apart from the kangaroo *mouse*, Horowitz could hardly have chosen a creature more evocative of *Dune*'s hopeful message about the possibilities of life on a desert world than the kangaroo rat.

Horowitz wrote his piece referencing the kangaroo rat a year after *Dune* was published, and his reference to the novel is clear but not overt. By contrast, more recent astrobiological work has cited *Dune* explicitly. In one article, entitled "Habitable Zone Limits for Dry Planets," the authors praise *Dune* for what they call "an exceptionally well-developed example of a habitable land planet" (Abe et al. 2011: 443). They delve somewhat deeply into the details about Arrakis, noting for example that there is evidence of liquid water in the planet's past, as well as the presence of polar ice caps and aquifers. "The tropics are exceedingly dry, but the polar regions are cool enough and moist enough to have morning dew," they write, recalling the brief scene in *Dune* where Duke Leto watches the morning dew collectors. Using a 3D model, they conclude that dry planets like Arrakis may be more likely to exist as habitable worlds than water worlds like our own, because water creates feedbacks that narrow the habitability range.[14] Abe et al. also show that it is possible for a planet, including perhaps the future Earth, to lose most of its water without experiencing a Venus-like runaway greenhouse effect that would sterilize life on its surface.

Following the Abe et al. article but performing his own reading of *Dune* (and several of its sequels) on his blog, *PlanetPlanet*, astrophysicist Sean Raymond wrote a post adding to the knowledge of Arrakis by working out the particulars of Arrakis's orbit and proximity to its star, Canopus, as well as describing what would happen to the planet's climate when Canopus goes supernova. Raymond seems to have engaged deeply with the *Dune* novels, as he notes that "the source of oxygen

---

14 As a vapor, H_2O contributes to the greenhouse effect, encouraging more evaporation, whereas when frozen it increases planetary albedo and cools the planet more quickly.

is sandworm metabolism instead of oxygenic photosynthesis," a detail from the novel that Pierrehumbert and others seem to have missed (Raymond 2014).

In fact, since the paper by Abe and colleagues, a discourse within astrobiology seems to have converged on the terms "Dune planet," "Dune-like planet," or sometimes "Planet Dune" to describe what another paper calls "hot, rocky planets with small water endowments and low obliquities [that] could conceivably remain habitable in their polar regions. Such planets would resemble the planet Dune in Frank Herbert's famous science fiction novel by that title; hence, the name 'Dune-like' planet has stuck" (Kasting et al. 2014: 12643).[15] This adaptation of the name of Herbert's desert world speaks to its iconic status, as well as to the speculative orientation of planetary science, especially in the world of astrobiology.[16]

In 2014, NASA scientists Ralph Lorenz and James Zimbelman published the geophysical science book, *Dune Worlds: How Windblown Sand Shapes Planetary Landscapes*. These planetary scientists, though highly gratified that Herbert dedicated his novel "to the dry-land ecologists, wherever they may be, in whatever time they work" (Herbert [1965] 2010: vii; Lorenz/Zimbleman 2014: 283), seem unsurprised that Herbert was so excited by sand dunes. They return the favor by citing Herbert, both in genuine attempts to extrapolate the plausibility of the novel's setting and in moments of lighthearted celebration of discoveries, as when the recent identification of Titan as the "most dune-covered world we know of" lead to a region of the moon being named "Arrakis Planitia" (Lorenz/Zimbleman 2014: 284). Not least of this homage to Herbert is the fact that they seem to have named the entire volume *Dune Worlds* after the 1963 serialization of *Dune* in *Analog: Science Fact and Science Fiction*, when it was titled *Dune World* (Herbert 1963).

To begin to explain the exemplary status that *Dune* seems to hold for planetary scientists, it is helpful to understand that the novel was itself already the result of feedback between science and science fiction. Frank Herbert's formula was simple but transformative. He took inspiration from mid-century ecology but reworked the pragmatic, local ideas he encountered there as globe-spanning patterns, extending them to cover a whole world. The remainder of this chapter will track this formula in Herbert's work, showing its kinship with climate modeling practices.

---

15 Cf. Cresto Aleina et al. (2013); Kalidindi et al. (2018); Catling/Kasting (2017: 426).

16 It's worth noting that these astrobiologists citing *Dune* are also using models of planetary climate as evidence of their claims.

Science Fiction's Sources

In 1957, Frank Herbert, then a journalist and modestly successful science fiction author, traveled to Florence, Oregon to report on a United States Department of Agriculture project to stabilize sand dunes that were migrating across a highway. According to literary biographer Timothy O'Reilly, Herbert "became fascinated by sand dunes—the irresistible way they move, swallowing roads, houses, and on occasion entire towns." He "imagined an entire planet that had been taken over by sand dunes, and an ecologist faced with the task of reclaiming it" (O'Reilly 1981: 39). Set 200 centuries in our future, *Dune* extends the Oregon dune project that Herbert visited in 1957, envisioning the dunes creeping inexorably across an entire planet over the course of deep time. The terraforming process that the ecologist Kynes is implementing on the desert planet Arrakis mirrors the Oregon dune stabilization project and the theory of ecological succession that was cutting edge in the middle of the twentieth century:

> Our first goal on Arrakis [...] is grassland provinces. We will start with these mutated poverty grasses. When we have moisture locked in grasslands, we'll move on to start upland forests, then a few open bodies of water. (Herbert [1965] 2010: 440)

The specific terraforming process enacted in the novel (and on the Oregon dunes) demonstrates an effort on Herbert's part to scale local working ecology up to a planetary size. This is made even more explicit if we consider Herbert's sources. In Herbert's initial imagining of the novel, the ecologist Liet Kynes was to be the main character. Kynes was partly styled on the ecologist Paul Sears, a mid-century scientist most famous as the author of *Deserts on the March*, a timely 1935 account of the Dust Bowl and the problem of soil erosion from the perspective of succession ecology. In his essay collection, *The Maker of Dune* (1987), Herbert says that he put the following quotation from Sears directly in the mouth of his character Kynes: "The highest function of ecology is the understanding of consequences" (104).[17] Actually, this is not the only thing that Herbert copied from Sears's work. Though Herbert claimed to have read "over two hundred books as background for this novel" (104), many of them about ecology, it is nonetheless possible to identify nearly every ecologically oriented statement in *Dune* as originating in one slim 1962 volume by Sears called *Where There Is Life*.

I have found more than twenty examples of Herbert lifting elements directly from *Where There Is Life* and duplicating them in *Dune*. A few are mere references.

---

17 Despite Herbert's claim, this is not a verbatim quotation of Sears. The precise wording in Sears's *Where There Is Life* is as follows: "For the highest function of science is to give us an understanding of consequences" (Sears 1962: 128).

For instance, Herbert transforms Sears's claim that only three per cent of the sun's light is captured by photosynthesis on Earth into the notion that, in order to create a self-sustaining ecological system on Arrakis, the Fremen need only control three per cent of the land's surface. But the majority of examples—at least fifteen—are direct reproductions of specific phrases and sentences from *Where There Is Life*. Many of them are uttered by the two planetary ecologists (Liet Kynes and his father Pardot Kynes), while others are in the voice of Paul or Duke Leto.

Table 2.1: Comparison of Sears's Where There Is Life *(left column) and Herbert's* Dune *(right column). Colored text indicates replicated language; underlined text indicates a shift of scales.*

From *Where There Is Life* (Sears 1962)	From *Dune* (Herbert [1965] 2010)
One cannot draw neat lines around such problems as these as he can in mathematical and experimental problems. [The] ecologist […] is like the general practitioner in medicine, obliged at all times to consult specialists in various fields (41).	"We are generalists," his father said. "You can't draw neat lines around planet-wide problems. Planetology is a cut-and-fit science" (439).
Nature, whether we relish the fact or not, is a vast, tightly interwoven fabric of activity (20).	A planet's life is a vast, tightly interwoven fabric (445).
This assurance seems to satisfy many [Americans] who forget that, beyond a certain critical point, freedom diminishes as numbers increase within a finite space. This is as true of humans on a continent as of gas molecules in a sealed flask. [The] real issue is not how many people can possibly survive, but what kind of existence will be possible if they do (23).	Beyond a critical point within a finite space, freedom diminishes as numbers increase. This is as true of humans in the finite space of a planetary ecosystem as it is of gas molecules in a sealed flask. The human question is not how many can possibly survive within the system, but what kind of existence is possible for those who do survive (797).
The Crusades, which had become a system of mutual pillage and extortion, also helped create great mercantile and shipping cities in the north of Italy (194).	"The historical system of mutual pillage and extortion stops here on Arrakis," his father said. "You cannot go on forever stealing what you need without regard to those who come after. The physical qualities of a planet are written into its economic and political record" (443).

As a creative method, Herbert seems to have repeatedly taken a localized, regional phenomenon—such as the Oregon dunes or a biographical sketch about a Chicago-based naturalist—and extrapolated that same phenomenon at a planetary scale. The following table provides a few examples. In it, I have used colored fonts to indicate words and phrases that Herbert copied exactly from *Where There Is Life* into *Dune*, while I have underlined the shifting scales of particular objects. In the case of Sears's *Where There Is Life*, the object is usually a specific ecosystem, while for Herbert it is the entire planet of Arrakis.

I have focused on these specific 'borrowings' on Herbert's part because they speak to the means by which *Dune* has become a touchstone amongst imaginary worlds. Imaginatively shifting local phenomena up to a planetary scale is what allowed a simple kind of mid-century working ecology to take on the proportions of planetary world-building that made *Dune* iconic. Even the concept of a 'climate' as applied to a whole planet results from this operation. The mid-century ecologist Sears never describes a planetary climate: even when he is talking about the history of geological epochs (i.e. climate *change*), he hedges about climate as a global phenomenon. Rather than describing an ice age as a single, unitary change, he writes that it is "reasonably certain the climatic changes responsible for [glaciers advancing and retreating] were general and fairly simultaneous in the Old and New Worlds and probably on northern and southern hemispheres" (Sears 1962: 152). He is aware that changes occurred globally, but he still differentiates climatic *changes* spatially. And why wouldn't he? From an Earthbound perspective, it is more interesting to think about the *various* climates of the planet, as proxies for describing the various kinds of ecosystems found on Earth. For Sears, the term "climates" is plural—a local or bioregional category, but not one that could characterize the atmosphere of the whole world. For example, he writes, "It is difficult to establish anything like precise boundaries between climactic provinces [...] In the transition belt between desert and oak woodland, one finds desert on the southwestern slopes and oak on the northeastern [...] The climates on two sides of a house differ" (Sears 1962: 150–151). In *Dune*, Frank Herbert posits a planetary climate—the singular term applied to the whole of Arrakis—but this is something that emerges from scaling a bioregional climate up to fill a whole planet.

A climate model, too, takes physics about specific phenomena and systems and extrapolates those connections to a planetary scale. In a general circulation model, the grid size is hundreds of miles. Climate models depict how clouds move across a square that is the size of a small state at each time step. This is the correct methodology with which to study a planet, at least until computing power allows finer-resolution models. Nonetheless, a climate model cannot help but have some of the same cartoonish enlargement of dynamics that we see in Herbert's exact duplication of passages from *Where There Is Life*. Speculative world-building in all of its forms requires generalizing phenomena and enforcing a kind of connectedness that speaks to the system as a whole. For example, a general circulation model ensures that local parameterizations communicate with one another in rule-bound ways: the conservation of mass and energy is adhered to at every time step, which prevents local errors from being amplified. Even though the specific modeled dynamics cannot represent the complexity of a real world, the causal connections between elements are enforced so that the 'world-ness' of the model is not at stake—circulations will still circulate, and no element will be magically conjured or disappeared between grid squares.[18]

I am not alone in identifying *Dune*'s world-building with climate modeling. In a discussion of terraforming narratives in science fiction, Chris Pak connects *Dune* with mid-century cybernetic theories. He writes, "Ecological principles fundamental to climate modelling, such as sensitive dependence on initial conditions, feedback systems, and cascading effects, are omnipresent in *Dune*, while Paul's prescience is described as being subject to the same limiting factors as climatological models" (Pak 2019: 204). Noting that Paul is the culmination of a Bene Gesserit project to create "a human computer," Pak reads *Dune* as a performance of cybernetic modeling in service of a critique of geoengineering. This warning, that computational modeling can never enable control or mastery over the future of a planetary system, is borne out especially strongly in the novel's sequel, *Dune Messiah*. But despite the critique, *Dune* displays a mode of explanation, common in planetary SF, that nonetheless seems to require a character or the narrator to try to envision (if not control) the planet. However much they may fail, such efforts are crucial to the planetary scale's emergence in the text.

For instance, in one scene, Kynes describes his realization about the atmospheric composition of the planet:

> So few people ever looked up from the spice long enough to wonder at the near-ideal nitrogen-oxygen-CO_2 balance being maintained here in the absence of large areas of plant cover. The energy sphere of the planet is there to see and understand—a relentless process, but a process nonetheless. There is a gap in it? Then something occupies that gap. [...] I knew the little maker was there, deep in the sand, long before I ever saw it. (Herbert [1965] 2010: 442)

In this passage, Kynes points to the nature of Arrakis as a chemical system and explains that a missing link in the cycling of nutrients around the planet was evident to him before he found the precise organism responsible for it. This moment exemplifies an epistemic habit of implicit causal completeness that is common in science fiction, but which *Dune* takes to an extreme. In the real world, there is

---

18 There are many overviews of climate modeling available. In writing this chapter, I consulted Edwards (2010), Neelin (2011), and Gettelman/Rood (2016), among others.

so much information that it would be impossible for a single person to infer the whole structure of a planet's energy sphere (this, in fact, is the whole project of climate modeling). It is only in a science fiction text like *Dune* that the reader is presented with a world that is absent of red herrings, causally complete, and simply waiting for its missing pieces to be slotted in by a science-minded observer.[19] As a performance of ecological knowledge, this scene makes sense: as we have seen in Sears's text, notions about ecology as made up of cycles and relationships were central to mid-century ecology.

But consider the following scene, in which the same kind of logic is performed but with a non-ecological (or only partially ecological) object. Here, Paul is just beginning to develop his prescient powers, while he and his mother are escaping from the Harkonnens by hiding in the desert. Paul begins to say that the Harkonnens have never truly ruled the planet, but Jessica doesn't understand:

> "Paul, you can't think that—"
> "We've all the evidence in our hands," he said. "Right here in this tent—the tent itself, this pack and its contents, these stillsuits. We know the Guild wants a prohibitive price for weather satellites. We know that—"
> "What've weather satellites to do with it?" she asked.
> Paul sensed the hyperalertness of his mind reading her reactions, computing on minutiae. "You see it now," he said. "Satellites watch the terrain below. There are things in the deep desert that will not bear frequent inspection."
> "You're suggesting the Guild itself controls this planet?"
> She was so slow.
> "No!" he said. "The Fremen! They're paying the Guild for privacy, paying in a coin that's freely available to anyone with desert power—spice. This is more than a second-approximation answer; it's the straight-line computation. Depend on it."
> (Herbert [1965] 2010: 311)

This passage is fascinating, as it attempts to mirror the same kind of logic that attended Pardot Kynes's claim, "There is a gap in [a process]? Then something occupies that gap" (Herbert [1965] 2010: 442). However, it also raises questions about

---

19 This feature of science fiction worlds is similar to what Fredric Jameson famously referred to as world-reduction, "a process of ontological attenuation in which the sheer teeming multiplicity of what exists, of what we call reality, is deliberately thinned and weeded out through an operation of radical abstraction and simplification" (Jameson 1975: 223). For Jameson, this enabled thought experiments with a kind of sociopolitical causal completeness that today looks oddly anti-ecological. In fact, he singles out *Dune* as inadequately 'reduced,' writing of *The Left Hand of Darkness* that its "peculiar ecology [...] along with the way of life it imposes, makes [it] something like an anti-*Dune*" (221). Nonetheless, the idea that SF represents simplified, implicitly causally-complete worlds is an analogy to modeling.

how a single process can be identified, and what constitutes a gap in the first place. Paul claims that "we've all the evidence" and begins to list the objects in the tent. Out of nowhere (or so Jessica thinks), he then adds the datum, "the Guild wants a prohibitive price for weather satellites." But the gap between the Guild's price for satellites and the desert survival technology in the tent is a bit more difficult to fill in than the gap in the cycling of atmospheric elements. This is why we are treated to a textual performance of causal closure as Paul's "hyperalertness [...] computing on minutiae" swoops in to make the non-obvious seem obvious. We are left inhabiting the same position as Jessica while Paul thinks, "she was so slow." In this case, just as in the case of the atmospheric cycle, the different elements of the process must be related to one another as part of some vast system of exchanges and relations. Here, the squares of the grid are so vast that only the fiction of Paul's immense processing power makes the leaps of association seem reasonable.

Like the scene about the atmospheric chemistry of Arrakis, this scene has the purpose of establishing a planetary scope to the science fiction narrative—while the significance of desert power has already been described at great length by this point in the narrative, this scene serves as an introduction to Paul's growing abilities. It communicates a way of thinking about how the different parts of the planet have to be connected in order to make it 'planet-shaped.' Paul's deductions leap from facts about the tent he is in, to satellites that are not in orbit around the entire planet, to the relationship between the Fremen and the Guild, and to the resources under the sand. These leaps connect the different aspects of the world in a way that makes a planet emerge, and the reason it works is because the ultimate object of each of its loops is explaining the planet itself.

Bruce Clarke writes,

> The planetary imaginary of any era is [...] an abiding creative resource that constitutes itself whenever an artist invents and communicates fictive images of living worlds—perhaps, also, of the cosmos that contains those imagined planets, or of the ecologies they sustain—and bodies these forth in some workable medium. (Clarke 2015: 152)

The reason *Dune* is such a touchstone for climate scientists isn't only that it depicts a planet with a single unique climate. Rather, it has to do with the mode of inference—the planetary imaginary—that the novel performs. This mode of inference is, the dual action of bringing explanations up to a planetary scale (as when a comment about the crusades in *Where There Is Life* becomes a comment about a planet's whole history) alongside the assumption of planetary closure. In Herbert's words, a planet is "a system. A system! [...] A system has order, a flowing from point to point" (Herbert [1965] 2010: 806) in wide, repeating cycles. In other words, Arrakis's construction is a form of speculative planetology: the closing of causal loops is assumed to happen at the planetary scale, and this is what makes it 'work' like a climate model.

Reading *Dune* in light of climate modeling helps to explain how science fiction texts make objects that cohere at the planetary scale. Speculative planetology involves the same kind of inference about how worlds cohere across disciplines. In Lisa Messeri's terms, planetary scientists are "literally world-builders," in that they are "invested in questions of what it is like to be on other worlds" (Messeri 2016: 5). For scientists as well as for the public, science fiction texts have helped to provide the templates for how to think about worlds and world-making. The discursive and computational construction of worlds by planetary scientists draws on 'SFnal' thinking, and on the fundamental premise of science fiction, the idea that things could always be different than they are. In *Dune*, when Duke Leto is introduced to Liet Kynes, the Duke refers to him as an ecologist: "'We prefer the old title here, my lord,' Kynes said. 'Planetologist'" (Herbert [1965] 2010: 174).

With this term, Herbert anticipated a science that has only begun coming into its own in the last few decades, alongside advances in Earth system modeling and the increasingly vigorous field of astrobiology. The strategies *Dune* uses to create a world out of a desert ecosystem exhibit a kind of planetary consciousness that is shared between science fiction and the planetary sciences, including climate modeling. As this chapter has shown, planetary and climate scientists refer to science fiction pedagogically and methodologically to communicate this form of speculative planetology. In doing so, they teach us that the ability to comprehend our own planet requires embedding it in a multiverse of imagined otherworlds.

References

Abe, Yutaka/Abe-Ouchi, Ayako/Sleep, Norman H./Zahnle, Kevin J. (2011): "Habitable Zone Limits for Dry Planets." In: *Astrobiology* 11, 443–460.
Beck, Ulrich ([1986] 1992): *Risk Society: Towards a New Modernity*. Mark Ritter (trans.). London: Sage.
Catling, David C./Kasting, James F. (2017): *Atmospheric Evolution on Inhabited and Lifeless Worlds*. Cambridge: Cambridge University Press.
Chakrabarty, Dipesh (2009): "The Climate of History: Four Theses." In: *Critical Inquiry* 35, 197–222.
Clark, Timothy (2015): *Ecocriticism on the Edge*. New York: Bloomsbury Academic.
Clarke, Bruce (2015): "The Planetary Imaginary: Gaian Ecologies from *Dune* to *Neuromancer*." In: Bruce Clarke (ed.): *Earth, Life, and System: Evolution and Ecology on a Gaian Planet*. New York: Fordham University Press, 151–174.
Connolley, William (2010): "Whats Wrong with the World." In: *Stoat*, September 28 (https://scienceblogs.com/stoat/2010/09/28/whats-wrong-with-the-world).

Conway, Erik M. (2008): *Atmospheric Science at NASA: A History*. Baltimore: Johns Hopkins University Press.

Cresto Aleina, Fabio/Baudena, Mara/D'Andrea, Fabio/Provenzale, Antonello (2013): "Multiple Equilibria on Planet Dune: Climate-Vegetation Dynamics on a Sandy Planet." In: *Tellus B: Chemical and Physical Meteorology* 65(1), article 17662.

Delany, Samuel R ([1978] 2009): "About 5,750 Words." In: *The Jewel-Hinged Jaw: Notes on the Language of Science Fiction*. Middletown, CT: Wesleyan University Press, 1–15.

Dick, Steven J./Strick, James E. (2004): *The Living Universe: NASA and the Development of Astrobiology*. New Brunswick: Rutgers University Press.

Edwards, Paul N. (2010): *A Vast Machine: Computer Models, Climate Data, and the Politics of Global Warming*. Cambridge, MA: MIT Press.

Gettelman, Andrew/Rood, Richard (2016): *Demystifying Climate Models: A Users Guide to Earth System Modeling*. Berlin: Springer.

Gillett, Stephen. L. (1996): *World-building: A Writer's Guide to Constructing Star Systems and Life-Supporting Planets*. Cincinnati, OH: Reader's Digest Books.

Grumbine, Robert (2007): "Cloudless Venus." In: *rec.arts.sf.science*, August 16 (https://groups.google.com/d/msg/rec.arts.sf.science/HMZCIAPC04k/Xc8Ae8XqDZAJ).

Grumbine, Robert (2008): "Science Fiction and Science." In: *More Grumbine Science*, November 26 (http://moregrumbinescience.blogspot.com/2008/11/science-fiction-and-science.html).

Gunn, James (2005): "Toward a Definition of Science Fiction." In: James Gunn/Matthew Candelaria (eds.): *Speculations on Speculation: Theories of Science Fiction*. Lanham, MD: Scarecrow Press, 5–12.

Heise, Ursula K. (2008). *Sense of Place and Sense of Planet: The Environmental Imagination of the Global*. Oxford: Oxford University Press.

Herbert, Frank (1963): "Dune World." In: *Analog: Science Fact and Science Fiction*, December, 17–71.

Herbert, Frank ([1965] 2010): *Dune*. New York: Ace.

Herbert, Frank (1969): *Dune Messiah*. New York: Putnam.

Herbert, Frank (1976): *Children of Dune*. New York: Putnam.

Herbert, Frank (1987): *The Maker of Dune: Insights of a Master of Science Fiction*. Tim O'Reilly (ed.). New York: Berkley.

Hitchcock, Dian R./Lovelock, James E. (1967): "Life Detection by Atmospheric Analysis." In: *Icarus* 7, 149–159.

Horowitz, Norman H. (1966): "The Search for Extraterrestrial Life." In: *Science* 151, 789–792.

Horton, Zach (2019): "The Trans-Scalar Challenge of Ecology." In: *ISLE: Interdisciplinary Studies in Literature and Environment* 26, 5–26.

Jameson, Fredric (1975): "World-Reduction in Le Guin: The Emergence of Utopian Narrative." In: *Science Fiction Studies* 2, 221–230.

Jameson, Fredric (1982): "Progress versus Utopia; Or, Can We Imagine the Future?" In: *Science Fiction Studies* 9, 147–158.

Kalidindi, Sirisha/Reick, Christian H./Raddatz, Thomas/Claussen, Martin (2018): "Two Drastically Different Climate States on an Earth-like Terra-Planet." In: *Earth System Dynamics* 9, 739–756.

Kasting, James F./Kopparapu, Ravikumar/Ramirez, Ramses M./Harman, Chester E. (2014): "Remote Life-Detection Criteria, Habitable Zone Boundaries, and the Frequency of Earth-like Planets around M and Late K Stars." In: *Proceedings of the National Academy of Sciences* 111, 12641–12646.

Latour, Bruno (1993): *We Have Never Been Modern.* Cambridge, MA: Harvard University Press.

Lorenz, Ralph D./Zimbelman, James R. (2014): *Dune Worlds: How Windblown Sand Shapes Planetary Landscapes.* Berlin: Springer.

Messeri, Lisa (2016): *Placing Outer Space: An Early Ethnography of Other Worlds.* Durham, NC: Duke University Press.

Milburn, Colin (2010): "Modifiable Futures: Science Fiction at the Bench." In: *Isis* 101, 560–569.

Neelin, J. David (2011): *Climate Change and Climate Modeling.* Cambridge: Cambridge University Press.

O'Reilly, Tim (1981): *Frank Herbert.* New York: Frederick Ungar.

Pak, Chris (2019): "Planetary Climates: Terraforming in Science Fiction." In: Adeline Johns-Putra (ed.): *Climate and Literature.* Cambridge: Cambridge University Press, 196–211.

Palmer, Timothy N. (2010a): "Is Science Fiction a Genre for Communicating Scientific Research? A Case Study in Climate Prediction." In: *Bulletin of the American Meteorological Society* 91, 1413–1417.

Palmer, Timothy N. (2010b): "Sunrise." In: *Bulletin of the American Meteorological Society* website, October (doi:10.1175/2010BAMS3187.2). Archived at: Oxford University Department of Physics website, October 12, 2016, (https://www2.physics.ox.ac.uk/sites/default/files/2016-10-12/sunrise_oct_2016_pdf_86437.pdf).

Pierrehumbert, Raymond T. (2005): "Science Fiction Atmospheres." In: *Bulletin of the American Meteorological Society* 86, 696–699.

Pierrehumbert, Raymond T. (2010): *Principles of Planetary Climate.* Cambridge: Cambridge University Press.

Pierrehumbert, Raymond T. (2012): "Successful Predictions." Tyndall History of Global Environmental Change Lecture. Fall Meeting 2012, American Geophysical Union, San Francisco, California, December 3–7. In: AGU, "Fall Meeting

2012 Tyndall Lecture: Successful Predictions," YouTube, December 7, 2012 (https://www.youtube.com/watch?v=RICBu_P8JWI).

Raymond, T. Sean (2014): "Real-Life Sci-Fi World #5: A Dune Planet (Arrakis)." In: *PlanetPlanet* October 10 (https://planetplanet.net/2014/10/10/real-life-sci-fi-world-5-a-dune-planet-arrakis/).

Sagan, Carl (1961): "The Planet Venus." In: *Science* 133, 849–858.

Sagan, Carl (1962): "Structure of the Lower Atmosphere of Venus." In: *Icarus* 1, 151–169.

Schmidt, Gavin A. (2018): "Under the Sun." In: *Motherboard*, April 16 (https://www.vice.com/en_us/article/3kj4y8/gavin-schmidt-fiction-under-the-sun).

Schmidt, Gavin A./Frank, Adam (2019): "The Silurian Hypothesis: Would It Be Possible to Detect an Industrial Civilization in the Geological Record?" In: *International Journal of Astrobiology*, 18, 142–150.

Sears, Paul (1962): *Where There Is Life*. New York: Dell.

Seitzinger, Sybil (2010): "A Sustainable Planet Needs Scientists to Think Ahead." In: *Nature* 468, 601.

Slonczewski, Joan/Levy, Michael (2003): "Science Fiction and the Life Sciences." In: Edward James/Farah Mendlesohn (eds.): *The Cambridge Companion to Science Fiction*. Cambridge: Cambridge University Press, 174–185.

Stocker, Thomas F./Clarke, Gary K. C./Le Treut, Hervé/Lindzen, Richard S./Meleshko, Valentin P./ Mugara, Richard K./Palmer, Timothy N./Pierrehumbert, Raymond T./Sellers, Piers J./Trenberth, Kevin E./Willebrand, Jürgen (2001): "Physical Climate Processes and Feedbacks." In: John T. Houghton/Yihui Ding/David J. Griggs/Maria Noguer/Paul J. van der Linden/Xiaosu Dai/Kathy Maskell/C. A. Johnson (eds.): *Climate Change 2001: The Scientific Basis. Contribution of Working Group I to the Third Assessment Report of the Intergovernmental Panel on Climate Change*. Cambridge: Cambridge University Press, 419–470.

Suvin, Darko (1979): *Metamorphoses of Science Fiction: On the Poetics and History of a Literary Genre*. New Haven, CT: Yale University Press.

Weart, Spencer R. (2019): "Venus & Mars." In: *The Discovery of Global Warming*, January (https://history.aip.org/climate/Venus.htm); expanded online version of Spencer R. Weart (2008): *The Discovery of Global Warning*, second ed., Cambridge, MA: Harvard University Press.

Winsberg, Eric (2010): *Science in the Age of Computer Simulation*. Chicago: University of Chicago Press.

Wolf, Mark J. P. (2012): *Building Imaginary Worlds: The Theory and History of Subcreation*. New York: Routledge.

Woods, Derek (2014): "Scale Critique for the Anthropocene." In: *Minnesota Review* 83, 133–142.

Chapter 3: The Rule of Productivity and the Fear of Transgression
Speculative Uncertainty in Digital Games

Felix Raczkowski

Regicide, it appears, is the ultimate crime in real-world monarchies, thus warranting capital punishment (Foucault [1975] 1977: 12). The same holds true for digital, ludic monarchies. Of all video game monarchies, none saw more regicide attempts than Britannia—the fictional, high-fantasy country in the long-running role-playing game series *Ultima* (Origin Systems/Electronic Arts 1981–1999). The reasons for this were twofold. Firstly, the ruler of Britannia, Lord British, was always conceptualized as the alter ego of the series's creator, Richard Garriott (cf. "Inside Ultima IV" 1986). With Lord British appearing in every installment of the series, his presence was a challenge for players, a chance to hurt the symbolic stand-in for the game's creator. Secondly, the challenge of killing Lord British was always situated in the rules of the games. He was simply very hard to kill in each installment of *Ultima*, so figuring out a way around his elevated hit points or various invulnerabilities became part of the fun of playing the game for some players (cf. "Killing Lord British" [2009] 2019). All of this contributed to the most well-known case of regicide in the history of the *Ultima* series, which also demonstrates the element of uncertainty that is at the core of games.

Shortly before *Ultima Online*—the massively multiplayer online game (MMO) in the *Ultima* series—was set to launch in August 1997, the developers attempted a stress test on their servers (Olivetti 2015).[1] They encouraged players to log on during that time to check whether the game's infrastructure was capable of handling large numbers of players at the same time. To increase participation in the test, Richard Garriott announced that he would be present in-game as Lord British, which offered players the chance to meet their world's creator as a character directly controlled by Garriott. Since *Ultima Online* was famous for its fairly loose set of rules, which allowed players to rob or kill each other at all times, the developers usually protected their own characters through an administrative command

---

1 There is some controversy over which day the assassination took place, with different sources claiming either August 8 or August 9, 1997 (Razimus Gaming 2016).

that granted them invulnerability. On the day of the stress test, a server reset happened shortly before Lord British was set to address his subjects. This removed his invulnerability, and since the reset went unnoticed by the developers, none of them thought of re-entering the command (Olivetti 2015). This enabled one player—to this day, known only by the character name of Rainz—to use a recently stolen magical fire field scroll on Lord British, killing him in a fiery inferno. In the aftermath of the assassination, all player characters that were present shortly after the event (Rainz had quickly fled the scene) were indiscriminately killed by the developers, while Rainz was later identified as the regicide and banned from *Ultima Online* altogether. The ultimate crime had warranted capital punishment, even in a virtual world. Indeed, because death is not permanent in Britannia (or in most games), banishment from the online world is the most severe punishment available in developer-monarchies. The character and their player are eliminated from the world altogether, in most cases leaving no trace of their participation in the game.

While interpreting the rules and the systems of punishment in online games with medieval subjects according to Foucault's analysis of sovereign power might be a fun exercise (and I will return to Foucault later in the essay), the anecdote of Lord British's assassination is relevant in this context because it tells us something about the unpredictability of games. The first notable observation is that it is possible to recount the events at all. Even though no video footage of the incident exists merely screenshots and 'eyewitness' accounts—the assassination of Lord British remains one of the most well-documented and discussed events in video game culture and MMO history.[2] The reasons for its notoriety relate to the unpredictability of the event itself and the openness of its immediate aftermath. *Ultima Online* proved that not only do all games encompass an element of uncertainty and openness, but also that this uncertainty affects players and developers alike. It produced a transgressive manifestation of uncertainty: the regicide. A game designer's perspective on this transgression may offer the mundane explanation that Rainz's actions did not violate the rules of the game (thus, they cannot be described as cheating), but instead owed to the emergent interplay of various systems in combination with the developers' oversight. In this view, the assassination proves the potential of *Ultima Online* as an early sandbox-style game and thus should either be framed as a positive experience or, at least, go unpunished. However, the immediate reaction by the developers (indiscriminate retaliation followed by a ban against the regicide) suggests that the matter is more complex. Apparently, while some degree of uncertainty and unpredictability in games is encouraged and supported, there can be transgressive uncertainty even without breaking the rules of the game.

---

2 Cf. Ramsay (2015: 128–130); and Olivetti (2015).

In this essay, I will take a closer look at the way uncertainty, unpredictability, openness, and speculative potential are discussed and framed in video game discourse. I am especially interested in the various measures taken to make ludic uncertainty productive and in the strategies employed by developers to limit or diminish transgressive uncertainties, both of which will here be discussed as practices of speculation. I differentiate between two basic modes of speculation: the speculation that aims to put uncertainty to work, to make it productive (for example, in the form of experiments or simulations that involve the players of online games), and the speculation that attempts to contain the risks of uncertainty (for example, in the form of experiments designed to produce formalized knowledge on toxic and antisocial gameplay, which then translates into systems designed to limit such behavior). Starting with anthropological and cultural-historical accounts of games and play, I will demonstrate that uncertainty is constitutive for games and play. It is then possible to outline the ways in which uncertainty in games is 'put to work' through strategies aiming to harness what I will describe as the speculative potential of digital games. In closing, I will focus once more on the paradox of necessary uncertainty and rule-bound predictability in games that has become apparent in the events surrounding the assassination of Lord British.

Uncertainty in Games and Play

The most well-known cultural-historical definitions of play, which informed early video game discourse, mention unpredictability and uncertainty as a core element of play. The Dutch historian Johan Huizinga refers to "tension" as a driving force behind the human tendency to play: "Tension means uncertainty, chanciness; a striving to decide the issue and so end it" (Huizinga [1938] 1980: 10). He later points to uncertainty as one of the unifying characteristics that motivate both playing by oneself (or single-playing, as we could call it from today's perspective) as well as group-play:

> There is always the question "will it come off?" This condition is fulfilled even when we are playing patience, doing jig-saw puzzles, acrostics, crosswords, diablo, etc. Tension and uncertainty as to the outcome increase enormously when the antithetical element becomes really agonistic in the play of groups. (47)

The difference between single- and group-play will become relevant for this analysis later on, albeit in a significantly different context. In game research, Huizinga is usually paired with French sociologist and anthropologist Roger Caillois, although both authors have little in common ideologically or regarding their disciplinary backgrounds, as Galloway points out (Galloway 2006: 19–20). Caillois cites Huizinga, building on his work to develop his own definition of play, which includes uncertainty as the third paragraph: "3. Uncertain: the course of which cannot be determined, nor the result attained beforehand, and some latitude for innovations being left to the player's initiative" (Caillois 2001: 9). While Huizinga emphasizes uncertainty in play as a source of tension or suspense, Caillois frames it as an essential prerequisite for play (7–8). In doing so, he is closer to contemporary game design discourse than to Huizinga's idealistic cultural-historical account.

Both Huizinga and Caillois draw upon anthropological research on rituals in their works, with Huizinga devoting several paragraphs of his study to the relationship between play and ritual (Huizinga [1938] 1980: 15–27). Play and ritual are seen as closely related phenomena, both taking place outside of ordinary life and in their own time, both adhering to special rules, both allowing for transgressive acts under specific circumstances. Game studies today even owes one of its key terms (and at the same time its most contested subject) to anthropological research on ritual: the "magic circle," introduced into video game discourse by Salen and Zimmerman, who in turn quote Huizinga (Salen/Zimmerman 2004: 95).[3] The magic circle marks the place and time of play and ritual, it separates transgressive acts from social order. The earliest mention of a magic circle in anthropological research can be found in the work of Dutch-German anthropologist Arnold van Gennep ([1909] 1960: 13), who studied rites of passage, meaning the transition between different social positions, for example, youth and adulthood or unmarried and married. The various rituals described by van Gennep already exhibit the precarious balance between non-negotiable, absolute rules and transgressive uncertainties. When discussing rites of initiation as a subset of rites of passage, van Gennep explains how novices in various cultures (he specifically mentions Liberia and Papua New Guinea) are allowed to break their respective societies' traditional rules:

> During the entire novitiate, the usual economic and legal ties are modified, sometimes broken altogether. The novices are outside society, and society has no power over them, especially since they are actually sacred and holy, and therefore untouchable and dangerous, just as gods would be. Thus, although taboos, as negative rites, erect a barrier between the novices and society, the society is defenseless against the novices' undertakings. That is the explanation—the simplest in the world—for a fact that has been noted among a great many peoples and that has remained incomprehensible to observers. During the novitiate, the young

---

3 For more detailed accounts on the magic circle and the debates surrounding it in game studies, see Consalvo (2009); Stenros (2012); and Zimmerman (2012).

people can steal and pillage at will or feed and adorn themselves at the expense of the community. (114)

One might be tempted to add "unpredictable" to van Gennep's list of qualities describing novices and gods alike, since they are both able to act with a degree of freedom that makes their "undertakings" unpredictable for their own people and "incomprehensible to observers." In short, rites of passage create uncertainty. However, there are three important differences between the way uncertainty works in transitional rites and the way it can be thought of in play. Firstly, the ritualistic uncertainty that van Gennep alludes to is experienced by everyone but the novices themselves. The players-novices create moments of uncertainty and unpredictability for all non-players, whereas play in the way it is theorized following Huizinga and Caillois needs to be unpredictable with uncertain outcomes for the players themselves. Secondly, the rites of passage are potentially threatening to society, since they cannot always be contained, as van Gennep describes. If the rites enable novices to break all common rules, society can only persist because the ritual is always limited in its duration. This is especially true for the rites of passage studied by van Gennep, because they enable the transition from one social position to the next—as soon as the novice has attained their new position, the ritual is over. Thus, the limited duration becomes the most important (and in some cases, the only) rule of rites of passage, whereas play can and must be governed by any number of rules, although they may constantly change. Thirdly, the rites of passage are productive (they enable transition) and potentially dangerous (they allow for the breaking of rules), whereas play, in its ideal form defined by Huizinga and Caillois, is unproductive and free of consequence.

We have seen that both play and ritual can be thought of as cultural practices generating a (more or less extensively) rule-governed time and space in which (more or less) unpredictable and uncertain events can play out. This broad characterization can be further abstracted to the relationship between a fixed frame and its freely moving contents, which is the central definition of play in early game studies and game design discourse. Katie Salen and Eric Zimmerman define play as "free movement within a more rigid structure" (Salen/Zimmerman 2004: 304), elegantly encompassing both Huizinga's theory as well as anthropological research on rituals.[4] Salen and Zimmerman's definition appears in the context of a game design handbook and has to be understood as an attempt to develop a definition of play that is operationalizable for game development. To this end, they discuss rules as systemic frames that are necessary for every kind of play. Inter-

---

4 Salen and Zimmerman cite Huizinga as the source of the term "magic circle" (Salen/Zimmerman 2004: 95), and it appears that they were unaware of earlier anthropological research on rituals.

estingly, Salen and Zimmerman account for the subversion and the breaking of rigid rules as an essential dimension of play, noting:

> When play occurs, it can overflow and overwhelm the more rigid structure in which it is taking place, generating emergent, unpredictable results. Sometimes, in fact, the force of play is so powerful that it can change the structure itself. (305)

Play can become transformative, unpredictably changing the rules framing it. Salen and Zimmerman perceive this as a source of creativity, maintaining that transformative play can bring about not only new rules or a new perspective on play, but new ways of playing or new games altogether.[5] Without explicitly addressing it, Salen and Zimmerman allude to the productivity of play that will be discussed in the following paragraphs.

When applying Salen and Zimmerman's definition to digital games and their ability to enable play, it seems obvious to equate the "rigid structure" with the respective computer program. The rules of the game are, after all, maintained by an algorithmic machine, as Juul argues (Juul 2005: 53–54). In this view, the game's rules are nearly absolute, since changing or violating them would require interfering with the game's code, necessitating specific technical knowledge (e.g. programming, using editors to change variables, or even physically altering consoles or cartridges). Consequently, it has been argued (especially by German media theorists) that there is no difference between the rules of the game and the laws of physics or space-time in digital games, since they all have to be programmed and then enacted through the code (Pias 2010: 14–15). Following this, all questions regarding the oft-discussed magic circle as the "place" of the game and its rules can be put aside, since algorithmic rules are neither permeable nor negotiable (Liebe 2008). The "magic" inherited from its ritualistic origins is exorcised from play, the danger for society is averted (although some media psychologists and worried parents think otherwise), and uncertainty can only manifest itself according to preset parameters. These manifestations include unpredictable emergent phenomena, but they can no longer encompass the rules themselves. Playing digital games comes down to reacting to the machine's commands (Pias 2010), enacting the designer's visions (Bogost 2007), or toying with flexible systems.

The introductory anecdote of Lord British's assassination proves, however, that matters are more complicated. There is an ontological uncertainty, an essential paradox at the core of play and games, as Markus Rautzenberg points

---

5 Following Salen and Zimmerman's account, there is a growing body of research dealing with transgressive play, although most publications tend to focus on an affirmative reading of transgression (in the sense of creativity and critique), e.g. Galloway (2006); Consalvo (2007); and Boluk/LeMieux (2017).

out. Drawing on the work of Gregory Bateson, he argues that there can be no instance of play in which the act of playing itself cannot be questioned (Rautzenberg 2015). "Are we playing?" or "Is this a game?" thus become essential questions that highlight the paradoxical situation of play. Every move or operation has to encompass two contradictory meanings at the same time, inside and outside of the game. Bateson illustrates this with the bite in animal play (Bateson 1987), but it is equally true of the regicide in *Ultima Online*. Is the attack on Lord British part of the game, or is it a personal affront to the lead developer? It is, of course, both (that is the reason it is still remembered today). In accordance with Bateson's theory and Erving Goffman's frame analysis, Rautzenberg goes on to describe games as "framed uncertainties," while also pointing out that "real" uncertainty is impossible in digital games:

> On the one hand computer games are celebrations of uncertainty, on the other, this uncertainty is not real. It's just pretend uncertainty because computers have a problem with real randomness in so far as they can't generate randomness due to their very nature as von Neumann architecture and Turing machines. This is a key distinction that separates computer games from other games. There are many forms of framed uncertainties but there is a certain edge to the notion when it comes to computer games because of their digital ontology. It almost seems as if there is a kind of longing for uncertainty, randomness and entropy in digital media that is articulated in computer games for us to explore. (Rautzenberg 2015: 95)

Rautzenberg's account offers an ideal point of departure for the close reading of digital games and their various strategies of self-referentiality that question the status of games and challenge the player's position. However, his accurate observation regarding the technical limitations of digital media is still too narrow to address the uncertainties that result from the cultural context of play or various player interactions. In other words, I maintain that the "frame" of a game is more than the sum of its algorithmic rules and that, therefore, a discussion of the uncertainties manifesting within this frame needs to take into account those phenomena that either lie outside the machine-enacted rules or that result from specific player interactions.[6] Multiplayer games such as *Ultima Online* especially manifest uncertainties that are not located in the algorithmic rules of these games, but instead emerge both from the way that players act with or on each other and

---

6 The game designer Greg Costikyan attempts to formalize different types of uncertainty, including "player unpredictability" and "randomness" (Costikyan 2013: 78–86), which would most closely correspond with Rautzenberg's theory and my critique. Yet, since Costikyan's taxonomy is mainly directed at game designers, it misses some of the theoretical nuance in the discussion of games as uncertain phenomena as such.

from the paradoxes that arise from the attempts to interpret these actions ("Was this a serious attack or a playful bite?" "Was this a legitimate player action or an act of aggression against a game developer?"). Thomas Malaby has called these properties of games their social and semiotic contingency (Malaby 2007: 108), while Mark Johnson describes these types of games in his Deleuzian reading of various forms of unpredictability in digital games as exhibiting a specific form of instability (Johnson 2019: 120–145). That is, they tend to generate unpredictable situations and results, regardless of whether or not they're designed to do so.[7]

Thus, the question of uncertainty in digital games is connected to an epistemological duality that shapes many debates in game studies: should the study of digital games focus on the technical artifacts (software programs, hardware platforms), or should it focus on the player expression and the cultural ramifications of digital games? And, if neither perspective is to be privileged, how can both approaches be combined with one another? This essay cannot solve these rather fundamental questions, but I will attempt to demonstrate how both the technical and the cultural dimension of digital games are intertwined when it comes to the point of speculating with the inherent uncertainty of digital games, either to harness it or to limit its consequences.

The Rule of Productivity: Uncertainty as Resource in Digital Games

Digital games have been likened to simulations, due to their conceptual relatedness as much as their technical similarities as early computer applications (Bogost 2006; Pias 2010; Crogan 2011; Frasca 2003; Aarseth 2004). As Pias demonstrates, there is a historical precedent of using heavily modified versions of chess as war games for educational purposes as well as for testing strategies in preparation for actual battles (Pias 2010: 203–228). Both games and simulations are rule-based structures that can offer ideal, consequence-free environments for learning or experimentation. At least a whole paper could be devoted to the history of games in thought experiments (the most influential of which would probably be Turing's imitation game), but I will focus on discussing several speculative applications of digital games that attempt to make their uncertainties productive.

As far as the history of games as simulations is concerned, uncertainty is introduced through elements of chance, such as dice rolls (Pias 2010: 218–223),

---

7 Johnson offers an ontological exploration of randomness and chance in (digital) games, in which he differentiates between randomness, chance, luck, and instability. Each of these concepts situates unpredictability at another level of gameplay, which allows Johnson to discuss a wide array of heterogeneous phenomena (e.g. procedural generation, glitches or grinding) in light of the question of how unpredictability is experienced during gameplay.

which are necessary to prevent 'perfect' information and absolute predictability in war games. In short, to reduce the gap between the perceived 'reality' of war and its rule-based representation (Bogost 2006: 107), it is necessary to address uncertainty and unpredictability in the simulation. It thus becomes apparent that epistemic simulations, by which I mean simulations that are not primarily designed as learning or training environments, have to allow for uncertainty to ensure that it is possible to adequately represent systems of imperfect information. One could even go so far as to presume that uncertainty is mandatory if epistemic simulations are supposed to contribute to the emergence of 'new' scientific knowledge, instead of merely enabling the testing of hypotheses. As soon as computer simulations come into play, the central problem with this approach is identical to the difficulty digital games have with randomness, as Rautzenberg points out: the machine can only ever simulate randomness for its human operator. Emergence is possible when the system is complex enough, but pure chance cannot occur. This is especially challenging for all simulations that attempt to represent systems in which human behavior plays a major part, such as traffic, economics, or epidemics.

The aspirations to solve these problems and to create simulations that more adequately manifest the uncertainties of human behavior are increasingly directed towards digital games, especially massively multiplayer games. The constitutive uncertainty of games and their paradoxical relationship to non-game conventions are to be made productive as part of epistemic simulations that attempt to answer questions from various disciplines, ranging from biochemistry and epidemiology to sociology, economics, and law. The uncertainty that players introduce into virtual environments thus becomes an object of speculation that is no longer framed as a source of concern for game developers trying to anticipate and foreclose transgressive player behavior. Two very different intensities of speculation can be discerned when it comes to ludic simulations, namely the concrete speculation with player behavior and the abstract speculation with games themselves. The propositions to make uncertainty in digital games productive all center around a specific duality of online games: on the one hand, their status as a frame that allows for interaction between players, and on the other hand, their nature as technological artifacts that enable measurement and tracking of player interactions. While uncertainty is introduced through the players, the outcome of most player actions is automatically formalized and measured, since that is a prerequisite for the computer program. This enables massively multiplayer online games to function similarly to agent-based simulations, while substituting 'real' players for simulated agents (Salazar 2009). Given a game of sufficient popularity and enough players, it becomes possible to enact (social) experiments inside an ostensibly consequence-free environment and with enough participants to produce results of statistical significance, while also accounting for the uncertainties of human behavior. There have been proposals by lawyers (Broekens 2008; Bradley/Froomkin 2004), epidemiologists (Lofgren/Fefferman 2007), economists (Castronova 2008), and communication scholars (Williams et al. 2011) to use MMOs for experimentation, e.g. to test legislation before it takes effect, to run simulations on the spreading of contagious diseases in pandemic scenarios, or to test economic policy. All of these proposals are speculative in nature not only because they suggest to use MMOs and their players as simulations, effectively turning the players into agents whose "playbour" (Kücklich 2005) produces or validates scientific knowledge, but also because, to date, they are only notices of intent, since it has proven difficult for the scientific community to initiate cooperation with developers or publishers of games with sufficiently large player-bases (cf. Williams et al. 2011: 165). While there have been ethnographic studies (cf. Taylor 2006) that were conducted inside MMOs, the large-scale problems of economic or legal research would require access to the game's rules and the data accumulated during gameplay, which both cannot be observed from the outside, but would have to be provided by the developers. Some of the most notable examples in which scientists have had access to this data are internships or consulting agreements initiated by the developers to solve specific problems (often relating to the economics of virtual marketplaces, cf. Seiler 2008; Suderman 2014).[8] An altogether different case compared to these examples might be considered when the game in question is built from the ground up to provide scientists with data. This happens as part of so-called citizen-science projects (Cooper 2014), which are usually employed to contribute to scientific certainties, e.g. to either minimize contingency, uncertainty, or chance or to make their inevitable appearance in play productive. However, at least one game has been developed with the explicit goal of producing specific uncertainties in the form of unpredictable human choices that were then used in Bell tests in physics (BIG Bell Test Collaboration 2018). These tests are dependent on sources for unpredictability, which poses problems that cannot be solved by computers alone but can be alleviated through unpredictable decisions by humans (in this case, quite literally through the production of bits by either pressing 1 or 0).

Attempts to make uncertainty productive in digital games could be discussed in more detail; however, for the scope of this essay, it is sufficient to note that we can observe what Patrick Crogan calls the "concretization of computer games":

> To play a computer game today—or to think and write about it—is to be part of this concretization, to adopt this facticity, to participate in its economic, logistical, technocultural becoming. Whether ignored, denied, sublated, or explicitly confronted, it is always a question of how to adopt this becoming. We are all betting

---

8 Among the best-known economists to cooperate with video game publishers in this way is the former minister of finance of Greece, Yanis Varoufakis (Suderman 2014).

on the future of computer games, with, against, or in some other orientation to their predominant becoming under the aegis of what Stiegler calls the "programming industries." (Crogan 2011: 31)

Crogan describes the mode in which players, scholars, and developers/publishers engage with digital games as gambling: to play, research, or develop digital games means placing a bet on their future. This form of speculation becomes especially interesting when we observe that the future of digital games may be concerned with predicting and preempting futures, often (according to Crogan and in line with Pias) continuing their historical legacy as military computer simulations. Thus, following Crogan, we can state that there is at least second-degree speculation taking place in the papers cited above. By proposing to use uncertainty in games to enact experiments, they speculate on the futures addressed by their specific disciplines while also speculating on the future of digital games themselves. This essay, discussing these phenomena in the context of speculation and uncertainty, could be regarded as a third degree of speculation; as the bet placed by certain disciplines in the humanities (media studies and game studies) on the future of digital games and game research.

The speculative practices I have discussed all aim to make digital games productive, to put game mechanics and players to work on problems and research questions, and even to conceive of new games and virtual worlds in an attempt to preempt some futures and close down others. I maintain that all of this becomes possible because of the uncertainty at the core of games that allows for unpredictable situations to arise in and around play, especially when several players are interacting with each other as well as with complex systems on the side of the machine. These uncertainties can enable not only potentially productive behavior, but also transgressive or harmful acts, which invite different forms of experimentation and speculation in the attempts to prevent them.

The Fear of Transgression: Uncertainty as a Challenge for Digital Games

Besides the rare cases in which the in-game representation of a game developer becomes the victim of aggression, which subsequently must be punished in an appropriately deterrent and terminal fashion, MMOs have developed communities in which transgressive acts in the form of verbal hostility, threats, harassment, and abusive in-game behavior between players are common. While it might be objected that verbal (or textual) abuse through chats or voice chat clients is not part of the game and thus cannot be compared to transgressions afforded by or enabled through the game's rules (such as the assassination of Lord British), game developers are recognizing so-called toxic behavior as a problem that is especially threatening to free-to-play business models (cf. Blackburn/Kwak 2014). These games depend on large player bases and a constant influx of new players, since the base game is free and the developers make money through in-game purchases. However, the low bar of entry for these games also means that the inhibitions regarding transgressive behavior are lowered—after all, the capital punishment of banishment holds little meaning anymore if you can just create a new account for the same game without any costs. Additionally, banning players has fallen out of favor with the developers even in games where it might work as a deterrent, since it always risks losing a customer permanently. In short, major online-game developers and publishers see themselves confronted with a situation that is marked by an ever-growing environment of toxicity (Alexander 2018), as well as the diminished efficiency and appeal of typical counter-measures against these behaviors. Bateson's paradox regarding the situation of play holds the potential of abuse in game environments: uncertainty can become hostility; the play bite can quickly come to be the real bite between players.

At this point, a disclaimer is in order. The issue of harassment in online games and the larger culture surrounding digital games in general is extremely broad and remains underexplored. It encompasses not only the toxicity that marks specific game communities, but also larger cultural debates regarding representation and gender in video games, as well as organized harassment campaigns such as GamerGate (Mortensen 2018). These concerns are far beyond the scope and topic of this essay and will not be addressed further. However, I am interested in harassment and toxicity because transgressive behavior such as this constitutes the 'dark' counterpart to the productive uncertainties inherent to gaming. While the transgressions function differently to the productive uncertainties, they both follow from and can be described through the ritualistic roots of play. Transgression is always possible and its most dangerous extremes have to be managed somehow. This problem of management is, moreover, where speculative practices once again come into play.

The game developers, confronted with increasing hostility inside the communities surrounding their games, attempt to solve these issues through technology. They develop systems that are supposed to encourage positive behavior and discourage negative behavior. These systems are constantly refined, adapted, tested, and evaluated. Players enter a speculative feedback loop in which their actions are permanently monitored by game systems that are designed (and periodically adjusted) to steer behavior in a productive or, at least, harmless direction. The most striking example of such systems was developed by Riot Games for the multiplayer game *League of Legends*. Released in 2009, the game has exploded with popularity. Since 2016, it boasts more than 100 million monthly players (Kollar 2016). However, it has also developed a reputation for having an unfriendly and

Chapter 3: The Rule of Productivity and the Fear of Transgression   89

aggressive community of players (LeJacq 2015). Riot Games has conducted several experiments in cooperation with psychologists, with Jeffrey Lin, a game designer with a PhD in cognitive neuroscience, serving as the project coordinator (Maher 2016: 569). Through the methods of psychology in conjunction with big data analysis, it has become possible to describe and formalize toxicity. The studies found that, in *League of Legends*, it was not merely a small minority of players responsible for most of the transgressive acts; rather, most players were overstepping the bounds of social conduct defined by Riot, at least from time to time (Maher 2016: 569).[9] This demonstrates that permanently banning the offenders is no longer a solution for *League of Legends*, because the game would lose a significant part of its players over time. We can now return to Foucault in the context of the introductory anecdote of Lord British's assassination. While the singular transgression (the regicide) can be met with the most severe punishment, a situation in which various transgressions are regularly committed by a significant part of the player population calls for reform. Foucault's analysis of the transition from sovereign to disciplinary society can be applied to online multiplayer games, as well, although the power structures and discursive formations are vastly different. What is interesting in the context of uncertainty and speculation is that, in the case of Riot Games, the focus on reform instead of punishment entails (again paraphrasing Foucault) a will to knowledge that is directed at the players and their behavior.

Online multiplayer games become the site of experiments once more. But this time, the players not merely participants in experiments that pertain to research questions and disciplines for which the game is just a scientific medium. Instead, they are the immediate objects of inquiry. To modify player behavior and make the community friendlier and more welcoming, there must be (scientific) knowledge about several factors. Which behaviors most need to change? How should 'good' or 'bad' behaviors be recognized and evaluated? What systems are best for encouraging change and reform? The various experiments conducted in *League of Legends* have posed such questions on a large scale:

> The Riot team devised 24 in-game messages or tips, including some that encourage good behaviour—such as "Players perform better if you give them constructive feedback after a mistake"—and some that discourage bad behaviour: "Teammates perform worse if you harass them after a mistake." They presented the tips

---

9   The code of conduct for *League of Legends*, called "The Summoner's Code," was introduced in 2010. Updated in 2017, the current version of the code states: "Play as a team, win as a team. Don't rage, blame or tear people down. Make allies on the Rift. Never feed intentionally and don't give up the fight! Lead the way for newbies, be helpful. Keep your account information private" ("The Summoner's Code" [2010] 2017). There is a clear emphasis on cooperation and a positive and welcoming atmosphere, which suggests that these are the norms that are violated the most.

in three colours and at different times during the game. All told, there were 216 conditions to test against a control, in which no tips were given. That is a ridiculous number of permutations to test on people in a laboratory, but trivial for a company with the power to perform millions of experiments each day. (Maher 2016: 569–570)

Experiments such as these turn *League of Legends* into what has been called "the largest virtual psychology lab in the world" (Hsu 2015). They contribute to various research papers in social psychology or information science (e.g. Kwak/Blackburn 2015). Moreover, they bring about tangible changes in the game itself, through which widespread behavioral reform is encouraged. These systems are all designed to shift decision and judgement regarding transgressive behavior from the developers to either the game's algorithms or the players themselves. Systems such as the Tribunal or the Honor System leave it to players to rate each other's behavior, which results in automatic rewards or punishments by the game. The current iteration of the Honor System offers players a level-based progression with rewards, depending on the way fellow players judge their behavior after each round of the game. Since Riot continuously evaluates the efficacy of their measures through new research, which then leads to changes in the game, it is difficult to discuss the various systems in relation to the current state of the game, as both are constantly changing. The important point is that the potentially transgressive uncertainties are subject to continuous and speculative experimental treatment, aiming to create a player community that no longer has to be threatened with capital punishment. The ideal player population governs and reforms itself, necessitating minimal interventions but maximal research effort from developers.

Closing Remarks

An element of uncertainty is necessary for play and games. This uncertainty is mobilized differently in rituals, child's play, sports, or digital games. Nevertheless, it brings with it potentials and threats that are comparable between vastly different forms of play and games: the thrill of unpredictability, the open outcome, the enjoyment of unforeseen moves, as well as the danger of transgression, the chance that play suddenly shifts into non-play, the risk that pretend aggression turns into real aggression, or even the possibility that the fabric of society itself becomes threatened through boundless rituals. Where digital games are concerned, I maintain that there are specific speculative practices that have emerged to address these uncertainties. Two modes of speculation have been discussed in this essay: productive speculation that aims to put uncertainty to work, and preventive speculation that attempts to limit the risks of uncertainty. Both modes of speculation are directed at players and systems alike. They both propose to address implications resulting from play and games taking place under the conditions of digital media. Ultimately, they both speculate on the future of digital games.

According to Crogan, to participate in gaming culture (even to study it academically) means to bet on the future of games (Crogan 2011: 30–36). These bets (or, as we may call them, speculations) have become far more tangible in some fields than others. There is keen interest in digital games as spaces for experimentation and simulation from researchers of various disciplines. The future of online games speculated by the scientific community frames them as laboratories, as epistemic toolboxes that, ideally, can be specifically designed to answer questions that are not related to the games themselves. This in turn means that research questions would have to be posed in a way that allows them to be formalized in game rules—the experiments have to work as games and vice versa. While these visions have not yet been widely realized, the experiments to limit transgressive behavior are already leading to results that warrant further study. As game developers such as Riot attempt to solve behavioral issues through systems and implemented design decisions, their repeated experimentation and refinement produces a specific knowledge on the way digital media can be used in large-scale behavior modification. In the case of *League of Legends*, the systemic solution means the implementation of a system of rewards and punishments, levels and scores, that relies on self-surveillance of the player populace. These strategies, which resemble neobehaviorist approaches and gamification (Raczkowski 2014), also demonstrate that such concepts can be successfully implemented on a large scale. Future research will have to focus on the consequences of these speculations, especially for implementations in non-game contexts—such as the Chinese social credit system (Mistreanu 2018)—that attempt to modify the behavior of whole populations through digital media and big data.

Digital games are currently entrenched in forms of speculation that are all directed toward the future of the medium, in one way or another. There is, therefore, a definite need to study these practices critically and, in doing so, to take part in the speculations regarding the futures and potentials of digital games.

Acknowledgments

I am indebted to Sylvia Mayer and Colin Milburn for their insightful remarks on the structure of the essay and on my arguments presented therein. Without their comments, the essay would undoubtedly lack clarity. I also want to thank Vera Butz for the thorough proofreading of the essay's first draft.

References

Aarseth, Espen (2004): "Genre Trouble: Narrativism and the Art of Simulation." In: Noah Wardrip-Fruin/Pat Harrigan (eds.): *First Person. New Media as Story, Performance, and Game*. Cambridge, MA: MIT Press, 45–55.

Alexander, Julia (2018): "League of Legends' Senior Designer Outlines How They Battle Rampant Toxicity." In: *Polygon*, March 20 (https://www.polygon.com/2018/3/20/17143610/league-of-legends-toxic-players-tyler1-riot-games).

Bateson, Gregory ([1955] 1987): "A Theory of Play and Fantasy." In: Gregory Bateson: *Steps to an Ecology of Mind: Collected Essays in Anthropology, Psychiatry, Evolution, and Epistemology*. Northvale/London: Jason Aronson, 138–148.

The BIG Bell Test Collaboration (2018): "Challenging Local Realism with Human Choices." In: *Nature* 557, 212–216.

Blackburn, Jeremy/Kwak, Haewoon (2014): "STFU NOOB! Predicting Crowdsourced Decisions on Toxic Behavior in Online Games." In: *WWW'14 Companion: Proceedings of the 23rd International Conference on World Wide Web*. New York: ACM, 877–888.

Bogost, Ian (2006): *Unit Operations: An Approach to Videogame Criticism*. Cambridge, MA: MIT Press.

Bogost, Ian (2007): *Persuasive Games: The Expressive Power of Video Games*. Cambridge, MA: MIT Press.

Boluk, Stephanie/LeMieux, Patrick (2017): *Metagaming: Playing, Competing, Spectating, Cheating, Trading, Making, and Breaking Videogames*. Minneapolis: University of Minnesota Press.

Bradley, Caroline/Froomkin, A. Michael (2004): "Virtual Worlds, Real Rules." In: *New York Law School Review* 49(1), 103–146.

Broekens, Joost (2008): "MMOGs as Social Experiments: The Case of Environmental Laws." In: *arXiv*, November 5 (http://arxiv.org/abs/0811.0709).

Caillois, Roger ([1958] 2001): *Man, Play and Games*. Meyer Barash (trans.). Urbana: University of Illinois Press.

Castronova, Edward (2008): *Exodus to the Virtual World: How Online Fun is Changing Reality*. New York: Palgrave Macmillan.

Consalvo, Mia (2007): *Cheating: Gaining Advantage in Videogames*. Cambridge, MA: MIT Press.

Consalvo, Mia (2009): "There Is No Magic Circle." In: *Games and Culture* 4, 408–417.

Cooper, Seth (2014): "Massively Multiplayer Research: Gamification and (Citizen) Science." In: Steffen P. Walz/Sebastian Deterding (eds.): *The Gameful World: Approaches, Issues, Applications*. Cambridge, MA: MIT Press, 487–500.

Costikyan, Greg (2013): *Uncertainty in Games*. Cambridge, MA: MIT Press.

Crogan, Patrick (2011): *Gameplay Mode: War, Simulation and Technoculture*. Minneapolis: University of Minnesota Press.

Foucault, Michel ([1975] 1977): *Discipline and Punish: The Birth of the Prison*. Alan Sheridan (trans.). New York: Random House.

Frasca, Gonzalo (2003): "Simulation versus Narrative: Introduction to Ludology." In: Mark J.P. Wolf/Bernard Perron (eds.): *The Video Game Theory Reader*. New York/London: Routledge, 221–235.

Galloway, Alexander (2006): *Gaming: Essays on Algorithmic Culture*. Minneapolis: University of Minnesota Press.

Hsu, Jeremy (2015): "Inside the Largest Virtual Psychology Lab in the World." In: *Wired*, January 27 (https://www.wired.com/2015/01/inside-the-largest-virtual-psychology-lab-in-the-world/).

Huizinga, Johan ([1938] 1980): *Homo Ludens: A Study of the Play Element in Culture*. London: Routledge and Kegan Paul.

"Inside Ultima IV" (1986). In: *Computer Gaming World*, no. 26, March, 18–21.

Johnson, Mark R. (2019): *The Unpredictability of Gameplay*. New York/London: Bloomsbury.

Juul, Jesper (2005): *Half-Real: Video Games between Real Rules and Fictional Worlds*. Cambridge, MA: MIT Press.

"Killing Lord British" ([2009] 2019). In: *Ultima Wiki*, February 20 (https://ultima.fandom.com/wiki/Killing_Lord_British).

Kollar, Phil (2016): "The Past, Present and Future of League of Legends Studio Riot Games." In: *Polygon*, September 13 (https://www.polygon.com/2016/9/13/12891656/the-past-present-and-future-of-league-of-legends-studio-riot-games).

Kücklich, Julian (2005): "Precarious Playbour: Modders and the Digital Games Industry." In: *Fibreculture*, no. 5, article FCJ-025 (http://five.fibreculturejournal.org/fcj-025-precarious-playbour-modders-and-the-digital-games-industry).

Kwak, Haewoon/Blackburn, Jeremy (2015): "Linguistic Analysis of Toxic Behavior in an Online Video Game." In: Luca Maria Aiello/Daniel McFarland (eds.): *Social Informatics: SocInfo 2014. Lecture Notes in Computer Science* 8852, 209–217.

LeJacq, Yannick (2015): "How League of Legends Enables Toxicity." In: *Kotaku*, March 25 (https://kotaku.com/how-league-of-legends-enables-toxicity-1693572469).

Liebe, Michael (2008): "There Is No Magic Circle: On the Difference between Computer Games and Traditional Games." In: Stephan Günzel/Michael Liebe/Dieter Mersch (eds.): *Conference Proceedings of the Philosophy of Computer Games 2008*. Potsdam: Potsdam University Press, 324–340 (https://publishup.uni-potsdam.de/opus4-ubp/frontdoor/deliver/index/docId/2550/file/digarec01.pdf).

Lofgren, Eric T./Fefferman, Nina H. (2007): "The Untapped Potential of Virtual Game Worlds to Shed Light on Real World Epidemics." In: *The Lancet Infectious Diseases* 7(9), 625–629.

Maher, Brendan (2016): "Good Gaming: Scientists are Helping to Tame Toxic Behaviour in the World's Most Popular Online Game." In: *Nature* 531, 568–571.

Malaby, Thomas (2007): "Beyond Play: A New Approach to Games." In: *Games and Culture* 2, 95–113.

Mistreanu, Simina (2018): "Life Inside China's Social Credit Laboratory." In: *Foreign Policy*, April 3 (http://foreignpolicy.com/2018/04/03/life-inside-chinas-social-credit-laboratory/).

Mortensen, Torill Elvira (2018): "Anger, Fear, and Games: The Long Event of #GamerGate." In: *Games and Culture* 13, 787–806.

Olivetti, Justin (2015): "The Game Archaeologist: The Assassination of Lord British." In: *Massively Overpowered*, October 3 (http://massivelyop.com/2015/10/03/the-game-archaeologist-the-assassination-of-lord-british/).

Pias, Claus (2010): *Computer Spiel Welten*. Zürich: Diaphanes.

Raczkowski, Felix (2014): "Making Points the Point: Towards a History of Ideas of Gamification." In: Mathias Fuchs/Sonja Fizek/Paolo Ruffino/Niklas Schrape (eds.): *Rethinking Gamification*. Lüneburg: Meson Press, 141–160.

Ramsay, Morgan (2015): *Online Game Pioneers at Work*. New York: Apress.

Rautzenberg, Markus (2015): "Navigating Uncertainty: Ludic Epistemology in an Age of New Essentialisms." In: Mathias Fuchs (ed.): *Diversity of Play*. Lüneburg: Meson Press, 83–106.

Razimus Gaming (2016): "The Death of Lord British." In: Razimus Gaming, "The Death of Lord British Ultima Online Aug 9 1997 (Razimus Gaming) Feat. 3pac RIP," YouTube, May 15 (https://www.youtube.com/watch?v=8Iww-cu1qds).

Salazar, Javier (2009): "Simulating a Quasi-Simulation: A Framework for Using Multi Agent Simulation Techniques for Studying MMORPGs." In: *DiGRA '09—Proceedings of the 2009 DiGRA International Conference: Breaking New Ground: Innovation in Games, Play, Practice and Theory* (http://www.digra.org/digital-library/publications/simulating-a-quasi-simulation-a-framework-for-using-multi-agent-simulation-techniques-for-studying-mmorpgs/).

Salen, Katie/Zimmerman, Eric (2004): *Rules of Play: Game Design Fundamentals*. Cambridge, MA: MIT Press.

Seiler, Joey (2008): "What Can Virtual-World Economists Tell Us about Real-World Economies?" In: *Scientific American*, March 17 (http://www.scientificamerican.com/article/virtual-world-economists-on-real-economies/).

Stenros, Jaakko (2012): "In Defence of a Magic Circle: The Social and Mental Boundaries of Play." In: *Proceedings of DiGRA Nordic 2012 Conference: Local and Global—Games in Culture and Society* (http://www.digra.org/digital-library/publications/in-defence-of-a-magic-circle-the-social-and-mental-boundaries-of-play/).

Suderman, Peter (2014): "A Multiplayer Game Environment Is Actually a Dream Come True for an Economist." In: *Reason Magazine,* June (http://reason.com/archives/2014/05/07/a-multiplayer-game-environment/).

"The Summoner's Code" ([2010] 2017). In: *League of Legends* website, July 2017 (https://na.leagueoflegends.com/en/featured/summoners-code). Original version: May 2010 (http://www.leagueoflegends.com/articles/The_Summoners_Code).

Taylor, T. L. (2006): *Play between Worlds: Exploring Online Game Culture.* Cambridge, MA: MIT Press.

van Gennep, Arnold ([1909] 1960): *The Rites of Passage.* Monika B. Vizedom/Gabrielle L. Caffee (trans.). Chicago: University of Chicago Press.

Williams, Dmitri/Contractor, Noshir/Poole, Marshall Scott/Srivastava, Jaideep/Cai, Dora (2011): "The Virtual Worlds Exploratorium: Using Large-Scale Data and Computational Techniques for Communication Research." In: *Communication Methods and Measures* 5, 163–180.

Zimmerman, Eric (2012): "Jerked Around by the Magic Circle—Clearing the Air Ten Years Later." In: *Gamasutra,* February 7 (https://www.gamasutra.com/view/feature/135063/jerked_around_by_the_magic_circle_.php).

Chapter 4: Lagging Realities
Temporal Exploits and Mutant Speculations

Joseph Dumit

How long does the beachball spin before you hard-reset your computer? Detecting the difference between a lag and a crash has become a fraught problem for everyone involved. Of course, our tolerance for different forms of delay changes historically: browser loading, phone dial tone, email response time. We adjust and readjust to them.

There is an early passage in Ellen Ullman's book *The Bug* (2003) in which the programmer protagonist is standing in a checkout line while the cashier rings out the purchases. Buttons press, numbers appear on display, chime, repeat, door open. There is a second-long delay between button pressing and the number display, however: a brief lag. The programmer realizes that this is a bug she never could track down fifteen years earlier and that the bug still exists, causing this unneeded lag. She meditates on how pervasive such delays are in our lives, how inevitable and unconscious they seem to us. A life of little waits, a real life of lags.

Lag often seems to be something we wait on, putting us on pause, while it does something in the background—like a traffic jam. We habituate to lags, up to a point. Adjustments are themselves lags: the time of adjustment. We often normalize them to ourselves and declare that others who adjust more slowly are lagging, therefore we are adjusting properly = no lag. But experienced time itself takes the form of durations, chunks, in which the chunking itself is the material of the experience. Just pause, for a moment, on all these lags: the time it takes for a cable box to switch channels, the phone to get a dial tone, a website to actually show up, your phone to switch gears, a friend to answer the phone, a student to turn in a paper, or a colleague to answer an email. What is lag and what isn't?

Lag is usually invoked when a delay is perceived as *too long*, calling attention to our own now frustrated anticipation, the speculation we didn't necessarily know we were involved in. The event is not proceeding as planned. If it is slowness, then it can be accounted for, anticipation reduced to calculation. Irritating when you don't know how long to wait. Psychologists have helped us program our devices to settle us down: the difference between the "Don't Walk" light that you wait impatiently for and the one that counts down. The difference with the countdown is the direct interpolation of time into the equation. Is there anticipation when you know *exactly* how long you have to wait?

Everything takes time. This seems a banal truism, but there is much more in it than we first suppose. The time that things/actions take is sometimes visible, but often not. When visible and noticed, we sometimes, like Ullman, see it as a mistake. We become sensitive to what we feel are unnecessary delays. We might call these lags. Something that could be corrected. Time saved. Literally, we have saved time from the monster of waste. In these cases, we embody a capitalist time that seems to be the opposite of speculation: we should not have to wait for the future!

> The desire of technologics, like that of the dual inheritors of rationalism called capitalism and science, is to obliterate the delay. Everything should be instantaneous and always the newest of the new—and, thus, the uncanny and its pluralized proxies. The just-in-time inventory of absolute information should be always at hand, at the click of a button, at my beck and call, so that there can be a quick turnaround. Waiting should be outlawed. (Kochhar-Lindgren 2005: 185)

Of course, this is not true at all. Capitalist speculation *depends* on futures and delays at the technical and social levels. Analyses from science and technology studies of corporate speculative power and reflexive market creation that draw upon and reinforce existing inequalities have investigated these speculative dynamics in genomics and biomedicine (Fortun 2008; Thacker 2005; Cooper 2008; Sunder Rajan 2006), pharmaceuticals (Peterson 2014; Dumit 2012; Sunder Rajan 2017), finance (LiPuma/Lee 2004), and security (de Goede 2012). Analyses of positive uses of speculation are rarer but include affirmative speculation (uncertain commons 2013), the affordances of glitches and delays in digital culture and gaming (Krapp 2011; Boluk/Lemieux 2017), and cultural resistance and invention (Moten 2003; Bhabha 1991).

Whereas Kochhar-Lingren and others (e.g. Lampert 2012) treat delay as something to universalize, asking about its ontology and its philosophical implications, in this chapter I am interested in the shared speculative experiences of lag. What happens when lags are persistent, when we encounter them as things we have to creatively adapt to? How do they in turn warp reality by warping time to be lagged time—never lagged-time-in-general, but always specific forms of lag? The empirical question is never: What is lag? Or much less: Is this lag? But rather: What kind of lag-time is this?

To study lag, therefore, to make it a method, we cannot start with a concept of time, of timescapes—or even of lag—but instead we follow where and how "lag" shows up, where it *must* be put into speech, how and where it becomes a matter of concern, a material-semiotic actor named into existence that has the potential to warp existence and time itself. My technique for following lag is that of empirical philosophy (Mol 1993)—following how "lag" is enacted in its naming—and substance as method, investigating how each lag is worked on, made into a substance that often transforms worlds by becoming its own form of time (Dumit 2020). In this chapter, I use thick description to treat texts (written accounts in textbooks, websites, chats, news) ethnographically for how they use lag to make lives. Lag, delay, latency, synchrony, etc. are all seen as active constructions—forms of time that are being tamed and strategized, even as they structure what one can do, how one can speculate.

Even basketball, like most competitive sports, can be looked at this way. There is a clock keeping track of game time, it counts down from twelve minutes to zero each quarter. But there are also actions that stop the clock, that lag the end of the game, stretching it out. These actions are part of the game but they can also be (perceived to be) abused, to the point where the rules committee has to institute new sanctions: "delay of game" penalties to prevent the lag strategies from overtaking the "proper" game strategies. At one point, a dominant player, Shaquille O'Neal (Shaq), was also a very poor free-throw shooter. A strategy against him developed: foul him repeatedly, bumping him, hitting him. "Hack a Shaq," it was called. Each foul stopped the clock, giving him the opportunity to shoot two free throws—which he would often miss, giving the hacking team the opportunity to get the ball back. As this strategy spread, new types of players were identified: those who can almost always make free throws (and who were now put onto the court in certain circumstances), and those who cannot. The examples can be multiplied, but the point is that the attempt to make a game fair within time depends on implicit lags that can be made explicit and warp the time of the game, making it unfair in unforeseen ways.

This may seem banal, but what fascinates here is that inside of every shared time is also a set of lags that can become actionable. They unshare the time. They recompose game time to the point where it becomes legitimate, over and over, to ask: What game are we playing? What time is it? What is happening? What happened to the time? And how to do things with lag?

Even as it slows things down, each lag (experienced as such) invents a kind of future: it provokes a sense that the future is being interrupted, that something is getting in the way of the smooth unfolding of time. This frustrates the forward rush, yet it presents unexpected opportunities, soliciting anticipatory practices that, by playing with the temporal disruptions, also try to exert control on *the future*. Each lag, by delaying a future, itself produces new ways of speculating: accelerating and even inventing some futures at the expense of others. In this chapter, therefore, we follow specific lags that have had transformative and disorienting effects on digital finance, games, and life, conjuring into existence new forms of temporality, creating new kinds of time. I dwell on gaming, in particular, because

I have been studying it as an anthropologist, and because lag is a continual explicit challenge to both game designers and players. Among other things, games are pastimes: many are literally designed and used to pass time, to lag life, until something else happens. Gaming thus offers a deeply reflexive site for noticing how lag is made into opportunity.

Lag Is a Bug, Lag Is a Feature

The delay that Ullman noticed does not mean that once it is fixed there is no time taken. Just normal delay = no lag. Or rather, no lag that matters ... until it does. Financial speculation, markets, depend upon information but also time. You can know more about what is going to happen, or you can know about it sooner. Both are advantageous in reducing the risk of your bets. Stock markets are full of spatial and temporal lags, small differences in prices between two markets that can be arbitraged, or the actual minute or microsecond delay between price changes and information about those changes. These are constant targets of algorithmic, network, and hacking exploitation that manipulate a presumed equality of speculation time (MacKenzie 2015, 2017; Hayles 2017; Miyazaki 2013).

Fidelity Investments, a behemoth financial services company based in the U.S. that holds my retirement funds, once sent me an email in 2011 pointing to their webpage on "Preventing Another Flash Crash." The webpage explained that, although it might look like they were up to something nefarious, they were just being competitive by "leveling the playing field for all market participants":

> Co-location facilities: Orders from data centers that are physically located near exchanges can shave milliseconds off of the time it takes to complete a trade. Being faster than rivals to the best price—that is, having the lowest "latency"—is an advantage that some traders seek in today's markets. Regulators are concerned that these facilities may give trading advantages to professional traders and thus disadvantage regular retail customers. (Fidelity Investments 2011)

This is Fidelity telling me not to try and trade on my own. They automatically lag less, and I have no chance. The truth was far worse, though.

The financial speculating act is often presumed to operate without delay, yet all speculations are a kind of exchange that takes time. Even for computers, time is materialized in chunks that are defined by its internal clocks and by the built-in sensors that make up *moments* of incoming and outcoming signals. The entire point of having a clock was to keep the variations in signals *in time*. Lag was only noticed when it was too long, when signals didn't arrive *on time*. Otherwise, moments were standardized and variations within them didn't matter. Speculations didn't take lag into account, at least, until a way was found to exploit it, to turn it into the difference that made a difference. A difference that mattered—materialized delay that became a new *kind* of speculation.

In 2015, Brad Katsuyama explained this transformation. He recalled that, back in 2006, a trader would see on his screen that there were 100,000 shares available on an exchange for a specific price, hit a button, and purchase them all. By 2007, however, the trader would only end up purchasing 80%, and by 2009, only 60%. This turned out to be because his one order would be divided up into four different exchanges, essentially server farms located in physically different buildings in different areas of New Jersey. Each 25,000-share part of his order would take a different amount of time to get to the four exchanges, depending on how much further out they were. Compared to the first exchange, the sixty-mile distance to the final exchange would take an additional two milliseconds for the order to arrive at it. Two milliseconds may seem fast (an eyeblink takes 300 milliseconds), but some high-frequency traders (HFT) had built special fiber optic cables that could race ahead four times faster (476 microseconds). These cables ran in a straight line rather than following the railroad tracks. *What had once been fast was now a significant lag.* The HFT computer could now see that someone had purchased the 25k shares and block them out of the other ones before their order arrived, forcing them to buy it at a higher price. *This was called "latency arbitrage," taking advantage of the fact that information, even at the speed of light, takes time to travel and can be outraced* (Katsuyama 2015; cf. Lewis 2014).

Many financial exchange institutions had morphed from the marketplaces where the trades take place—a kind of neutral institution that would take a small fee from each transaction for providing that neutrality—into time brokers, selling new forms of speed for extraordinary amounts of money. They sold "fast data," access to data with less lag. "Why do people pay hundreds of millions of dollars for the technology to be right next to stock exchanges? Because it gives them the ability to trade hundreds of times, thousands of times, before that same piece of information makes it to the last person" (Katsuyama 2015).

The standardized lag of clicking contained within it not just delay but its own form of time. This was truly insider trading, trades taking place inside the time of speculation. This warped the very possibility of previous kinds of speculation: now you couldn't speculate because you would always be late, always lag behind those who paid for the new time. Speculation here created the need to talk about microseconds and then nanoseconds: new forms of financial time that now mattered.

One brilliant response by a Canadian group was to create a new kind of exchange, one that aimed not to race time but to freeze it:

> What we've done at IEX is we've slowed everyone down by an equal amount. We actually did this, we simulated physical distance [in a little box]. We've coiled 38 miles of cable in a box, and it creates 350 microseconds—millionths of a second—of a delay. And that delay actually deters many of the high-speed trading strategies. (Katsuyama 2015)

Literally turning space into time, the spool of fiber optic cable means that all trades have to travel an extra 38 miles at the speed of light to get into and out of the exchange. This "speed bump" or "magic shoe box," as it is called, creates a new level of lag that renders speculative trades relatively equivalent in time, eliminating the ability to conduct latency arbitrage.

What we learn from this example is that lag can become an exploit, which in turn transforms/terraforms the market (situation) it inhabits. This is not an aberration or a bug but a feature of lag: each lag can make its own kind of time, and has the potential to take over the form of time of the system it started in. The story I just narrated from the financial industry takes place over and over in the digital gaming world.

Lag Is (In)tolerance Is Reality

The first thing to realize about lag is that most of it is tolerated. We adapt to lag so that it becomes our background, the environment within which we act. Adrian Mackenzie writes,

> Players habituate themselves to the delay in the circuit between hand and eye and eventually, within certain limits, do not even regard it as an obstacle. Embodied anticipation can 'overcome' the delay, or render it latent, so that delays in the flux of images are not even obvious to the player. (Mackenzie 2006: 166–167)

The "input lag" time between clicking a button and one's digital character jumping is unnoticed, incorporated, literally part of our bodies—we do things with this time.

And yet, there is a limit. Overly long delays in the digital world become frustrating: the environment effect breaks down and the jump feels not like the *same* thing as the button press, but instead like *another*, separate thing. And yet, the limit is different for different people. Some people feel this annoyance and separation at 200 milliseconds (ms); most people, like this author, notice it around 100 ms. But a few notice even *small* lag, as little as 13 ms. It bothers them, interrupts their play, and they complain that they cannot stand it. It seems to rattle their nervous system.

Discussions of input lag are riven by these differences in people: "People like to throw that idea out there [that 100 ms input lag is okay], but they are wrong. I can clearly notice and it's impossible to play serious games with that kind of lag" (RRettig responding to GivingCreditWhereDue 2016). Psychologists have researched this problem and have investigated the effects of too much input lag on people.

Lag intolerance marks the human edge of digital interactivity shaping the very features of devices and interfaces. Most multiplayer digital games, like most multi-person digital interfaces, balance on the edge between better resolution with more features and less lag. Skype and other video-chat programs try to upgrade and downgrade video quality to prevent delay-degradation from becoming too annoying. But the internet is finicky, with its own ebbs and flows and jitters and stutters. We adjust, we switch to audio, we hang up and try again, we blame the wifi, the cell service, the program.

Lag is also the reality of multi-person online interaction. Whether you are Zooming or working on a document together or playing a game in "real time," you cannot escape the experience and frustration of lag. Multiplayer game designers in particular have to design their games not only to minimize frustration but to maximize fairness. For turn-based (asynchronous) games such as chess or *Scrabble*, this is not a problem. But synchronous, high-speed reaction "twitchy" games such as first-person shooters, races, and brawlers need to be played across the internet. This means figuring out how to balance the fact that each player's computer must communicate to a server somewhere (with some at a delay of 50 milliseconds and others over 300) which registers all the players' moves (key presses or joystick actions), coordinates them, and sends them back (with another delay). This turnaround time between a message from one computer to the server and back is called "ping" (the imagined sound of sonar hitting an object and returning).

In a first-person shooter game such as *Quake* (a real-time game simulating soldiers shooting at each other in a building complex), everyone is simultaneously moving, shooting, and speculating on where everyone else will be moving and shooting, as fast as their thumbs can twitch. Yet because they are separated by lags longer than twitches, the results of everyone's actions are a bit behind and possibly conflicting: I shoot where you are right now (from my perspective on my machine), but you have already moved (from your perspective on your machine).

The server-side software coordinating the various players' actions must therefore split the difference and sometimes rewind time to make the best of the simultaneously delayed actions. Players can adapt to this lag (even when they see their avatars jitter), but oftentimes some of the players are only delayed by 50 ms (a low ping) while others are delayed by 200+ ms (or 4+ times more). This is asymmetry in relative action time: the machines that have a low ping can literally act and react before the high-ping machines even know that something is happening.

According to one player, "A Low Ping Bastard (ping under ~100 ms) was generally able to see and kill you before you had a chance to react" (fappaderp, responding to TokingMessiah 2016). Another player writes,

> I was an LPB (low-ping bastard) thanks to my job—I worked for a national ISP and we had a T3 [high-speed internet connection] in our call center, which had all of 6 people using it when I worked the overnight shift. It was glorious, that quarter-second edge we had against the majority of players made you feel like you were the best player in the world and everybody else was a slow loser. Me and my co-workers would find a busy server near us (we worked in Dallas), all join at once, and dominate the top of the scoreboards until the admin would almost invariably boot us. (MelsWhitePubes, responding to TokingMessiah 2016)

The author here describes himself as a "Low Ping Bastard," a name that arose to describe the unfair advantage that less lag accorded over "High Ping Bastards," whose machines were too many internet hops away to react as speedily. The term has oscillated between insult, envy, and admiration as the lag difference came to create new kinds of players and interactions based on virtual–real spacetime differences that are not linear.

This lag difference formed not only player types but divided games into types: "Quake 1 introduced a scoreboard that not only had someone's name and score, but also their ping time in milliseconds. This allowed players to judge who was an LPB and HPB (and hope to justify their skill or lack thereof)" (fappaderp, responding to TokingMessiah 2016). Players created servers that were limited to HPB or LPB only. Other players developed playstyles that depended on their system's lag: "I lived in Alaska. My ping averaged about 900–1000. I practiced playing the maps blind, because relying on what you could see would throw you off and get you stuck in a doorway or falling into lava" (Shalrath, responding to TokingMessiah 2016).

Players from the days of extreme lag report that they have compensatory "muscle memory": "Whenever I have lag, the muscle memory to compensate kicks right in. If it's server side lag, it's actually a bit of an advantage, since most of the other players never learned to play that way" (definitely_not_cylon, responding to TokingMessiah 2016). While others had their bodies trained to play with lag so much that when new systems decreased it, or they played not over the internet but by LAN (physically connecting the systems together with cables), they had to unlearn these habits: "I can remember my first LAN, we played Team Fortress and Unreal tournament. I was so used to lag it was impossible for me to get used to 0 ping" (Stupidpuma1, responding to TokingMessiah 2016).

The above mutations in game play were player driven. As twitchy multiplayer games gained in popularity and "seriousness," including tournaments, game designers increasingly had to find ways to make the games more fair across unequal lag differences. The result was a unique and evolving set of "Lag Compensation Algorithms" that attempted to manage this sense of playing on an even battlefield:

> In fast-paced action games, even a delay of a few milliseconds can cause a laggy gameplay feeling and make it hard to hit other players or interact with moving objects. Besides bandwidth limitations and network latencies, information can get lost due to network packet loss. To cope with the issues introduced by network communication, the Source engine server employs techniques such as data compression and lag compensation which are invisible to the client. The client then performs prediction and interpolation to further improve the experience. (Valve Developer Community 2005)

Lag compensation algorithms turn out to be a collection of modifications and tricks because player experience is the key variable: how to give the player the *sense* that the game world is fair and predictable. David Aldridge, network designer for *Halo*—one of the most popular online shooter games with tens of millions of players—has noted that "player perception is everything," describing how he needed to become friends with everyone on the design team in order to make the game feel fair (Aldridge 2011). Creating the sense of a fair, lagless world involved several tricks: limiting the data sent between computer and server in order to maximize the data that matters; changing the appearance of certain actions, such as throwing a grenade, by partially blocking the player's view and thus disguising the delay between hitting the button and lobbing the grenade; pulling back the in-game camera during a knife attack to hide the fact that the other player is also moving and may not be there; and so on. As Aldridge suggested, "Players fill in the gaps. So—no visible latency, no complaints of lag" (Aldridge 2011). The physics of the game engine often had to be altered in order to prevent lag from becoming noticeable to players. Aldridge summed this up with four rules:

1. [Decide:] Which parts of your gameplay need to be adjudicated by a single authority?
2. Always ask: where am I hiding the lag?
3. Don't be afraid to change game mechanics to improve networking.
4. Reserve time to iterate. (Aldridge 2011)

Network lag, in other words, was not a problem to be overcome, but the fabric of reality that had to be designed. The challenge was to make speculative risk-reduction equitable, and there were multiple solutions to this. Where *Halo* aimed to create a seamless lagged world, other games created lag compensation algorithms that created multiple universes within one game according to their lag. Some first-person shooter war games, such as *Call of Duty: Black Ops 2* (2012), altered game physics according to one's lag:

> It's really hard to explain lag comp in a simple way. Really, really hard. BUT....I can explain its effects on players relatively simply [...] Low latency/good connection [experiences] faster bullets, faster movement into cover, [but] appears out from cover/corner earlier [...] High latency/bad connection [is experienced as] Sneaky—your appearance is delayed to enemies when coming out of corners/cover [...] enemies are slower to escape into cover, [but your] bullets travel slower, [and] your movements are [more] sluggish. (Darius510 2012)

The intended effect of these coexisting multiple physics was to create a shared world in which the tradeoffs of different lags could be equalized. But players took this further, with some purposefully throttling their own internet connection speed in order to "get the lag comp that players with poor internet get" (Noteful, responding to TemperVOiD 2016). These players were choosing the physics that fit their playstyle. In response, other games have revised their lag compensation scheme in response to this type of advantage and now explicitly "favor players that have the faster and more stable connection [..., giving them] the best experience possible while maintaining the accessibility for higher ping players" (*Rainbow Six Siege* Developers 2017).

Game designers often build in extra lag (similar to the financial "magic shoebox") in an attempt to mitigate the vicissitudes of various latencies. Solving this sometimes means that they also give a bit too much control to players' consoles. One game allowed the player with the fastest connection to "be the server" rather than having a central server that everyone connected to. This created better experiences for many players but some found a way to take advantage of it. For example, numerous YouTube videos instruct gamers on how to build a "lag switch," in which you cut open the Ethernet cable connecting your Xbox to the internet and install an old-fashioned light switch. You are then able to temporarily cut yourself off from the internet. If your Xbox happens to be the server for a first-person shooter game, then all of your opponents experience lag but you do not—during which time you run up and kill them. Then you reopen the switch and they find themselves dead without knowing why.

In other games, such as the online role-playing game *Runescape*, which hosts thousands of players simultaneously playing fighters and wizards in a shared digital world full of dungeons, dragons, and magical runes, the system is tuned to as much fairness in speed as possible. Of course, in a competitive world, if you lag even slightly while fighting, you die. Yet lag is always there—due to slow computers, internet delays (especially around 5:00 PM), wireless connections, and so forth. The game stutters, freezes, jumps—and players take advantage.

Some players have found a place in the game where two servers meet, meaning that everyone crossing an invisible line experiences a slight delay as their character is ported from one server to the next. The players in the know call this a "lag line" and wait on the other side of it for someone to cross. For a second or two, they appear frozen, but can be attacked. In what they call a "lagxploit," the nefarious players rush the laggard. The little delay now means that when the laggard unfreezes, they are dead by dozens of hits and their corpse has been looted. Again, there are countless videos online explaining how to take advantage of a lagxploit. Playing the game requires not overcoming but attuning to the reality of lag.

Are these invented playstyles cheating? And/or are they forms of affirmative speculation, making each kind of lag itself into something new out of the previously predictable digital world? At minimum, they are thick descriptions of the ways in which people do things with lag.

To combat this type of invention, most competitive e-sports, especially those with money on the line, have to invent a notion of complete uniformity for competition between players at different computers. Everything down to inches of Ethernet cable must be identical:

> One concern is uniformity, or verifying that playing conditions are equal for all players in a match. This is important because it would be an unfair advantage for one team to get lightning fast computers while the other is stuck with the spinning hourglass. This starts with installing identical hardware on all computers in the arena, including those used by the referees and elsewhere, Veiser said. Additionally, when they first set up an event, they create a master image of a single hard drive and copy it onto every computer, so that every single bit is the same. This level of attention to evenhandedness even extends to the length of Ethernet cable that connects players to the game. Both teams in a match will sit symmetrically in a row of computers, so that there is no speed advantage for being positioned very slightly closer to the local router. This might sound like overkill, something that no one would notice, but these players are so good that a few milliseconds could be the difference between a win and a loss. (Johnson 2015)

Lag, in other words, defines and splits and then invents game physics as well as players and playstyles. Whereas games like finance may initially imagine an idealized world without lag, a world where pure speculation and play can take place, taking account of lag requires a complete reinvention of the firmament of the world, even whole new worlds.

Lag Is Human, Humans Lag

Lag doesn't just shape digital gaming, it is also the very foundation of many games, especially multiplayer role-playing games (RPGs). Digital RPGs are fascinating in part because they are incredibly time consuming; many are designed to pass time, to lag life. Some games brag about 100+ hours of content! Online forums reviewing and discussing games often compare the price of a game to the number of hours it takes to complete. Many players agree, for example, that a game that takes forty hours to play is worth more than one that can be completed in twenty. From an outside perspective, these players have a lot of excess time to pass! The challenge for game companies is how to monetize this excess, speculating on how to get players to pay to lag.

Massively multiplayer online RPGs (MMORPGs, such as *Runescape* and *World of Warcraft*) can have thousands to tens of thousands of players sharing in a virtual world, each controlling their own character, each spending hundreds to thousands of hours adventuring with that character (or serially with multiple characters). The games have developed complicated processes to enable characters to advance in ability and power regularly, though slowly, through repetitive activities that are derisively and approvingly called "grinding." Gaining more skill in woodcutting, for instance, means clicking on a tree, waiting five seconds until the tree is cut, then clicking on another tree, waiting five more seconds, and so forth, until 250 trees have been cut down. At that point, one "gains a level" in woodcutting and can use a better axe to cut down harder-wood trees—which one then does 500 more times to gain the next level to cut down even bigger trees, now 1000 of them, and so on: exponentially more clicks regulating the real-world time it takes for one to achieve status and power within the game.

This enforced lag in advancement spreads out those who have "put the time" into the game. Lag = Power. The more time one has spent not living outside but inside the game, the more advancement one's characters have. From the game and most gamers' perspective this is a desired type of fairness. Unlike the first-person shooter games where one's status comes from being very skilled with high-speed twitching, in most MMORPGs one's status is a fairly direct measure of the time one has put into the game, as well as the social networking and information-gathering one has managed to acquire during all of this clicking time through in-game chatting and out-of-game forum browsing.

But grinding is tedious. Too tedious for many. Game designers face an array of challenges in providing enough micro-rewards alongside repetitive activities to keep them interesting, or at least tolerable, and providing shortcuts to advancement that risk making the "equal lag for equal advancement" patently unequal. Many games offer "pay-to-win" options, in which players can make cash payments to advance their characters. Pay-to-win is a variation on decades of some players putting in the clicking-time and then selling their advanced characters to others who have money but either no time or no patience. For contemporary game designers, advancement lag has in turn become the new economy: how to design a game so that the delay is not ideally suited to equal status, but instead just frustrating enough that more and more players pay a little to get a little jump, or pay a lot to get a big jump. Lag, in other words, is no longer about passing time but about generating enough temporal friction against just enough desire to get players to speculate that skipping the lag is worth it.

Around most massively multiplayer games there is also a lively economy crossing in-game and out-of-game worlds. I might spend two days clicking on enough high-value trees in *Runescape* to make a superb magic weapon and trade it to you for a rare Pokémon in another game, or perhaps sell it to you for cash. At eleven years old, my son referred to the in-game accumulation of items by clicking as "work," and he made money at it. There are various methods employed by the *Runescape* company Jagex to prevent too-rapid accumulation. Most of these methods involve delaying acquisition. It takes a lot of mouse-clicks to get a thousand runes. There is labor—prosumption—being paid for.

But when he was twelve years old, he was banned from *Runescape* for a week because he was detected using "bots," in other words, macros that automatically repeat the mouse-clicking process in precise ways over and over. These bots saved him the tedium of becoming a robot himself. His bot activities were not detected by a human, however; he was "auto-banned" by the system itself. A program detected the too-quick clicking: the lack of normal human lag was the key to detecting that my son was using a bot. Here, this autoplay was not allowed. He was not playing fair, he was banned.

Runescape was using its own automated programs—"botcops"—to speculatively detect the difference between a human player doing something robotically and a bot pretending to be a human doing something robotically. Here is another flipside of passing time: the entire premise is that the human finds the activity repetitive and boring and dreams of automating it to do it faster, or at least, to do something else while it is happening.

One of the first solutions *Runescape* employed to prevent bots was to create "anti-macro monsters," special creatures that would appear whenever someone spent a lot of time doing the same thing repeatedly. For players attentively clicking, the monsters were easy to dispatch; but for bots mindlessly clicking, the monsters could be deadly. That is, until they could be anticipated.

Soon the bots became more sophisticated. In the world of "botting" today, one uses programs that simulate all manner of human-appropriate lags—curved mouse movements, mis-clicks, programmed random breaks (to represent time away from the keyboard, perhaps for eating, bathroom use, sleeping), and even mini-conversations—in order to mimic the mindlessly robotic behavior of a human stretched to the limits of boredom playing the game. Whereas simulation is often used as a form of reductive speculation, calculating an array of possibilities in order to reduce the risk of being surprised, here the hackers reverse engineer the surveillance in order to give the company exactly what it wants to see, precisely in order to get away with something underneath. In this metagame, the hacker-simulated human is designed not to figure something out, but to jam the speculative practices of the humans at the game company trying to programmatically detect the difference between these robots imitating humans playing robotically and actual humans playing robotically.

The following summer, my son took up botting again. This time, he ran an entire bot farm, with each bot on a different account, each one running as fast as it could. He was playing two metagames at once. In one, he was participating in forums discussing the best bot strategies with meta-contests to see who could last the longest before getting caught and banned. This was "Getting Banned Is Fun." Videos and descriptions of epic "suicide botting" runs were posted on sites such as *powerbot.org*.

In his other metagame, he was accumulating gold as fast as possible, then trading it online for cash—PayPal, Amazon gift cards, and so on. He got scammed more than once, but he made enough money to buy some high-end bots. Then, he got banned from PayPal. Not fun.

I learned that there were entire forums devoted to bot makers; but even more fascinating were the forums devoted to bot *users* who would create new accounts, program their bots, and run them in different types of competitions. Similar to the speed runs analyzed by Stephanie Boluk and Patrick LeMieux (2017), these bot users had all sorts of categories to differentiate: how long a bot could run, how much gold it could accumulate by chopping down trees, killing monsters, and so forth, before it got banned. The game was not so much to elude banning altogether, but to elude capture longer or better than others.

In the *Pokémon Go* hacking world of 2016, tens of thousands of hackers gathered on Reddit and Facebook and Github to exchange tips in order to spend less time catching the digital Pokémon that they wanted. Many of them instead spent their time making bots: programs running on laptops that did not need the phone apps at all but instead pretended to be phones. *Pokémon Go*'s maker Niantic was overwhelmed by the millions of mobile players in the first six months and spent most of its time upgrading its server capacity rather than preventing the relatively few creative hackers. The main challenge for the hackers was what they explicitly called "'human' randomization": making one's pretend phone behave as if it were in the hands of an actual human moving at walking speed and clicking with "human like" delays (jabbink 2016). These automated human lags were imagined to aid in evading detection by Niantic.

Much more collective action went into this practice than can be discussed here, but for our purposes, the lag in detection was being exploited. Speeding up Niantic's change detection, checking every millisecond, would be possible in theory—but the detection itself takes time, and the effect would be to slow the entire system down. This reveals a Heisenberg uncertainty problem plaguing digital security: the act of checking is an action that changes the system it is checking, because it lags everything else. In Cory Doctorow's novel *For the Win* (2010), an internet worker revolution occurs through this exact speculative strategy: namely, causing security measures to escalate so much that the whole system lags catastrophically and crashes. Some video game players today find out that the security settings of their home routers, inspecting every packet of data coming in or out of their homes—normally a virtue for preventing viruses and attacks—actually slow down their ping to the point where the game may not be worth playing.

Lest all this seem a bit removed from everyday life, let us recall that Alan Turing's classic 1950 essay, "Computing Machinery and Intelligence," defined machine intelligence through a test: using a typing interface, can a man tell the difference between a computer pretending to be a woman, on the one hand, and a man pretending to be a woman, on the other? Turing noted that the computer would have to be prevented from answering questions (for example, math or chess questions) inhumanly fast: its programming would have to ensure appropriate lags. (The answer Turing had the computer give was also wrong.) Lagging in behavior and conversation is part of what we recognize as human. Temporality proper to humans involves normal delays, normal lags. Responding too quickly can be as suspicious as responding too slowly.

Humans take time to make decisions, they are made up of delays that define them. Experimental psychology was founded, in no small part, on reaction time measurements. Different lags in reading words, for instance, provided clues to psychic mechanisms and their diagrams. Though everyone takes time to respond, lags have their social limits, wherein too much delay in response is read as meanness, cognitive deficit, disease, and so forth. Americans often use the language of lag—for example, "that person is slow" and "mental retardation"—to define proper and improper lag. These lags vary historically and culturally.

In researching sufferers of Chronic Fatigue Syndrome (CFS) and ADHD, I found many instances where the asynchronous lag of email enabled them to achieve a fluency not achievable in net-chatting or phone or face-to-face talking (Dumit 2006). In person, people with CFS were often frustrating to other people, because they were experienced as too slow to respond to the speed of neurotypical conversation. But a two-hour message-typing session resulting in a paragraph reads quite fluently when received in email or on a bulletin board. In one, I found that a slowly written description by one CFS sufferer about her experiences convinced a friend (who read it quickly) that she was actually suffering.

Lag temporalities that are proper to humans need to be investigated. Human lags are part of interaction, and delays are not simple at all. It is our temporalities, with our lags, that are in fact the measure of what matters for us in machines and games. In 2019, the fact that computers can beat the best players at Go has been hailed a breakthrough. A computer beating someone at tic-tac-toe or even checkers is uninteresting: we expect that these finite games are computationally solvable, and it as silly to compare humans to computers in regard to these games as it would be for humans to compete with a calculator at long division. Similarly, the fact that a computer could beat someone at chess if it had hundreds of years to make a move is not meaningful. We all might agree that, given enough time, chess is finite—unimaginably huge, but computationally solvable. Like all games, chess is, in fact, defined by time. Matches give each player a limited amount of time to play their moves (sometimes each move has a time limit, sometimes the total move time is limited, as in speed chess). The fact that players lag in making a move (but not too much) and that computers initially could not play fast enough to seem human meant that, in the last forty years, we could witness *computers catching up*.

Lag Is Another Time

Lag is a gateway twixt worlds. On one side, it is ignored, devalued. We speculatively leap over it, seeing only what it delays. We treat it as compressible, imagine it quantitative—to be reduced to zero if possible, or else to become imperceptible. No one need care much about it. On the other side, it gnaws apart our reality, inventing new times, new forms of temporality. It terraforms our metric life—transforming standardized milliseconds into gaping eons of profit, an in-breath into an opening, a server switch into a kill zone, thirty seconds into thirty minutes of clutch basketball, an injury in the moment of defeat into a delay of game into a victory, awesome hair into a crashed system. That which had been tolerated as part of the duration of the world (page loading, switching servers, enough time to trust a transaction) becomes a strategy to put the world into disarray.

While there is no time to go into the technical details, I would be remiss if I did not mention the most ironic and vile combination of speculation and lag: bitcoin. The darling of investment speculation in the twenty-first century, bitcoin and the blockchain ledger promise a fully trustable digital currency that does not require banks or governments. Its value soared and now remains a core icon of a speculative future cyber-economy. Yet at its material core is an endless need for more computing power: its trust model requires that a large number of computers solve a cryptographic puzzle so difficult that the world's fastest computers need ten minutes to calculate it. This prevents any one group from being able to cheat the system: it is truly a brilliant form of crowdsourced trust. The tragic side effect of increasing computing power is that bitcoin mining never gets efficient; rather, the very lag that enables trust requires more and more energy to stay trustworthy (Bitcoin Wiki 2010). As one analysis put it, "if more computing power joins the network, the result isn't that more bitcoins get created. Instead, it takes more computing power to produce each bitcoin, making existing mining hardware less profitable than before—and driving up the energy consumed per bitcoin" (Lee 2018). By the end of 2019, bitcoin-mining computers, run mostly in giant clusters—and often located in cold climates to reduce the hardware cooling costs—were consuming as much electricity as Belgium, now somewhere around 0.33 per cent of the entire world's energy consumption and rising (Cambridge Centre for Alternative Finance 2019).

As with other forms of lag, this one also transmogrifies the form of time it is supposed to inhabit. Here, the lag that is supposed to create trust among humans starts to contribute to global warming and the end of humanity. The ten-minute lag becomes a speculative contributor to a planetary countdown.

Clock time, which was supposed to standardize us, turns out to be an excuse to not pay attention to how each type of lag makes a new form of time measured by a new kind of clock (Galison 2004; Bender/Wellbery 1991). This is not the impossibility of measuring time that Wittgenstein ([1977] 1980) talked about, but the time of measuring itself which turns out to be reflexive of the world. And it is not generalizable: in fact, it is ever specifying. Each lag is unique. Each generalization is precisely what is turned on its head: to generalize is to speculate that time remains the same—and therefore to be caught flatfooted when it varies within itself.

What varies in lag time is the very consistency of what is in time and what is out. Each form of time also has its exceptions, the ineradicable metagame of the outside that time pretends to keep out. And because it is time, which has its limits, that becomes intolerable when it goes on too long, intolerable by humans and machines, it opens itself to more lags. Because they are in time, the very rulings and interruptions and reflections all too take time. And then we have to ask again, which kind of time do they take? What kind of lag time is this?

References

Aldridge, David (2011): "I Shot You First: Networking the Gameplay of HALO: REACH." In: *GDC Vault*, March 3 (https://www.gdcvault.com/play/1014345/I-Shot-You-First-Networking).
Bender, John B./Wellbery, David E. (eds.) (1991): *Chronotypes: The Construction of Time*. Stanford, CA: Stanford University Press.
Bhabha, Homi K. (1991): "'Race,' Time and the Revision of Modernity." In: *Oxford Literary Review* 13, 193–219.

Bitcoin Wiki: "Difficulty" (2010): In: *Bitcoin Wiki*, December 19 (https://en.bitcoin.it/wiki/Difficulty).

Boluk, Stephanie/LeMieux, Patrick (2017): *Metagaming: Playing, Competing, Spectating, Cheating, Trading, Making, and Breaking Videogames*. Minneapolis: University of Minnesota Press.

Cambridge Centre for Alternative Finance (2019): "Cambridge Bitcoin Electricity Consumption Index." In: Cambridge Centre for Alternative Finance, Judge Business School, University of Cambridge website (https://www.cbeci.org/comparisons/).

Cooper, Melinda (2008): *Life as Surplus: Biotechnology and Capitalism in the Neoliberal Era*. Seattle: University of Washington Press.

Darius510 (2012): "An Easy Way to Understand the Effects of Lag Comp....in Terms Everyone Understands: Perks." In: Reddit, November 29 (https://www.reddit.com/r/blackops2/comments/1402p0/an_easy_way_to_understand_the_effects_of_lag/).

Doctorow, Cory (2010): *For the Win*. New York: Tor.

Dumit, Joseph (2006): "Illnesses You Have to Fight to Get: Facts as Forces in Uncertain, Emergent Illnesses." *Social Science & Medicine* 62, 577–590.

Dumit, Joseph (2012): *Drugs for Life: How Pharmaceutical Companies Define Our Health. Experimental Futures*. Durham, NC: Duke University Press.

Dumit, Joseph (2020): "Substance as Method." In: Brit Ross Wintereik/Andrea Ballestero (eds.): *How to Do Ethnography?* Durham, NC: Duke University Press, forthcoming.

Fidelity Investments (2011): "Preventing Another Flash Crash." In: Viewpoints, Fidelity Investments, July 25 (https://guidance.fidelity.com/viewpoints/preventing-flash-crash).

Fortun, Michael (2008): *Promising Genomics: Iceland and DeCODE Genetics in a World of Speculation*. Berkeley: University of California Press.

Galison, Peter (2004): *Einstein's Clocks, Poincaré's Maps: Empires of Time*. New York: Norton.

GivingCreditWhereDue (2016): "(PSA) Sony Removes 90+ Pages Thread on Their Community Forums with Users Reports on Input Lag Issues with 2016 Bravia Models, Any New Threads Regarding It Instantly Locked—Amid Holiday Season." In: Reddit, November 22 (https://www.reddit.com/r/technology/comments/5edhty/psa_sony_removes_90_pages_thread_on_their/).

Goede, Marieke de (2012): *Speculative Security: The Politics of Pursuing Terrorist Monies*. Minneapolis: University of Minnesota Press.

Hayles, Katherine (2017): *Unthought: The Power of the Cognitive Nonconscious*. Chicago: University of Chicago Press.

jabbink (2016): response to wartickler, "Catching Too Quickly" (issue #59). In: jabbink, *PokemonGoBot*, GitHub, August 15 (https://github.com/jabbink/PokemonGoBot/issues/59).

Johnson, Jason (2015): "Behind the Scenes at a Major eSports Event." In: *iQ* (Intel), July 22 (https://iq.intel.com/behind-the-scenes-major-esports-event/).

Katsuyama, Brad (2015): "Building a Market That Works for Investors." In: PRI, "PRI in Person 2015 - Day 2 - Keynote: Brad Katsuyama," YouTube, September 10 (https://www.youtube.com/watch?v=N9hoqFpDjVs).

Kochhar-Lindgren, Gray (2005): *TechnoLogics: Ghosts, the Incalculable, and the Suspension of Animation*. Albany: State University of New York Press.

Krapp, Peter (2011): *Noise Channels: Glitch and Error in Digital Culture*. Minneapolis: University of Minnesota Press.

Lampert, Jay (2012): *Simultaneity and Delay: A Dialectical Theory of Staggered Time*. London: Continuum.

Lee, Timothy B. (2018): "New Study Quantifies Bitcoin's Ludicrous Energy Consumption." In: *Ars Technica*, May 17 (https://arstechnica.com/tech-policy/2018/05/new-study-quantifies-bitcoins-ludicrous-energy-consumption/).

Lewis, Michael (2014): *The Flash Boys: A Wall Street Revolt*. New York: Norton.

LiPuma, Edward/Lee, Benjamin (2004): *Financial Derivatives and the Globalization of Risk*. Durham, NC: Duke University Press.

Mackenzie, Adrian (2006): *Transductions: Bodies and Machines at Speed*. London: Continuum.

MacKenzie, Donald (2015): "Mechanizing the Merc: The Chicago Mercantile Exchange and the Rise of High-Frequency Trading." In: *Technology and Culture* 56, 646–675.

MacKenzie, Donald (2017): "A Material Political Economy: Automated Trading Desk and Price Prediction in High-Frequency Trading." In: *Social Studies of Science* 47, 172–194.

Miyazaki, Hirokazu (2013): *Arbitraging Japan: Dreams of Capitalism at the End of Finance*. Berkeley: University of California Press.

Mol, Annemarie (1993): "What Is New? Doppler and Its Others: An Empirical Philosophy of Innovations." In: Ilana Löwy (ed.): *Medicine and Change*. Paris: Inserm, 107–125.

Moten, Fred (2003): *In the Break: The Aesthetics of the Black Radical Tradition*. Minneapolis: University of Minnesota Press.

Peterson, Kristin (2014): *Speculative Markets: Drug Circuits and Derivative Life in Nigeria*. Durham, NC: Duke University Press.

Rainbow Six Siege Developers (2017): "Dev Blog: Ping Abuse, Peeker's Advantage, and Next Steps." In: *Tom Clancy's Rainbow Six Siege* official website, October 18 (https://rainbow6.ubisoft.com/siege/en-us/news/152-303559-16/dev-blog-ping-abuse-peekers-advantage-and-next-steps).

Sunder Rajan, Kaushik (2006): *Biocapital: The Constitution of Postgenomic Life*. Durham, NC: Duke University Press.

Sunder Rajan, Kaushik (2017): *Pharmocracy: Value, Politics, and Knowledge in Global Biomedicine*. Durham, NC: Duke University Press.

TemperVOiD (2016): "Please Tone down the Lag Compensation." In: Reddit, November 6 (https://www.reddit.com/r/Infinitewarfare/comments/5bfy8e/please_tone_down_the_lag_compensation/).

Thacker, Eugene (2005): *The Global Genome: Biotechnology, Politics, and Culture*. Cambridge, MA: MIT Press.

TokingMessiah (2016): "TIL That During the 1990's Joe Rogan Paid $10,000 per Month to Have a T1 Internet Connection Installed in His House in Order to Play Quake without Dealing with Lag." In: Reddit, June 20 (https://www.reddit.com/r/todayilearned/comments/4oz06z/til_that_during_the_1990s_joe_rogan_paid_10000/).

Turing, A. M. (1950): "Computing Machinery and Intelligence." In: *Mind* 59, 433–460.

Ullman, Ellen (2003): *The Bug*. New York: Nan A. Talese/Doubleday.

uncertain commons (2013): *Speculate This!* Durham, NC: Duke University Press.

Valve Developer Community (2005): "Source Multiplayer Networking." In: *Valve Developer Community* wiki, July (https://developer.valvesoftware.com/wiki/Source_Multiplayer_Networking).

Wittgenstein, Ludwig ([1977] 1980): *Culture and Value*. G. H. von Wright/Heikki Nyman (eds.). Peter Winch (trans.). Oxford: Blackwell.

Embodiment: Speculating with Matter

Chapter 5: "La vie impossible"
Germfree Life in the Microbiome Era

Melissa Wills

David Vetter spent his entire life waiting for the future to arrive. Diagnosed prenatally with Severe Combined Immunodeficiency (SCID), he was delivered by sterile Cesarean section in 1971 and transferred immediately to the plastic-film isolator that would earn him the nickname "Bubble Boy." The bubble was his refuge, a place of therapeutic safety against the microbes that would otherwise devastate his vulnerable body. And there he lived for twelve years, eating sterilized food and drinking sterilized water, reading sterilized books and doing schoolwork on sterilized paper, his entire world structured to preserve the integrity of the membrane surrounding him.

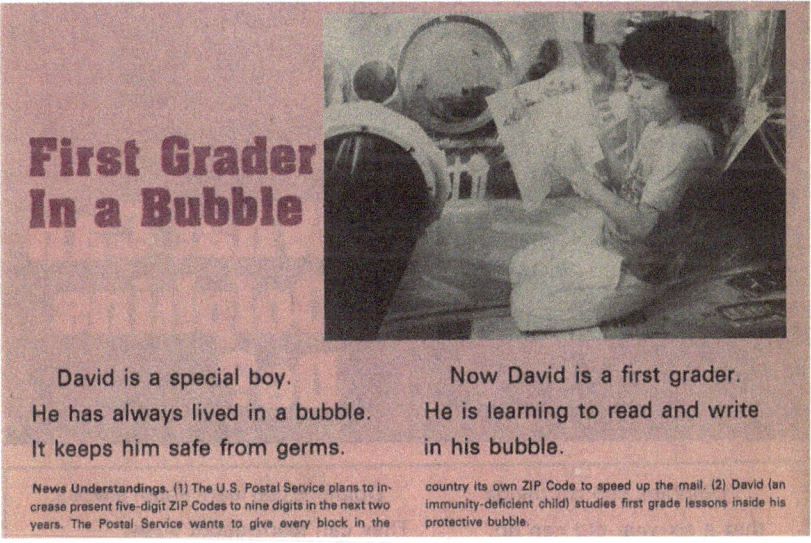

Figure 5.1: David Vetter featured in "First Grader in a Bubble," Buddy's Weekly Reader, *January 1979.*

David—and the worldwide audience following his story—looked toward his eventual exit from that bubble, as medical researchers searched for a cure that would liberate him to a coexistence with the germs, and the people, of the world. In the public eye, David's confinement was often bemoaned, with news reports and magazines emphasizing the experiences and social contacts he lacked. Yet above all, his life was a medical miracle, "a triumphal tale of technological innovation and medical mavericks" (Elman 2014: 30). His bubble was, if regrettable, a place of safety. It was a refuge, a haven in which to wait (fig. 5.1).

As the first child to be kept alive long-term in a germfree space, he was also the biomedical future made manifest. David's case—his survival, normal development, and general good health—seemed to prophesy the salvation of other immunodeficient children, whose bodies would otherwise be fatally wracked in infancy by contact with microorganisms. But even more people stood to benefit, as well, as doctors and scientists began to wonder whether the technology extending his life might be used to treat ailments spanning the entire lifespan.

David's bubble had been made possible by eight decades of progressive refinement of isolator technology in the field of *gnotobiology*, the study of organisms possessing either no microbes or only a small, specified contingent of them. With the creation of David's bubble, the *human* germfree future appeared both achievable and imminent. When David was a year old, the keynote speaker at a prominent conference on germfree research, Wallace Herrell, predicted "that gnotobiotic research may have some clinical application in nearly every medical specialty and sub-specialty ranging from pediatrics to geriatrics" (Herrell 1973: 11). He called for researchers "to immediately initiate extensive use of these germfree programs" (16). In the space age, that mission appeared as noble and as transformative as landing on the moon. Herrell asked, "if we can spend billions of dollars getting to the moon to find out among other things that it is germfree, why not spend a few million on the germfree programs?" (16–17). To many, David was an astronaut on Earth—a pioneer of life without germs.

Such boundless optimism in the saving power of medical technology was largely warranted in David's case. He lived to the age of twelve, fully a decade beyond the life expectancy of untreated SCID patients. The isolator technology was nearly flawless, and while he did acquire some microorganisms over time and was thus not strictly germfree, he evaded infection until the end of his life. His death, in fact, resulted from efforts to bring him out of the bubble: a bone marrow transplant meant to confer a functional immune system harbored an undetected virus that cost him his life. David emerged from his bubble only in his last days, already grievously ill. It was the cure, then, and not the enclosure that killed him. Until the end, his bubble remained a protective space within which to survive and to thrive. Or so the story used to go. But that is not the David Vetter story of today.

In this time of the human microbiome, living without germs seems a bizarre, even contradictory prospect. With large-scale genomic sequencing initiatives such as the Human Microbiome Project in the U.S., the sheer scope and variety of microorganisms associated with the human body—the microbiome—are coming into focus. It is increasingly clear that microbes confer vital health benefits and that reduced microbial biodiversity can propel illness. Such findings have driven a major shift in the public conversation surrounding microbes and disease, predominantly through the vast body of popular science writing on the microbiome. This discourse, which I term "microbiome writing" in this chapter, spans news reports, journalistic interviews, books, videos and other media narrating microbiome research and its applications. Microbiome writing generally shares a common persuasive goal of convincing readers to leave behind outdated ideas of microbes as disease-causing invaders, to recognize their necessity to human life, and to live more intentionally with them. We simply cannot do without our microbes, these texts insist. We are barely human at all, according to Alanna Collen's book 10% *Human: How Your Body's Microbes Hold the Key to Health and Happiness* (2015). We must attend to the tiny legions inside, according to Ed Yong's book *I Contain Multitudes: The Microbes within Us and a Grander View of Life* (2016). Or, as Rob Knight suggests in his TED talk, "How Our Microbes Make Us Who We Are" (2014), we must acknowledge our microbes, ourselves.

Even as microbiome writing celebrates the teeming abundance of microbial life, the thought of life without germs is never far from mind. Particularly in the book-length texts that are the focus of this chapter, authors almost universally argue that microbiome research overturns the pervasive modern attitude of what might be termed *antibiosis*: a philosophy of "anti-life" in which microorganisms are viewed chiefly as antagonists to be eliminated at all costs.[1] Antibiosis encompasses antibiotic therapy as well as a host of contemporary practices, from hand sanitizers and Clorox wipes to hospital birth and processed foods, that systematically exclude the organisms with which humans coevolved. Microbiome books assert that the regime of antibiosis has resulted in a dramatic rise of noncommunicable diseases associated with the loss of microbial diversity. Almost in unison, authors claim that modern humans are on the brink of antimicrobial crisis. In his book *Missing Microbes: How the Overuse of Antibiotics Is Fueling Our Modern Plagues*, Martin Blaser even predicts an "antibiotic winter" of apocalyptic suffering should we fail to correct course (Blaser 2014: 6).

Germfree life emblematizes that threat. David Vetter appears frequently in microbiome books, alongside gnotobiotic mice in their miniature bubbles. Au-

---

1 While I draw this term from Landecker (2016: 20), where it is used specifically in the context of antibiotic drugs, it accurately describes a more comprehensive attitude of "anti-life" in microbiome writing.

thors recount visits to germfree animal facilities, cite research on gnotobiology, and delve into the history and technology of germfree isolators. Microbiome writers sometimes emphasize the research utility of germfree animals, namely, their role as negative controls in elucidating the influence of microorganisms on mammalian physiology, development, and neurobiology.[2] As research organisms, germfree animals are generally studied for their relevance to human biology; murine pathologies lead to inferences about human counterparts. In this sense, germfree mice serve as model organisms within biomedicine.[3]

In microbiome writing, however, germfree life is primarily deployed for its symbolic value. Gnotobiotic mice and David the Bubble Boy become figures for the microbially depleted modern body, products of the regime of antibiosis. This symbolism is made possible by a significant shift in their status. As represented in microbiome writing, the germfree state is no longer an achievement but rather a catastrophe, no longer lifegiving but rather intrinsically risky. If gnotobiotic organisms are model organisms in biomedicine, in microbiome writing they are more properly what anthropologists Heather Paxson and Stefan Helmreich have termed *model ecosystems*, functioning "in a prescriptive sense, as tokens of how organisms and human ecological relations with them *could*, *should*, or *might* be" (Paxson/Helmreich 2014: 165). In this chapter, I show how microbiome writing employs germfree bodies as model ecosystems in reverse, as non-ecosystems held up prescriptively to illustrate how humans and microbes should not be, that is, separate. Germfree life signals grave costs to body, psyche, and society; it germinates a moral imperative to live with germs in the wider world.

The David Vetter story of today is a parable for the folly of attempting to live without germs, in which their absence, not their presence, is lethal. In this chapter, I show how microbiome writers accomplish the rewriting of his life and legacy into a register suited to the microbiome era. Conducting a close-reading analysis of ten popular science microbiome books, I examine how the history and status of germfree life—animal and human—are subtly reframed to align with the authors'

---

2 For a scientific perspective on microbiomics and gnotobiology see Falk et al. (1998). For a more comprehensive view of gnotobiology's applications, including in infectious disease research, see Carter/Foster (2006). The philosophers O'Malley/Skillings (2018) also discuss germfree animal research in relation to the history of microbiomics. Microbiome writing's engagement with gnotobiology occurs almost exclusively in the more capacious space of full-length books. Such texts began appearing with frequency around 2008, after the launch of the Human Microbiome Project in the U.S.

3 They are model organisms in the sense that they produce findings generalizable beyond themselves and model whole-organism processes, such as human–microbe interactions (Ankeny/Leonelli 2011). See Davies (2013) on the structuring role of narrative in shaping relations between animal biology and human disease, and Rader (2004) on the standardization of laboratory mice.

critiques of antibiosis. Through a subtle web of historical disjunctions, recurring tropes, a touch of misquotation, and a dose of hyperbole, germfree life in the microbiome era becomes sick. Transforming the germfree isolator from a historical invention to a modern one, from a protective space to an imminently dangerous one, microbiome writers reconceptualize germfree bodies as profoundly suffering, urgently in need of reintegration with the microbial world.

I argue that reappraisal of germfree life in microbiome writing is unified by a recurrent speculative maneuver in which the germfree body signifies the materialized future, a small-scale perfection of antibiosis. Microbiome writers continually forge parallels between germfree organisms and human bodies overexposed to antibiotics, asking readers to identify the conditions of their own bodies replicated in the space of the gnotobiotic isolator. Germfree life comes not only to exemplify the present suffering of human bodies but also to foretell the devastating failures of body and society that are the terminus of antibiosis. As embodiments of a catastrophe already underway in the antibiotic-laden modern world, germfree mice and bubble boys are deployed as interventions in the present: they function as deterrents to the trajectory of antibiosis, revealing the crisis of life without germs as foretold by the bodies of germfree mice and David Vetter.

Germfree Dreaming

Germfree animals have a long scientific history that is seldom recognized in microbiome writing. They were first conceptualized in 1885 by Louis Pasteur, who proposed deriving a sterile chick in order to assess the impact of microorganisms on vertebrate biology. Supposing the interior of the egg to be free of microbes, he suggested that this state could be preserved by transferring the newborn chick to a chamber supplied with sterile air, water, and food. Pasteur believed microbes to be vital to the physiological functioning of higher organisms, especially in digestion; he hypothesized that the germfree state would be biologically untenable, "que la vie, dans ces conditions, deviendrait impossible" (Pasteur 1885: 68).

By 1895, two German researchers, George Nuttall and Hans Thierfelder, challenged that hypothesis by providing the first indication that the survival of germfree life was in fact possible. Adapting Pasteur's proposal to vertebrates, they surgically extracted a guinea pig fetus from the sterile space of its mother's uterus, raising it for eight days inside a massively complex apparatus of glass, metal, and rubber that was kept sterile using steam, chloroform, and wax (Nuttall/Thierfelder 1895). Across Europe, researchers modified these methods to isolate germfree goats, mice, tadpoles, insects and more, including at last Max Schottelius's derivation of the germfree chicken in 1899 (Schottelius 1899).

Germfree organisms in the early twentieth century were technological marvels, encased in meticulously engineered chambers that required constant and intensive maintenance to prevent the onslaught of environmental microbes. Still, they lived.

It was how they lived that now became controversial, as researchers found that these organisms generally failed to gain weight, suffered from malnutrition, exhibited a range of physiological anomalies, and lived only a short time. It seemed that microbes, while not strictly required for life, were indeed necessary for long-term health. Yet scientists gradually developed modified feeding and supplementation regimes to compensate for the loss of microbes. These, alongside refinements in isolator technology by the American machinist James Reyniers, enabled germfree organisms—especially mice—to be maintained long-term in breeding colonies by the mid-twentieth century. And with the engineering of flexible-film plastic incubators, they eventually became cheap and transportable, extensively used in biomedical research as tools for the study of host–microbe ecology.[4] They now appear in laboratories around the world, still dependent on their isolators and careful nutritional management, but thriving.

The existence of breeding colonies of germfree animals, as documented in the scientific literature, demonstrates that life without microbes is quite possible. Contemporary microbiome writers, however, have recurrently resurrected Pasteur's hypothesis to affirm the sentiment that we simply cannot do without our microbes. "La vie impossible" thereby comes to signify not the life and death of a particular, isolator-bound chicken but rather the impossibility of human life in the absence of microorganisms—technical achievability aside. Pasteur's prediction becomes detached from his task of proposing the strategic exclusion of microbes, becoming remade into a claim, in the model-ecosystem mode, about the absent modern microbiome in an age of antibiosis.

The twenty-first-century rewriting of Pasteur is accomplished through a distortion of the historical development of germfree life that situates it in our more recent past. The misrepresentations I detail below are largely innocuous, likely arising from the simple fact that science writers are not historians; nor are they specialists in gnotobiology. Nevertheless, their renarrations of the historical record matter, helping to articulate an imminent crisis of post-microbial life looming large in microbiome writing.

Although they almost universally reference Pasteur's 1885 hypothesis, microbiome writers consistently obscure the long and largely successful early history of gnotobiology; the proposed experiment is generally suggested to have been left unexplored. In *Good Germs, Bad Germs: Health and Survival in a Bacterial World*, Jessica Snyder Sachs writes that "Pasteur's greatest protégé, the Nobel Prize-winning

---

4 On the history of gnotobiology, see Kirk (2012a, 2012b) and Luckey (1963).

Elie Metchnikoff," believed that people would be better off without their bacteria, and he "openly scoffed at what he considered his mentor's naïveté" (Sachs 2007: 29). Sachs frames Metchnikoff's rejection as the disdain of an insolent student, with material consequences: identifying Metchnikoff as leading the "winning" side in gnotobiological debates, she implies an institutional diminishing of the proposal, setting Pasteur in opposition to the (prize-winning, great) microbiological mainstream (30).

More broadly, microbiome writers steadily minimize the substantial successes of gnotobiology in the early nineteenth century. Sachs neglects to mention Metchnikoff's own deep investment in germfree animal research, casting him solely as critic of Pasteur. Similarly, she entirely overlooks his wife Olga's derivation of germfree tadpoles, crediting her instead with an "unsuccessful attempt to keep tadpoles alive under sterile conditions" (30).[5] Other microbiome writers repeat the pattern. In *The Psychobiotic Revolution: Mood, Food, and the New Science of the Gut-Brain Connection*, Scott C. Anderson and his coauthors note the eventual implementation of the germfree chicken isolation proposed by Pasteur. But rather than mentioning that germfree guinea pigs and other animals had already been isolated by 1899, they describe only the "decade of failure" before Schottelius was "finally able to breed germ-free chickens" (Anderson et al. 2017: 31–32). Likewise, in *The Wild Life of Our Bodies: Predators, Parasites, and Partners That Shape Who We Are Today*, Rob Dunn depicts early experiments in gnotobiology as relying on ineffective, low-tech methods of "scrubbing the germs off [...] a kind of Mr. Clean approach [...] Those attempts had failed" (Dunn 2011: 68).

After decades of neglect or failed efforts, this narrative goes, germfree life finally emerged with force in the mid-twentieth century. While it is true that germfree research accelerated at this time, with specimens becoming more transportable and more commonly studied, microbiome writers generally suggest them to have been *invented* or even conceived of at this moment. The timeline is a point of general consensus among microbiome writers. Anderson as well as Yong place its origins in the 1940s, while others are somewhat less precise. In *I, Superorganism: Learning to Love Your Inner Ecosystem*, Jon Turney says "50 years ago" (Turney 2015: 55). In *The Human Superorganism: How the Microbiome Is Revolutionizing the Pursuit of a Healthy Life*, Rodney Dietert says "forty to fifty" years ago (Dietert 2016: 44). In *An Epidemic of Absence: A New Way of Understanding Allergies and Autoimmune Diseases*, Moises Velasquez-Manoff simply puts it in the "mid-twentieth century" (Velasquez-Manoff 2012: 169).

In this vein, Dunn suggests Reyniers's isolator technology to have been the invention of a lone genius, first dreamed up in a heady era of technological innovation. He writes, "the iron lung had just been invented, as had the first robot.

---

5 Five of Metchnikoff's tadpoles lived, and remained sterile, beyond 63 days (Metchnikoff 1901).

What if, Reyniers thought, he used the same sorts of technologies to construct a microbe-free world?" (Dunn 2011: 68). Dunn's account assigns key insights from the first decade of gnotobiology, including Pasteur's recognition of the sterility of the chicken egg and the extension of this concept to the guinea pig by Nuttall and Thierfelder, to Reyniers himself.[6] He concludes, "if Reyniers could accomplish his goal, he might be the first person in history to produce an animal devoid of germs [...] Such an animal would be fascinating and modern" (68–69). In light of the longer history of gnotobiology I have been discussing, of course, such an animal was neither modern, nor invented by Reyniers.

If Dunn frames gnotobiology as a continuation of the technological advances of the mid-twentieth century, other authors link it more specifically to the antimicrobial advances of the same period. Anderson and his colleagues introduce Pasteur's hypothesis but only mention the actual existence of germfree animals following their section on penicillin, implying that it was only in the wake of antibiotics that germfree mice were "finally created" via C-section birth (Anderson et al. 2017: 33). Similarly, Velasquez-Manoff writes,

> Beginning in the mid-twentieth century, following a hundred years of almost miraculous progress in medicine—including the triumph of germ theory, the advent of antibiotics, and the polio vaccine—scientists finally looked into Pasteur's idea. They delivered mice by C-section, fed them sterile food, and raised them in germfree bubbles [...] (Velasquez-Manoff 2012: 169)

Velasquez-Manoff suggests Pasteur's vision to have lain dormant for a half century, emerging only after the solidification of a systemic program of microbial eradication, and from a cultural moment in which such progress was hailed as "miraculous" and a "triumph." Each of these books, then, suggests that Pasteur's vision of germfree animals could only be realized in the wonder-drug era.[7] Gnotobiology, disjointed from its historical origins, becomes symptomatic of a prevailing attitude of antibiosis.

Indeed, microbiome writers share a preoccupation with antibiotic drugs, which often function as symbolic distillations of a less-than-rational quest for control over germs and disease. Antibiotics metonymize an obsessive vision of

---

6 The suggestion that the Cesarean delivery of germfree mice was an innovation of the mid-twentieth century is also made in Anderson/Cryan/Dinan (2017: 33) and Velasquez-Manoff (2012: 169).

7 The historian Robert Bud has documented the robust cultural legacy of penicillin, namely, the drug's "associat[ion] with unprecedented power, science, and modern medicine" (2007: 74). Microbiome writers inherit these associations, with the gnotobiotic isolator recapitulating the familiar linkage between antibiotics and technological achievement.

microbial transcendence pursued at any cost. Transported into the era of wonder drugs and vaccines, then, germfree animals become products of an ill-advised desire for life beyond germs.

For microbiome writers, germfree fantasy rather than technological rationality has guided the development of gnotobiology. Dunn's account in *The Wild Life of Our Bodies* features a Reyniers driven to the pursuit of germfree steel isolators by a fantasy of both personal and biological transcendence: he "dreamed of germfree rats and, with them, grandeur" (Dunn 2011: 68). A lengthy discussion of Reyniers's work describes him as nearly crazed in his obsessive pursuit of the "dream" of germfree life, "interested, beyond reason" (67) in Pasteur's hypothesis and irrationally driven to disprove it. Dunn repeatedly emphasizes Reyniers's youth—he was nineteen—and calls him "a boy" (69, 70). Dunn also plays up Reyniers's unorthodox training as a machinist rather than as a biologist and his appointment to academic posts without the expected degrees. Dunn's Reyniers is an audacious dreamer, carried beyond reason in his imagination of germfree life. While other microbiome writers treat Reyniers with more circumspection, the situation of gnotobiology in a post-antibiotic world is widely echoed: the germfree animal in its germfree world is framed as the terminus, and culmination, of antibiosis.

Accusations such as Dunn's—that the pursuit of germfree life is rooted in unreasonable fantasy—recur throughout microbiome writing, particularly in discussions of the material elimination of microorganisms through antibiotics. In microbiome-era retellings of gnotobiological history, the discovery of penicillin is said to have launched the persistent imagination of a germfree human future. As Anderson and his collaborators put it,

> The world began to wonder: Could germs be completely eliminated? The idea of living in a sterilized world—a world free of disease—was tantalizing. People fantasized about a future in which children would be brought up as superkids, liberated by their germ-free environment. Without bacteria, they would never be sick and could live for hundreds of years. It was a vision of purity, a sparkling biological utopia. (Anderson et al. 2017: 32–33)

Wonder, fantasy, vision: penicillin gives rise irresistibly to the possibility of germfree utopia, to the wild dream of liberation from illness and death.

With germfree animals, microbiome writers suggest, the dream became real. Dunn attributes an irresistible allure to Reyniers's animals, suggesting that even scientists were led astray by the discovery that it was, after all, possible to live without microbes:

> Reyniers spoke often and with the weight of his institute and accomplishments. His voice came to dominate the field [...] Each new talk or study added punctua-

tion until one could almost hear it, a drumming chorus of "Kill the germs!" *Kill the germs!*" and we would be free of our past. Kill the germs and we would be healthier and happier, just like the guinea pigs in their giant metal worlds. (Dunn 2011: 74)

The scientific response to Reyniers's guinea pigs, Dunn implies, has actually been a collective mania in which biologists' own antibiotic fantasies are recursively amplified by the materialization of germfree animals. Significantly, Dunn presents the scientific aspiration toward microbial transcendence as being motivated by an explicit desire to kill the germs, not merely to study life without them: gnotobiology is synonymous with microbicide.

The public, Dunn suggests, has been similarly affected by appearance of germfree animals. Noting that germfree animals generally outlive their conventional counterparts, he writes that Reyniers "had inspired the imagination of the masses, inspired them to believe that we all might live like his guinea pigs, germ-free and nearly forever" (73). Germfree guinea pigs were more than scientific model organisms, becoming also "a model of what was possible" and foretelling "the chambers of the future, where we were completely removed from the plagues of our past" (72–74). But the imagined germfree future does not remain hypothetical: Dunn suggests that it has also driven efforts to manifest a germfree state in the present. For the public, such efforts take shape not as elaborate isolators but rather as more ordinary antimicrobial compulsions, attempts to "make our lives more like the lives in those guinea pig chambers" (74). Dunn declares antimicrobial actions to be attempts toward a literal germfree bubble, reinforced by the "barriers we attempt to erect with antibiotic wipes, antibiotic sprays, and the like" (76).

For Dunn, the familiar antimicrobial practices of daily human life are consistent with the same germfree dreaming that produced gnotobiology. This sentiment recurs across microbiome books, with authors continually equating modern life with a deeply rooted and irrational desire to eliminate, not just to manage, microorganisms. Dietert, in *The Human Superorganism*, laments our "modernized world of antibiotic-administered, formula-fed, cesarean-delivered babies growing up in urban environments, surrounded by hand sanitizers and antibacterial wipes" (Dietert 2016: 6). Dietert suggests a spatial boundedness to this antibiotic lifestyle in which babies, not unlike germfree mice, are born and raised within strict barriers keeping germs at bay—as if living in a bubble.

The scientific literature characterizes the effects of depleted microbiome biodiversity as *dysbiosis*: a lost biodiversity reflected in an imbalance in the expected proportions, but not the total volume, of species comprising a body's microflora.[8] In popular science writing, however, dysbiosis is often reinvented as a state of microbiological barrenness. Microbes are not imbalanced, but rather gone entirely

---

8 For a philosophical critique of the explanatory potential of dysbiosis: O'Malley/Skillings (2018).

in an "epidemic of absence" (Velasquez-Manoff 2012) and a crisis of "missing microbes" (Blaser 2014). The human body perceives the loss: Blaser describes "a dance without a partner," Dunn a "longing" or "an ache for the context you miss," like the "pain of a missing limb" (Blaser 2014: 122; Dunn 2011: 23, xii, xiii). These tropes are supplemented by microbiome writing's proliferation of environmental destruction metaphors, such that the antibiotic-laden modern body is said to suffer like a landscape that is scorched, deforested, desolate without its extinct species, and polluted by nuclear fallout.[9] Contained within antibiotic barriers rigorously maintained, the human body becomes figuratively germfree.

Microbiome writers do not hold that our bodies are literally germfree, but rather that the germfree imagination continues unabated in a continual striving toward germfree utopia. It is in this trajectory that they seek to intervene. The solution to germfree fantasy, according to these authors, is scientific rationality. They suggest that microbiome science, with its sobering attention to the consequences of microbial depletion, can puncture the inflated dream of life beyond germs. Microbiomic rationality exposes the germfree dream to be a germfree nightmare; it defines the microbeless body as disastrous rather than transcendent.

In advocating for a saner approach to germs, microbiome writers take on the rhetorical mantle of historical antibiotic reformers: mid-twentieth-century infectious disease researchers who sought to curb the overzealous use of antibiotics. According to Scott H. Podolsky, reformers defined the overuse of antibiotics as driven by a deep-seated irrationality, and they advocated for "therapeutic rationality" in response (Podolsky 2015: 2). For microbiome writers, too, accusations of irrationality sharpen arguments for a more sparing use of antibiotics as well as a more deliberate approach to living with microorganisms.[10] Time and again, the yearning for life without microbes is countered by an emphasis on the risks of such a life. As we will see, the "impossible life" of the germfree organism comes to mean something worse than death: a life of unbearable suffering.

---

9 Blaser (2014) employs these metaphors relentlessly, but they abound across microbiome writing. They are inherited, in part, from antibiotic reformers' tendency toward natural destruction metaphors (Podolsky 2015) and contemporary catastrophe discourse in microbiology (Nerlich 2009).

10 On hysteria surrounding microbes and the "gospel of germs," see Tomes (1998); on American culture's particular obsession with cleanliness, see Hoy (1996).

Germfree Suffering

Living without germs leaves a mark. From the outset of gnotobiology, scientists have identified multiple physiological and immunological anomalies of gnotobiosis: altered anatomical features, digestive and metabolic anomalies, heightened nutrient requirements, and more.[11] Yet these anomalies are familiar, well characterized, and manageable. When successfully accommodated with the appropriate supplements and care, germfree animals thrive. In itself, germfreeness is not an obstacle to long-term survival. Gnotobiotic animals even tend to outlive their conventional counterparts.

The gnotobiotic isolator might reasonably be considered a triumph of engineering and, given its success in medicine, a lifesaving innovation. But microbiome writers define the technology almost exclusively as transgressive—as Dunn writes, "monstrous" (Dunn 2011: 73). Monstrosity, not achievement, characterizes the mission to separate an organism from its microbes. Other authors also describe germfree isolators as violations of the natural order, emphasizing their strangeness, awkwardness, or sheer technological immensity: Ed Yong calls them "some of the strangest environments in the world" (Yong 2016: 112); Turney, "an expensive and awkward business" (Turney 2015: 55). The monstrous space of the isolator extends to the bodies enclosed within, as microbiome writers consistently transform the familiar physiological anomalies of the germfree mouse into indicators of suffering. Difference becomes abnormality; isolation becomes pathology. Germfree mice are remade as victims, irreparably harmed and decisively artificial.

The artifice of germfree life, for instance, is highlighted in microbiome writers' frequent assertion that all germfree mice are Cesarean-delivered before being transferred to their isolators.[12] While this procedure has remained in use since the nineteenth century, it has largely been eliminated—except in the establishment of new colonies—due to the development of breeding colonies in which animals give birth without intervention. Rampant C-section birth is a convenient suggestion, however, for writers wishing to establish these animals as thoroughly artificial—reproductively inviable—from birth to death. With assisted obstetrics a condition of their very existence, they embody a horrifying vision of technological intrusion: babies wrested from mothers, skin replaced with iron.

The pattern repeats in discussions of the distinctive physiologies of germfree mice. Microbiome writers seldom acknowledge that scientists modify the care of germfree animals to ensure their long-term survival, instead defining difference itself as pathological. Influential microbiologist and proto-microbiome writer

---

11 See Carter/Foster (2006) and, for a historical perspective, Gordon/Pesti (1971).

12 E.g. Turney (2015); Rosebury (1969); and Velasquez-Manoff (2012).

Theodor Rosebury set this tone in his 1969 book, *Life on Man*, writing that germfree animals "turn out to be puny and deformed [...] with deficiencies and weaknesses yet to be counted" (Rosebury 1969: 149).[13] Contemporary writers follow Rosebury's lead, almost always portraying these animals as both deformed and deficient. Sachs recites a litany of defects: "unusually thin" intestinal tracts, and bodies "unusually vulnerable" to toxins and "unusually susceptible to deadly infections" (Sachs 2007: 45). Sachs does not mention that these differences are managed by researchers; rather, the unusual physiology of the germfree mouse becomes intrinsically problematic.

Germfree mouse bodies are sometimes more overtly characterized as grotesque. Yong notes the "weird biology of germ-free animals" (Yong 2016: 54), while Velasquez-Manoff depicts them as having a "really weird" physiology that is "off," "abnormal," "malformed," "strange," "shrunken," and "arrested" (Velasquez-Manoff 2012: 169–170). For Collen, they are revolting: an animal researcher she interviews recalls "that the first time she dissected a germ-free mouse, she was horrified by the size of the caecum, which took up most of the space in the abdomen" (Collen 2015: 128). The researcher's horror is recreated for the reader thanks to the inclusion of colored images of flayed mouse guts, in which the conventional as well as the germfree cecum might well be repulsive to the average reader. For these writers, the normal physiological differences of the germfree body are equated with suffering.

Significantly, in these accounts the research utility of germfree animals is rarely discussed; their crucial contributions to the study of human-microbial ecology go unnoticed. Instead, they are deployed primarily for their symbolic value. Transformed into bodily victims of a regime that values germfreeness above function and accepts countless deformities as the cost of its achievement, germfree mice are meant to be startlingly familiar. As depicted by microbiome writers, the grotesque germfree body is both alien and deeply resonant with the human bodies also suffering the consequences of antibiosis. Mice and humans are common victims of the dream of a germfree world.

Microbiome writers generally suggest that the microbially-depleted human body suffers profoundly in its "dance without a partner." Blaser even describes the lost biodiversity of the human microbiome as "exacting a terrible price":

> We are suffering from a mysterious array of what I call "modern plagues": obesity, childhood diabetes, asthma, hay fever, food allergies, esophageal reflux and cancer, celiac disease, Crohn's disease, ulcerative colitis, autism, eczema [...] Un-

---

13 I include Rosebury's work in this chapter because it has been particularly influential for microbiome scientists as well as popular science writers, and because it prefigures many of the themes and narratives of contemporary microbiome books.

> like most lethal plagues of the past that struck relatively fast and hard, these are chronic conditions that diminish and degrade their victims' quality of life for decades. (Blaser 2014: 6, 2)

In Blaser's assessment, these modern plagues are unleashing an unprecedented misery that is subtler than infectious diseases—the "lethal plagues of the past"—but no less profound. He suggests an urgent need to become attuned to these newer, more nuanced illnesses produced by the damaged microbiome.

We are meant to recognize ourselves within the space of the germfree isolator, identifying the bodily afflictions wrought by our own antimicrobial dreams. Contemporary human bodies mirror the "monstrous" germfree mice in microbiome writing, even if they do not (yet) appear so grotesque. In this sense, germfree animals might be understood as serving a *diagnostic* function, presenting afflictions that allow humans to identify their own dysbiotic suffering even in a not-quite-germfree world. The gnotobiotic isolator and the modern human world thereby become parallel spaces, limned spatially or rhetorically by a sterile boundary within which life suffers.

But the key innovation of microbiome writing's reappraisal of germfree life is that it is more than merely diagnostic of present human illness, also serving a crucial *deterrent* function; the virtual witnessing of germfree catastrophe is mobilized to intervene in the future. Microbiome writers generally suggest that the crisis of noncommunicable diseases, already dangerously out of control, threatens to worsen as the germfree fantasy draws ever closer to completion. Germfree mice and David Vetter, as early manifestations of that dream, suggest humanity's trajectory. Revealing the germfree dream to be a biological catastrophe, they are deployed to startle the reader into a more rational apprehension of microbial life and to forestall the devastations of antibiosis.

There is abundant cultural precedent for this speculative neutralization of the germfree dream. Science fiction authors pioneered the narration of germfree life's damages as a means of critiquing dominant, eradicative attitudes toward microorganisms. For instance, Michael Crichton's novel *The Andromeda Strain* (1969) imagines the development of Kalocin, a "universal antibiotic" that fully eliminates a patient's microbial load to horrifying effect. Crichton emphasizes the risk of superinfection, the uncontrolled influx of microorganisms into the germfree body. In the novel, the clinical volunteers who test this powerful antibiotic suffer painful deaths upon discontinuing treatment:

> The forty volunteers each had died of obscure and horrible diseases no one had ever seen before. One man experienced swelling of his body, from head to foot, a hot, bloated swelling until he suffocated from pulmonary edema. Another man

fell prey to an organism that ate away his stomach in a matter of hours. A third was hit by a virus that dissolved his brain to a jelly. And so it went. (Crichton 1969: 266)

This side effect is so severe that the drug is ultimately denied even to a key scientist who becomes infected with the gruesome Andromeda Strain. "It might cure you for a while," the lead researcher explains, "but you'd never survive later, when you were taken off" (267). Germfreeness is the greater evil, a state not to be pursued even under the gravest circumstances—not even in the face of a ghastly death.

Scientific discourse has also historically relied on the power of the apocalyptic imagination to counter prevailing germophobias, through thought experiments exploring the catastrophic disappearance of microorganisms in the global ecosystem. The foundational example is bacteriologist Otto Rahn's 1945 popular press book *Microbes of Merit*, featuring an epilogue that summarizes the diverse roles of bacteria by imagining their disappearance in the wake of an antimicrobial comet. Rahn observes that the immediate resolution of bacterial diseases would be welcomed, but any celebration would quickly cease with the unfolding of successive global crises: stalled agriculture, the accumulation of undecomposed bodies, devastated landscapes, undrinkable water. These consequences reveal the demonization of microorganisms to be short-sighted, thinkable only by those who "take the cooperation of microbes for granted" (Rahn 1945: 274). The imagined hellscape of a world without microbes is meant to return readers to a more holistic attitude in which they join Rahn in concluding: "Let us hope that we never collide with the tail of such a comet" (274).

In their engagements with germfree life, microbiome writers largely reprise the lessons of Crichton's Kalocin, Rahn's antimicrobial comet, and countless other devices historically recruited to illustrate graphically the toll of the germfree aspiration. Yet where these precursors have always announced themselves as thought experiments or as science fiction, microbiome writers extract the same insight from real, embodied organisms. One need no longer turn to the imagination, it would seem; looking into the gnotobiotic isolator brings the germfree nightmare to life before our very eyes. As perfections of an abiotic state dreamed of but not hitherto attained in the human world, germfree animals materialize antibiosis and its costs.

Rosebury first brought this speculative maneuver to microbiome writing in his discussion of gnotobiology. He writes that the numerous deficiencies of germfree animals demand we "abolish at once any notion we might have had that the animal would be generally better off without his germs [...] The germ-free animal is, by and large, a miserable creature" (Rosebury 1969: 49). Rosebury here comments on more than simply the status of germfree animals: his detailing of their miseries serves to rebut the notion that life without germs might be desirable—for humans. Animal misery forebodes human misery. He continues, "Knowing things like this, would you willingly separate your infant from his microbes if you could? Or ought you to be glad you can't?" (54). The paired questions affirm the stubborn persistence of gnotobiotic fantasy, despite the recognition that its achievement would be devastating. For Rosebury, that aspiration might only be dispelled by a speculative intervention: by asking the reader to imagine their own infant as germfree and therefore subject to the atrocities wreaked upon gnotobiotic animals.

Contemporary microbiome writers also turn to germfree animals as indicators of human suffering, though they generally assert a stronger potency for the deterrent possibilities of germfree imagination. Dietert is perhaps the most explicit in identifying the speculative mode animating microbiome writers' engagements with germfree life. He explicates at some length a 1971 gnotobiology review article summarizing the physiological anomalies of germfree animals.[14] Significantly, Dietert interprets the article as a catalogue of present and future *human* horrors, despite the fact that it makes no claims about human applications. He argues that it "foretells exactly what happens when we are a single mammalian species. Without those microbes, we face a life of biological deficiencies, illnesses, and death" (Dietert 2016: 44). From the bodies of gnotobiotic animals, he extrapolates to a dire human future of required nutritional supplements, swelling, immune susceptibility, and imminent death. It is germfree animals that lead him to conclude that "there are consequences to degrading or damaging the human microbiome garden," which is absolutely required in order "to have a healthy and prolonged life" (45).

For Dietert, germfree animals are more than model organisms; they also foretell our impending germfree future. It is a vision from which the reader is meant to recoil, to be surprised into a new appreciation of microbial life. Recognizing the kinship of this maneuver with the sorts of science fictional devices I mentioned above, Dietert explains his symbolic use of germfree organisms through the lens of speculative fiction:

> A wealth of studies in rodents and other animals shows us what happens when the microbiome is degraded, damaged, or even lost. The storyline strikes me as a little similar to the classic Frank Capra movie *It's a Wonderful Life*. We have the information to look ahead and see what the future brings for living with a damaged microbiome. It is not pretty. It is not something we would want for ourselves or our children. (44)

Germfree animals, then, are our future. In them we are meant to glimpse the culmination of antibiotic fantasy, and to find it so appalling that we are provoked to

---

14 The review, which goes uncited, is likely Gordon/Pesti (1971).

reject such fantasy. With this digression, Dietert asks his readers to take on the role of George Bailey, the protagonist of *It's a Wonderful Life* (1946) who wishes he'd never been born. The film narrates Bailey's glimpsing of a world without him—that is, a world in which impulsive dreams of absence are actualized. Merely a glimpse is enough to affirm for Bailey the necessity of reintegrating with his social and familial context. The same is meant to be true for readers of Dietert's book: merely a glimpse of the post-microbial future, as embodied in germfree mice, should affirm the necessity of reintegrating with one's micro-ecological context. An apocalyptic vision of the future thus comes to prevent that vision coming true.

The Germs That Bind

Nowhere is the imminent futurity of gnotobiosis more evident than in the case of David Vetter, whose bubble-bound form is continually recruited by microbiome writers to define the costs of life without germs. Where gnotobiotic animals generally illustrate physiological effects, however, David's humanity enables an argument for the social consequences of germfree life. Paxson and Helmreich write that as model ecosystems, microbial communities are "made to signify larger biological worlds and socialities, wider perils and promises, in worlds imagined yet to come" (Paxson/Helmreich 2014: 171). David's story is only nominally about a celebrity of the past. As told by microbiome writers, it also entails a model-ecosystem claim in which David signifies the promises and, especially, the perils of imagined worlds without germs. As with the germfree mice discussed above, his story is retold as a deterrent: the recitation of his struggles is intended to guide readers to step out of their own bubbles and into a life interconnected with human and microbial bodies.

In microbiome writing, David's enclosure in the bubble is generally suggested to have been motivated by irrational germophobia more than any therapeutic agenda. He becomes the product of the persistent dream of life beyond germs first realized in gnotobiology. In *The Psychobiotic Revolution*, Anderson and his coauthors claim that penicillin launched dreams of "superkids" raised in "a sparkling biological utopia" (Anderson et al. 2017: 32–33)—and David seemed to materialize those dreams. They write that "in 1971 the ultimate germ-free animal was created: a human."[15] As *ultimate* germfree animal, David here becomes the culmination—the dream come true—of both antibiotics and gnotobiology. It is a claim echoed by Dunn in *The Wild Life of Our Bodies*, writing that David's life and eventual death

---

15 Kirk details the early history of gnotobiological therapeutics, writing that these precedents "helped determine David's role as an object of scientific interest, comparable, if not directly akin, to the laboratory animal" (2012a: 269).

resulted from the belief that "we might achieve some germ-free utopia for ourselves" (Dunn 2011: 76).[16]

Framed as the achievement of germfree utopia, David is transformed into gnotobiotic specimen. His SCID diagnosis recedes; his dramatically improved lifespan is forgotten. Instead, he is made to exemplify the catastrophically missing contemporary microbiome. In reality, he was not germfree, possessing a limited microflora due to leaks and contaminations (Williamson 1977). Microbiome writers consistently disregard that fact. Anderson and his colleagues insist that this "ultimate germ-free animal" was "freed from germs" (Anderson et al. 2017: 34). That point is echoed by Dietert, who asserts that he had "no immune system and no microbiome to co-mature with him and to enable him to function biologically in the environment of the world" (Dietert 2016: 73–74)—a phrasing that strongly implies that it was gnotobiosis, rather than SCID, from which David suffered.

In the context of microbiome writing's preoccupation with gnotobiology, readers are encouraged to consider David's putative germfreeness with the deformity and physiological suffering so consistently attributed to germfree animals. No longer an engineering triumph, no longer a safe space, the bubble comes to signify a violation of the natural order. Crucially, though, David's own story complicates this narrative: microbiome writers must confront the inconvenient fact of his physiological normalcy. Physically healthy, typically developing, charismatic and curious even under the circumstances of his confinement, David fails to exhibit the deficiencies so insistently associated with germfree life in microbiome writing.

In *10% Human*, Collen reconciles this contradiction by allowing David to have been less-than-fully germfree. She explains his microflora as the result of medical failure: "[D]espite their best efforts to keep David germ-free, from birth onward his gut had been colonised by more and more species of bacteria" (Collen 2015: 127). Collen suggests those bacteria to have been his salvation; had the bubble been executed as intended, the results would have been disastrous. The hypothetical here becomes an occasion to invoke the speculative-deterrent mode of germfree life once more:

> Had David been truly germ-free, the coroner at his autopsy might have discovered that David's digestive system was drastically out of proportion. The first tennis-ball-like section of the large intestine—the caecum—to which the appendix is attached, might have been more like a football than a tennis ball. The folded surface of the small intestine would probably have had a much smaller surface area than normal, and fewer blood vessels supplying it. As it was, David's digestive system was as normal as any other child's. (128)

---

16 Weinstein (2010: 17–27) describes gnotobiology's perennial invitation of utopian dreaming.

Might have been, but was not: Collen composes an alternative history in which David's body, enclosed in a perfected germfree isolator, bears identity with the anomalies of germfree mice. Her enumeration of digestive aberrancies that might have been is reinforced by her description and graphic illustration of the 'horrifyingly' enlarged mouse cecum, as noted above. Gnotobiotic disaster has been forestalled by the lifesaving presence of a few accidental microbes. It is a maneuver meant to correct the course of germfree dreaming, not only for David but also for the reader.

Other microbiome writers resolve the apparent contradiction of healthy germfreeness by rewriting his biography into a story of unrelenting anguish that is not physical but rather social, emotional, and societal. In this they align with the robust cultural censure of isolator life and bubble boys that has emerged since David's death. Movies, songs, and literature have for decades portrayed bubble boys as both miraculous and victimized, heroically surviving in the face of profound, if intangible costs. More generally, the phrase "living in a bubble" has come to signify a perspective that is sheltered or shortsighted, divorced from intellectual context.[17] Microbiome writers harness these diverse meanings, transmuting them into a condemnation of antibiosis. The bubble is not the problem; the missing microbiome is the problem. Taking David to be the embodiment of the epidemic of absence, these authors rewrite his legacy, together crafting a consistent narrative of profound social suffering.

In these accounts, David is simply "bubble boy," sometimes anonymous beyond this familiar nickname, and always defined by deprivation. Collen narrates a life of total social isolation:

> David was born in 1971 by Caesarean section into a sterile plastic bubble. He was handled through plastic gloves and fed sterilised infant formula. He never knew the scent of his mother's skin, or the touch of his father's hand. He never played with another child without plastic sheeting preventing the sharing of toys and laughter. (127)

Collen narrates his life almost exclusively in the negative, through a list of things never known and sensations never felt. Gone is the celebratory tone with which the media documented David's story while he lived; here and elsewhere, microbiome writers emphasize only lack.

And from that lack follows an encompassing desolation. In *The Psychobiotic Revolution*, Anderson and his colleagues emphasize the boy's psychological distress:

---

17 Elman (2014) has extensively charted the cultural memory of Vetter's life. For the political resonances of "living in a bubble," see Safire (1993).

David didn't take long to realize that he was doomed to be cut off from the world, and he started questioning his life. He was depressed, but whether that was from being germ free or just because he lived in a plastic bubble with no physical human contact is debatable. (Anderson et al. 2017: 34)

Again, David is defined exclusively by isolation and lack. His depression is suggested to be due either to his germfree state or to his isolation; it is therefore remediable only by integration with the human and germy world, an integration incompatible with his own survival.

Figure 5.2: David Vetter with his parents, sister, and family dog. Photograph archived in the David Vetter Collection (1971–1986): Box 9 (David Vetter and Family, 1976–1983). Courtesy of Archives Center, National Museum of American History, Smithsonian Institution, Washington, DC.

In Dunn's *The Wild Life of Our Bodies*, social isolation appears to be the indirect cause of death. Omitting the contributions of David's very involved parents and sister (fig. 5.2), Dunn writes that "inside his chamber, he was raised by doctors until the age of twelve" (Dunn 2011: 76).

Like some Mowgli raised by wolves, this David exists entirely beyond the human realm, a separation that he attempts to transcend with grave consequences. Dunn continues, "at twelve, he wanted out. At twelve, something needed to change and so he was given a bone marrow transplant in an attempt to restore his immune system" (76).[18] That this transplant ultimately ended his life consolidates David's status as a sufferer of the fatal pathology of isolation. To live with people is to live with germs; their lack is unsustainable on any level.

In retelling David's story, these authors highlight the denial of desires universal to human experience—for a parent's touch, for friendly interaction, for shared laughter and a bit of teenage rebellion—and so forge an argument for the *social* suffering of the germfree state. Microbiome writers generally describe the toll of dysbiosis for ordinary people in similar terms, suggesting that the resulting illnesses resulting from a too-clean environment force sufferers into conditions of social withdrawal. In *Good Germs, Bad Germs*, Sachs details the plights of two young boys whose severe food allergies force them to withdraw from friends, classmates, and even family (Sachs 2007: 7, 73). In *An Epidemic of Absence*, Velasquez-Manoff describes "asthmatic teenagers wondering if they'll be able to join friends in a game of baseball" (Velasquez-Manoff 2012: 6). David's case shows this social cost at its most extreme. Once more, germfree life is invoked as a deterrent to the dream of life beyond germs.

In microbiome writing, however, David symbolizes more than merely individual isolation. His germfreeness also forebodes a societal breakdown felt well beyond his bubble. In *The Human Superorganism*, Dietert pivots from David to expansive claims about the consequences of microbial depletion at the societal level, depicting a dramatic rise in "microbially incomplete" babies—an entire "incomplete generation" (Dietert 2016: 73). Dietert takes David's bubble to be an outward indicator of his own "microbial incompleteness," a state that kept him "removed from the world's normal environment and segregated into a completely artificial environment" (74). Dietert, in other words, identifies David's segregation as the fate awaiting the incomplete generation. He observes that the skyrocketing rate of dysbiotic illness means that "increasing numbers of us may have severely restricted environments in which we can safely function" and "restrict[ed] access to the full environment normally enjoyed by others" (74). The result is a widespread "social fracturing," detectable in a breakdown of social cohesion (76). With food allergies, for instance, familiar social rituals come unglued:

> Individuals may [...] have to withdraw from what used to be routine social gatherings and interactions with friends, family, and business colleagues [...] Holiday dinner celebrations, wedding receptions, community dinners, summer picnics, conference meals, and even single-family meals are increasingly affected. (76)

---

18 Dunn's implication of adolescent rebellion is consistent with representations of David's life as a coming-of-age tale, especially in film adaptations (Elman 2014).

Dietert calls these deprivations a "new cost in human capital, our capacity to congregate around a meal, and a type of freedom humans used to have" (77).

David thus portends the looming societal disasters produced by the pursuit of life beyond germs. Echoing his description of Vetter as "segregated" into his bubble, Dietert suggests that the social withdrawal necessitated by dysbiotic illness threatens to solidify into full-fledged institutionalized injustice. He predicts a recapitulation of the "physical segregation of people in the course of human history" due to factors such as "race, religion, lifestyle [...] politics, and wealth" (77). Invoking leper colonies and the Indian caste system, Dietert here articulates the most sweeping extrapolation possible from David's isolator, looking to a future fractured by "an ever-increasing divide among humans" (78).

In microbiome writing, then, David represents both the individual and the social costs of antibiosis. Further, his life comes to represent a germfree catastrophe threatening all of society, in which people are held apart from one another as from the germs that bind—from the germs that constitute the very fabric of functional society.

David's story comes to represent how much we stand to lose should we fail to stop dreaming of a world without microbes. He thus becomes, for Anderson and his colleagues, the "ultimate germ-free animal" in a second sense: the last and final germ-free animal, such that there will be no more bubble boys. The authors write of his death:

> The public was taken aback by this human experiment that had gone so wrong, and at a stroke, it seemed, we awoke from the dream of a germ-free world. David, freed from germs, was not a superkid. The microbes, it seemed, had won a reprieve. (Anderson et al. 2017: 34)

A sudden, unified awakening: this is the impact of witnessing David's life and death, in a phrasing that encapsulates the use of germfree life in microbiome writing more broadly. David and his various miseries, like the deformities attributed to germfree mice, are suggested to carry with them the power to rouse an entire society (or at least, a diligent reader) from a decades-long dream of life beyond germs. Fantasy is countered with a speculative glimpse of our own future and, at a stroke, we awake.

Conclusion

The specter of germfree life haunts our dreams of the future. As this chapter has shown, in microbiome writing the miseries of microbeless bodies—whether animal or human—reflect onto the present. Authors identify the deformities of the germfree mouse, or the social ruptures of David the Bubble Boy, as the terminus of a trajectory already in progress. Glimpsing our own germfree futures, microbiome writing suggests, we are compelled to intervene.

In this context, it is unsurprising that microbiome writers unanimously suggest ways of emerging from the bubbles of our modern, sanitized existence. They champion responsible means of rewilding bodies devastated by antibiotics, whether through consumption of fermented foods, through "natural" ways of birthing and feeding babies, or through the dictum to *get your hands dirty*. As we have seen, not only human bodies but the very functioning of society and community are at stake. In the post-microbiome vision of the future, we step out of our bubbles, awaken from the dream, and build for ourselves better, and germier, lives.

References

Anderson, Scott C./Cryan, John F./Dinan, Ted (2017): *The Psychobiotic Revolution: Mood, Food, and the New Science of the Gut-Brain Connection*. Washington, DC: National Geographic.
Ankeny, Rachel/Leonelli, Sabina (2011): "What's So Special about Model Organisms?" In: *Studies in History and Philosophy of Science Part A* 42, 313–323.
Blaser, Martin J. (2014): *Missing Microbes: How the Overuse of Antibiotics Is Fueling Our Modern Plagues*. New York: Henry Holt.
Bud, Robert (2007): *Penicillin: Triumph and Tragedy*. Oxford: Oxford University Press.
Carter, Philip B./Foster, Henry L. (2006): "Gnotobiotics." In: Mark A. Suckow/Steven H. Weisbroth/Craig L. Franklin (eds.): *The Laboratory Rat*. 2nd ed. Amsterdam: Elsevier Academic Press, 693–710.
Collen, Alanna (2015): *10% Human: How Your Body's Microbes Hold the Key to Health and Happiness*. New York: Harper Collins.
Crichton, Michael (1969): *The Andromeda Strain*. New York: Knopf.
David Vetter Collection (1971–1986). Collection NMAH.AC.1133. Archives Center, National Museum of American History, Smithsonian Institution, Washington, DC.
Davies, Gail (2013): "Mobilizing Experimental Life: Spaces of Becoming with Mutant Mice." In: *Theory, Culture and Society* 30, 129–153.
Dietert, Rodney (2016): *The Human Superorganism: How the Microbiome Is Revolutionizing the Pursuit of a Healthy Life*. New York: Dutton.
Dunn, Rob (2011): *The Wild Life of Our Bodies: Predators, Parasites, and Partners That Shape Who We Are Today*. New York: Harper Collins.

Elman, Julie Passanante (2014): *Chronic Youth: Disability, Sexuality, and U.S. Media Cultures of Rehabilitation*. New York: New York University Press.

"First Grader in a Bubble" (1979). In: *Buddy's Weekly Reader*, January 1979, 2. Archived at: David Vetter Collection (1971–1986). Collection NMAH.AC.1133. Box 4. Archives Center, National Museum of American History, Smithsonian Institution, Washington, DC.

Falk, Per G./Hooper, Lora V./Midtvedt, Tore/Gordon, Jeffrey I. (1998): "Creating and Maintaining the Gastrointestinal Ecosystem: What We Know and Need to Know from Gnotobiology." In: *Microbiology and Molecular Biology Reviews* 62, 1157–1170.

Gordon, Helmut A./Pesti, Laszlo (1971): "The Gnotobiotic Animal as a Tool in the Study of Host Microbial Relationships." In: *Bacteriological Reviews* 35, 390–429.

Herrell, Wallace E. (1973): "Thoughts on the Role of Gnotobiotics in Clinical Medicine." In: James Heneghan (ed.): *Germfree Research: Biological Effect of Gnotobiotic Environments*. New York: Academic Press, 9–17.

Hoy, Suellen (1996): *Chasing Dirt: The American Pursuit of Cleanliness*. Oxford: Oxford University Press.

Kirk, Robert G. W. (2012a): "'Life in a Germ-Free World': Isolating Life from the Laboratory Animal to the Bubble Boy." In: *Bulletin of the History of Medicine* 86, 237–275.

Kirk, Robert G. W. (2012b): "Standardization and Mechanization: Germ-Free Life and the Engineering of the Ideal Laboratory Animal." In: *Technology and Culture* 53, 61–93.

Knight, Rob (2014): "How Our Microbes Make Us Who We Are." In: TED, February (https://www.ted.com/talks/rob_knight_how_our_microbes_make_us_who_we_are?).

Landecker, Hannah. (2016): "Antibiotic Resistance and the Biology of History." In: *Body and Society* 22, 19–52.

Luckey, Thomas D. (1963): *Germfree Life and Gnotobiology*. New York: Academic Press.

Metchnikoff, Olga (1901): "Note sur l'influence des microbes dans le développement des têtards." In: *Annales de l'Institut Pasteur* 15, 631–634.

Nerlich, Brigitte (2009): "'The Post-Antibiotic Apocalypse' and the 'War on Superbugs': Catastrophe Discourse in Microbiology, Its Rhetorical Form and Political Function." In: *Public Understanding of Science* 18, 574–590.

Nuttall, George H. F./Thierfelder, H. (1895): "Thierisches Leben ohne Bakterien im Verdauungskanal." In: *Zeitschrift für Physiologische Chemie* 21, 109–121.

O'Malley, Maureen A./Skillings, Derek J. (2018): "Methodological Strategies in Microbiome Research and Their Explanatory Implications." In: *Perspectives on Science* 26, 239–265.

Pasteur, Louis (1885): "Observations relatives à la note précédente de M. Duclaux." In: *Comptes rendus hebdomadaires des séances de l'Académie des Sciences* 100, 68.

Paxson, Heather/Helmreich, Stefan (2014): "The Perils and Promises of Microbial Abundance: Novel Natures and Model Ecosystems, from Artisanal Cheese to Alien Seas." In: *Social Studies of Science* 44, 165–193.

Podolsky, Scott H. (2015): *The Antibiotic Era: Reform, Resistance, and the Pursuit of a Rational Therapeutics*. Baltimore: Johns Hopkins University Press.

Rader, Karen (2004): *Making Mice: Standardizing Animals for American Biomedical Research, 1900–1955*. Princeton, NJ: Princeton University Press.

Rahn, Otto (1945): *Microbes of Merit*. Lancaster, PA: Jacques Cattell Press.

Rosebury, Theodor (1969): *Life on Man*. New York: Viking Press.

Sachs, Jessica Snyder (2007): *Good Germs, Bad Germs: Health and Survival in a Bacterial World*. New York: Hill and Wang.

Safire, William (1993): "On Language: The Man in the Big White Jail." In: *The New York Times Magazine*, January 24 (https://www.nytimes.com/1993/01/24/magazine/on-language-the-man-in-the-big-white-jail.html).

Schottelius, Max (1899): "Die Bedeutung der Darmbacterien für die Ernährung." In: *Archiv für Hygiene und Bakteriologie* 34, 210–243.

Tomes, Nancy (1998): *The Gospel of Germs: Men, Women, and the Microbe in American Life*. Cambridge, MA: Harvard University Press.

Turney, Jon. (2015): *I, Superorganism: Learning to Love Your Inner Ecosystem*. London: Icon Books.

Velasquez-Manoff, Moises (2012): *An Epidemic of Absence: A New Way of Understanding Allergies and Autoimmune Diseases*. New York: Scribner.

Weinstein, Matthew (2010): *Bodies Out of Control: Rethinking Science Texts*. New York: Peter Lang.

Williamson, Alice P. (ed.) (1977): "A Special Report: Four-Year Study of a Boy with Combined Immune Deficiency Maintained in Strict Reverse Isolation from Birth." In: *Pediatric Research* 11(1), 63–64.

Yong, Ed (2016): *I Contain Multitudes: The Microbes within Us and a Grander View of Life*. New York: Harper Collins.

Chapter 6: Spores of Speculation
Negotiating Mold as Contamination

Christoph Schemann

This essay reflects on some of the often worrying worldings[1] of well-known fungal companions called "mold."[2] It highlights the speculative character of mold-related negotiations and practices that originate from encounters in different contexts and settings. More specifically, it argues that we can usefully distinguish between a "firmative" and an "affirmative" mode of speculation, as proposed by the uncertain commons (2013) collective. Efforts that are determined to proceed by encoding and fixing mold as a signifier of contamination for human health and the inhabited built environment are framed here as firmative speculation. While mold can undoubtedly be harmful to humans (and to other organic materials especially when becoming its substrates), such attempts are nevertheless rife with obstacles and uncertainties. They are speculative, insofar as the individual susceptibility to mold is highly variable—depending on the conditions of one's own immune system, for example, acute or chronic immunodeficiencies and allergic dispositions—and the principle of cause and effect is hardly linear or generalizable when it comes to providing a clear-cut diagnosis once symptoms occur. Furthermore, considering the extent and duration of exposition, the complex of problems needs to be related not only to the human body but also to the fungi, taking into account the quantity and quality of the diverse sorts of mold and their biomaterial characteristics, substrates, metabolisms, and varying forms of spatialization. Thus, other convergences with mold that open up rather contingent ways of negotiation and cohabitation can instead be understood as actualizing an affirmative mode of speculation. Attending to such affirmative engagements also signals possibilities

---

1 Drawing upon the work of Donna Haraway (2008), the notion of "worlding" or "becoming with" (301) "insists on the coconstitution, the material-semiotic interplay, that shapes what is" (van Dooren/Kirksey/Münster 2016: 12).
2 While I use the semantics of "mold" and "fungus" interchangeably here, they do not necessarily denominate the same objects. Their respective meanings—along with those of related terms, such as "mildew"—have been shaped in different contexts, e.g. biology, medicine, vernacular language, metaphoric usage, and so forth (cf. Bates 2015: 49–50).

of shifting from speculations *about* mold toward ways of speculating *with* mold as contamination.

In proposing this shift, this essay connects to what Donna Haraway has termed the "Chthulucene." Challenging the anthropocentric perspective aimed at controlling far-reaching socio-ecological entanglements between humans and nonhumans in what has become known as the Anthropocene, the Chthulucene is instead about ways of "staying with the trouble" and "making kin" with such potentially risky creatures as mold (Haraway 2015, 2016). In exploring different ways of speculating, I also draw on Karen Barad's elaborations on "agential realism." Barad's entwined onto-epistemological concepts of the "apparatus"[3] and "intra-action"[4] will be deployed here as an analytical framework to avoid essentializing the living entities commonly assembled under the term "mold" and to highlight the performative (and necessarily selective) character of knowledge production around mold and contamination within the cases discussed. As Barad puts it: "Intra-actions always entail particular exclusions, and exclusions foreclose any possibility of determinism, providing the condition of an open future" (Barad 2003: 826). Hence, apparatuses are themselves materializing practices that perform "particular ways of drawing boundaries between 'humans' and 'nonhumans'" (Barad 2012: 31)—so-called "agential cuts" that produce knowledge around what mold can be and do within specific settings.

In what follows, I examine the performativity of mold in relation to four apparatuses for "cutting together-apart the mould" (Bates 2015). My analysis draws on ethnographic research conducted between winter 2016 and fall 2017 in a variety of sites.[5] The first two apparatuses, the "distributed sporesmeter" and the "(human) ventilator," bring into relief firmative modes of speculation connected to

---

3 Barad presents her outline of an apparatus in the fourth chapter of *Meeting the Universe Halfway* (2007: 132–185). Importantly, an apparatus does not necessarily denote a given sociotechnical device in the classical sense but can refer to any material-semiotic assemblage through which knowledge regarding certain phenomena can be perceived. Furthermore, apparatuses do not exist in themselves but only through intra-active practices that perform them.

4 Barad coins the term "*intra-action* (in contrast to the usual "interaction," which presumes the prior existence of independent entities/relata)" to highlight that the entities isolated by an apparatus that examines them do not exist as individual elements independently from this apparatus (2003: 815; cf. Barad 2007).

5 All research has been done by the author. Based on an ethnographic multi-sited research design, the data collected draws on field notes from participatory observations, review of specialized literature, ethnographic photography, conversations with experts in the fields of microbiology, mycology, sanitation, the building sector, and pest control, interviews with activists engaged in urban exploration and food saving, and discussions with concerned laypeople who shared their own personal experiences with me. In addition, the research also involved an experiment with a rapid testing device for analyzing the moldy load of indoor air, which will be described in detail in the section on the "sporesmeter."

mold in common housing spaces. The last two apparatuses, labelled as "ruin-archive" and "waste container," help to spotlight affirmative modes of speculation by drawing on the example of a decaying industrial ruin and the linkage of mold to both edibles and waste. In addition, these two latter cases of speculation emanate not from already prescribed regulative material-semiotic practices but from much less enclosed performances related to urban exploration and potentialities of affect, disclosing much more unanticipated apparatuses in turn. Finally, differentiating between a firmative mode and a more dynamic, affirmative mode of speculation will allow for modifying the prevalent understanding of contamination as threat, indicating a more contingent translation of contamination as collaborative encounters with diversity (Tsing 2015). This, I suggest, can further our understanding of human entanglements with mold and contribute to cultivating a more attentive and immersive notion of multispecies conjunctions (van Dooren/Kirksey/Münster 2016).

Part One: Speculating *about* Mold

The Distributed Sporesmeter: Making Spores Visible

Mold in buildings is a key area of mold-related interventions. Such interventions involve a range of actors, including technical experts and their various instruments, apart from the visible and invisible components of mold itself. Thereby, apparatuses of visualization for scientifically reducing uncertainties and the fuzziness of risk are key to such efforts.[6] Attempts to fix the problem of uncertainty, which constantly challenges the field of expertise, can here be viewed as bounding practices of speculation that deploy technologies within a rigorously outcome-oriented mode that predominantly anticipates mold as contamination. All sorts of mold, along with their spores and material entanglements, are expected here to fit within technological frameworks meant to discipline them. Interventions in relation to mold in houses are enacted not only by professionals that often command the most up-to-date technical equipment but also by concerned laypeople.

The distributed apparatus I would like to discuss here is what I call the "sporesmeter." A sporesmeter is a biotechnological device designed to diagnose the degree of contamination in the ambient air of closed rooms. Its main component, the "Sporometer," is simply a kind of Petri dish or contact plate coated with agar

---

6 Questions of visualization have been discussed extensively in science and technology studies and other disciplines; for context, see, Burri/Dumit (2008); Rheinberger (2009); and Heßler/Mersch (2009).

as typically used in biological and medical sectors (fig. 6.1).[7] It features a seemingly professional instructional manual containing descriptions for correct handling and can be purchased on the internet or in larger hardware and home-supply stores. The whole testing kit includes: a neatly vacuum-packed Sporometer with a contact plate that is pre-coated with an undefined agar; a brochure that informs the purchaser about fungi, possible health problems, and options for remediation, as well as advertising the manufacturing company; and an operating manual that provides further information about the testing procedure. The manual also includes an exemplification, a chart with specific values to denote the factor of contamination, and a protocol form for recording the findings as handwritten notes (fig. 6.2). An impartial volunteer, a 29-year-old student, carried out the entire test in her apartment with no visible mold in any location and no history of mold-related damage.

To start the experiment, the Sporometer was placed on a table in the living room of the flat, leaving the lid of the Petri dish open for thirty minutes, as stipulated by the operating manual. The little plastic box was then closed and sealed and put in a shaded place, leaving the agar and its potential new but yet invisible inhabitants to their own resources. Interestingly, after the recommended five days of incubation, the Petri dish transformed into a plastic greenhouse accommodating colorful bouquets of diverse mold cultures (fig. 6.1). The next step scheduled in the operating manual was to count out the visibly evolved spores that had taken residence and to make them readable in the protocol (fig. 6.2, third section from top). Apart from gathering information about the surveyed location as well as the date and the timespan of testing, the protocol offers a picture of the Sporometer segmented into two major quadrants—each further segmented into four minor quadrants—to locate and measure the concrete spots of the colonies, even though they appeared to be hardly separable. In fact, distinguishing them turned out to be the most challenging task in the entire test. Finally, the entities were pinned down to an approximate number of twenty discrete bio-settlers made visible in the Sporometer. In accordance with the chart provided, the degree of contamination in the apartment was classified as category C: "critical pollution" (fig. 6.2, second section from top).[8]

---

7 The manufacturer calls this agar-coated plate a "Sporometer." In modifying this name, I use the term "sporesmeter" to refer to the entire buyable test setup, which includes Petri dish, instruction manual, protocol, and so on.

8 The contamination levels in the chart are: A (<10) = noncritical pollution; B ($10–16$) = increased pollution; and C (>16) = critical pollution.

Chapter 6: Spores of Speculation 149

Figure 6.1: The incubated Sporometer.

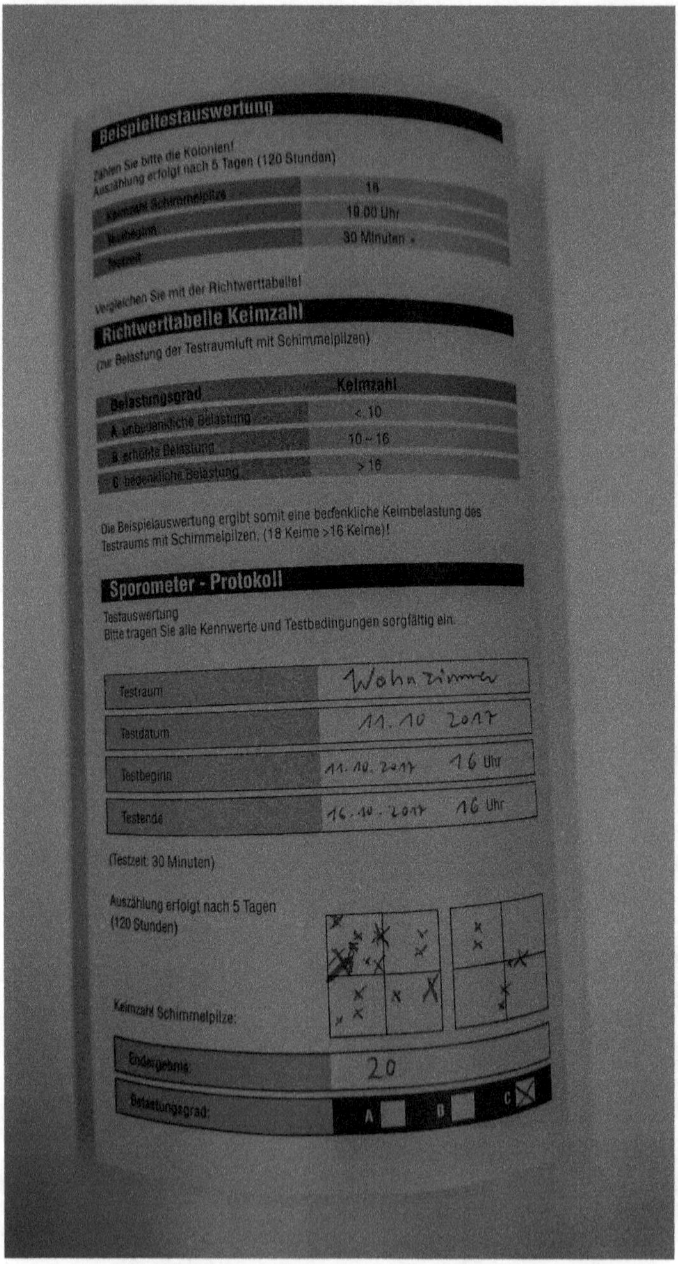

Beispieltestauswertung

Zählen Sie bitte die Kolonien!
Auszählung erfolgt nach 5 Tagen (120 Stunden)

Keimzahl Schimmelpilze	18
Testbeginn	19.00 Uhr
Testzeit	30 Minuten

Vergleichen Sie mit der Richtwerttabelle!

Richtwerttabelle Keimzahl

(zur Belastung der Testraumluft mit Schimmelpilzen)

Belastungsgrad	Keimzahl
A unbedenkliche Belastung	< 10
B erhöhte Belastung	10 – 16
C bedenkliche Belastung	> 16

Die Beispielauswertung ergibt somit eine bedenkliche Keimbelastung des Testraums mit Schimmelpilzen. (18 Keime >16 Keime)!

Sporometer - Protokoll

Testauswertung
Bitte tragen Sie alle Kennwerte und Testbedingungen sorgfältig ein.

Testraum	Wohnzimmer
Testdatum	11.10.2017
Testbeginn	11.10.2017 16 Uhr
Testende	16.10.2017 16 Uhr

(Testzeit: 30 Minuten)

Auszählung erfolgt nach 5 Tagen (120 Stunden)

Keimzahl Schimmelpilze:

Endergebnis:	20
Belastungsgrad:	A ☐ B ☐ C ☒

Figure 6.2: The completed protocol form.

Despite the fact that, strictly speaking, there was no mold visible or perceivable by any other senses in the apartment, the student volunteer's feeling of being at ease with her living situation—which had been considered healthy prior to these findings—subsequently eroded. The mere presence of the incubated Sporometer exposing such an amount of unexpected beings in her flat had discomforted her during the preceding days, when she had to watch the mold colonies slowly grow up from day to day underneath her table. Moreover, having heard about the potential threat of respiratory problems connected to the molding of potting soil, she started to be concerned about the potted plants and flowers decorating her flat. However, besides searching for a reasonable cause of the contamination within the realm of her own responsibility, she nevertheless started to question the alarming outcome of the procedure.

She was not the only one to express doubts. In the course of research, I met a microbiologist who runs an accredited and renowned environmental health institute that provides mold- and dampness-related damage assessments (among other services, such as drinking water analysis and hospital hygiene consultation). According to this specialist, there are quite a few obstacles to conducting such a do-it-yourself test with scientific rigor. Indeed, a failure of scientific standards is almost inevitable, as there are just too many misleading factors and potential sources of disruption that cannot be controlled by this lay practice. How constant was the temperature during the five days of incubation? Was there a window open or any other ventilation going on in the room during collection of the spores? What is the domestic architecture, and how does the arrangement of the room's interior—including the array of all possibly relevant objects and materials such as plants and flowers, furniture, radiators, etc.—influence the test? Has the box been placed in a spot protected from sunlight? What exact kind of agar has the Petri dish been coated with? Despite the fact that the manual of the sporesmeter informs the user about avoiding some of these obstacles, they are nevertheless hard to control completely—at any time. Seen from the perspective of scientific expertise, the distribution of such an apparatus does not make much sense, as its very application will multiply rather than reduce uncertainties regarding degrees of contamination.

Tellingly, the device also includes an advertising leaflet for mold-decontamination products as well as a printed form for submitting an analysis order (for an additional fee). The order form instructs the user to send the protocol with the recorded results and the mold-charged Sporometer to an assigned microbiological contractor to verify the findings and clarify the magnitude of threat.[9] The

---

9 Even if the results are sent in to a laboratory, they cannot be taken as fully correct and exact under scientific premises, as any ex post facto evaluation would be incapable of reconstructing the actual testing situation that occurred in the user's place.

spore-catching and visualizing apparatus of this measuring instrument, with all its complementary components and processes, can therefore best be understood as what Muniesa, Millo, and Callon call a "market device": "the material and discursive assemblages that intervene in the construction of markets" (Muniesa/Millo/Callon 2007: 2). Here, the necessary intervention to be made is to trap spores, turn them into distinct visible mold and translate the now (ac)countable colonies into an official form, making the results immutable and mobile so that they can easily be negotiated as supposedly reliable facts.[10] Thus, the acts of selling and buying the gadget, on the one hand, and the fee-based follow-up requirements of sending in and defining what is at stake, on the other, represent the economic surplus of a market construction that relies on the ability "to stabilize a particular state of power relations by associating the largest number of irreversibly linked elements" (Callon/Latour 1981: 293). In this case, the major linkage at stake that needs to be stabilized consists of all the elements that get folded into the sporesmeter (test kit, spores of mold, temperature, moisture, humans, and so on), pushing speculation into the one-way street of always anticipating—and therefore calculating, imagining, and performing (Anderson 2010: 787)—contamination as economic payoff.

The (Human) Ventilator: Keeping Spores in Circulation

Frequently, the inhabitants of buildings are warned to avoid mold straight from the outset. In particular, what is often stated as having gone wrong when there are visible occurrences of residential fungi—not least by landlords—is the maintaining of sufficient circulation of air, which prevents spores from settling down in too large numbers. Despite the practical limitations of keeping air in circulation in every part of a building, despite the existence of other factors for mold to grow, and despite the fact that mold does not necessarily impair human health, having mold in one's residence is therefore often connected to feelings of guilt. As one person I interviewed ("Lynn") aptly elaborated,

> Mold can always be taken as a sign, indicating that something goes wrong, that something happens, which normally shouldn't. [...] It's just like some people have a bad conscience when mold occurs in their homes, when they get the feeling that because something like this happens they might be living in the wrong way. For example, that they are not airing their apartment enough or something like that. [...] And mold always shows that things are somehow out of control, that these norms

---

10 Here I draw on the concept of translation as developed in actor-network theory (e.g. Callon 1984) to highlight the sociotechnical process of (re)formatting the inscription of mold/contamination as "material semiotics" (cf. Law 2008) and on Latour's notion of "immutable mobiles" (e.g. Latour 1987: 227; cf. Law/Mol 2001).

of conduct are not applicable or at least that one can't meet these obligations properly. I think this is felt as a personal failure rather quickly, because actually you know what to do so that something like this doesn't happen.[11]

Just like in the experiment concerning the sporesmeter—where the person carrying out the test suspected that the potting soil might be the problem and that she simply possesses too many plants—discomfort and a sense of personal failure can be felt. In both cases, what brings mold into appearance is an accumulation of risk factors that are related to blocking the flow of spores. The inscription of responsibility and guilt into people's practices of circulation can thus be viewed as a key driver for the apparatus I call the "ventilator."

To keep spores from accumulating, settling down and spawning up to potentially harmful levels due to ventilation signals a shift in mold apparatuses away from measuring a concrete process of contamination toward a mode of preemption aiming at the virtual (cf. Massumi 2009). In contrast to the prevention of a concretely contoured thread in the making, preemption "is a mode of power that takes threat, which has no actual referent, as its object" (Massumi 2010: 59). In this case, the practice of 'airing' is not dependent on anticipating calculable contamination because it is framed around diligent behaviors steadily integrated into normal, uncontaminated daily life. Diligence, in turn, gets empowered through principles of guidance and regulation, as Foucault ([2004] 2007, [2004] 2008) has analyzed in his works on (neo)liberal political economy. This governmental power-mechanism is key to an understanding of the ventilator as a decidedly 'conductive' apparatus on behalf of a biopolitical precautionary principle regarding spatial purity connected to human health. It is also a savagely preemptive apparatus against the nonhuman life cycle of mold. As Ben Anderson has also noted, the logics of preemption, precaution, and preparedness, as soon as they foster societal implementation of normalization and standardization, work even without any occasion of concrete suspicion (Anderson 2010: 787–792). The ventilator apparatus, in other words, seeks to preempt any (bio)material outcomes, and even any breeding of mold, by instigating cautionary actions independently of any specific indication of contamination.[12]

Nevertheless, in preempting the growth of mold by keeping spores in circulation, the ventilator retains mold as a key signifying component—but only its semiotics, not its bio-essential materiality and diversity. This indicates its major dif-

---

11 Translated from German by the author. Besides being concerned with indoor mold, this highly reflective interviewee is also a food-saving activist and will be cited again in the section below on the "waste container" apparatus.

12 Or the behavior-relieving installation of permanent technological solutions with aeration equipment, such as automated ventilation systems.

ference in terms of the material-semiotic outcome in relation to an anticipating apparatus such as the sporesmeter: 'mold' primarily gets passed on discursively as a guilt-laden and shame-ridden sign, indicating a socially ostracized and personally felt loss of control. In turn, to preempt such an unpleasant situation of contamination where feelings of guilt and shame affect the assigned human polluter, mold becomes a semiotic element that does not necessarily need a projected material correlate anymore as mold is exactly the materiality that is to be avoided. Firmative speculation functions here by stabilizing mold as contamination detached from any actual threat or risk to health. Even though firmatively minimized to the highest possible extent, the process is still—or even more—speculative in general, precisely because there is no factual evidence or even any predictable consequence regarding what the mobile spores might actually do once they are no longer ventilated. Thus, this preemptive variation of firmative speculation is based on exactly the kind of uncertainty that the anticipating sporesmeter pretends to overcome by intentionally producing and visualizing mold in contrast. However, both differentiations—anticipation and preemption—correspond to a firmative modus of speculation "that seeks to pin down, delimit, constrain, and enclose—to make things definitive, firm" (uncertain commons 2013: ch. 1).

Yet, regarding mold in buildings, there are also deviant and subversive behavioral patterns that withdraw from preemptive conduct by tolerating at least a certain degree of mold in residential spaces. Some people remove spatially quite limited mold spots from time to time with cleaning agents or enclose them with wall paint. Others even choose to strategically "stay with the trouble" (Haraway 2016) of growing mold without any attempts to eradicate it—for instance, in order to enforce an abatement of rent[13]—keeping the fungi more or less as "'domestic' organisms [...] whose species being has changed to a form that survives for human needs" (Tsing 2018: 232). However, the mechanisms that link anticipation to visualization and preemption to ventilation undermine the affirmative speculative potential of these more-than-human microbial apparatuses.[14] Thus, in contrast to these firmative speculative practices that are more interactive than intra-active, arising from largely predefined material and semiotic apparatuses, the following

---

13 This can normally only be the case (sometimes even negotiated before the law) if it can be asserted that the spatialization of mold is due to defects or deficiencies in the construction and not by misconduct on behalf of the tenant(s), and if the landlord does not fix the problem in time. However, as I have been told by experts from the building sector as well as individual renters, not all tenants actually want to get rid of residential mold, just as clarifying cause and effect is not always a fast problem to deal with.

14 The sporesmeter is also rife with possible speculations, both in handling the apparatus and negotiating the outcomes. Likewise, for the yet unsettled spores in circulation, it remains unknown what specific effects a failure of ventilating may actually cause to matter (and meaning) in particular spaces and places.

two negotiations fairly invert this ratio by highlighting more contingent practices of speculation and bringing more unorthodox settings into scope.

Part Two: Speculating *with* Mold

The Ruin-Archive: Exploring Spores out of Time

To negotiate material-semiotic assemblages of mold differently from a firmative orientation requires an openness to uncertain ways of knowing. Akin to Caitlin DeSilvey's idea to follow "the invisible bookworm into the encyclopaedia" (DeSilvey 2006: 322), this can also mean to occasionally follow spores on their metabolic flights through the (sub)urban environment into rather unruly edgelands (Farley/Roberts 2011). Here an industrial ruin was one such destination.

The ruin I entered in the course of research used to be an iron foundry in the northern part of Bavaria, flame-cut by a fire accident and subsequently vacated in 2012. Since fire brigades flooded the remaining building blocks with huge amounts of water and subsequently left the area largely unsheltered, moisture had been able to enter, facilitating a range of biological processes that had been contributing to the ruin's progressive decay. The proliferation of fungi like mold within the entire complex, but especially in its remaining semi-closed rooms, forms part of this larger process. Not only do such places as ruins abandoned by humans provide an asylum for rats, pigeons, insects and other pollutants like mold, they also allow these critters to literally 'take place' and to grow and foster the very sorts of contamination that are typically eliminated by "papering over the mold and cracks" in our buildings and by covering "the world with a chemical armory [...] to escape rot's degenerative force" (Lorimer 2016: 236). In this sense, places left to rot, where the preemptive mechanisms for keeping spores in constant circulation through human and nonhuman ventilators are no longer operative, can also be seen as blended, unpurified spaces of defilement (Sibley 1995: 49–89).

Exploring ruins as assemblages where all kinds of human and nonhuman, living and nonliving materials and actors are no longer kept apart has the potential of giving rise to an affirmative apparatus where time is not necessarily linear and space is rarely Euclidean. As will be shown, the appearance of mold can be an index of the sort of 'topological' spatiality here, which Michel Serres has famously illustrated through the allegory of a handkerchief crumpled in a pocket, which brings points once far apart into an unexpected close contact (Serres 1995: 60–61). This means that a full-grown mold can be seen as a continuous reminder of an initial point of contamination lying in the past while being diffractively able to affect and alter encounters of contamination in the present: instants of time and materiality get refolded in mold–substrate amalgams through the biochemical mode of decomposition that mold spores induce in their manifold substrata.

But it is not only the rotting materials that get transformed over time through decomposition. Their semiotics are also time-shifting, as they retain connections to the ruin's remaining "phantom networks" (Edensor 2005a: 63) where mold and their substrates are spatially embedded in history. As Dylan Trigg notes:

> In the ruin, time runs off, so becoming timeless. The convergence of temporal categories means that linear progress loses its power of persuasion. We are confronted with an ambiguous space. Time has ceased, yet simultaneously attracts the impression of becoming. (Trigg 2006: 185)

It is precisely the persistent tension between an activating impression of becoming, on the one hand, and the overall impression of loss and decay in a seemingly passive state of ceasing progress, on the other, that the unpredictable melding of mold with its various material substrata can bring into relief. Therefore, past points of contamination in time can be encountered in the present, insofar as mold contains the potential to alter time-relations due to affirmative contingent impressions. In the vocabulary of agential realism, the processual experiencing of moldy materialities in ruins can be referred to as "spacetimemattering," denoting "a dynamic ongoing reconfiguring of a field of relationalities among 'moments,' 'places,' and 'things' (in their inseparability)" (Barad 2017: G111). This is the case especially when ruins are engaged in the intra-active practices of "urban exploration" (Garrett 2010, 2014). Entering such spaces where the presence of absence becomes mediated through all kinds of waste material provokes an affirmative mode of speculating with the lost and the found-again. This is because the

> political assumptions and desires which lie behind the ordering of matter in space are thus revealed by the effects of objects in ruins, and they provoke speculation about how space and materiality might be interpreted, experienced and imagined otherwise. (Edensor 2005b: 330)

What speculations with mold can look like then becomes patently apparent in the foundry's decaying archive (figs. 6.3 and 6.4).

The old foundry's management and employment archive in one of the administrative offices is still filled up with files and folders that include staff lists, labor time schedules, conference protocols, accounting sheets, technical instructions and proceedings, guidelines, diaries, and so on. Ecologies of rot and decay have taken over the lead in (dis)ordering the materials over time. Intruding human and nonhuman visitors have moreover been walking through the archive, leaving their tags and marks behind, just as the flames had done before. Peter, one of the

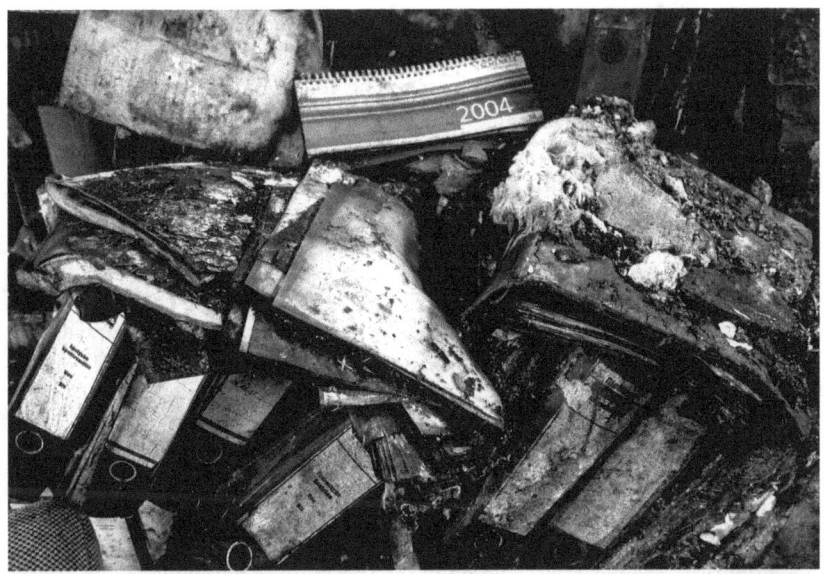

Figures 6.3 and 6.4: Exploring the old foundry's former archive. Photographs by Christoph Schemann.

human visitors I accompanied, an urban explorer who had been drawn to ruins and other lost places for years, highlighted this archive as being exceptional because of its contradictory character: all these documents were once archived to be sustained and preserved for future times and to be retrieved whenever required;

now they are left to rot and be forgotten, with some of the files already almost unreadable and sooner or later possibly completely inaccessible. What has attracted various visits on the part of this explorer and his colleagues is just this paradoxical situation of the archive still being right in place yet falling apart in time. While browsing and flicking through the files, these explorers fantasized what this place might have been like for the workers, what kind of data the firm might have collected, scrutinizing which names can still be read on the schedules and wondering how many employees eventually tried to cheat management with sick notes. As Peter expressed it to me, they have become some kind of "contemporary witness" of a dying place with a gradual loss of memory to be eaten away by natural agents like fungi. Or, as Miles Ogborn reasons, "memory is chemical and biological"—and for spores of "archival fungi," this is nothing but a favorable opportunity to live it up: "These fungi absorb nutrients from the dead or living organic matter on which they grow. For them books are good sources of cellulose and starches, albeit hard to digest" (Ogborn 2004: 240–241).

Affirmative speculations "produce futures while refusing the foreclosure of potentialities," even as they "hold on to the spectrum of possibilities" (uncertain commons 2013: ch. 1). Therefore, ruins and their degrading walls, rooms, artefacts, and material leftovers can be seen as birth-giving substrates for mold and other commonly suppressed organisms that, in entanglement, stimulate commemorative intra-actions that render possible more contingent interpretations and engagements with the surroundings "presented in a speculative spirit" (DeSilvey 2006: 335). Urban explorers can speculatively realize productive possibilities, memories and desires to sense ruins (Edensor 2007; DeSilvey/Edensor 2012: 471–478) that otherwise would have been spoiled and demolished by virtue of administrative politics and economic (re)investments. When it comes to negotiating contamination in all this, it is especially the intertwining of human-nonhuman (de)composition of history and memory that can be speculated-with in an affirmative mode of exploring the material semiotics of the present past in ruins.

The Waste Container: Affecting Spores of (Dis)gusto

In contrast to the already mentioned contaminated fungal substrates, I will now highlight some affirmative speculations regarding mold on edibles.[15] The main argument here is that what links mold to waste lies in the material capability of

---

15 Leaving out edible mold as a delicacy—for example, on certain kinds of cheese—I am solely focusing on mold as unintended contamination at this point. Concerning the microbiopolitics of crafting cheese and its relation to mold where "post-Pasteurians move beyond an antiseptic attitude to embrace mold and bacteria as allies" (Paxson 2008: 18), see the work of Heather Paxson, especially her monograph, *The Life of Cheese* (2013: 46–49, 158–186; cf. Paxson 2014).

mold to bodily affect people, urging them to react in one way or another when encountered. The notion of a "waste container" as an apparatus enacted by practices related to affect has at least two dimensions in this context. First, a container can physically be something like a bin for household garbage, used to get rid of rotten and contaminated foods, which detains spores and prevents smells from circulating. Therefore, the possibility of placing food in a container is what distinguishes mold on edibles from mold on house walls and other spatially fixed materials. Here, attention turns first and foremost to the hedging or enclosure set in process when moldy food is thrown away. Second, as Mary Douglas has shown in her study *Purity and Danger* ([1966] 2002), waste is commonly culturally coded as impure and disorderly. As devices for minimizing contact with such impure matter and dissociating it from the domestic space, the refuse sacks of waste bins can easily be handled and bundled to carry garbage off—putting it out of sight and out of scent—highlighting the semiotic aspects of containment.

Mold that is becoming perceptible on food causes many people to displace the infected comestibles directly into the bin, as it often triggers an affective response of bodily repugnance—if not self-protection against poisoning and disease. Importantly, this response indicates a material-semiotic threshold, as tasty edibles become 'dis-gusting' and transform into something potentially unhealthy—rendered mere waste, accompanied by the foul-smelling odor of lingering decomposition. In consequence, there often does not seem to be much tolerance for the affects that the emergence of food-related mold can trigger. Thus, mold's biomaterial capacity to elicit affective reactions of concern and disgust can be understood as a demarcation or agential cut (Barad 2012), indicating that what used to be food has just exceeded edibility.

Nevertheless, there is a diverse range of ways in which contaminations can be kept at unproblematic levels, for example, isolating the still fresh and tasty pieces from the rotten ones or cutting off molded bits. Even though such forms of customary knowledge among many people might not lead to a more generous approach to mold, they do indicate more affirmative modes of speculating with mold: they call attention to different practical possibilities to (re)negotiate and concretely localize the threshold between edibility and waste, disgust and gusto. The threshold between enjoyable food and repellent waste therefore cannot be seen as a fixed boundary. One possibility here consists of differentiating between diverse material qualities of foods as substrate: edibles with a rather soft texture such as marmalade, meat or certain sorts of fruits and cheese are more likely to be completely binned when contaminated with mold than bread, vegetables or other foods of a harder and more solid consistency. Rational reconsideration, alongside a more relational evaluation, can thus foster a more contingent engagement with mold, while at the same time also altering the affective predisposition for disgust.

Such an altered embodiment of mold intra-actions is particularly pronounced in the case of food-saving activists who, due to their socio-ecological orientations and their interventionist approach to the waste of food, engage in "dumpster diving." Technically legal in the U.S. but illegal in Germany, this practice consists of reopening and climbing down the commercial waste containers of grocery stores, which dispose of large quantities of still edible foods due to strict legal regulations. In diving down these containers, the activists I interviewed speculatively reevaluated (dis)gusto in relation to what has been thrown away, inverting the waste container apparatus by containing their responsivity (and not the rotting food). They therefore maintained the ability to respond differently in speculating with contamination:

> ["Mario"] Well, I don't know the risk, I can't really estimate it. That's why ... it's a very unknown risk. I don't know, I mean you can't ... Well it is hard to relate. Either way, I eat a rotten tomato, or I take a smoke from a cigarette, so to say. I can't compare that. And I do smoke cigarettes from time to time. [...] It's just the same if you go dumpster diving. You take a look in the container and see: There, at the corner, is a molded lemon that is completely green and next to it, there is a perfect eggplant that has been in contact for, I don't know, two or three hours—I nevertheless take out the eggplant and just wash it off.

> ["Lynn"] Sure! The brink of disgust has totally been reduced! Well, three, four years ago, before I started food-saving—that's when the reduction of disgust initially started—then, five years ago, I wouldn't go dumpster diving. I thought it was totally disgusting and I found it completely repulsive.

What can be fleshed out from these passages is that the practice of diving into the sometimes unpleasant interior of containers situates subjects within a state of affairs where the affects of (dis)gusto can be altered and acted upon differently. While the problematizing of an unnecessary binning of food, capitalistic overproduction, sell-by dates and the like may certainly be the key drivers for these engagements, it is the ability to partly resist and resituate the negative affective intensities of moldy waste that allows the activists to renegotiate the degree of biomaterial contamination. In turn, both aspects—material and discursive—taken together could actualize and reframe the potential to critically address broader societal questions ranging from negotiations about consumption and value to sociocultural demands on the freshness of perishable foods (Freidberg 2009). The "affective life" (Hutta 2015) of this multifarious, living semiotic being called food mold—which frequently enters the encountering subject's expressive registers by provoking deprecatory facial expressions or a shift in vocal intonation—is therefore the intra-active nexus that can either constrain the scope of speculating with mold or open it up to the possibility of reassessing its substrates again and again.

Conclusion

This essay began by picking up Donna Haraway's invitation to stay with the sometimes troubling entanglements of humans and nonhumans in favor of "chipping and shredding and layering like a mad gardener, mak[ing] a much hotter compost pile for still possible pasts, presents, and futures" (Haraway 2016: 57). As the likewise colorful and pillowy compost piles of mold are regularly seen as threat to humanly colonized environments, 'contamination' is one of the key categories we can use to describe related negotiations. In turn, such negotiations rely on practices that are speculative inasmuch as they need to produce knowledge about a vital entity that cannot easily be reduced to a set of fixed qualities or a fixed scope of inferences—much less when seen in connection to its numerous metabolites and ingrowing substrates.

While the first two apparatuses have been identified to demonstrate how the practices related to them get firmatively restricted in their speculative potential due to sociotechnical endeavors to anticipate and preempt mold as a material-semiotic signifier for unpleasant contamination, the last two agential practices can aptly be termed speculating *with* instead of *about* mold to draw attention to the fact that entering into active collaboration denotes a necessarily contingent shift in terms of what can (and not must or should) be encountered. Picking up Anna Tsing's notion of "contamination as collaboration," contamination itself can further be categorically expanded, denoting yet-to-be-known speculations that simultaneously reaffirm fungi such as mold (or Matsutake, in Tsing's case) and human subjects (Tsing 2015: 27–34). As for Tsing, "we are contaminated by our encounters" whereas "purity is not an option" (27). Likewise, Donna Haraway points in a similar direction by referring to "sympoiesis" (in contrast to a self-referencing "autopoiesis") as the central attunement to face the Anthropocene/Chthulucene, where "making-with" becomes the crucial condition of living in common (Haraway 2016: 58–98, 2017: M25–M31). Finally, engendering perceptive apparatuses that always cut together and apart such sympoietic contaminations requires an "accountability for the cuts that are made and the constitutive entanglements that are effected" (Barad 2012: 31). Hence, to perform speculations *with* mold in an affirmative manner also means to queer and blur demarcations in negotiating the role of the human and the nonhuman, the predefined and the possible, while remaining attentive toward the alterations made.

To negotiate mold and other cohabitants fraught with risk *in* a state of contamination can therefore be detached from a fixed understanding of contamination as mere threat, irregular and something to be avoided by any means necessary. Instead, it can be understood as creative and productive in a world whose future can only be speculated about but will definitely need further exploration of its awkward[16] multispecies entanglements and constitutive contaminations.

Acknowledgments

I would like to thank Uli Beisel, Christine Hanke and Matthew Hannah for their thoughtful remarks on this essay at different stages. I am particularly grateful to Jan Simon Hutta who accompanied the whole evolution of this text from the moment of drafty spores to the point of substantial bloom and moldy splendor with his passionate reading. An earlier version of this paper was presented at the conference Neue Kulturgeographie XVI at the Catholic University of Eichstätt-Ingolstadt where I received a lot of fruitful comments and shared some speculative conversations on this topic. Furthermore, I have to thank all the activists, experts, and individual participants who shared their experiences, expertise, and concerns with me while continually advancing and enriching the scope of research.

References

Anderson, Ben (2010): "Preemption, Precaution, Preparedness: Anticipatory Action and Future Geographies." In: *Progress in Human Geography* 34, 777–798.
Barad, Karen (2003): "Posthumanist Performativity: Toward an Understanding of How Matter Comes to Matter." In: *Signs* 28, 801–831.
Barad, Karen (2007): *Meeting the Universe Halfway: Quantum Physics and the Entanglement of Matter and Meaning*. Durham, NC: Duke University Press.
Barad, Karen (2012): "Nature's Queer Performativity." In: *Kvinder, Køn og Forskning*, no. 1–2, 25–53.
Barad, Karen (2017): "No Small Matter: Mushroom Clouds, Ecologies of Nothingness, and Strange Topologies of Spacetimemattering." In: Anna L. Tsing/Heather A. Swanson/Elaine Gan/Nils Bubandt (eds.): *Arts of Living on a Damaged Planet: Ghosts and Monsters of the Anthropocene*. Minneapolis: University of Minnesota Press, G103–G120.
Bates, Tarsh (2015): "Cutting Together-Apart the Mould." In: *Antennae* 32, 44–66.
Burri, Regula V./Dumit, Joseph (2008): "Social Studies of Scientific Imaging and Visualization." In: Edward J. Hackett/Olga Amsterdamska/Michael Lynch/

---

16 See also Ginn/Beisel/Barua (2014) and Lorimer (2014) in this context.

Judy Wajcman (eds.): *The Handbook of Science and Technology Studies*. Cambridge, MA: MIT Press, 297–317.

Callon, Michel (1984): "Some Elements of a Sociology of Translation: Domestication of the Scallops and the Fishermen of St Brieuc Bay." In: *The Sociological Review* 32, 196–233.

Callon, Michel/Latour, Bruno (1981): "Unscrewing the Big Leviathan: How Actors Macro-Structure Reality and How Sociologists Help Them to Do So." In: Karin Knorr-Cetina/Aaron V. Cicourel (eds.): *Advances in Social Theory and Methodology: Toward an Integration of Micro- and Macro-Sociologies*. London: Routledge, 277–303.

DeSilvey, Caitlin (2006): "Observed Decay: Telling Stories with Mutable Things." In: *Journal of Material Culture* 11, 318–338.

DeSilvey, Caitlin/Edensor, Tim (2012): "Reckoning with Ruins." In: *Progress in Human Geography* 37, 465–485.

Douglas, Mary ([1966] 2002): *Purity and Danger: An Analysis of Concepts of Pollution and Taboo*. London: Routledge.

Edensor, Tim (2005a): *Industrial Ruins: Space, Aesthetics and Materiality*. New York: Berg.

Edensor, Tim (2005b): "Waste Matter: The Debris of Industrial Ruins and the Disordering of the Material World." In: *Journal of Material Culture* 10, 311–332.

Edensor, Tim (2007): "Sensing the Ruin." In: *The Senses and Society* 2, 217–232.

Farley, Paul/Roberts, Michael S. (2011): *Edgelands: Journeys into England's True Wilderness*. London: Jonathan Cape.

Foucault, Michel ([2004] 2007): *Security, Territory, Population: Lectures at the Collège de France 1977–1978*. Michel Senellart (ed.). Graham Burchell (trans.). Basingstoke: Palgrave Macmillan.

Foucault, Michel ([2004] 2008): *The Birth of Biopolitics: Lectures at the Collège de France 1978–1979*. Michel Senellart (ed.). Graham Burchell (trans.). Basingstoke: Palgrave Macmillan.

Freidberg, Susanne (2009): *Fresh: A Perishable History*. Cambridge, MA: Harvard University Press.

Garrett, Bradley L. (2010): "Urban Explorers: Quests for Myth, Mystery and Meaning." In: *Geography Compass* 4, 1448–1461.

Garrett, Bradley L. (2014): "Undertaking Recreational Trespass: Urban Exploration and Infiltration." In: *Transactions of the Institute of British Geographers* 39, 1–13.

Ginn, Franklin/Beisel, Uli/Barua, Maan (2014): "Flourishing with Awkward Creatures: Togetherness, Vulnerability, Killing." In: *Environmental Humanities* 4, 113–123.

Haraway, Donna (2008): *When Species Meet*. Minneapolis: University of Minnesota Press.

Haraway, Donna (2015): "Anthropocene, Capitalocene, Plantationocene, Chthulucene: Making Kin." In: *Environmental Humanities* 6, 159–165.

Haraway, Donna (2016): *Staying with the Trouble: Making Kin in the Chthulucene.* Durham, NC: Duke University Press.

Haraway, Donna (2017): "Symbiogenesis, Sympoiesis, and Art Science Activisms for Staying with the Trouble." In: Anna L. Tsing/Heather A. Swanson/Elaine Gan/Nils Bubandt (eds.): *Arts of Living on a Damaged Planet: Ghosts and Monsters of the Anthropocene.* Minneapolis: University of Minnesota Press, M25–M50.

Heßler, Martina/Mersch, Dieter (eds.) (2009): *Logik des Bildlichen: Zur Kritik der ikonischen Vernunft.* Bielefeld: transcript.

Hutta, Jan Simon (2015): "The Affective Life of Semiotics." In: *Geographica Helvetica* 70, 295–309.

Latour, Bruno (1987): *Science in Action: How to Follow Scientists and Engineers through Society.* Cambridge, MA: Harvard University Press.

Law, John (2008): "Actor Network Theory and Material Semiotics." In: Bryan S. Turner (ed.): *The New Blackwell Companion to Social Theory.* Chichester: Wiley-Blackwell, 141–158.

Law, John/Mol, Annemarie (2001): "Situating Technoscience: An Inquiry into Spatialities." In: *Environment and Planning D: Society and Space* 19, 609–621.

Lorimer, Jamie (2014): "On Auks and Awkwardness." In: *Environmental Humanities* 4, 195–205.

Lorimer, Jamie (2016): "Rot." In: *Environmental Humanities* 8, 235–239.

Massumi, Brian (2009): "National Enterprise Emergency: Steps Toward an Ecology of Powers." In: *Theory, Culture and Society* 26, 153–185.

Massumi, Brian (2010): "The Future Birth of the Affective Fact: The Political Ontology of Threat." In: Melissa Gregg/Gregory J. Seighworth (eds.): *The Affect Theory Reader.* Durham, NC: Duke University Press, 52–70.

Muniesa, Fabian/Millo, Yuval/Callon, Michel (2007): "An Introduction to Market Devices." In: *The Sociological Review* 55, 1–12.

Ogborn, Miles (2004): "Archives." In: Stephan Harrison/Steve Pile/Nigel Thrift (eds.): *Patterned Ground: Entanglements of Nature and Culture.* London: Reaktion Books, 240–242.

Paxson, Heather (2008): "Post-Pasteurian Cultures: The Microbiopolitics of Raw-Milk Cheese in the United States." In: *Cultural Anthropology* 23, 15–47.

Paxson, Heather (2013): *The Life of Cheese: Crafting Food and Value in America.* Berkeley: University of California Press.

Paxson, Heather (2014): "Microbiopolitics." In: Eben Kirksey (ed.): *The Multispecies Salon.* Durham, NC: Duke University Press, 115–121.

Rheinberger, Hans-Jörg (2009): "Sichtbar Machen: Visualisierung in den Naturwissenschaften." In: Klaus Sachs-Hombach (ed.): *Bildtheorien: Anthropologische und kulturelle Grundlagen des Visualistic Turn.* Frankfurt a. M.: Suhrkamp, 127–145.

Serres, Michel (1995): *Conversations on Science, Culture and Time: Michel Serres with Bruno Latour.* Ann Arbor: University of Michigan Press.

Sibley, David (1995): *Geographies of Exclusion: Society and Difference in the West.* London: Routledge.

Trigg, Dylan (2006): *The Aesthetics of Decay: Nothingness, Nostalgia, and the Absence of Reason.* New York: Peter Lang.

Tsing, Anna L. (2015): *The Mushroom at the End of the World: On the Possibility of Life in Capitalist Ruins.* Princeton: Princeton University Press.

Tsing, Anna L. (2018): "Nine Provocations for the Study of Domestication." In: Heather A. Swanson/Marianne E. Lien/Gro B. Ween (eds.): *Domestication Gone Wild: Politics and Practices of Multispecies Relations.* Durham, NC: Duke University Press, 231–251.

uncertain commons (2013): *Speculate This!* Durham, NC: Duke University Press.

van Dooren, Thom/Kirksey, Eben/Münster, Ursula (2016): "Multispecies Studies: Cultivating Arts of Attentiveness." In: *Environmental Humanities* 8, 1–23.

Chapter 7: Enacting Speculation
The Paradoxical Epistemology of Performance as Research

Wolf-Dieter Ernst and Jan Simon Hutta

The generation of knowledge—i.e. predominantly propositional knowledge in Western traditions of science—depends on embodied and situated practices, as the sociology of knowledge and the feminist discussion of situated knowledges have made clear. But apart from this well-rehearsed argument that all knowledge is situated, what precisely constitutes embodied, performative dimensions of knowledge production, and how these relate to cognitive and propositional dimensions, has remained rather unclear. Are embodiment and performativity aspects that ought to be controlled or critically reflected upon, or are they generative resources to be affirmed? Are there any particular strategies for fostering or intensifying performative dimensions of knowledge generation? Which kinds of settings, formats and collaborations does this entail? And what are some of the concrete implications regarding the practice of teaching and research? This essay tackles these questions by relating the issue of speculation, which has received increasing interest across the humanities and social sciences, to discussions on performative research and "performance as research" (Kershaw 2008, 2009; Stutz 2008). As a way of thinking that goes beyond existent propositional knowledge, speculation enables the formation of new knowledge. But as an embodied activity, speculation also supports ways of knowing that exceed cognitive reasoning. In this essay, we examine some of the conditions of possibility of this double capacity of speculation, of generating knowledge and fostering embodied ways of knowing. We consider especially the role that performative enactments play in facilitating speculative moments as they unsettle entrenched hierarchies between cognitive and bodily, abstract and situated practices. More specifically, we highlight the productive role of paradoxical constellations of scientific inscription and practical performance.

Our discussion focuses on the 2016 interdisciplinary seminar "Mapping Bayreuth" that we conducted, in collaboration with Matt Adams from the arts collective Blast Theory, with our students at the University of Bayreuth. Practically speaking, the seminar offered a welcome context for experimentation and exemplification around issues of speculation and embodied knowledge. But we also focus on teaching and collaborative learning/research here, as we see potential in using interdisciplinary seminars to foster the kinds of speculative practice on which learning as well as research depends. In fact, following Paulo Freire (1970), any real learning might be productively viewed as a form of research in the first place. In what follows, we will begin by situating our approach within the wider shift from critical rationalism to "abductive" and "affirmative" epistemologies. We then introduce our strategy of enacting speculation in order to unpack some concrete ways of, and challenges in, performing speculative research.

From Critical Rationalism to Affirmative Speculation

Every theory needs speculation. Even Karl Popper (1959), who sought to purge speculation from the realm of science, had to admit the relevance of something like Henri Bergson's ([1907] 1911) "creative intuition" in regard to the generation of new hypotheses. Yet, for Popper, epistemology proper had no business engaging with speculation. Rather than proceeding through speculative forms of induction or abduction, only the persistent elimination of unwarranted assumptions through the method of falsification could ultimately yield scientific results. In Popper's critical rationalism, which provided an epistemological foundation to the quantitative approaches developed since World War II, science was thus ultimately distinguished from other kinds of practice if it succeeded in operationalizing the rational capacity to negate.

In demonstrating the limits of abstraction, negation is credited here for purifying scientific knowledge from subjective beliefs, imaginations or speculations. At the methodological level of research practice, this focus on negation has also entailed eliminating any 'confounding factor' in the objects studied as related to context, situation or body. To do so, positivistic science has deployed technologies such as containment, reiteration and controlled observation to arrive at reliable and valid statements. In the terms of the uncertain commons collective (2013), such a research practice can also be viewed as a "firmative" mode of speculation in its orientation towards the unknown. Firmative speculation, in this sense, seeks to predict and control uncertainties, "turning uncertainty into (external, calculable, knowable) risk" (uncertain commons 2013: ch. 2). Following in the footsteps of Western enlightenment as imprinted from Descartes to Kant and Hegel, this negativist bias—along with its devaluation of the body—still reverberates through both mainstream and critical social research. It also chimes with an instrumental view on research as the gradual 'filling of gaps' and piling up of knowledge. Even in a work such as Bruno Latour's *Science in Action* (1987), which shifts the focus from rational reasoning to the powerful, embodied and messy social practices that enable science in the first place, processes of knowledge production are still depicted as the result of rational-instrumental accumulation cycles.

By the time Latour's book was first published in the late 1980s, though, a more *affirmative* undercurrent had already appeared in philosophy and the social sciences—not to mention the humanities, which had never succumbed to the positivistic agenda in the same ways. For instance, the narrative turn in 1980s social and cultural anthropology cast the "poetic" dimensions of knowledge production into relief (cf. Clifford/Marcus 1986), and the growing interest in complexity theories drew attention to the spontaneous emergence of novelty (Thrift 1999). Along with the surge in feminist and participatory methodologies, the 'turn to affect' of the 1990s and 2000s, and the more recent 'speculative turn,' these engagements have helped reopening the epistemological door to those speculative dimensions of knowledge production that had accompanied pre-World War II epistemologies all along—from Romanticism and Dilthey to Freud, Whitehead or Bergson. A bridge between, say, the 1920s interest in desire and the post-war agenda of a positivist science was constructed in the 1950s and 1960s by Guy Debord and the Situationist International. Using what Debord called "dérive" (drift), by which he meant an 'aimless strolling' in urban space, the researchers-activists still sought to study "the precise laws and specific effects of the geographical environment, whether consciously organized or not, on the affective behavior of individuals" (Debord [1955] 2006; translation altered).

Epistemologically speaking, we might frame the broader move beyond critical rationalism since the 1970s and 1980s in terms of an "abductive turn" (cf. Reichertz 2010). Credited with the potential of generating new orders of knowledge and meaning, Charles Sanders Peirce's ideas around abductive inference (e.g. Peirce [1901] 1958)—in contradistinction to deductive and inductive interference—have struck a chord with researchers from a range of disciplines.[1] Following Peirce, abduction is generally understood here as a kind of careful guessing in search of plausible explanations for given observations, as opposed to rigid explanations derived from causal connections that have already been established in advance. While in Popper's critical rationalism it is irrelevant how the hypothesis to be tested came into being, abduction is all about speculative hypothesizing. This *affirmative* mode of speculating stays with these uncertainties and seeks new ways of relating to the future's inherent complexity—it "progresses and lives by attending to what it does not know" (uncertain commons 2013: ch. 2).

---

[1] As Jo Reichertz summarizes: "educationists, linguists, psychologists, psychoanalysts, semioticians, theater-scientists, theologians, criminologists, researchers in artificial intelligence, and sociologists announce in their research reports that their new discoveries are due to abduction" (Reichertz 2010: 6).

Some of the most consequential elaborations of such an affirmatively speculative approach have emanated from Anglophone experimental, performative and live methodologies, which have also increasingly interconnected the humanities and the social sciences, as well as the practical fields of curating, arts, political activism or the use of social media.² Intersecting with the reinvigoration of dynamic, processual and interactive ontologies in discussions of affect or the so-called new materialism, some of these approaches can also be related to earlier generations of researchers proposing ecological approaches to thought and practice, including Gregory Bateson, Félix Guattari or eco-feminists. On a conceptual level, an affirmatively speculative project has moreover been formulated in engagements with Gilles Deleuze, and Deleuze's readings of Spinoza, Nietzsche and Bergson in particular (Deleuze [1969] 2004).

In our endeavor to explore the epistemological potentials of speculation in an embodied and affirmative register, we follow in the footsteps of some of these wider debates, from Situationism to engagements with Deleuze. However, whereas especially in Deleuze-inspired discussions, ideas of 'affirmation' and 'becoming'—along with the vitalist ontology that has often underpinned these terms—have tended to be embraced in celebratory and idealized ways, abstractly denying negativity (Harrison 2015), we would like to argue here that affirmative speculation does not need to ignore the firmative strategies of falsification and critique, nor scientific technologies such as containment and inscription. Instead, we suggest that a performative approach to speculation teases out, and thrives on, the paradoxes that arise as such firmative epistemological strategies and technologies are performatively enacted and combined with affirmatively speculative strategies. In other words, we suggest that new knowledge, as well as embodied ways of knowing, are prone to be generated as the firmative closures of containment, reiteration, observation and inscription are paradoxically constelled with the affirmative openings of embodied enactment. Paradoxicality is therefore our ally.

The Paradox of Scientific Inscription and Performative Enactment

A key strategy for moving from positivistic reasoning to the speculative generation of new ideas is the use of paradox. Deriving from Ancient Greek παράδοξος (parádoxos), meaning "unexpected, strange," the notion of paradox addresses apparently self-contradictory statements, such as, "this sentence is false," or counterintuitive conclusions, for instance, "drinking a lot of water can make you

---

2 Examples include Bay-Cheng (2010), Back/Puwar (2012a), and Thompson/Independent Curators International (2009); cf. Law (2004), and Wilkie/Savransky/Rosengarten (2017).

feel thirsty." Often, paradoxes also arise when contradictory ideas or elements simultaneously coexist, as in "not having a fashion is a fashion." Authors such as the logician Lewis Carroll have spotlighted a creative capacity in paradoxicality, showing that what at first sight seems to be absurd or self-contradictory might lead to realistic explanations when looking at complex problems. Among the most prominent discussions in this line is Denis Diderot's elaboration on the paradox of the actor's passion: Should an actor playing a murderer feel what a murderer feels? While intuitively one might agree, this soon leads into murky waters in ethical terms. Wouldn't then the best preparation for the actor be to commit murder? Contemplating this ethical intricacy, Diderot then goes on to claim the opposite: The more an actor identifies with a character's passion, the less they will be able to act. This is the formulation of a counterintuitive paradox that leads to the elaboration of how the best actor is the 'cool' actor who shows no personal affective disposition whatsoever; the one "too apt for too many things," then, is the best actor (Diderot [1835] 1957: 18).

The use of paradoxes and the effects of surprise or puzzlement they elicit can thus foster the generation of new insights and ways of reasoning. As a strategy for using paradox as an epistemological resource, we want to highlight in particular ways of dealing with the simultaneous presence of contradictory elements. Going beyond the formulation of paradoxical statements, we take paradoxicality to the level of research practice by exploring the generative potentials that arise from the combination of scientific inscription and performative enactment.

In *Science in Action*, Bruno Latour showed how the modern science system has tended to accumulate knowledge in central locations, whereby it supports and stabilizes hegemonic political and economic processes. This accumulation of knowledge necessitates a great variety of technologies that make the researched objects controllable and mutually combinable. Moreover, it uses what Latour calls "inscription devices," such as cartography, laboratory instruments, ethnography and so on, which transfer local knowledge into the abstract grids of scientific texts. In return, only knowledge that appears as part of these grids counts as scientifically sound (Latour 1987). While this conception of scientific knowledge production assists in illuminating some of the logics and power-effects of modern science, more recent ethnographies of science have directed attention at the specific "enactments" of scientific methods, which relationally shape both objects and actors (e.g. Mol 2002). Following this interest in the contingent ways in which subjects and objects of knowledge are relationally enacted in actual practice, we want to push the discussion a step further by asking what embodied ways of learning take place as scientific methods are enacted, not within their apparatuses of control and inscription, but in experimental and performative processes that also involve putting these very methods in new ways on display. The field "performance as research" offers useful practical and discursive queues for pursuing this investigation.

Performance as Research

In collaboration with Matt Adams, cofounder of the artist collective Blast Theory, we offered a series of workshops in 2016 for graduate students from human geography (Hutta) and opera studies (Ernst), using the rather ambitious title "Embodying Speculation." Among other issues, the workshops addressed how digital media and the increasing digitalization of everyday life impact both research and the subjects conducting it. As a starting point, we combined teaching in a seminar room with performative experiments in the urban spaces of the midsize town of Bayreuth. Considering the distinctive kinds of activity and interaction taking place in urban space, it became clear that a text-based approach to the cultures of speculation can productively be enhanced by some kind of performance and embodied practice. A workshop was therefore scheduled to introduce all participants to basic principles of body work, including warm-up, movement and expression exercises as well as theatre games. Drawing on the work developed by performers, researchers and educators such as the Californian dancer Anna Halprin, these activities focused especially on sensual awareness and a very rough introduction into movement techniques.

On a conceptual level, we introduced the "live-methods" discussion in sociology, which advocates the use of embodied and creative research techniques (Back/Puwar 2012a, 2012b), as well as arts-based approaches in human geography and examples from performance art and theory. We then moved towards the following idea, generally shared by all participants: we can understand performative research as taking place when theories and methods are both a way of doing research and an object studied in the process of enactment. In this double gesture of applying and reflecting on theory and methods, performative research is particularly suited for engaging with digital interactive practices, such as gaming and mapping, as they share its volatility and anti-expert character. Yet, the practical consequences of opting for performative research were less than evident, to say the least. Admittedly, there are easier—and more predictable—course designs at hand than delivering such a theory-practice mashup. Would we gain any usable results by moving around Bayreuth, equipped with Open Street Map and interactive applications on our mobile devices? Or would that mean merely repeating some of the insights we could learn from books? What kind of site-specific learning environments and situated knowledges might we encounter and produce through conducting performance as research in and around Bayreuth?

Our experiment was influenced by extant reflections in the 'pedagogics' of performance as research. On the website of one of the leading research projects in this field, *Practice as Research in Performance,* led by Baz Kershaw at the University of Bristol from 2000–2006, we find a helpful explanation:

> Broadly speaking, practice as research is an attempt to see and understand performance media practices and processes as arenas in which knowledge might be opened. The institutional acceptance of practice as research in the higher education sector acknowledges fundamental epistemological issues that can only be addressed in and through theatre, dance, film, TV and video practices. (PARIP 2002)

So, practice as research generates or reveals enactive ways of knowing, which are stimulated by the materiality and mediality of its very production and distribution or circulation—for instance, among university students. Knowledge emerging through ways of speculating with what Kershaw and colleagues call "performance media practices and processes" can and should thus be studied through embodied methods. Practice as research makes use here of the paradoxes arising as different media and knowledge practices are engaged simultaneously: "One kind of knowledge—theory, books, libraries, archives—is challenged profoundly by another" (Kershaw 2008: 23). What is emphasized in particular is that speculative *ways* of knowing—'knowing *how*' instead of 'knowing *that*'—are best achieved when they are embodied.

We were therefore confronted with a series of paradoxical shifts, moving from text-based to embodied knowledge practices and back again. While in other frameworks, different speculative ways of generating knowledge might occur, our approach opened up in particular disciplinary boundaries inasmuch as it invited reflections on how knowledge is usually generated, accumulated and evaluated. These reflections started with the researcher's own position in space. Are the students sitting at a table with text in front of their eyes, which they decode using their silent inner voice? Or are they standing or moving around in the theatre lab or in urban space? As long as they are in the seminar room, they will most likely understand themselves as listening and arguing academics. Once they are undergoing their physical warm-up, they gradually enlarge their awareness and add to it layers of their casual, private and artistic habits and experiences.

For example, one of the workshop exercises asked participants to move around in space and think of another person present in the room. Upon a certain cue, they were asked to address that person with their index finger as quickly and accurately as possible, calling them loudly by their name. This exercise performatively transformed the bodily order of the class room with its triangulation of silent voice–text–teacher into a diffusely interactive situation, where silent and loud voice constantly alternated. This also entailed shifts in the very ways we addressed each other. The formal "Mr./Mrs." or "Dr." with family name, or "*Sie*," commonly used in German seminar rooms, gave way to a non-hierarchical '*du*' and first name for the time of the exercise. This address turned out to be just more fitting to the kind of deliberate collaboration that emerged in the lab, not least fueled by "kinesthetic empathy" (Foster 2008). Such a collaborative atmosphere might as well emerge when students are confronted with new methods in the seminar room. In most cases, such new methods are considered as new tools for gaining knowledge, but would not necessarily change the way of knowledge production itself. Performance as research aims precisely at this.

It might therefore be one of the crucial characteristics of performance as research that it both confronts and paradoxically aggregates the firmative knowledge practices of standard learning environments together with affirmative ways of knowing that emerge through performative enactment. No doubt, following such an approach would lead us into uncharted waters, posing a series of thorny questions, some of which we will discuss in the following sections. In particular, there are three paradoxical problems ahead: 1) the paradox of facts becoming fictional; 2) the paradox of boundless specificity; and 3) the paradox of inscribing the ephemeral. All three paradoxes are part and parcel of the issue of whether and how we acknowledge a performance's effect as a way of knowing something. Does knowledge obtained in performance encounter its limits in the attempt to systematize and chart it? Or does it, by contrast, comment on or even change existing regimes of truth?

Paradox 1: Facts Becoming Fictional

The first paradox addressed in our workshop emerged from the performative enactment of scientific factuality. 'Facts' in a positivistic framework are sensory 'data' registered through controlled, reproducible and mutually combinable means and inscribed into abstract grids. Standard cartographic methods, for instance, deploy a clearly defined set of operations to transpose real-world spatial data onto a two-dimensional plane. This plane then contains an apparently stable yet portable set of spatial data that can be moved around, combined with other such planes and decoded by means of another set of procedures. It thereby also enables firmative processes of speculation, whereby new data are included into extant grids. But what happens when the map is manipulated in ways that exceed these well-defined encoding and decoding operations, when mapping and reading follow as yet undefined strategies? What kinds of cartographic practice does this inspire? What insights regarding maps and mapping are solicited by such kinds of performance? How do these insights reflect back on understandings of 'facts'?

Some may think that the kind of knowledge such performance-as-research activities generate was related to the arts and theatre in particular and thus neither real nor relevant to scientific exploration. This objection does not fully acknowledge, though, that 'performance' equally refers to artistic, scientific, *and* everyday practice.³ Not least, in anthropology and sociology, as well as in gender studies—particularly fueled by Judith Butler's (1990) work on the social construction of both sex and gender—the concept has opened up a critical semantic spectrum for considering the efficacy of embodied acts inside and outside the performing arts.⁴ We would therefore agree that not only actions on stage but literally any scripted behavior can be understood as performed by someone and for someone, including the scripted behavior of scientists. Hence, it should come as no surprise that the performance paradigm demands a broader understanding of what theatre is. Yet, to conversely also consider scientific facts and data as subject of a *mise-en-scène* is another challenge, as it undermines the status of the apparently neutral scientist. (It is precisely this insight into science's constructed nature that performance studies shares with science and technology studies and the history of science.) The method of performance as research is therefore critical as it forces the researcher to consider whether their data should be taken as self-evident or make-believe, and according to what standards this decision should be taken. Drawing on Donna Haraway, we might approach any knowledge production as a type of "sf worlding," where the signifier "sf" is extended beyond its common use as abbreviating "science fiction" to signal how "speculative fiction and speculative facts" are necessarily entangled (Haraway 2007: 93).

In the workshop sessions, this paradoxical simultaneity of facticity and fictionality was purposefully intensified and performed through a series of techniques. Matt Adams, for instance, introduced 'play' as a vital dimension of creative interaction (resonating with Haraway's discussion of the role of play in sf—science fiction, speculative fiction, speculative facts—as worlding). Encouraging playfulness, one of our workshops focused on speculative experimentations with mappings, following on from our theoretical engagement with Situationism, critical cartography and the uses of cartography in choreography and performance arts. Our focus was here on cartography's capacity to conjure inversions of the tradi-

---

3 Within the discipline of performance studies, one distinguishes performance art from cultural performance such as sport events, rituals, and festivities. In performance theory, the concept is further stratified into performance signifying any 'show' in the broadest sense, a 'cultural performance' manifesting a certain culture; and a 'radical act' able to unsettle given oppositions (cf. Ernst et al. 2014).

4 In philosophy, the concepts of performance and the performative have unfolded similar border crossings, starting with J. L. Austin's lectures on the speech-act to the debate between Jacques Derrida and John Searle about the citationality of performance. See the helpful introductions by Carlson (1996), Wirth (2001), Shepherd (2016), and Schechner (2002).

tional relationship between (firmative) inscription and (affirmative) performance: as the scientific inscription of world onto map tends to fix the world's inherent processuality, so the map's practical, performative use and modification are able to remobilize this processuality. Thus, students who embark on experiments in drawing alternative maps and walking rare itineraries—for example, by symbolically rearranging significant locations of Bayreuth on the theatre-lab floor—do so in real space and with regard to the way maps work as inscription devices. Yet, as they simulate and change what is given, the students also approach their learning task in a playful manner, and nothing can prevent them from switching into a theatrical as-if mode. The use of maps thus invites fictitious reinscriptions of the real. This way, inscription and performance are able to penetrate each other, initiating a process of factual-fictitious speculation.

How can we better understand the way firmative knowledge is opened up by affirmative speculation? Inspired by the Situationists' experiments around the manipulation and reinterpretion of already existing cartography, one of our exercises was to manipulate Bayreuth city maps that were available for free, in order to read them differently.

Students were therefore invited to manipulate copies of the map. The maps could be folded, torn, crumpled, inscribed, or edited in another form (performance). The resulting map object should then be provided with a new legend (re-inscription), from which paradoxical jumps and a-logic connections (speculation) arouse. For this exercise, no fictional framing was necessary. The assumption that one would rearrange the map as a fictional character in the context of a fictional action would have been far too complex. It was rather a 'task performance' that, abstaining from overt fiction, simply asked participants to alienate the existing map and add a new legend. And yet the task appealed more to associative thinking, imagination, and hands-on experimentation than to rational-cognitive abilities of scientific inscription alone. Additionally, the manipulation was performed while other participants could watch it. It thereby revealed its theatrical merits. Probably, the location of this experiment was also of some importance, as all participants seemed to consider the folding maps as props rather than navigation devices. In the center, therefore, was the experience of creating and perceiving practical-performative approaches to cartography and setting them in paradoxical relation to accustomed forms of inscription and analysis. In a certain way, this experience compares to the one you may have when you become a cartographer by using an open-source online mapping tool. However, in our experiment the changes included the map's destruction and other absurd acts, such as when the second was transferred to the third dimension through folding, or when gaps and fragments appeared in place of the overview.

This suggests that the participants took the experiment very far, namely, in the direction of an implicit idea of art as a possible space of performative rewriting.

The a-logical jumps articulated in the feedback discussions also indicated that new insights into the map's/city's reality were produced precisely by the 'alienation' of the real finding. Participants implicitly displayed an exact idea here of what a map performs and of what logical and functional use it might be. Staged knowledge, therefore, can be viewed as located right between fictional assertion and factual knowledge. Kershaw also speaks of a "dislocation of knowledge" here that is typical of performance as research:

> Such dislocation of knowledge by action is characteristic of performance practice as research, especially in its more radical forms. [...] As a result, any facts, truths, ideas, principles attributable to the scene become as fleet and wayward as autumn breezes; like all performance, there but not there. (Kershaw 2009: 4)

What is at stake is therefore no different or radically new propositional knowledge, but a shift and dynamization of the solid ground, on which we tend to believe exact knowledge is based. With regard to the contemporary rhetoric of 'alternative facts,' one might be concerned about this loss of certainty. Yet, if we accept what Haraway (1988) calls "situated knowledges" or what Hans Blumenberg ([1971] 2001) describes as the rhetorical constitution of human existence, it is not a question of whether, but of how and with what interest knowledge is dislocated and subject to change. What we want to emphasize, though, is that in dislocating firmative knowledge, the paradox of facticity and fictionality—"there but not there"—also opens up a space of affirmative speculation, as it calls for a response. It "produce[s] undecidability and in Derrida's sense: implying a decision that makes us responsible for their meaning" (Kershaw 2009: 4). It is this space of affirmative speculation that we want to further explore through a second experiment.

Paradox 2: Unlimited Embodiment

One of the key ways in which performance as research solicits affirmative speculation has to do with its capacity to touch upon the somatic and subjective dimensions of knowledge production. For it is not concerned with filtering out influences that would blur our sensory perception—a problem for which different disciplines have developed sophisticated methods. Instead, performance as research attempts to make productive use of the somatic, subjective and situational dispositions as a source of knowledge. It thus engages the issue of embodiment also raised in ethnographic approaches as well as in the feminist discussion of situated knowledge. Where these approaches understand knowledge production as a necessarily embodied process, performance as research goes a step further. It seeks out and affirms the conditions of embodiment, amplifying them as much as possible, so that we can obtain new findings precisely from what is seemingly not at hand or adequate. What Haraway (1988) has called "the privilege of partial perspective" is brought down here to the concrete enactments of all participants in a given research setting. In this regard, performance as research subscribes to a "boundless specificity" (Kershaw 2008: 26) as its constitutive paradox. The method oscillates between an unlimited expansion of its subject area, on the one hand,[5] and its condition to consider each performance as embodied and specifically localized, on the other. Every human behavior can be understood as a performance, in line with Goffman, and complementary to this observation, every performance is a highly subjective act. Paraphrasing John Cage, Schechner thus notes, "simply framing an activity 'as' a performance—viewing it as such—makes it into a performance" (Schechner 2003: 22).

The decision to conceive every possible situation as a performance and, at the same time, to jeopardize the distinction between observers and performers, can be illustrated by the following experiment. The workshop participants were asked to take their lunch break in the cafeteria as an exercise in collective disability—in the sense of the alienation of everyday activities mentioned above. For this purpose, the group assembled within a rubber-cord loop of approximately twenty feet. The task was to have lunch together, while ensuring that everyone remained in the loop without letting the rope touch the ground. It was agreed that any communication should be limited to the most necessary, as the exercise was primarily about bodily and interpersonal coordination. Metaphorically speaking, any tension within the group had to be controlled, as an individual, existential need was being satisfied. The ensuing complications were predictable and unfolded on three complementary levels, each expressing specific issues of embodied performative research.

First of all, we observed that most of us focused on the in-group, as our own bodies became the central points of performative action. We thereby continued the performative exploration processes that had been prepared and started in the previous workshop exercises. Concentration and attention to one's own body and the bodies of others was thus rather high compared to usual lunch breaks. Only a few participants showed signs of what we called "being private." On a second level, though, the workshop atmosphere, which was characterized by a certain intimacy, collided with the cafeteria setting and the specific habitus in which we usually take our meals. At times, students were approached by fellow students; at times, it became obvious how they routinely maneuvered around the canteen crowds, acting strategically in order to get the food they liked. In some cases, participants lost sight of the task, the rubber cord threatening to be stretched or relaxed. At

---

5 As Schechner notes, "there is no cultural or historical limit to what is or is not 'performance'" (2002: 2).

the same time, these were also the moments in which other participants decided to de-privilege their own needs and to step in for the others, which served the common goal. This in turn led other participants to organize a portion for others, and so on.

The intermingling of habitual action and exceptional, situational experiment required a constant reorientation of one's own actions. On a third level, this was further intensified by the performative character of the exercise and the boundless specificity of the performance, as we were noted by the involuntary spectators in the cafeteria. The way spectators and actors looked at each other suggested that everyone knew they were dealing with a non-everyday action—despite the ordinary nature of the activity of picking up a meal and taking it in. The experiment thus intentionally intersected the expansion of the concept of performance with a specificity here and now. It was clear to everyone that the actions could be carried out with little effort, as few special skills were required. Putting Cage's definition of performance to practice, you could even dispense with the rubber band and see the intake of the meal itself as a performance. For instance, our constriction within the rubber band was curiously mirrored by the balustrade surrounding the terrace on which some of the other eaters were sitting, enacting a kind of involuntary reverse performance. What is considered a performance cannot be limited, then—it is 'boundless'—and, metaphorically speaking, also not to be delimited by a rubber band. At the same time, this experiment took place with very specific participants and in a very specific place, namely, 'our' cafeteria, which is connected to the conditions of student and teacher life, to our biographies, as well as to our relationships to others.

These three aspects—group focus versus private action, habitus versus situational practice, everyday activity versus performance—are all generative of speculative processes, as they constantly evoke paradoxes that call for new responses. The rubber band, as constitutive element of the exercise, illustrates their mutual imbrication. On the one hand, the band functioned semiotically as a sign of an 'as-if' situation—especially for the unprepared spectators. The spectators reacted to it as in a 'hidden camera' trick—with joy and astonishment, but also relatively relaxed as soon as they understood what was going on. The participants, in turn, answered questions, said "hello" to friends, but mostly remained with their task. In addition to the semiotic function, the rubber cord also unmistakably had its material qualities, which allowed to provide immediate embodied feedback. It took on an extreme form when an uninvolved person, for example, pressed themselves into the group or wanted to cross their path and gradually became aware of the rope. Or, there was the moment when the group agreed on how to sit down at the tables. The most extreme situation, however, occurred when all of the participants were back in the theater and were reluctant to leave the rope.

From such extreme feedbacks, those feedbacks are to be distinguished which point to continuous bodily attention, the feeling that figures as somatic and subjective knowledge. However, this knowledge, in the sense of an abductive process, only arises in the interplay of the mentioned complications that are related to the paradoxicality of embodiment and boundlessness: the persistent intersecting of demarcation and expansion as concerns group and individual, habitus and situation, routine and performance, stipulates new practical responses and intellectual reflections. The bodily as well as intellectual knowledge thus generated is affirmatively speculative as it defies any clear definition of the research field—spatially and epistemologically. The open-ended setup of the experiment therefore does not lend itself to the firmative control of predictable repetition. Instead of lending itself to the deductive testing of pre-established hypotheses, each repetition will invariably incite slightly different knowledge. Despite its essential association with the local, this knowledge ironically cannot be controlled or restricted to the local circumstances. Haraway speaks of irony as an essential moment of such paradoxical knowledge production: "Irony is about contradictions that do not resolve into larger wholes, even dialectically, about the tension of holding incompatible things together because both or all are necessary and true. Irony is about humour and serious play" (Haraway [1985] 2001: 291). The paradoxical formulation "serious play" nicely captures the simultaneously consequential and circumstantial nature of the boundless specificity of performative research.

Paradox 3: Ephemerality and Inscription

The rubber-cord experiment has demonstrated how intensifying paradox through performance incites affirmative speculations that are enacted by embodied subjectivities, while persistently challenging the boundaries of situated embodiment. Returning to our overarching paradox, we now want to consider further the relation between knowledge derived from performance as research and the abstract knowledge generated through scientific inscription devices. The map experiment has already indicated how the performative enactment of scientific inscription enables new *ways* of knowing cartography. But if it is thus possible to performatively open up scientific inscription, does it conversely also make sense to inscribe performance? What kinds of inscription devices are useful here, and how can paradoxes of the firmative and the affirmative be productively mobilized in the process of inscription?

Kershaw points out two distinct problems, one relating to ephemerality, the other one to inscription:

Firstly, how can the ephemeral be of lasting value; that is, how might valid knowledge claims emerge through the ephemerality of performance events? Secondly, how can the "live" of the past be revived through its remains; that is, how might knowledge created by the liveness of performance be transmitted in its documentary traces? (Kershaw 2008: 26)

While the first question contemplates possibilities of creating "lasting value" precisely in the absence of (traditional) inscription devices, the second question calls for new techniques of inscription. Such techniques should be capable, not only of fixing performance events for the sake of knowledge accumulation, but to *revive* the eventful past in the present. How, in other words, might the eventful, paradox-ridden past come to bear on the present? And to what extent does paradoxicality itself need to be conjured in the present if the past's liveness is not to be deadened by the inscription?

Let's take this text as an example. At one level, our essay has enacted an abductive process of speculation oriented towards abstractable knowledge regarding the paradoxical relations of performance and inscription. This abstractive abduction has entailed recursive forms of evoking the workshop's live events through description and distancing ourselves through analytic accounts. The more we have distanced ourselves from what happened in the 'live' of the workshop, the more we have been able to build up a new hypothesis from our initial assumptions around speculative knowledge. In order to do so, the performance's diverse traces needed to be read over and over again, which allowed us to reflect on how knowledge is both embodied and inscribed. Similar abductive abstractions already happened during the workshop itself where participants responded to given tasks with different commitments and based on different experiences, reflecting on these responses in discussions and writing.

Recursive evocation has thus been a key element in our affirmatively speculative inscription device. Performance studies provide us with helpful tools to record, remember and re-evoke the ephemeral event. In some respects, this tool-kit also corresponds to ethnographic methods in social research (e.g. Emerson/Fretz/Shaw 1995). However, whereas such techniques of documentation and analysis often serve to inscribe ephemeral events into grids of apparently neutral-objective knowledge, they might also be used to cast into relief the ways in which the concrete paradoxes that have animated research-performances of the past have been responded to. They might thus be deployed to retrace these events on a dynamically unfolding and situated—rather than fixed and neutral—level of analysis. Perhaps more than we have managed to do here, this therefore entails not only factually tracing the eventful past, but rather affectively evoking it, for instance, through narrative and poetic means (which also connects to the ethnographic discussion on "writing culture"). Feminist researchers, especially, have productively connected scientific inscription to such "evocative" descriptions and fabulations (cf. Hutta 2015). Methodological attentiveness to the evocative potential of analysis moreover suggests nuanced engagement with visualization beyond mere representation and illustration. This signals the value of collaborative formats that connect text-based research with expertise in areas such as visual arts, as also proposed in the discussion around live methods and live sociology.[6]

As Back and Puwar (2012a) have noted, "live sociology"—or what we have termed performative research—is enhanced as researchers become increasingly "crafty" in making use of the evocative inscription devices developed in visual or performance arts or curation. This imbrication of research and arts concerns processes of empirical research as well as of analysis and presentation. Regarding the empirical process of engaging with real-world objects such as maps of Bayreuth, the students of our workshops 'artistically' manipulated these objects and combined them with other material and semiotic objects. They speculatively in-folded various elements—map, signs, gestures, and spatial arrangements in the theatre lab—into their performative activity, which went along with a process of fictionalizing empirical facts. As our discussion has suggested, such creative speculation can be instigated through the use of play, irony and the creation of 'as-if' situations, especially in contexts like theatre or urban spaces. At the level of analytically and curatively reengaging with the various traces thus performatively produced, on the other hand, what has been performatively 'in-folded' is evocatively *un*-folded.

This brings to mind the ethnographic understanding of "thick description" as a process of "explicating" (which literally means 'unfolding') social events and interactions (Geertz 1973). In performance as research, however, what is to be explicated are not merely cultural sets of meanings and practices, but rather the creative responses participants have formulated in relation to paradoxes of fact and fiction, embodiment and privacy, group and privacy, habitus and situation or everyday situation and staged performance. While analysis and presentation retrace some of the material and factual processes 'im-plicated' (infolded) in a fictionalized performance, they simultaneously need to re-evoke these fact-fictions in the here and now—thereby necessarily altering whatever components have entered into the performance as these are selectively related to a different context.

Regarding the mode of analysis, we see a shift in focus here from the firmative inscription of events to the affirmative re-evocation of their paradoxical intensities. In such an approach, conceptual abstractions—such as group focus versus private action, habitus versus situational practice, everyday activity versus performance—cease to function as the neutral grids of universal knowledge. Instead, they become vital means enabling thought to open itself up towards the eventful-

---

6 In their discussion of "curating sociology," Nirmal Puwar and Sanjay Sharma (2012) have insightfully demonstrated this value.

ness that unfolds through perceptual and affective registers (cf. Deleuze/Guattari [1991] 1994). If there is thus considerable potential for analysis to be enhanced through techniques of evocation, however, this does not stop the paradox of inscription and ephemerality from reappearing all along—persistently demanding our response. Paradoxicality thus re-emerges in the very process of eventful inscription.

A variant of this paradox has surfaced in our double role as observers and participants. While conducting the workshop, we were also part of the group—for instance, during the cafeteria experiment or the warm-up sessions—and thus shared to some extent the somatic and subjective dimensions of the project. At no point were we able to observe the group from a safe distance. In ethnographic research, the simultaneity of bodily participation and analytic observation is commonly discussed under the rubric of "participant observation"—an activity that, starting from the haphazard jottings of ephemeral situations and continuing with the descriptive re-creation of significant scenes, leads, step by step, to the formulation of analytic claims and insights (cf. Emerson/Fretz/Shaw 1995). This ethnographic activity, though, tends to posit the observant participant-researcher-author as the central subject of knowledge. Yet, the text you are reading is only one of many possible traces of the workshop. Other such traces exist, for example, as feedback discussions, notes, photographs, a weblog, various notes—and likely the embodied memories of mapping exercises and lunch breaks. This suggests that knowledge formation ought to be conceived as more dispersed.

What is more, the ethnographic approach commonly centers the generation of knowledge on the sphere of textual production and analysis, sidelining the bodily levels on which it simultaneously occurs. A more consequential interrogation of the paradox of inscription and ephemerality calls instead for considering the body itself as a possible device for what we have called the evocative inscription of knowledge. This brings us back to speculation's double capacity of generating knowledge and fostering embodied ways of knowing.

To Conclude: Researching Performance, Performing Research

What is the epistemic status of the knowledge generated by means of performance? To the extent that the speculative cartography of performance as research is concerned with the formulation of propositional statements relating to the concrete issues engaged with, there might appear to be few new or substantially different findings compared to what one can read in academic literatures on performance art or live sociology. There are two ways in which this affirmatively speculative knowledge production matters, though. On a formal level, this knowledge is radically different inasmuch as it is embodied. This suggests not only a different pedagogical approach in academic teaching, but also a different approach to knowledge production. Performance as research relates to the everyday practice of orientation in space by means of maps, digital devices and so on, only to transfer it to the instable, or 'multi-stable,' space between the theatre lab and its others (including experience, city space, social research and so on). It has turned out to be much easier to open up and unsettle existing grids of knowledge in the theatre lab as well as in public space than in the seminar room, where this might be a bigger challenge. Performance as research, then, claims to unsettle that which, as an effect of its accumulation, is considered self-evident. It does so by means of embodiment and in reference to implicit knowledge, which has always already been transferred more via evocation and performance than by being stored in neutral grids of knowledge. Thus, after the experiment, we can claim that we 'know' the meaning of navigation through public space in close proximity to another. We 'know' how our awareness can shift from the usual perspective of a sitting or standing body to a bodily awareness of the space. We 'know' how to imagine a-logical itineraries and cartographies that juxtapose and challenge existing regimes of navigation.

Additionally, on the meta-level we have used to frame this essay, we can now more profoundly evaluate the strategies, potentials and limitations of experiments and research endeavors in the performance arts, the Situationists' movement or abductive approaches. For instance, in focusing on the dynamic conjunction of firmative and affirmative speculation, we have sought to rework a paradox that has implicitly accompanied approaches from Situationism to the turn to abduction. As Reichertz points out, abduction's "secret charm" resides in the fact that "it is a *logical* inference (and thereby reasonable and scientific), however it extends into the realm of profound insight (and therefore generates new knowledge)" (Reichertz 2010: 7). Similarly, the Situationists have affirmed the desiring fluxes of embodied subjects that speculatively drift through space, while at the same time seeking to articulate "precise laws," to use Debord's above-cited formulation. Various approaches that can be credited with promoting affirmatively speculative research designs are therefore founded on a paradoxical simultaneity of firmative and affirmative registers. Yet—not least in the German social sciences—the endeavor to generate 'scientific' knowledge has frequently gotten the upper hand, whereas affirmatively speculative moments have been relegated to the secondary status of generating hypotheses to be deductively tested—and potentially falsified.[7] Rather than making productive use of paradoxes of emic and etic, concrete and abstract, affirmative and firmative, these approaches have therefore ambiv-

---

7 Qualitative approaches seeking to embrace abduction have been especially haunted by the specter of 'neutral objectivity'—avowals of the emic, contextual and explicatory notwithstanding.

alently oscillated between different registers, often hierarchically subordinating the affirmative to the firmative.[8]

As we have argued, though, it is precisely the dynamic coexistence of heterogeneous elements in the paradox that has a potential for generating new practices and insights (cf. Hutta 2010). Instead of warding off paradoxicality by integrating the affirmative into the firmative, we have sought to discuss settings of learning and research that open up space for paradoxicality to be enacted. In a certain way, we have returned to some of Peirce's own elaborations on abduction.[9]

There is thus more at stake than a mere reproduction of artistic or theoretical ideas. In fact, rather weak criteria such as expectation, empathy and suspense need to be considered as equally important and productive aspects for conducting a performance analysis as the instruments that enable scientific inscription. This entails productively accepting the limitation of our interpreting efforts, as set by the mere fact of performance's ephemerality. It also asks us to develop forms of re-inscription that proffer affective evocation in place of neutralizing distance. Therefore, the fact that we might find ourselves distanced from positive knowledge as a modern certainty even in the act of remembering it should not leave us in despair, for it is more and more a lesson to learn in digital culture.

References

Back, Les/Puwar, Nirmal (2012a): "A Manifesto for Live Methods: Provocations and Capacities." In: *Sociological Review* 60, 6–17.
Back, Les/Puwar, Nirmal (eds.) (2012b): *Live Methods*. Malden, MA: Wiley-Blackwell.
Bay-Cheng, Sarah (2010): *Mapping Intermediality in Performance*. Amsterdam: Amsterdam University Press.
Bergson, Henri ([1907] 1911): *Creative Evolution*. Arthur Mitchell (trans.). New York: Henry Holt.
Blumenberg, Hans ([1971] 2001): "Anthropologische Annäherungen an die Rhetorik." In: Hans Blumenberg: *Ästhetische und metaphorologische Schriften*. Aus-

---

[8] In a similar vein, Antke Engel has argued that paradox has often been conceived merely as a problem to be warded off or to be transposed into binary oppositions. Axel Honneth and the Frankfurt Institute for Social Research, for instance, call for a transposition of paradoxes into a normative politics of oppositions and contradictions (cf. Engel 2009: 125).

[9] For instance, discussing strategies that facilitate abduction, Peirce mentions bodily emergency situations, such as the self-induced pressure to act or fear of failure, as well as—diametrically opposed—the daydreaming, *dérive*-like activity he calls "musement" (cf. Davis 1972). Such a strategic re-embodiment of epistemology also indexes its paradoxical relation to scientifically inscribed knowledge.

wahl und Nachwort von Anselm Haverkamp. Frankfurt a. M.: Suhrkamp, 406–431.

Butler, Judith (1990): *Gender Trouble: Feminism and the Subversion of Identity.* New York: Routledge.

Carlson, Marvin (1996): *Performance: A Critical Introduction.* London: Routledge.

Clifford, James/Marcus, George E. (ed.) (1986): *Writing Culture: The Poetics and Politics of Ethnography.* Berkeley, CA: University of California Press.

Davis, William H. (1972): *Peirce's Epistemology.* The Hague: Martinus Nijhoff.

Debord, Guy ([1955] 2006): "Introduction to a Critique of Urban Geography." Ken Knabb (trans.). In: Ken Knabb (ed.): *Situationist International Anthology,* Revised and Expanded Edition. Berkeley, CA: Bureau of Public Secrets, 8–11.

Deleuze, Gilles ([1969] 2004): *The Logic of Sense.* Mark Lester/Charles J. Stivale (trans.). London: Continuum.

Deleuze, Gilles/Guattari, Félix ([1991] 1994): *What Is Philosophy?* Hugh Tomlinson/Graham Burchell (trans.). New York: Columbia University Press.

Diderot, Denis ([1835] 1957): "The Paradox of Acting." Walter Herries Pollock (trans.). In: Wilson Follet (ed.): *The Paradox of Acting* [Denis Diderot]/*Masks or Faces?* [William Archer]. New York: Hill and Wang, 11–71.

Emerson, Robert M./Fretz, Rachel I./Shaw, Linda L. (1995): *Writing Ethnographic Fieldnotes.* Chicago: University of Chicago Press.

Engel, Antke (2009): *Bilder von Sexualität und Ökonomie: Queere kulturelle Politiken im Neoliberalismus.* Bielefeld: transcript.

Ernst, Wolf-Dieter/Mungen, Anno/Niethammer, Nora/Szymanski-Düll, Berenika (eds.) (2014): *Sound und Performance: Positionen, Methoden, Analysen.* Würzburg: Königshausen und Neumann.

Foster, Susan Leigh (2008): "Movement's Contagion: The Kinesthetic Impact of Performance." In: Tracey C. Davis (ed.): *The Cambridge Companion to Performance Studies.* Cambridge: Cambridge University Press, 46–59.

Freire, Paulo (1970): *Pedagogy of the Oppressed.* New York: Herder and Herder.

Geertz, Clifford (1973): "Thick Description: Toward an Interpretive Theory of Culture." In: Clifford Geertz: *The Interpretation of Cultures, Selected Essays.* New York: Basic Books, 3-30.

Haraway, Donna J. ([1985] 2001): "A Cyborg Manifesto." In: Simon During (ed.): *The Cultural Studies Reader.* London: Routledge, 271–291.

Haraway, Donna J. (1988): "Situated Knowledges: The Science Question in Feminism and the Privilege of Partial Perspective." In: *Feminist Studies* 14, 575–599.

Haraway, Donna J. (2007): *When Species Meet.* Minneapolis: University of Minnesota Press.

Harrison, Paul (2015): "After Affirmation, or, Being a Loser: On Vitalism, Sacrifice, and Cinders." In: *GeoHumanities* 1, 285–306.

Hutta, Jan Simon (2010): "Paradoxical Publicness: Becoming-Imperceptible with the Brazilian Lesbian, Gay, Bisexual and Transgender Movement." In: Nick Mahony/Janet Newman/Clive Barnett (eds.): *Rethinking the Public: Innovations in Research, Theory and Politics*. Bristol: Policy Press, 143–161.

Hutta, Jan Simon (2015): "The Affective Life of Semiotics." In: *Geographica Helvetica* 70, 295–309.

Kershaw, Baz (2008): "Performance as Research: Live Events and Documents." In: Tracy C. Davis (ed.): *The Cambridge Companion to Performance Studies*. Cambridge: Cambridge University Press, 23–45.

Kershaw, Baz (2009): "Performance Practice as Research: Perspectives from a Small Island." In: Shannon Rose Riley/Lynette Hunter (eds.): *Mapping Landscapes for Performance as Research: Scholarly Acts and Creative Cartographies*. London: Palgrave McMillan, 3–13.

Latour, Bruno (1987): *Science in Action: How to Follow Scientists and Engineers through Society*. Cambridge, MA: Harvard University Press.

Law, John (2004): *After Method: Mess in Social Science Research*. Abingdon: Routledge.

Mol, Annemarie (2002): *The Body Multiple: Ontology in Medical Practice*. Durham, NC: Duke University Press.

PARIP (2002): "PARIP FAQs." In: *Practice as Research in Performance*, University of Bristol (http://www.bris.ac.uk/parip/faq.htm).

Peirce, Charles S. ([1901] 1958): "Abduction." In: *The Collected Papers of Charles S. Peirce*, Vol. 7. Arthur W. Burks (ed.). Cambridge, MA: Harvard University Press, 136–144.

Popper, Karl R. (1959): *The Logic of Scientific Discovery*. London: Hutchinson.

Puwar, Nirmal/Sharma, Sanjay (2012): "Curating Sociology." In: *Sociological Review* 60(S1), 40–63.

Reichertz, Jo (2010): "Abduction: The Logic of Discovery of Grounded Theory." In: *Forum: Qualitative Social Research* 11(1) (http://dx.doi.org/10.17169/fqs-11.1.1412).

Schechner, Richard (2002): *Performance Studies: An Introduction*. London: Routledge.

Schechner, Richard (2003): *Performance Theory*. London: Routledge.

Shepherd, Simon (ed.) (2016): *The Cambridge Introduction to Performance Theory*. Cambridge: Cambridge University Press.

Stutz, Ulrike (2008): "Performative Forschung in der Kunstpädagogik am Beispiel von Szenen aus dem Seminar 'Erforschen performativer Rituale im Stadtraum'." In: *Forum: Qualitative Social Research* 9(2) (http://dx.doi.org/10.17169/fqs-9.2.411).

Thompson, Nato/Independent Curators International (eds.) (2009): *Experimental Geography: Landscape Hacking, Cartography, and Radical Urbanism*. Brooklyn: Melville House.

Thrift, Nigel (1999): "The Place of Complexity." In: *Theory, Culture and Society* 16, 31–69.

uncertain commons (2013): *Speculate This!* Durham, NC: Duke University Press.

Wilkie, Alex/Savransky, Martin/Rosengarten, Marsha (eds.) (2017): *Speculative Research: The Lure of Possible Futures*. New York: Routledge.

Wirth, Uwe (ed.) (2001): *Performanz: Zwischen Sprachtheorie und Kulturtheorie*. Frankfurt a. M.: Suhrkamp.

Figuration: Speculating with Fiction

Chapter 8: Scale and Speculative Futures in Russell Hoban's *Riddley Walker* and Kim Stanley Robinson's *2312*

Matthew Hannah and Sylvia Mayer

Any fictional text can be regarded as speculative—in the sense that all fiction invents alternative realities and thus engages with questions of how we understand our present worlds and ourselves, our knowledge of the past, and our conceptualizations of the future. As readers we enjoy the "cognitive provisionality" fictional texts provide us with, the opportunity to suspend disbelief, engage in "imaginative play" (Gallagher 2006: 347), and speculate about the (im)probable, the (im)possible, the (un)desirable of proposed realities. Some genres, however, have lent themselves particularly well to speculation about possible futures. Whether labeled "utopia," "dystopia," "science fiction," "speculative fiction," or "post-apocalyptic fiction," future-oriented fictional texts all engage in the imagination of possible future worlds, thereby responding to the political, social, economic, or cultural challenges of the times in which they are written. In some way or another, these genres all share the qualities that Fitting (2010) regards as characteristic for modern science fiction. They represent "a response to the effects of the scientific transformation of the world beginning around the end of the eighteenth century: in the European awareness of history and the future, and in the increasing impact of the scientific method and of technological change on people's lives" (136).[1]

This essay addresses two novels that create speculative future worlds as responses to the economic, scientific, and technological challenges that marked the times of their writing: Russell Hoban's *Riddley Walker* and Kim Stanley Robinson's *2312*. Each of these novels responds very differently to "the terrors and delights of technological modernity" (Luckhurst 2005: 170) that science fiction explores.

---

1 On the speculative quality of any fictional text, see Chu's science-fictional theory of mimesis, which argues that realism and science fiction "exist on a continuum" (Chu 2010: 7), and Freedman's claim that even the most realistic fiction reveals "an irreducible degree of alterity and estrangement" (Freedman 2000: 21). For a survey of more recent scholarship on such genre categorization, including discussions on the distinction between science fiction and speculative fiction, see also Fitting (2010); Vieira (2011); and Voigts (2015).

Riddley Walker engages in an exploration of the challenges of twentieth-century nuclear technology and develops a thoroughly dystopian far-future scenario. *2312* engages in an exploration of the challenges of early twenty-first-century computer, biomedical, and geo-engineering technologies and develops a future scenario marked by a mixture of utopian and dystopian features.

Hoban's novel, published in 1980, imagines the far-reaching effects of nuclear catastrophe. Variously labeled "apocalyptic sf" (Mousoutzanis 2009), "post-apocalyptic science fiction" (Branscomb 1991; Maynor/Patteson 1984), or "post-nuclear dystopia" (Horstmann 2015), the novel envisions a geographically isolated, rural society in southeast England some 2,500 years after a nuclear war. The depiction of this future society's habits of living, political and economic structures, and religious beliefs positions it in what can be identified as a new iron age where daily work routines lack the mechanical assistance of an industrial age existence and life expectancy is low. To Natalie Maynor and Richard F. Patteson, Hoban's account of this post-apocalyptic world, as well as his invention of an English language variant that reflects the dramatically altered conditions of social reality, turns *Riddley Walker* into one of "the most sophisticated work[s] of fiction ever to speculate about man's future on earth and the implications of a potentially destructive technology" (Maynor/Patteson 1984: 18).

Robinson's novel, published in 2012, is set 300 years in the future, when humanity has successfully colonized the solar system, while planet Earth still struggles with ecological devastation, overpopulation, and political strife that extends into space. The local settings of the novel include planets, moons, and asteroids that have been terraformed—in part, to preserve biomes that had been destroyed on Earth due to anthropogenic global climate change—and, in the case of the asteroids, are not only inhabited by humans but also used as means of rapid transportation. Dramatic advances in science and technology have made such terraforming possible while also accelerating travel and mobility for the privileged, spurring bodily human enhancements, creating flexible sexualities and genders, and significantly increasing life expectancy. *2312* can be classified as a critical utopia (Moylan 1986) that engages with the social, economic, political, and cultural risks, the chances and threats, generated by the ongoing technological processes of modernization.

While the speculative genre of science fiction is clearly defined by its future orientation, the relevance of spatiality for the genre has also increasingly been acknowledged, especially in the wake of postmodern theorizing and the spatial turn in literary and cultural studies. In 1987, drawing on his notion of the predominance of space in postmodern culture, Fredric Jameson argued that "we need to explore the proposition that the distinctiveness of SF as a genre has less to do with time (history, past, future) than with space" ([1987] 2005: 313). More recently, James Kneale (2009) claimed that the genre of science fiction lends itself particularly well to the analysis of the shapes and functions of spatial structure in light of current work in human geography as well as literary spatial studies, since it imagines alternative worlds without a referent in so-called real life. As "representations of places that do not or cannot exist" (424), science fiction draws particular attention to the relationality, heterogeneity, and process-character that mark the construction of space and place—whether in fiction or in the 'real' world.

Drawing on these ideas, we focus our analysis on the significance of "scale" for the spatial representation of the two novels' speculative future worlds. The category of scale, too, has become increasingly relevant in human geography and in literary spatial studies. In geography, there are two general kinds of scale definition, one quite technical and cartographic, the other "a kind of shorthand to describe either an areal unit on the Earth's surface (as when studying a phenomenon 'at the regional scale') or the extent of a process's or a phenomenon's geographical reach (as when suggesting that a particular process is 'a regional' or 'a national' one)" (Herod 2011: xi). The literary critic Hsuan L. Hsu offers a more encompassing transdisciplinary definition:

> At once an epistemological framework, an imaginative construct, and an idea materialized in real spaces and activities, scale can only be understood through interdisciplinary analysis that attends to its fictive, geographical, and political economic properties. (Hsu 2017: 125)

In this essay, we understand scalar concepts to pertain to graduated scales in this geographical sense as treated in literary works. Focusing on the role of scale in the novels, we explore how scale is employed in *Riddley Walker* and *2312* for the purpose of drawing attention to processes of spatial structuring and to specific thematic preoccupations in the two novels.

In the next section, we provide definitions of the scale concepts that we turn into tools for textual analysis and interpretation. We then explore the 're-scaled' worlds of the two novels, attending to the loss of the global or planetary scale in *Riddley Walker* and the expansion of scale in *2312*. By explaining processes and outcomes of re-scaling, we shed light on the local, temporal, and social settings from which the novels' respective plots unfold. We compare scale-related strategies in the two novels, including failed attempts at scale-jumping in *Riddley Walker* and key instances of successful scale-jumping in *2312*. Our analysis focuses on the desperate and misguided mimetic attempts in *Riddley Walker* to regain access to atomic and molecular knowledge that promises to reopen access to distant parts of the planet, and on the plan to save Earth in *2312* by making use of the opportunities of an expanded scale system.

Scale, Human Geography, and Science Fiction

In international debates in human geography since the 1970s, a number of key concepts have played central roles for addressing the mutual constitution of social and spatial relations. Bob Jessop, Neil Brenner and Martin Jones (2008) identify four such concepts: territory, place, scale, and networks. These concepts have each been the focus of lasting discussion. In the course of examining them, it has become clear that all four can be seen as socially constructed (and often contested) heuristic devices, which, through the understandings of social actors, nevertheless produce real effects in socio-spatial organization of life. It is by now also clear that specific constructions of territory, place, scale, and network influence each other in complex ways.

In everyday parlance, scale is usually assumed to refer to a nested hierarchy of geographical levels. More broadly, scale is a way to structure our understandings of relative geographical size or extent not along a continuous spectrum but with reference to a small number of conventionally accepted 'levels.' In public and scholarly discourses about social life in the twentieth and twenty-first centuries, a differentiation is typically made between 'local' or 'urban,' 'regional,' 'national,' and 'global' scales. These constructs, of course, can have real effects—in political terms, for instance, where scale structures are usually fixed in legal and constitutional documents as administrative hierarchies: as 'municipal' or 'local,' 'state' or 'provincial' and 'national' governmental units, or in reference to the 'international' scale (Herod 2011: ch. 1). However, as human geographers have delved ever more deeply into the concept of scale, they have fundamentally complicated our understanding of what scale is and how it plays a role in social life. Starting in the 1980s, prominently in Neil Smith's theorization of the historical geography of capitalism and capitalist reconfigurations of 'nature,' scale came to be understood as a contingent, contestable way of framing reality that has real effects (Smith 1990; cf. Herod 2011: 25).

Changes in conventionally accepted scale structures are often termed *re-scaling*, which is defined, for example, in the literature on political scale as "the process in which policies and politics that formerly took place at one scale are shifted to others in ways that reshape the practices themselves, redefine the scales to and from which they are shifted, and reorganize interactions between scales" (McCann 2003: 162).

Re-scaling "necessarily entail[s] a disruption and recomposition of the networks of power that tie political actors together within and across scales" (McCann 2003: 163). Finally, it is important to note that re-scaling can mean 'down-scaling' as well as 'up-scaling.' The development of scale concepts in the context of seeking to understand the historical geography of capitalism has led scholars to focus much more often upon expansions than upon contractions or narrowings of scale structures. Yet, the latter type of re-scaling is also a possibility. As these discussions of re-scaling suggest, the specific scale levels within any one scale structure (such as local, national, or global) each only make sense in relation to the other levels (Agnew 1997: 100). Scale, in other words, is not only constructed but relational.

Since scale can be understood "not just as an outcome of social process but also an instrument for reshaping power dynamics" (Gruby/Campbell 2013: 2048)—what Smith calls the "politics of scale" (Smith 1990: 173–175)—a number of authors have focused upon "scalar strategies" or ways of using specific scalar levels to achieve something at the same or other scalar levels (Lindseth 2006: 740). A specific kind of scalar strategy is identified by Smith as "scale jumping" (1990: 174–175), a strategy he illustrates in his analysis of local protests against gentrification in New York City and their successful attempts to become more broadly visible at the neighborhood and city levels.

Recently, human geographers have begun to extend the scope of their research beyond the confines of the Earth itself, with an eye to how long-standing disciplinary research themes may be taken up and potentially transformed by a broadened engagement with extraplanetary realms. In a 2017 forum in *Progress in Human Geography* entitled "Geographies of Outer Space: Progress and New Opportunities," the forum editors argue that, in this enterprise, "[h]uman geographers are well-placed to draw on a breadth of conceptual developments from its range of subdisciplinary perspectives, including an established engagement with concepts of scale" (Dunnett/Maclaren 2019: 315). And yet, this connection is not developed. Instead the contributors to the forum take up other concepts and subfields: labor geographies and astro-capitalism; environmental geographies and human-nature relations; geographical imaginations of outer space and geographies of knowledge about it; landscapes and moral geographies of outer space; and connections between exploration and control of space and nationalism.

Regarding scale as a meaning-making feature not only in the 'real world,' but also in fictional future worlds, the starting point of literary analysis is the same as that in the geographical literature. When David Delaney and Helga Leitner argue that geographical scale is considered "socially constructed rather than ontologically pre-given" and that "the geographic scales constructed are themselves implicated in the constitution of social, economic and political processes" (Delaney/Leitner 1997: 93), they refer in part to the constructing power of language and narrative. Such an analytical approach needs to be taken with science fiction texts, which, whether utopian or dystopian in outlook, have for a long time imagined spaces in which humanity has increased the geographical extent of its presence in the universe beyond what is currently the highest conventionally understood geographical scale we inhabit, the global or planetary scale. It also needs to be taken with texts centered on contact with or invasion by extraterrestrial beings, exploring the question of how scales conceived as being beyond that of the Earth might impact life on the planetary scale. And it needs to be taken with texts such as *Riddley Walker* that draw attention to the shrinking of geographical reach due to technological catastrophe.

The Re-scaled Future Worlds of *Riddley Walker* and *2312*

Riddley Walker is set about 2,500 years after a nuclear catastrophe that occurred in the late 1990s and returned the southeast of England (and probably most other regions of the world) to a level of cultural, technological, and economic sophistication comparable to the prehistoric iron age. The region is known to its inhabitants as "Inland" (after "England"). Inland serves as the highest-order level of geographical reference or scale at which human life relevant to the narrative is organized. The chief economic activities in Inland are some rudimentary farming, salvaging of metals left over from pre-catastrophe civilization, and basic manufacturing of iron tools fueled by charcoal. Social organization is at the level of small, loosely organized groups of roughly between ten and fifty people who either control stationary farms or travel around doing salvage jobs. Life expectancy has dramatically dropped. Travel on land is by foot. The fastest form of communication is by carrier pigeon.

The society in which Riddley Walker, the novel's protagonist and autodiegetic narrator, grows up is marked by a ritualized search for long-lost knowledge that would allow the reconstruction of a technologically much more advanced way of life. It is in ritualistically performed narratives that some rudimentary knowledge about the ancient world as well as the causes of its catastrophe have been preserved. This knowledge, however, proves to be insufficient. In focusing on a future scenario marked by an inability to overcome scientific and technological ignorance, *Riddley Walker* presents a cautionary tale about the effects of nuclear technology and a narrative of a failed quest for essential scientific knowledge.

Loss of knowledge is reflected in—and mediated by—the language used by Riddley and by the other characters, a language that itself seems to have been ruined by the catastrophe. Many words have survived from pre-catastrophe times, but with spellings mangled almost to the point of unrecognizability. The place names in what used to be late twentieth-century Kent and surrounding areas likewise survive only in twisted form. More poignantly, the referents of many words no longer exist, and the novel's characters must rely on imprecise, often simply false understandings of what these words once meant.

The culture in which these (mis)understandings are preserved and relayed has been almost exclusively oral, though some people can write. The tenuous grasp the characters have of human history and their place in it is thus still largely conveyed by storytellers. The most important story to be interpreted, and the meager core of the shared culture of Inland, is the Eusa Story—an adaptation of the story of St. Eustace, a painting of whom in Canterbury Cathedral was the original inspiration for the novel.

The tellers of the Eusa Story are Abel Goodparley and Erny Orfing, two representatives of the "Mincery" ("ministry"), which passes for the rudimentary government of Inland. Goodparley, the "Pry Mincer," and Orfing, the "Wes Mincer," travel around Inland periodically in a circuit, accompanied by "hevvys" (a category of bodyguards) and tell the Eusa Story through a puppet show in the style of the Punch and Judy tradition, using the same kind of puppets and miniature stage or "fit-up." This periodic circuit by representatives of the Mincery is the chief way in which Inland as the largest effective scale is produced and reproduced. All local groups are aware of the extent of territory covered by Goodparley and Orfing, and this serves as their widest geographical reference.

The Eusa Story centers upon Eusa, a pre-catastrophe scientist who worked out how to harness nuclear power but was forced to surrender this knowledge to Mr. Clevver (modeled on the devil figure in Punch and Judy shows). Mr. Clevver then built and detonated the bomb that destroyed civilization. For giving up the technical knowledge that led to catastrophe, Eusa was beheaded, but his disembodied head, as Goodparley explains to Riddley, instructed survivors to tell his story for posterity:

> Make a show of me for memberment and for the ansers to your askings. Make a show with han figgers put a littl woodin head of me on your finger in memberment of my real head on a poal. Keap the Eusa folk a live in memberment of the hardship they brung on. (Hoban [1980] 2002: 122)

The Eusa story is thus in part a cautionary tale. But it also includes some distorted information about the chemistry of gunpowder and nuclear fission, as does a related story circulating in Inland called "the hart of the wood" (2–4). The Eusa story cryptically holds out the promise of recovery of the knowledge necessary to rebuild civilization:

> Out of that hardship let them bring a Ardship 12 years on and 12 years come agen. Let the head of Inland ask the Ardship then. Let the head of Inland road the circel ful and to the senter asking what he wants to know for all of Inland. When the right head of Inland fynds the right head of Eusa the anser wil come and Inland wil rise up out of what she ben brung down to. (122)

Goodparley, Orfing and others, eventually including Riddley, are tantalized by the hints handed down in the Eusa story as to how nuclear power might once again be understood and harnessed, though the stories they rely on lead them to conflate the secrets of nuclear fission with the recipe for gunpowder.

Riddley and others are keenly aware that they live in a degraded situation. Often the focus of the novel is upon the loss of technological capabilities and the mathematical and physical knowledge that underlies them. But the "clevverness" that brought this knowledge is portrayed as dangerous, as in Lorna Elswint's telling of the story "Why the Dog Wont Show Its Eyes": "They had the Nos. of the rain bow and the Power of the air all workit out with counting which is how they got boats in the air and picters on the wind. Counting clevverness is what it wer" (19).

Probably because of the skepticism encouraged in these stories, Riddley is at first not particularly interested in trying to regain such lost technological knowledge. But then he has a moment of conversion at Fork Stoan (Folkestone), where the ruins of what seems to be a nuclear power plant elicit unexpected emotions: "How cud any 1 not want to get that shyning Power back from time back way back? How cud any 1 not want to be like them what had boats in the air and picters on the wind? How cud any 1 not want to see them shyning weals terning?" (100). Imagining the "boats in the air and picters on the wind," Riddley begins to link the loss of technological knowledge with the disappearance of larger scales. The lost ability to fly and to transmit information refers metonymically to the loss of global reach. Later, Goodparley spells out more clearly the connection between the molecular sources of power and the possibility of travel and communication over much larger distances:

> What wer it put them boats up there in the air dyou think? Power it musve ben musnt it. Youve got to have the Power then befor youwl have the res of it havent you. Which theres Power in this here Salt 4 we know that much. Its 1 of the Nos. of the 1 Big 1. All weve got to do is put it to gether with the others. (143)

In the Eusa Story itself, Eusa's scientific abilities are depicted essentially as the ability to convert one scale into another: "Eusa wuz a noing man he noet how tu bigger the smaul & he noet how tu smauler the big" (30). The 'smaller—bigger' relation is at the core of all specific scale constructions. This is the question of relative size in a nutshell, to which conventional scale hierarchies provide handy practical guides. The re-scaled world of *Riddley Walker* is a world that has failed to recover the necessary knowledge of processes at what we would call the molecular and atomic scales that is needed to reconstruct larger geographical scales, to put "boats in the air and picters on the wind."

In its re-scaling of a future world, *2312* differs dramatically from *Riddley Walker*. In contrast to the latter's narrowing of scale or down-scaling, *2312* imagines a world that is marked by the expansion of scale, by an up-scaling beyond the planetary scale taken for granted as the largest geographical extent relevant to most human social life. The 300 years that lie between the early twenty-first century and the novel's fictional future have seen a multitude of fundamental disruptions and reorganizations of scale. The twenty-first and twenty-second centuries—designated in the novel's system of historical periodization as "The Dithering: 2005–2060" and "The Crisis: 2060–2130"—experience climate collapse on Earth and "catastrophic death on all continents" (Robinson 2012: 277), but also first successes in the settlement of the moon and Mars. Depending on their geographical position and socioeconomic status, people experience down-scaling and up-scaling simultaneously during these periods. The periods of "The Turnaround: 2130–2160" and "The Accelerando: 2160–2220" then see an accelerated expansion of spatial reach with the "[f]ull application of all the new technological powers, including human longevity increases; terraforming of Mars [...]; full diaspora into solar system [...]; start of terraforming of Venus" (278). While this acceleration slows down somewhat in the following two periods, "The Ritard: 2220–2270" and "The Balkanization: 2270–2320," due largely to political tensions, the solar system is by then firmly established as the highest geographical reference for the human population's "place-based identification, economic activities, and access to mobility across space" (Hsu 2017: 125).

Dramatic advances in the sciences and massive technological innovation have revolutionized transportation and terraforming capabilities, shifting the political and economic focus from a planetary to an interplanetary perspective. New forms of transportation, new ways of inhabitation, but also striking biomedical advances and advances in computer technology form the basis for an interplanetary civilization still in the making. While Earth is still the socioeconomic, political, and cultural reference point of the thousands of small and larger communities that have formed in the solar system, it is no longer portrayed as the highest level of human scale configuration. The new absolute limit for humanity is the space beyond the solar system, the universe: it is now the stars, and no longer the planets, that "exist beyond human time, beyond human reach" (Robinson 2012: 375). Of course, any expansion beyond the traditional terrestrial scale-system can be refined much further: "Thinking through the nuances of the 'spaces of outer space' through terms such as extraterrestrial or extra-global space, earth-orbital space (involving polar, parabolic, or geostationary trajectories), interplanetary space, exo-planetary space, interstellar or celestial space, the cosmos, or even the heavens, invokes a variety of scales" (Dunnett/Maclaren 2019: 315). These nuances are secondary in *2312*, where tensions between terrestrials and "spacers" are represented in a binary fashion.

In the year 2312, the enormous increase in transportation capabilities has become manifest most significantly between planets but also on individual planets, including Earth. Some of the characters regularly travel by spacecraft between different terrestrial planets, as well as to—and on—asteroids, called "starships"

(Robinson 2012: 281), that were formed into terraria. On Mercury, the entire city of Terminator moves on giant tracks, always slightly ahead of the sun's rays, which threaten to destroy it but also drive it forward by thermally expanding the tracks on which it moves (29–30). The available range of geographical mobility is most conspicuously expressed in the movements of one of the protagonists, Swan Er Hong. These movements extend from slow travel by foot underground, to fast travel by trains and airplanes on Mercury and Earth, to wave-surfing on the F-ring of Saturn, to interplanetary trips in space ferries, space elevators, and various other types of spacecraft. Swan is a spacer, the novel's version of the typical science fiction traveler who introduces readers to the fictional future world. Spacers are humans who live most of the time in space and enjoy the privilege of regular space travel. They need to return to Earth with some regularity to maintain their health and longevity; they know that "neglect of this practice leads to a high risk of dying many decades before" (94). Spacers thus personify the new superordinate scale, the highest level of spatial mobility and communication encompassing human life throughout the solar system.

Advances in terraforming have made possible extensive and politically, economically, and culturally diverse inhabitation of the solar system. Not only do humans inhabit terrestrial planets such as Mercury, Mars, and Venus, but they also inhabit some of their moons. They create terraria on asteroids, and in 2312 they have even begun to inhabit the moons of low-density giant planets such as Saturn. A more recent innovation that enhances the attractiveness of some already colonized solar bodies is the large-scale transfer of light from a set of small "Vulcanoid" asteroids in a belt between the sun and Mercury (397–398). The novel here provides the reader with a very direct and physical sense in which the solar-system scale is being configured.

The solar system emerges as a space not only characterized by an ongoing intensification of human inhabitation, but also by an interplanetary political and socioeconomic order originating in space exploration and colonization by the powerful nations on Earth. Thus, the scale hierarchy typical of the twentieth and twenty-first centuries, in which the national scale is placed below the global scale, is no longer adequate as a shorthand. The emerging interplanetary order is marked by conflict that reflects the conflict-ridden situation on Earth, which is to a large extent caused by competing economic models. At the time of the "Accelerando," there were "several competing economies on Earth, all decisively under the thumb of late capitalism" (139). In the year 2312, "feudalistic" economies are competing with the "non-market economy" of the Mondragon settlements and with the type of capitalist system practiced on Mars, a "social-democratic system" in which political regulation plays a prominent role (139). All these systems influence social and political organization: they are fundamental to the "power geometry" (cf. Massey 1994) of the interplanetary order and the power geometry of single solar bodies, as they determine access to resources and to the means and experiences of mobility. When Wahram muses at one point that "[a]ll trouble comes from Earth" (Robinson 2012: 301), he indicates that, despite existing political conflicts on the interplanetary level, power struggles originate and are still fiercest on Earth.

In 2312, Earth has become "a mess, a sad place," as Swan muses at one point, but it still remains "the center of the story" (99). After climate collapse in the twenty-first century, Earth is still an overpopulated place with an ecology at breaking point. After an eleven-meter-sea-level rise, all the coastlines of the twentieth century are gone, and with them many plant and animal species; existing social systems are unable to respond adequately to the environmental needs of both humans and non-humans; political conflict and social ills are widespread. For survival, the human population on Earth has become increasingly dependent on resources from space. Operating on the new solar-system scale to alleviate planetary ills has thus restructured the scale system and created new networks of power.

The expanded and restructured scale system in 2312 is formally reflected by the novel's expansive, open, and ultimately epic aesthetics that diametrically contrast with the closed aesthetics of *Riddley Walker*, where the reader, caught in the perceptions and thoughts of a single narrator-focalizer, is denied information essential for understanding the situation more fully. 2312 presents a diversity of narrative voices that provide information in a collage of different types of texts. The major plot strand of the novel, the attempt of a small group of people to uncover a conspiracy that involves the manipulation of humanoid beings—beings made of "human material" and "qubes" (quantum computers)—and thereby secure peaceful interplanetary cooperation, is presented in sections that are focalized by several of the major characters. Additional information about the solar system and about the history of its colonization is given in sections called "lists," in sections named after planets and moons, and in sections called "extracts." The latter are paragraphs taken from history books that look retrospectively at the year 2312, at the centuries that precede it, and at the decades immediately following. This collage technique recalls a prevalent mode of representation for the planetary scale, as Ursula Heise has suggested: "Epic, one of the oldest allegorical forms of narrative in which the fate of the entire known world is usually at stake, has made a comeback as a way of establishing a planetary scope in storytelling." Epic, she argues, is able to "accommodate ecological dynamisms, disequilibria, and disjunctions along with ecosystems' imbrications in heterogeneous human cultures and politics" (Heise 2008: 64). One narrative element that signals the shift to levels of geographical reach beyond the planetary scale may be seen in the fact that both the lists and the "extracts" that consist of syntactically incomplete paragraphs convey an overall sense of incompleteness and openness. They also convey a sense of a continuing lack of knowledge that characterizes the world of 2312—albeit on a strikingly different level compared to *Riddley Walker*.

In 2312, a lack of knowledge is also signaled by the novel's main plot, a mystery plot. The group of spacers, first assembled by Swan's grandmother Alex, then joined by Swan and led by inspector Genette, has to find out the sources of the acts of sabotage that have accumulated in recent years and that threaten the interplanetary political order the group finds most desirable. Moreover, all the major scientific and technological advances continue to produce the unknowable side-effects or unintended consequences that have characterized industrial modernity since the eighteenth century: there is a lack of knowledge concerning the consequences of some biomedical technologies, and there is a lack of knowledge concerning the capabilities of advanced artificial intelligence. Despite the enormous successes in terraforming thousands of solar bodies, finally, there is still a lack of technological knowledge needed for improving the environmental situation on Earth:

> It was one of the ironies of their time that they could radically change the surfaces of the other planets, but not Earth. The methods they employed in space were almost all too crude and violent. Only with the utmost caution could they tinker with anything on Earth, because everything there was so tightly balanced and interwoven. (Robinson 2012: 347)

Scalar Strategies in *Riddley Walker* and *2312*

In Hoban's post-apocalyptic future, the characters' yearning for the rediscovery of molecular processes and the reconstruction of larger geographical capabilities this would allow fuels a range of attempts to rediscover the forgotten or misremembered technological secrets. It is here that we can see a "scalar strategy" (Lindseth 2006) come into play, that is, a way of trying to move from the relatively small to the relatively big or the reverse. In effect, this strategy is an attempt at "scale jumping," the transference of events or phenomena at one scale to other scales.

Riddley, Goodparley, and others are severely hampered by ignorance of the electrical and chemical processes needed to produce the power to restart a lost civilization. But this ignorance is compounded by a second level of ignorance about how to put the knowledge they do possess to work. Not all of their beliefs about chemistry are completely wrong, and Granser, one of the itinerant charcoal burners, reveals to Goodparley and Riddley that gunpowder, "the 1 Littl 1," is not to be confused with nuclear power, "the 1 Big 1" (Hoban [1980] 2002: 188–189). Granser uses the sulfur yellowcake Riddley has found to mix and detonate gunpowder late in the novel—in the process killing himself and Goodparley. Even the myths surrounding atomic fission, preserved in the figure of the "Littl Shyning Man" split in two, are not completely unconnected to what we would consider valid science.

But what science is and how scientific method works is completely beyond the characters. This is clear from the way Goodparley describes the efforts he and others have gone to:

> Weve got to work the E qwations [equations] and the low cations [locations] weve got to comb the nations [combinations] of it. We ben looking for Eusas head 1 way and a nother this long time. We ben digging in the groun for it we ben spare the mending [experimenting] we ben tryl narrering [trial-and-erroring] for it. (143)

Scientific terms—if in highly distorted forms—are invoked here, but without the faintest hint of understanding of what they mean or entail.

The figure of the ring or circle is at the heart of the scalar strategies pursued by Goodparley and Riddley in trying to make sense of how Eusa discovered the secret of radiation by splitting the atom (the "Littl Shyning Man"):

> Owt uv thay 2 peaces of the Littl Shyning Man the Addom thayr cum shyningness [radiation] in wayvs in spredin circels. Wivverin & wayverin & humin with a hy soun. Lytin up the dark wud. Eusa seen the Littl 1 goin roun & roun insyd the Big 1 & the Big 1 humin roun insyd the Littl 1. He seen thay Master Chaynjis uv the 1 Big 1. Qwik then he riten down thay Nos. uv them. (32)

The path to rediscovering the "Nos." needed to generate nuclear power, according to the disembodied head of Eusa, is to mime or reproduce this circular motion at the scale of Inland itself, that is, to "road the circel": "Let the head of Inland road the circel ful and to the senter asking what he wants to know for all of Inland. When the right head of Inland fynds the right head of Eusa the anser wil come and Inland wil rise up out of what she ben brung down to" (122).

Roading the circel, traveling with the puppet show counter-clockwise around through Bernt Arse to Fork Stoan and back northwards to "the senter" (Canterbury), is what Goodparley—as "Pry Mincer" the "head of Inland"—had been doing for years, performing the scalar strategy of jumping scale downwards, seeking to invoke molecular-level knowledge of electron orbits and fission by traveling in analogous circles through Inland. He had tried to "smauler the big" (32). The ultimate goal is to deploy the knowledge thus gained in putting "boats in the sky and picters on the wind," that is, to "bigger the smaul." Ultimately, however, all of this is in vain, in technological terms. There is no rekindling of advanced technology. Riddley and his contemporaries must continue "slogging through the mud," haunted by the knowledge of lost scales.

In contrast to the failure of the scalar strategy in *Riddley Walker*, *2312* provides two major examples of effectively employed scalar strategies. The successful interaction and interpenetration of scales becomes visible, first, in the implementation of Alex's plan to stabilize environmental and thus political and socioeconomic conditions on Earth, and second, in the course of action of the group of spacers that investigate the various acts of sabotage that threaten the power symmetry of the solar system.

After Alex's death, Swan learns that she and her allies had been working on a plan to help save Earth from itself. Alex planned "the re-wilding of Earth" (458) for the purpose of triggering an ecological recovery, that is, the reintroduction of a multitude of species that had become extinct on the planet. Alex and the interplanetary community that supported her had stockpiled "food and animals in the terraria" (81) over many years, intending to reintroduce them on Earth. While the terraria had already been providing an important part of Earth's food, more unilateral, interventionist attempts by spacers or interplanetary organizations to 'help' Earth were highly controversial and often resented. All attempts at larger-scale or more invasive terraforming of Earth had upset its delicate balances, causing widespread death and destruction (304). Therefore, Alex and her associates had been working in secret.

On August 5, 2312, Alex's friends decide to execute her scheme, sending tens of thousands of animals taken from the terraria down to the Earth's surface, first in big landers, then in smaller parachuted landers, then in aerogel balloon bags, "each transparent bubble holding inside it an animal or an animal family" (395). Thus, a scalar strategy comes to fruition, in which endangered species are initially moved systematically beyond the global scale to secure their longer-term survival, but then reintroduced on Earth to help shore up or revitalize struggling or disappearing ecosystems. This re-wilding by spacers also illustrates one of many ways in which the specific scale levels in any scale structure are never independent of each other but are reshaped or acquire different meanings when the overall structure itself changes.

The second example of a successfully employed scalar strategy is the sabotage that endangers several places in the solar system and their inhabitants. The group of spacers around Alex is also concerned with a more acute danger, namely, a possible plot among qubes, the miniaturized but ultra-powerful computers displaying artificial intelligence. Inspector Genette and Wang, two leading members of the group, have begun to detect strange patterns of qube activity and wonder whether this activity is related to seemingly unconnected incidents throughout the solar system. This suspicion intensifies dramatically when a huge and unexplained explosion wrecks the tracks on which Terminator glides along the surface of Mercury, ultimately destroying the city.

The group eventually figures out that the explosion could only have been caused by the simultaneous convergence upon one location of thousands or millions of objects, each too small by itself to trigger Mercury's protective systems. These objects had to be launched from a vast array of different places in the solar system at different times. Genette realizes that only the most powerful qubes would have been able to carry out the calculations necessary to calibrate these launches with such precision. One of the most impressive of all the imagined technological feats in *2312* is thus centrally about the interpenetration of the solar and the local scales, or, in the language of *Riddley Walker*, of "bigging the smaul."

Conclusion: Shifting Scales and the Instability of Scale Systems

The analytical focus on scale as narrative strategy has shown that the speculative futures of *Riddley Walker* and *2312* draw attention to processes of spatial structuring and to the instability of any scale system, which depends strongly on the inextricable link between spatial and social—or, to be more precise, socioeconomic and cultural—construction. The re-scaled worlds of these novels challenge twentieth- and twenty-first-century scale systems by envisioning dramatically different consequences of technological modernization. On the one hand, *Riddley Walker* provides a devastating assessment of nuclear technology, the employment of which causes a narrowing of scale and the breakdown of civilization. On the other hand, without ignoring their dangers, *2312* emphasizes the opportunities that risk technologies such as geo-engineering or biomedical and computer/AI technologies provide by presenting a new civilization characterized by an expansion of scale. In both novels, the global scale remains a pivotal construct—but it functions very differently in the respective scale systems. In *Riddley Walker*, the global scale is lost in practical terms, but it remains central to the entire narrative as a 'present absence' that acts as the focus of desire and a motivation for the actions undertaken by the story's main characters. In this dystopic world, the global scale is present as a haunting. By contrast, in *2312*, the global scale remains very much alive. Its significance, however, has been fundamentally altered by the fact that it is no longer the largest level of spatial extent structuring human society. Earth still remains utterly central, both because it is still home to the vast majority of human beings and because spacers must return to Earth periodically for health and longevity reasons. But its lingering or worsening environmental, social, and economic problems can now be addressed 'from below' at smaller scales and also 'from above,' that is, from other planets and by interplanetary alliances, consortia, or groups.

In both novels, re-scaling is thus not only a matter of adding or subtracting specific scale levels in a way that leaves the other previously accepted conventional scales intact. In *Riddley Walker*, the absence of knowledge of molecular processes and of access to other parts of the globe intensifies the significance of what we would call local and bodily scales. In *2312*, the Earth is changed by its new position in the solar system not only in ways discussed above, such as the re-wilding episode, but also by the emergence of "Solar System Cities" or "Interplanetary Cities" (which can be seen as amplifications of the economically important "global cities" of the twentieth and twenty-first centuries). These cities support the terrestrial spaceports, thus giving them a crucial interscalar position.

Finally, in their exploration of the relevance of knowledge, science, and technology for the construction of geographical scale, the novels draw attention to environmental crisis and to the significance of energy sources on which spatial practices and configurations of scale ultimately depend. *Riddley Walker* presents a civilization in which the non-human environment has again become a threat to humans. Lacking basic scientific knowledge as well as machines to sustain the economy and to ensure protection in daily life, this civilization creates a space that leaves its inhabitants acutely vulnerable. In terms of energy, the result of an earlier nuclear catastrophe is that this civilization relies almost exclusively on charcoal, a source of energy that locks the characters in place and effectively rules out the establishment of a geographically wider scale. In contrast, the energy regime in *2312* consists of a large variety of sources—most importantly, solar energy in a variety of physical forms—that allow for various types of movement and the expansion of scale toward the solar system. While Earth is still plagued by ecological crisis, the spatial practices that the expansion of scale makes possible offer at least some hope that the situation will, after all, be remedied at some point. Exploring these shifting meanings and functions of scale in the novel thus contributes to what Eric C. Otto (2012) has called "green speculations," in other words, science fictional engagements with the contemporary global environmental crisis.

References

Agnew, John (1997): "The Dramaturgy of Horizons: Geographical Scale in the 'Reconstruction of Italy' by the New Italian Political Parties." In: *Political Geography* 16, 99–122.

Branscomb, Jack (1991): "Knowledge and Understanding in *Riddley Walker*." In: Nancy Anisfield (ed.): *The Nightmare Considered: Critical Essays on Nuclear War Literature*. Bowling Green: Bowling Green State University Press, 106–113.

Chu, Seo-Young (2010): *Do Metaphors Dream of Literal Sleep? A Science Fictional Theory of Representation*. Cambridge, MA: Harvard University Press.

Delaney, David/Leitner, Helga (1997): "The Political Construction of Scale." In: *Political Geography* 16, 93–97.

Dunnett, Oliver/Maclaren, Andrew (2019): "Introduction." In: Oliver Dunnett/Andrew Maclaren/Julie Klinger/K. Maria D. Lane/Daniel Sage: "Geographies of Outer Space: Progress and New Opportunities." In: *Progress in Human Geography* 43, 314–336.

Fitting, Peter (2010): "Utopia, Dystopia and Science Fiction." In: Gregory Claeys (ed.): *The Cambridge Companion to Utopian Literature*. Cambridge: Cambridge University Press, 135–153.

Freedman, Carl (2000): *Critical Theory and Science Fiction*. Hanover, NH: Wesleyan University Press.

Gallagher, Catherine (2006): "The Rise of Fictionality." In: Franco Moretti (ed.): *The Novel. Vol. I: History, Geography, and Culture*. Princeton, NJ: Princeton University Press, 336–363.

Gruby, Rebecca/Campbell, Lisa (2013): "Scalar Politics and the Region: Strategies for Transcending Pacific Island Smallness on a Global Environmental Governance Stage." In: *Environment and Planning A: Economy and Space* 45, 2046–2063.

Heise, Ursula K. (2008): *Sense of Place and Sense of Planet: The Environmental Imagination of the Global*. Oxford: Oxford University Press.

Herod, Andrew (2011): *Scale*. London: Routledge.

Hoban, Russell ([1980] 2002): *Riddley Walker*. Twentieth anniversary edition. London: Bloomsbury.

Horstmann, Ulrich (2015): "Post-Nuclear Dystopia: Russell Hoban, *Riddley Walker* (1980)." In: Eckardt Voigts/Alessandra Boller (eds.): *Dystopia, Science Fiction, Post-Apocalypse: Classics, New Tendencies, Model Interpretations*. Trier: WVT, 303–316.

Hsu, Hsuan L. (2017): "Literature across Scales." In: Robert T. Tally Jr. (ed.): *The Routledge Handbook of Literature and Space*. London: Routledge, 125–134.

Jameson, Fredric ([1987] 2005): "Science Fiction as a Spatial Genre." In: Fredric Jameson: *Archaeologies of the Futures: The Desire Called Utopia and Other Science Fictions*. London: Verso, 296–313.

Jessop, Bob/Brenner, Neil/Jones, Martin (2008): "Theorizing Sociospatial Relations." In: *Environment and Planning D: Society and Space* 26, 389–401.

Kneale, James (2009): "Space." In: Mark Bould/Andrew M. Butler/Adam Roberts/Sherryl Vint (eds.): *The Routledge Companion to Science Fiction*. London: Routledge, 423–432.

Lindseth, Gard (2006): "Scalar Strategies in Climate-Change Politics: Debating the Environmental Consequences of a Natural Gas Project." In: *Environment and Planning C: Government and Policy* 24, 739–754.

Luckhurst, Roger (2005): *Science Fiction*. Cambridge: Polity Press.

Massey, Doreen (1994): *Space, Place, Gender*. Minneapolis: University of Minnesota Press.

Maynor, Natalie/Patteson, Richard F. (1984): "Language as Protagonist in Russell Hoban's *Riddley Walker*." In: *Critique* 26, 18–26.

McCann, Eugene (2003): "Framing Space and Time in the City: Urban Policy and the Politics of Spatial and Temporal Scale." In: *Journal of Urban Affairs* 25, 159–178.

Mousoutzanis, Aris (2009): "Apocalpytic SF." In: Mark Bould/Andrew M. Butler/ Adam Roberts/Sherryl Vint (eds.): *The Routledge Companion to Science Fiction*. London: Routledge, 458–462.

Moylan, Tom (1986): *Demand the Impossible: Science Fiction and the Utopian Imagination*. New York: Methuen.

Otto, Eric C. (2012): *Green Speculations: Science Fiction and Transformative Environmentalism*. Columbus: Ohio State University Press.

Robinson, Kim Stanley (2012): *2312*. New York: Orbit.

Smith, Neil (1990): *Uneven Development: Nature, Capital, and the Production of Space*. Oxford: Blackwell.

Vieira, Fátima (2011): "The Concept of Utopia." In: Gergory Claeys (ed.): *The Cambridge Companion to Utopian Literature*. Cambridge: Cambridge UP, 3–27.

Voigts, Eckardt (2015): "Introduction: The Dystopian Imagination—An Overview." In: Eckardt Voigts/Alessandra Boller (eds.): *Dystopia, Science Fiction, Post-Apocalypse: Classics, New Tendencies, Model Interpretations*. Trier: WVT, 1–11.

Chapter 9: The Lifecycle of Software Engineers
Geek Temporalities and Digital Labor

Jordan S. Carroll

Saturday Night Live played an important role in defining the geek: beginning in 1978, the show ran a series of comedic skits that introduced the American public to the term "nerd" and cemented many popular conventions for representing geeks (Lane 2018: 4–8). This process of mythmaking culminated in the infamous 1986 sketch featuring William Shatner. Shatner, playing himself, appears on the fourth day of the sixteenth annual *Star Trek* convention. The trekkers in the crowd seem to be trapped in a time warp. They experience *Star Trek* as if it is still ongoing, recalling the minutest details with perfect precision, and they expect Shatner to do the same. Frustrated, Shatner shouts at his fans, "You have turned an enjoyable little job that I did as a lark for a few years into a colossal waste of time!" (*Saturday Night Live* 1986: 4:22). The star of *Star Trek* then goes on to berate them for never having "kissed a girl" or moved out of their parents' basements, screaming at the geeks to "[g]row the hell up!" Here, the irate Shatner clearly speaks on behalf of chrononormativity, that is to say, a socially determined temporality oriented toward capitalist production and heterosexist reproduction (cf. Freeman 2010: 3). Instead of wasting his years on fannish pursuits, a young Shatner made time with women and advanced his career, moving beyond the show. The geek figure, however, stands for a very different temporal order. What others see as ephemeral, geeks treat as a ceaseless project, a way of life they refuse to relinquish even when it is no longer considered mature or fashionable. Although this life-aesthetic may be portrayed as regressive in the tirades of moralists like Shatner, many self-described geeks work hard to embody the temporality of *Star Trek*'s extreme fans.

The geek figure has become increasingly popular in recent years, both as a cultural phenomenon and an object of academic inquiry. Once a term of derision, "geek" now serves as a source of identity, pride, and belonging. Geeky practices including technical tinkering, gaming, and science fiction fan culture are becoming mainstream, shedding their old stigmas. Geek culture's growing importance has drawn the attention of scholars such as Andrew Ross, who theorized geek identity in the digital labor force by arguing that a geek is someone who refuses to distinguish between play and labor, allowing their time spent coding to swallow up any leisure time (Ross 2004: 10). Fan studies takes a similar approach to the geek figure: Kathryn E. Lane (2018: 10) and Matthew Hills (2002: x) suggest that a geek is someone who spends an unusual or even excessive amount of time on their favorite medium, even after others have moved on to other pursuits.

When we see geekiness as a matter of time, we begin to see some of the contradictions within the geek ethos. On one hand, geek workers often give themselves over to being hyper-exploited, enthusiastically allowing their work to commandeer their entire lives.[1] On the other, however, geek culture offers an alternative way of inhabiting time that refuses to follow the rhythms and temporal patterns of heterosexual temporality.[2] As Elizabeth Freeman suggests, normative time governs productive citizens, subjects who follow a preordained timeline of personal and economic life-achievements, "[accumulating] health and wealth for the future" (Freeman 2010: 3–4). Geeks, however, may choose to pursue ludic and subcultural achievements while postponing or foregoing life-events such as marriage or career advancement. When mainstream culture pathologizes geekdom, it does so in part because geeks' lives move at rhythms very different from normative life schedules.

Frequently, mainstream discourse describes geeks in ways that connote backwardness or delay. Terms such as "fanatic" or "cult" cast geeks as archaic survivals from a non-secular and therefore pre-modern era (Hills 2002: 117–130). The etymology of the epithet "geek" suggests madness and mental disability, while its usage to describe animal-devouring circus performers evokes abject savagery.[3] The geek appears in these constructions as throwbacks. More often, though, the stock denunciations of geek culture present fans as childish yet queer. Geeks' refusal to abandon old media—including narratives marketed for younger audiences—becomes equated with a refusal to grow up. Geeks, we are often told, fail to meet the developmental milestones associated with heterosexual maturity. The most common stereotype here is the man-child, but the rogue's gallery of geek deviants also includes the celebrity stalker, the obsessive fangirl, and the negligent gamer parent, figures whose addictive or psychotic forms of fandom seem to preclude progress in social and familial relations (Jenson 1992: 9–29). In these cautionary tales, geeks often present as perverse, frustrated, or asexual, lagging behind their age cohorts to remain in childhood or adolescence. Thus, popular culture lauds the stereotyped tech geek for youthful precocity while condemning him or her as a perpetual virgin. Geek temporalities remain in tension with normative time, alternately exploited and disavowed.

---

1   I offer a longer discussion of geek temporality and capitalist exploitation in Carroll (2019).

2   For an excellent overview of the temporal turn in queer theory, see Lothian (2018: 5–14).

3   See "Geek, n." (2018). For an exploration of "geek" as a keyword, see Dunbar-Hester (2016).

Robots and artificial intelligences from speculative fiction often serve as figures for this temporality. For example, Data from *Star Trek: The Next Generation*—who became a focal point for many fans—inhabits a very different time scale than that of his crewmates. Data not only learns cognitive skills much faster than social or emotional ones, but also he experiences the outside world as glacially slow compared to his own interior life thanks to his positronic brain's rapid processing speed. Data and other geek figures appear as space cadets, desynchronized and separated from their mundane, earthbound counterparts by signal latency and time dilation.

The equation between geekiness and artificial intelligence is explored throughout Ted Chiang's *The Lifecycle of Software Objects* (2010). Chiang's novella is particularly useful here given that it reflects the author's experience working within the technology field, where he wrote technical documents for Microsoft (Clark 2015). Moreover, speculative fiction is an especially effective way of giving an account of geek time because, as Alexis Lothian suggests, the genre frequently thematizes other temporalities, offering visions of inevitable progress or apocalyptic redemption alongside alternative temporal modes including nondevelopmental or otherwise queer futurities (Lothian 2018: 19–22). However, I would go even further. Speculative practices in fan culture do more than allow audiences to sense or imagine other times—they also entrain media consumers to follow alternative temporalities. Speculative fiction, in particular, invites the reader to become absorbed in the genre, encouraging timeless moments of wonder and sustained devotion to time-consuming practices such as conventions, fanzines, fan fiction, and cosplay.[4] Even otherwise heteronormative fans often find themselves negotiating under strained circumstances when the time required for geek activities competes with the temporality of the couple and family forms. *The Lifecycle of Software Objects*, although a relatively short text, presupposes and comments upon a much longer engagement with more demanding forms of speculative world-making.[5]

Set in the near future, Chiang's narrative follows the story of digients—sentient, commercially-produced software objects living in an online virtual world. Although they have been designed to look like anthropomorphic baby animals and cute steampunk robots, the digients behave more like the so-called child-machine envisioned by Alan Turing. Through a "genomic engine" under the brand name Neuroblast, the digients have been programmed to learn through experience (Chiang 2010: 4).[6] This makes them incredibly adaptive, but it also makes their care and

---

4 On this "timeless" or "atemporal" sense of wonder, see Landon (2002: 20).

5 Time also proves to be a major concern throughout Chiang's work. See "Story of Your Life" and "Understand" in *The Story of Your Life and Others*.

6 For an exploration of Blue Gamma digients and artificial intelligence, see Shaviro (2015: 71–102).

training very time-intensive, prompting the digient developer—Blue Gamma—to hire former zookeeper Ana Alvarado to help prepare the company's models or mascots for the consumer market. Ana, along with avatar designer Derek Brooks, geeks out about the digients, devoting her life to furthering their upbringing and, later, promoting their cause. In the process, she alienates several successive boyfriends and earns the disdain of expecting parents who see digients as pallid substitutes for children. Similarly, Derek's marriage founders partly due to his wife's frustration with the amount of time he puts into his digient hobby. Prolonged and indefinite immersion into the lives of digients seems to strain against the dictates of heteronormative time, including the schedule demands of domestic life.

Although Ana and Derek's tireless engagement with digients springs from a real ethical commitment, their geeky affinity is clearly captured and exploited by Blue Gamma. As home life diminishes and deteriorates to accommodate greater work hours, the postindustrial workplace seems to become a site of refuge, meaning, and play (Hochschild 1997). Ana and Derek join the ranks of the nudist on the late shift, the programmer sacked out in the nap corner, and the fast-track employee using company subsidized oocyte cryopreservation so they can spend their most productive years focused exclusively on career advancement.[7] This geek devotion manifests itself as a science-fictional *novum* in the world of *Lifecycle*, where many employers require their employees to wear smart devices that inject compounds of oxytocin and opioid hormones into their bodies while they are on the job. InstantRapport transdermals—originally designed to "strengthen rocky marriages and strained parent-child relationships"—now make frustrated employees feel like they are spending quality time with their work families (Chiang 2010: 104). By fostering the geek disposition, managers work to overcome any psychic or social barriers to labor's colonization of leisure time.[8]

Ana's experience reflects a very real problem in the video game industry of our present moment. Gaming company employees often report grueling schedules and unfair labor practices, especially in the weeks or months before launch day: crunch time. A widely shared Livejournal entry by an anonymous family member of an Electronic Arts employee—EA Spouse—reported that her partner worked 90 hours a week with no overtime pay or compensation time off. After detailing the immiseration of EA employees—many of whom burn out and leave—she asked EA CEO Larry Probst, "When you make your profit calculations and your cost analyses, you know that a great measure of that cost is being paid in raw human dignity, right?" (EA Spouse 2004). EA Spouse's husband ultimately succeeded in winning

---

[7] As this last example suggests, women have been hit hardest by this development, taking on additional hours of paid labor while still also performing more unwaged housework than men (Brennan 2003: 22).

[8] For a broader discussion of this temporal phenomenon, see Crary (2013).

a class action lawsuit for unpaid overtime, but the practice of crunch time still persists in the industry in part because employers have become adept at exploiting tech worker's geeky love for what they do. As one developer put it, "It has gotten so bad that a lot more experienced [developers] will see the word 'passion' on a job description as a red flag" (quoted in Schreier 2015). In technology industries, geek ardor has become a method for rationalizing if not palliating excessive hours on the clock.

Although geeks often prove to be eager and efficient workers, they do not always remain on schedule. Like their owners, the digients inhabit an alternate temporality. They can be suspended and rolled back to previous states, leading some owners to replay certain periods in digient life over and over in order to optimize their behavior or avoid more difficult growth periods. Digients can also experience rapidly accelerated time in what are termed hothouses. In some ways, the reader shares their time-sense: although the narrative takes place in the present tense, it skips forward between sections, sometimes years at a time, like a digient consciousness being suspended and reactivated. Furthermore, like their geek counterparts, the digients do not follow normative, human life-paths. Their patterns of development do not match up with expectations for children, and it is possible that they will keep learning and changing forever. Only time will tell how they will turn out, and there is no way to circumvent this by programming them with given knowledge or already formed attributes. As Ana comes to realize through her travails with the digients, "experience is algorithmically incompressible" (Chiang 2010: 138). To borrow a phrase from Kathryn Bond Stockton's work on queer children, instead of growing up, digients seem to "grow sideways," evolving in ways that are not teleological, finite, predictable, or stagist (Stockton 2009: 52).

In this regard, the digients follow the same Darwinian temporality suggested by their genomic engines. Digients are not built or programmed—they "evolve" from "biomes" (Chiang 2010: 65). As Elizabeth Grosz argues, in Darwinian time every biological change or mutation is an unforeseen event that introduces unpredictability and chance into the Newtonian world of deterministic cause and effect (Grosz 2004: 8–9). Because evolution depends on selecting from among these seemingly random variations, Darwinian temporality severs the present and future from the past, making it impossible to predict the direction of evolution with any precision. Innovation in the digient genome, then, can only be described retrospectively. Years after the digient launch, there are still geeks holding how hope that "[t]he Alan Turing of Neuroblast digients is just waiting to be born" (Chiang 2010: 135). Digients could very well become anything.

Ongoing uncertainty about digient capacities leads to an intense debate within the fan community depicted in the novella about when to end their nonage and allow them to own themselves as corporations. The question of digient age of consent becomes particularly pressing when digients ask to be copied and sold to a virtual sex doll manufacturer. Although the debate is never completely resolved, this discussion makes clear that the temporal patterns governing the digients' lives and our own are both radically contingent. Blurring between childhood and maturity replicates the same experience documented by Lynn Spigel and Henry Jenkins in their work on fans of the *Batman* television series (Spigel/Jenkins 1991: 117–148). As they suggest, returning to the favorite media of their youth allows fans to take an impish, child-like perspective, calling into question adult norms while generating playful and even utopian possibilities. This geek temporality suggests that the proper lifeline for fans, as well as digients, can only be determined through experimentation free from pre-given plans or timelines.

Their openness toward an unknowable future allows the digients and the caretakers who follow their twists and turns to resonate, at moments, with a postfordist labor landscape that no longer offers stable careers. Fernando Flores and John Gray argue that the "wired mode of life" inhabited by tech workers does not follow "a single narrative of gradual development, but by a number of discrete, even discrepant, achievements—brief lives as Nietzsche calls them" (Flores/Gray 2002: 21). As workers are forced to give up job security, they also shed their "lifelong identities," coming to experience their biographies as discontinuous and fragmentary (Flores/Gray 2002: 24). As in the present day, the tech workers in Chiang's novella are accustomed to a peripatetic work life that often requires them to take layoffs or short-term gigs in stride. Although geeks may no longer be tied down to a dream that ends with paying off a thirty-year mortgage on a family home, they also often find themselves unable to plan ahead for any other life project that they might want to pursue.

Because of its orientation toward a radically different future, Chiang's novella contains an implicit critique of the kind of nostalgia found in geek narratives that exploit the pleasure of recognition and the pride of insider knowledge, rewarding media consumers for liking what they already like and knowing what they already know. Although the mainstream videogame industry monetizes this impulse through an array of reboots, mashups, and sequels, the indie game has often displayed a very different relationship to twentieth-century video game history. Both technical feasibility and personal affinity have pushed many small video game developers to reimagine Nintendo Entertainment System (NES) genres such as platform and roguelike games. Some of the most popular indie games call attention to the creator's emulation of 8-bit console technology by narrating stories of innocence lost. Thematizing how audiences now see NES graphics and gameplay with different eyes, games such as *Braid*, *The Binding of Isaac*, and *Undertale* feature adorable, *kawaii* characters who gradually shift into more sinister or pathetic figures over time. To borrow Maria B. Garda's useful distinction, these are "reflective" rather than "restorative" retro games: while restorative nostalgia in game design attempts to somehow recreate the past, reflective nostalgia reworks and reinterprets historical aesthetics (Garda 2013: 2).⁹ Opposed to the restorative nostalgia, these games urge players to renegotiate their relationships to previous attachments.¹⁰

We see much the same sentiment in Chiang's novella. Initially, the digients appear cute in the manner of super deformed anime characters: their heads are disproportionately large compared to their bodies, giving them babyish appearances. As the narrative continues, however, they alter their avatars to match their learned behaviors. The uncontrollable passage of time is integral to the digients, leading Derek to remind one user that "a digient is not a videogame that you replay until you get a perfect score" (Chiang 2010: 20). Although the digients move beyond what seems like infantilism, they are not simply putting away childish things. Instead, they reveal how alien they are by demanding, for example, the ability to "edit [their] reward maps" (125). When majority comes with the right to don a new body or reprogram one's psychology to enjoy previously unpleasant or neutral activities, we are talking about a very different form of coming of age. Indeed, digients do not even have to maintain personal identity as they evolve: because a digient can be copied, it can split into multiple versions and explore many different life trajectories simultaneously. Embodying the dream of fandom, a digient is not so much a bounded entity as it is a living matrix of speculative possibilities.

Because digients have a potentially unlimited capacity for self-transformation, they do not always turn into docile virtual pets or charming helpers, making them a very unsafe investment. The Blue Gamma company goes under and the platform for their virtual world loses its user base and product support after the advent of newer, state-of-the-art, online environments. The market for digients crashes because most owners expect them to act like preprogrammed digital pets and quickly grow impatient with them when it becomes clear that they require years of care to flourish. Struggling to find money to port their software, the digient community dwindles and eventually becomes stranded in an online ghost town, living impoverished lives cut off from their favorite pastimes and online friends.

Here we catch a glimpse of the utopian promise contained within geek temporality. While capitalism increasingly demands flexibility and opportunism in

---

9 See Svetlana Boym on the distinction between restorative nostalgia (a yearning to recreate the past with absolute fidelity) and reflective nostalgia (a more ironic attitude toward the past that explores history's unrealized potentials while also admitting that lost time can never be relived or retrieved) (Boym 2001: 49–50). As Boym argues, U.S. popular culture tends to trade on restorative nostalgia (33–39).

10 Author Jo Walton has even come up with an entire mythology to describe the temporality of geek reflections on the mutability of the cherished childhood media: when a book turns bad between one reading and the next, it has been visited by the Suck Fairy, a magical creature who ruins narratives that have been sitting on the shelf for too long (Walton 2010).

an age of job instability and creative destruction, geeks remain fixated on ways of being associated with media from years gone by. Thus geek culture may serve as a reaction against the precariousness of late capitalism. Ana and Derek's fidelity to their digients suggests a geek ethic that might challenge capital's heedless presentism. As Alexander Cho puts it, fan practices mobilized around "cyclicality, repetition, and refrain" suggest a "possible resistant queer politics rooted in the interplay of cyclical, erotic, and melancholic queer temporalities that linger in a stubborn persistence of the past" (Cho 2015: 44).[11] Through the way they move through time, the digients resist their legal and economic status as disposable property. What makes them worthy of "respect" is that by the end of the novella they possess all of the memories and capacities that can only be achieved through "twenty years of being in the world" (Chiang 2010: 138). Ana and Derek devote their lives to shepherding the digients over onto a new platform and into a future that is increasingly hostile toward any form of loyalty to a life project outside of work. In a moment when both people and commodities become expendable while any attachment becomes a potential liability, geeks seek the reassurance of meaning and belonging through fandom.

Some digients, however, are made for the temporal regime of late capitalism. The only kinds of digients with financial backers to be ported out of the failing platform are ones produced by other companies to perform menial tasks, digients whose personalities have been engineered with neurotic anxieties and stereotyped behaviors that equip them with the superhuman ability to focus exclusively on their appointed functions. Produced by the Sophonce company, the Drayta models have an obsessive focus on problem solving. When asked any question, the Drayta anxiously repeats, "Wanna solve puzzles" (Chiang 2010: 67). Unlike the Neuroblast digients, their singlemindedness means the Sophonce digients do not require regular human interaction. This immense capacity for concentration allows them to disengage from human time and disappear into virtual worlds where time speeds up. The Drayta's accelerated microcosms parallel the distorted time-reckoning of the so-called flow experience, in which lived time speeds up as the geek gets into a groove or slows down as they focus on a difficult move (Csikszentmihalyi [1990] 1991: 66).

Despite its productivity, there is something masochistic about the flow state. The temporality of flow often proves inimical to the reproductive labor involved in maintaining one's own life. The geek figure is often portrayed as negligent of self-care, too absorbed in his or her obsessions to pay attention to sleep, diet, exercise,

---

11 Boym makes the case that reflective nostalgia draws on aspects of both mourning and melancholia insofar as it successfully grieves—realizing as it does that its lost object can never be fully recalled—even as it also turns inward to ruminate and reflect on its bereavement (Boym 2001: 55).

or grooming. Neal Stephenson's *Reamde* encapsulates this idea in Devin Skraelin, a "freakishly prolific" fantasy author who works ceaselessly producing back-stories for a game development company (Stephenson 2011: 41). Devin has built a protective shell around his workspace to maintain flow—he writes in a trailer without windows, his screen and keyboard mounted on robotic arms that follow his every movement. Biometric sensors attached to Devin's body register whether he is in flow and, when he is, a signal is given to his assistants to pass out a "Flow State FAQ" to any incoming visitors to explain why he cannot see them in a timely manner (222). Everything about Devin's body is carefully controlled to keep him in constant flow and thereby maintain his extremely fast writing pace—"all he's doing is applying scientific management principles to a hundred-million-dollar production facility (i.e. Devin) with an astronomical profit margin" (224). Before he began writing content for the videogame industry, Devin could not easily sit in an airplane seat. Now that he does all of his work while on a treadmill, exercising many hours a day, his body fat has dropped to a painful 4.5 per cent and his skin has become as thin as "shrink wrap laid directly over nerve and bone" (224). Behind his back, people in the company call him Skeletor, after the cadaverous villain of *He-Man and the Masters of the Universe*. Devin represents very real stories in game development. One author writing content for a text-heavy video game reportedly lost 10 per cent of her body weight, falling to 99 lbs., after a nine-month long period of working 80-hour weeks (Schreier 2015). This is what Teresa Brennan refers to as the bioderegulated body (Brennan 2003: 19–22, 29–31). As the laws and norms that protect time outside of work fall before the onslaught of capitalism, the worker must keep pace with ever-faster automated processes, laboring at a tempo and duration that preclude any time for rest and regeneration. Labor expands to intrude upon the normal cycles of sleep and relaxation, a disruption that employees experience as stress, anxiety, and illness (Dyer-Witheford/de Peuter 2011: 59). Although highly praised by managers, the flow state is an intimate of premature death.

Nevertheless, this morbid state of suspended self-consciousness can be extremely enjoyable. As we can see in *The Lifecycle of Software Objects*, the flow subject strives toward a queer antirelationality. When Drayta digients work, they exit from the social entirely, dropping down into timeless black holes.[12] The Draytas do not work toward building relationships with their masters, nor do they seem

---

[12] The tech geek's antisocial attitude is fundamentally bound up in gendered and economic inequalities. Flow allows the geek worker to appear to transcend the hassles of everyday life, including the concerns associated with care work, which is either foisted onto feminized others or left undone. Moreover, as Sarah Sharma argues, the accelerated, 24/7 temporalities of privileged workers such as business travelers often depends on an entire infrastructure maintained by hyperexploited workers such as taxicab drivers and hotel cleaning staff, whose time is not equally valued or supported (Sharma 2014: 139).

interested in self-improvement or becoming more human. While the Neuroblast digients move along an open-ended and unpredictable temporality, the Draytas ignore everything except for the impulse to repeat the assigned tasks they were evolved and selected to complete.[13] As such, the Draytas represent a refusal of the future. Following the stereotype of geek as stunted child, the standard avatar for the Drayta model is a "hydrocephalic dwarf," a feature that, along with its limited language abilities, gives it the semblance of an overgrown baby (Chiang 2010: 20). However, the Drayta—being a software object—represents not a return to childhood but a return to inorganic matter. Indulging in the cyberpunk's masculinist contempt for the body as meat, the temporality of geek work feeds into a repetition-compulsion not unlike the death drive (Edelman 2004: 9–11; Hayles 1999). The Draytas' self-shattering urge propels them whether they are tasked with playing games, writing code, or providing erotic gratification: we later learn of "a harem of Draytas dressed in Marilyn Monroe avatars, all bleating *Wanna suck dick*" (Chiang 2010: 20). As Gabriella Coleman points out, hackers—whom she later calls "geeks"—seem to merge with their machines when they enter flow, experiencing an ecstasy comparable to *jouissance* (Coleman 2013: 46, 13). In the brief moments before the crash, the flow state allows geeks to feel the obliterating rush of being propelled by accelerating forces beyond their control.[14] Even as it serves capital, the geek figure enjoys a transgressive pleasure.

Geek temporalities prove to be politically ambiguous. They can provide support for capital's ever-growing need for labor and consumption and they can also subtend a restorative nostalgia for media that sometimes precludes cultural innovation or social change. Increasingly, managers have worked to harness the lived experience of geek time to produce disciplined workers who willing participate in their own hyperexploitation.[15] Nevertheless, the desynchronized forms of life found in the work of Chiang and others show that geek temporalities maintain the capacity to unsettle rhythms that have come to seem natural and inevitable. The fannish desire to hold onto the past can motivate protests against capital's destruction of other modes of temporality. Whether they seem to cast forward into the future or backward into the past, geek temporalities offer speculative alternatives to the present.

---

13 For an ethnographic account of this work experience, see Ullman (1995).
14 Csikszentmihalyi himself goes so far as to name the Marquis de Sade as a master of flow (Csikszentmihalyi [1990] 1991: 69).
15 An entire school of management science has arisen around geek temporality. See, for example, Glen (2003).

References

Brennan, Teresa (2003): *Globalization and Its Terrors*. New York: Routledge.
Boym, Svetlana (2001): *The Future of Nostalgia*. New York: Basic Books.
Carroll, Jordan (2019): "Geek Temporalities and the Spirit of Capital." In: *Post45*, no. 3, August 21 (http://post45.org/2019/08/geek-temporalities-and-the-spirit-of-capital/).
Chiang, Ted (2002): *The Story of Your Life and Others*. Easthampton, MA: Small Beer Press.
Chiang, Ted (2010): *The Lifecycle of Software Objects*. Burton, MI: Subterranean Press.
Cho, Alexander (2015): "Queer Reverb: Tumblr, Affect, Time." In: Ken Hillis/Susanna Paasonen/Micheal Petit (eds.): *Networked Affect*. Cambridge, MA: MIT Press, 43–58.
Clark, Taylor (2015): "The Perfectionist." In: *The California Sunday Magazine*, January 4 (https://story.californiasunday.com/ted-chiang-scifi-perfectionist).
Coleman, Gabriella (2013): *Coding Freedom: The Ethics and Aesthetics of Hacking*. Princeton, NJ: Princeton University Press.
Crary, Jonathan (2013): *24/7: Late Capitalism and the Ends of Sleep*. New York: Verso.
Csikszentmihalyi, Mihaly ([1990] 1991): *Flow: The Psychology of Optimal Experience*. New York: Harper Perennial.
Dunbar-Hester, Christina (2016): "Geek." In: Benjamin Peters (ed.): *Digital Keywords: A Vocabulary Information, Society, and Culture*. Princeton, NJ: Princeton University Press, 149–157.
Dyer-Witheford, Nick/de Peuter, Greig (2011): *Games of Empire: Global Capitalism and Video Games*. Minneapolis: University of Minnesota Press.
EA Spouse (2004): "EA: The Human Story." In: *ea_spouse—LiveJournal*, November 10 (http://ea-spouse.livejournal.com/274.html).
Edelman, Lee (2004): *No Future: Queer Theory and the Death Drive*. Durham, NC: Duke University Press.
Flores, Fernando/Gray, John (2000): *Entrepreneurship and the Wired Life: Work in the Wake of Career*. London: Demos.
Freeman, Elizabeth (2010): *Time Binds: Queer Temporalities, Queer Histories*. Durham, NC: Duke University Press.
Garda, Maria B. (2013): "Nostalgia in Retro Game Design." In: *DiGRA '13—Proceedings of the 2013 DiGRA International Conference: DeFragging Game Studies*, August 2014 (http://www.digra.org/digital-library/publications/nostalgia-in-retro-game-design/).
"Geek, n." (2018). In: *Oxford English Dictionary Online*, June (http://www.oed.com/view/Entry/77307).

Glen, Paul (2003): *Leading Geeks: How to Manage and Lead People Who Deliver Technology*. San Francisco: Jossy-Bass.

Grosz, Elizabeth (2004): *The Nick of Time: Politics, Evolution, and the Untimely*. Durham, NC: Duke University Press.

Hayles, N. Katherine (1999): *How We Became Posthuman: Virtual Bodies in Cybernetics, Literature, and Informatics*. Chicago: University of Chicago Press.

Hills, Matthew (2002): *Fan Cultures*. New York: Routledge.

Hochschild, Arlie Russell (1997): *The Time Bind: When Work Becomes Home and Home Becomes Work*. New York: Metropolitan.

Jenson, Joli (1992): "Fandom as Pathology." In: Lisa Lewis (ed.): *The Adoring Audience*. New York: Routledge, 9–29.

Landon, Brooks (2002): *Science Fiction After 1900: From the Steam Man to the Stars*. New York: Routledge.

Lane, Kathryn E. (2018): "How was the Nerd or Geek Born?" In: Karthryn E. Lane/Palgrave Macmillan (eds.): *Age of the Geek: Depictions of Nerds and Geeks in Popular Culture*. Cham: Palgrave Macmillan, 1–20.

Lothian, Alexis (2018): *Old Futures: Speculative Fiction and Queer Possibility*. New York: New York University Press.

Ross, Andrew (2004): *No-Collar: The Humane Workplace and Its Hidden Costs*. Philadelphia: Temple University Press.

Saturday Night Live (1986): "Trekkies." In: NBC.com (http://www.nbc.com/saturday-night-live/video/trekkies/n9511).

Schreier, Jason (2015): "The Horrible World of Video Game Crunch." In: *Kotaku*, May 15 (http://kotaku.com/crunch-time-why-game-developers-work-such-insane-hours-1704744577).

Sharma, Sarah (2014): *In the Meantime: Temporality and Cultural Politics*. Durham, NC: Duke University Press.

Shaviro, Steven (2015): *Discognition*. London: Repeater.

Spigel, Lynn/Jenkins, Henry (1991): "Same Bat Channel/Different Bat Times: Mass Culture and Popular Memory." In: Roberta Pearson/William Urichio (eds.): *The Many Lives of Batman: Critical Approaches to a Superhero and His Media*. London: BFI, 117–148.

Stephenson, Neal (2011): *Reamde*. New York: William Morrow.

Stockton, Kathryn Bond (2009): *The Queer Child, or Growing Sideways in the Twentieth Century*. Durham, NC: Duke University Press.

Ullman, Ellen (1995): "Out of Time: Reflections on the Programming Life." In: James Brook/Iain Boal (eds.): *Resisting the Virtual Life: The Culture and Politics of Information*. San Francisco: City Lights, 131–144.

Walton, Jo (2010): "The Suck Fairy." In: Tor.com, September 28 (http://www.tor.com/2010/09/28/the-suck-fairy).

Chapter 10: Uncertainty between Image and Text in Ben Templesmith's *Singularity 7*
Interdisciplinary Perspectives on Narrative and Performance

Jeanne Cortiel and Christine Hanke

Comics perform a peculiar mediality in the interplay between image and text, which serves as the basis of their specific aesthetic quality and their storytelling capacity. This interplay sets the comics medium apart from written text (as in novels or short stories, for example) and audiovisual media. Many scholars who have discussed comics as a medium argue that comics require a specific imaginative input by the reader (McCloud [1993] 1994: 65–66; Saraceni 2003: 9, 51–52). While every text works with gaps of information the reader needs to fill, comics deploy visible gaps (the gutter) to modulate the pacing and development of the narrative. In this way, comics rely on a fundamental uncertainty as each gutter opens a space of speculation on how the reader is to interpret the difference between two frames. Between what the panel shows and what the gutter hides, speculation in comics makes thinkable what is inaccessible to propositional knowledge at the moment. Because of this intrinsic quality, comics may help us analyze acts of speculation more generally. Reflecting on or filling in gaps, speculation is, after all, a way of dealing with the uncertainty of not knowing for sure.

Yet unlike in written text, visuals in comics also introduce a different instance of apparent certainty in tension with another form of uncertainty. This has to do with their mode of showing and the visual pleasure they offer (Mersch 2005, 2011; cf. Boehm 2007). Images seem to suspend speculation, because what one sees has a certain presence for the beholder. The image in comics makes the fictional world present in a way that a written text cannot. Yet, as has been emphasized by phenomenology, this sense of presence in image objects has a particular quality: they bear an "artificial presence"—"a presence precisely without substantial attendance" (Wiesing [2005] 2009: 20). Although comics work through varying degrees of abstraction and a conventional visual 'language' is recognizable to readers familiar with the code (Varnum/Gibbons 2001; Saraceni 2003), they retain this quality of evidence beyond or before speculation and narrative. This artificial presence introduces a paradox for the role of the image in acts of speculation: the image object is both present and absent at the same time. It is, after all, no coincidence that the etymology of "speculation" connects to the spectacle and to an act of looking. This paradoxical relationship of the image to a mode of presence has important implications for how comics modulate uncertainty between image and text.

Comics specifically use and play with these tensions between certainty and uncertainty in any act of reading and viewing, which opens up space for speculation in a performative rather than a narrative mode. Image and text in comics thus not only work together to tell a story, but to produce an effect: they can create speculative worlds that have a reality effect for the reader/viewer. This bifurcation of realities does nothing to bring the story forward, but it adds another level of uncertainty—and, with *Singularity 7*, of discomfort—unsettling meaning-making. In comics, this bifurcation enables conscious acts of producing uncertainty, demanding equivalent acts of speculation by the reader that both maintain and suspend the ambiguity between present tense and past (or future) tense. While the box commentary may speak in the past tense, the images and the speech bubbles unfold the story in the present. In comics, seeing, deciphering, speculating, world-making, and storytelling operate on several layers that the act of reading and seeing keeps together and in tension. This is how comics work as a medium.

While all comics share this quality, there are comics that make this type of speculation their central concern. *Singularity 7* (2004) by Ben Templesmith is such an example.[1] *Singularity 7* creates a fascinating and disturbing aesthetic experience between its apocalyptic narrative and haunting images. Pushing the conventions of both science fiction and horror to their limits, the comic engages with forms of non-knowing and uncertainty in narrative and scientific speculation—always contending with the (illusory) certainty of the visual. *Singularity 7* makes use of the language of comics to present worlds within the tension between the possible, the probable, and the impossible in science fiction, in ways that are relevant to thinking about how speculation works. This tension plays out in the comic between the written text, the visual image, the narrative, and the performative in multiple layers.

Although comics studies is now an established field if not a discipline, approaches to comics as a medium differ between disciplines. Scholarship has long understood comics as imagetext, and comics studies has been an interdisciplinary endeavor from its inception.[2] However, disciplinary proclivities continue to shape perspectives. Scholars trained in literary studies tend to focus on comics as

---

1 All citations of *Singularity 7* in this chapter refer to the 2011 digital edition.
2 On comics as both text and image and neither, see Robin Varnum and Christina T. Gibbons's edited volume, *The Language of Comics: Word and Image*, which focuses explicitly on "the balance of power between words and images" (Varbum/Gibbon 2001: ix). The journals *Image[&]Narrative* and *ImageTexT* likewise focus on this synthesis, attending not only to comic strips and comics but

narrative (Kukkonen 2013; Groensteen [2011] 2013). Scholars trained in fields that focus on mediality or visual culture tend to look at comics as sequential art—following the lead of comics artists Will Eisner (1985) and Scott McCloud ([1993] 1994), and continuing with Jan Baetens's work (2011), to name just a few examples. These different perspectives produce discrepant, sometimes contradictory readings, calling for an interdisciplinary approach to comics that makes these conflicts productive. Such a dual perspective informs our study of comics as a specific practice of speculation. An interdisciplinary dialogue between literary studies and image studies enables us to show how the comic accomplishes this conscious play with uncertainty by tapping and interrelating two principal modes of speculation: narration and performance.

Furthermore, because of the unique relationship between image and text, comics favor affirmative (exploratory) types of speculation. In *Speculate This!*, the uncertain commons conceptualize "affirmative speculation" through its openness: "To speculate affirmatively is to produce futures while refusing the foreclosure of potentialities, to hold on to the spectrum of possibilities while remaining open to multiple futures whose context of actualization can never be fully anticipated" (uncertain commons 2013: ch. 1). The sometimes uneasy tension between image and text constitutive of comics opens up spaces of speculation instead of shutting them out.

How does *Singularity 7* engage in such speculative practices? Most obviously, the narrative is speculative fiction—a dystopian science fiction story that imagines an unusual alien invasion, in which the aliens terraform the earth for future colonization. The sequence of images, however, encourages speculation by the reader, as well, and this is crucial to the narrative. Without such guesswork, the story does not come together to make sense as a dystopian narrative. Combining and layering images and written text to present a dystopian world, the comic creates a disturbing narrative flow that culminates in extinction (even of the alien invaders) and an uncertain new beginning. Box commentary and character speech, then, work together (or across one another) to undermine the stabilizing tendencies of both story and image.

From the perspective of narrative analysis, *Singularity 7* engages virtually all speculative genres. Not only that, the comic reflects upon the act of storytelling as speculation, as well as on the fundamental uncertainty and non-knowing that emerge from science and technology knowing too much. All comics tell a story through the interaction between text and image, yet *Singularity 7* adds another layer through narrative embedding, a story within a story. Even though the narrative holds the comic together, there is much more to speculation in this comic

---

also to illustrated fiction and children's books. The journal *ImageTexT* takes its title from W. J. T. Mitchell's coinage of "imagetext" in *Picture Theory* (Mitchell 1994: 83).

than just storytelling, and this other aspect does not yield meaning or reveal itself through interpretation. Image studies, a young field of research in the European humanities, enables us to inquire into the specific visual experience that comics offer. The images give the comic as a whole a completely new dimension—a dimension that does not have to be directly linked to narration. *Singularity 7* features particularly striking visuals. The images are richly colorful, deliberately working with the vivid contrasts between complementary colors and juxtaposing different design styles (typographies, graphics, schemata, scientific scribblings). There is so much to see in each panel and across the pages; even photographic layers are included—for example, a photograph of the UN headquarters (Templesmith [2004] 2011, #1: 7). *Singularity 7* fully engages visual pleasure—even scopophilia. While the images in this comic attract attention and stimulate a positive affective response, they also encourage a strong repulsion that throws the reader from the realm of pleasure into a sense of disgust, horror, and anxiety. The images show grotesquely distorted characters, physical destruction of the landscape, human bodies suffering atrocious violation. This strange tension between attraction and repulsion produces a discomfort that works hand in hand with the story told—yet it is the visuals and the mixed response they elicit that make *Singularity 7* so disquieting. The pleasure one experiences regarding these images is deeply disturbing.

Responding to these observations from two distinct methodological angles allows us to focus on narrative embedding, voice, and intertextuality, as well as on visual layers, artificial presence, and sequencing to explore how uncertainty shapes the interactions between these differing medial practices. Which textual and visual strategies are performed by *Singularity 7*? How do these strategies work together to tell a speculative story? Which effects are produced by the visuals, and how do they relate to those produced by the text? How do the images enact a paradoxical presence of speculation? How does this presence interact with the narrative of disappearance? Addressing these questions together will enable us to investigate the comic's specific intermedial performativity in relation to storytelling, and to explore the potential of intermedial comic assemblages in general.

Narration and Sequential Images

In the interplay between images and text in comics, one may regard the narrative as the backbone or hinge, the element that keeps all parts together even as they tend to drift apart. The embedded narrative enables *Singularity 7* to reflect upon and disrupt the act of fictional speculation, but it also interweaves major speculative genres and tropes, including genesis and apocalypse. The narrator turns out to be a character in the story: an old man with all the paraphernalia of a teacher.

Figure 10.1: Mapping the night sky. Singularity 7 *(Templesmith [2004] 2011, #1: 3).*

He speaks to a group of young children in an enclosed space that looks like a cave. He is telling a story of origin for the dystopian narrative world, and his narrative connects with biblical Genesis. The box commentary floating on the opening page duplicates what is shown in the image, but it also gives it specific meaning in relation to the narrative: "So, it started with a light in the sky" (fig. 10.1).

The image and the text perform together here: the mise-en-abîme, the act of storytelling within the story, enables a rupture in the narrative voice right from the beginning. This embedded narrative comes to an abrupt end when the Gosiodo—the creatures whose simultaneous approach has been traced at the bottom of the page—invade the enclosure and kill the whole group, including the narrator and the children listening to him. This is especially disturbing, since many of these characters are named as if they were going to feature as central characters in the story. This disruption of the first narrative strand introduces a second: an alien invasion narrative with nanotechnology as its central risk technology. So, the dystopian narrative is cut short by the intrusion of the science-fictional apocalypse, with a new narrator voice that speaks in the present tense and shifts the performance of storytelling to another diegetic level. This shift dissolves the temporal distance between narrative and image. All inhabitants of the human enclosure have been killed, with one exception: Chon, the boy with the dragon tattoo. A third narrative strand emerges that centers around a group of special human beings who are immune to the nanites and in fact are enhanced by them. These characters introduce a connection to superhero fiction. The three narrative strands—story of origin (dystopian world), catastrophe (alien invasion), and balked rescue (superhero narrative)—correspond with three central biblical narratives: genesis, apocalypse, and redemption. Repeatedly disrupting the plot arcs it sets up, continually gesturing toward completion without fully suturing the ruptures in the storyline, this comic demands reflection upon acts of speculation that too easily rest on well-worn narrative expectations.

Time and narrative sustain an uneasy relationship in this comic, not only on the level of narrative voice but also in how the images work with the text to create a world and a story. First of all, there is a tension between the presence and immediacy of a whole page as image and the temporalization that only comes into being through an image sequence, frame by frame, gutter by gutter. But temporalization is not the same as narrativization—some uncertainties remain. For example, the three narrow panels on the top of page 6 (fig. 10.2) can be understood (according to McCloud's terminology) either as moment-to-moment—that is, temporal—transitions that show the transformation of Bobby into the Singularity, or as aspect-to-aspect transitions that depict the very moment of change. Due to the narrowness of the frames, they appear like three stroboscopic snapshots happening at almost the same time. Time itself appears unhinged, jagged, disrupted.

Chapter 10: Uncertainty between Image and Text in Ben Templesmith's *Singularity 7*   227

Figure 10.2: Moment-to-moment or aspect-to-aspect transition? Singularity 7 *(Templesmith [2004] 2011, #1: 6).*

Figure 10.3: Looking straight at the beholder. Singularity 7 *(Templesmith [2004] 2011, #1: 6).*

Singularity 7 deploys a number of visual strategies to further increase the uncertainties about the comic's temporality and its relationship to the moment of reading. The gaze of Bobby the Singularity breaks the 'fourth wall' of the narration: at the moment of reading, he is looking directly at us, the audience (fig. 10.3). This is anathema to classic cinematography, but quite common in comics. The Singularity addresses us directly—*we* are hailed. This disturbing sense of being watched, of the image gazing back at us, is an effect of the image—not the text. It invokes a Christian iconography of the Messiah realizing the medial performativity of the image: "what we see looks back at us" (Didi-Huberman 1992). The same pages of the comic use parallel montage, a cinematic strategy. In the blue frames below the embedded narrative, a parallel storyline unfolds. While the narrator tells his story, unaware of the imminent threat, the reader sees the Gosiodo approaching. The color contrast between the frames and the repetition of this pattern on several pages separates them as two realms and indicates this as a parallel montage, although this second realm initially emerges almost unnoticed and then merges with the first in a subtle way. Two layers of the story are pictured in different colors: a swarm of nanites attacking and Chon being attacked. But the colorful contrasting images produce uncertainties. While the story tells us that the nanites arbitrarily form a protection buffer making Chon special, which depends on a spatial continuity, the images present two worlds that, on some pages, are sharply separated by colorful contrasts. These contrasts both distinguish two spaces and suggest simultaneity, creating a tension between the two presented spaces as well as between the written text and the visuals. *Singularity 7* incorporates other cinematographic temporalizations, as well—ones that support the narration. We see Chon cry out loud (#1: 17), requiring us to translate a drawing of an open mouth into another medium: sound. What happens with Chon in this panel? The end of the page acts like a cliffhanger and turning the page opens a new chapter in the story (#1: 18). Here, the frames slowly fade in and, for these three frames, we suddenly have a subjective perspective of Chon, the new hero, reopening his eyes. However, while cinema deploys parallel montage, color contrasts, and—at least in conventional cinema—a correlation between image and sound, the comic intrinsically retains an indeterminacy between simultaneity and sequence. The sound remains imagined, the pitch, timbre, and accent of the narrative voice unspecified (adding other indeterminacies, as well, including the gender of the speaker). The mise-en-page and each individual panel suggest both a temporal sequence enabling narrative flow and an immediate presence, drawing attention away from this flow. *Singularity 7* makes full use of the medium's ability to push the story forward and to encourage a lingering gaze at the image, both at the same time.

In this comic, different narrative layers thus come together and collide, creating a structure of uncertainty that engenders or even presents and performs speculation itself. The images participate in telling the speculative story, but the speculation is already realized: we see what happens, a disturbing and new strange world, the events unfold in front of our eyes, the world becomes present and, in the moment of seeing, is no longer speculation.

Presence Effects of the Image

How to understand the medial differences between images and texts, between narrativity and showing? To take up an idea from Lessing's *Laokoon* (1766), we could differentiate iconic and textual qualities as follows: while verbal text as a *discursive* medium operates in a linear progression, the image as an *aisthetic* medium presents itself in a spatial mode, where the whole image is visible at once.[3] Comics, however, show how these distinctions intersect with each other. The sequentiality of images in comics operates in a mode between image and text: similar to reading, it enables a linear and thus discursive progression in the perception of a series of panels. Usually the panels in a comic are organized according to the reading direction of the respective language. Therefore, comics in English start at the top of the page, beginning with the first frame, and move from left to right and downwards, very much like written text does. At the same time, the performativity of the image and the specificity of visual perception guides the reception of comics. While texts have to be read to be understood and to be interpreted, images address our sensual perception. Thus, even if we start looking at a comic according to our writing and reading conventions, the whole page and the juxtaposition of the images will be in sight and call for our perception—we will not be able to *not* see the contrasting colors and figures of the whole page. The medial specificity of the image allows us to see the panels as separated (by the gutter) as well as connected, an ensemble image that spreads over a whole page, since all panels on a page are present at the same time. In a similar way, written text in comics—to be precise, its 'writtenness' (cf. Krämer 2003)—also has iconic qualities: its typography might indicate its function as speech via italics, or as commentary via boxing and capitalization, or as sound via onomatopoetic visualization. The visual mode of showing (Mersch 2002b, 2011) is why the image is connected to a certain presence, thereby producing effects of evidence.[4] This is what we propose to call the "visual performativity of comics." As the image produces presence, it generates visibility, it shows something and shows itself. The presence of what is shown stands in conflict with claims of the possibility of subjunctive images (cf. Wolf 1999; Buckland 1999; Metz 2008). The grammatical format of the subjunctive, like the possibility of negation, seems instead to belong to the medial logic of the text/language in a literal sense. This becomes evident, for example, when the image performs an act of immediate interpellation—as when the character looks out of the panel as a

---

3   In order to underline that focus is not on "aesthetics" (with its associations of beauty and the arts) but instead on a mode of sensory perception (Ancient Greek: αἴσθησις, *aísthēsis*), we use the term "aisthesis" here with respect to the dimensions of showing/looking related to the image.

4   A textual mode of showing in literature might also yield instants of a peculiar presence, which Roland Barthes named the "reality effect" (Barthes [1969] 1989).

disturbing presence addressing us, the beholders (fig. 10.3). This visual evidence-effect exceeds the meaning-making process of the narrative, while the text narrates the event as in the past. Two realities, two worlds, two narrative possibilities face the reader at the same time. The staring face addresses us as readers in the here and now, drawing us not only into the story but into the story world, while the narrative instance situates us both somewhere else and in another time.

Textual and Visual Layering

The textual and the visual dimensions of the comic therefore engage us in different ways. Images address our visual perception, they can affect us before or beyond any cognitive process, before or beyond understanding: we see them and they might look back (Didi-Huberman 1992) or puncture our perception (Barthes [1980] 1981). Text addresses our cognition, requires us to read and understand words and sentences. The boundaries between these two aspects of the comic are blurry since text has to be seen in order to be read and images frequently have to be read in order to be understood. It is this imbrication of modes that makes comics so interesting as a medium of speculation. The narrative emerges between the text and the image, a process that requires our imagination, our ability to speculate, to fill in gaps. But the interplay between text and images also has an effect that goes beyond their function in creating a narrative—together, they perform a presence that counteracts the temporal flow of the sequence and the story. In other words, they are performative, in the sense of J. L. Austin's definition of a performative speech act: they do something by saying and by showing (Austin 1962: 6).

Singularity 7 not only uses the performative and narrative means of comics as a medium, but also reflects upon the act of storytelling through speculation, and its images reflect upon their status as images as well as their relation to spoken and written text. This raises the question of how *Singularity 7* deals with uncertainty and speculation specifically. One of the most prominent features of *Singularity 7*, one which it shares with many other speculative comics, is the use of multiple layering techniques. As explained above, the images give the comic as a whole a completely new dimension—a dimension that does not have to be directly linked to narration. They are characterized by a richness and a distinctive layered aesthetic that is a result of the specific production process, which Ben Templesmith describes as follows:

> [T]he art is all hand drawn, on tonal paper, then I ink it, lay in some grey tones and white highlights using paint and markers and anything that comes to hand. Then I scan them in and add photographic layers, be it textures of cracked walls, collages I've made and bits of faces, before adding color, all in Photoshop. At the end of the

day it's still about 80% drawn and 20% computer. But I don't actually draw on it, I just use Photoshop as a composition and layering tool really. (Templesmith quoted in Ambush Bug 2008)

This layering process allows Templesmith to superimpose very different techniques and textures. Yet while the layers remain visually effective, we have to concede that, superimposed upon each other, they melt into one visual experience, one picture, in which the different layers become at the same time indistinguishable as they constitute the initial visual effect.

Figure 10.4: Layering with photographic images. Singularity 7 *(Templesmith [2004] 2011, #1: 9).*

It is this interweaving of different layers and different styles that make it difficult to notice why the characters in *Singularity 7* are so disturbing. Many of the drawn faces are layered with photographic images (fig. 10.4; cf. #1: 9, panel 1). A careful look reveals that some parts of the faces include photographic traces: parts of the chin, the eyes, but mostly the regions around the nose. To understand the strange effect and affect of this photographic layer, we have to take into account that the photographic medium in our culture is understood as indexical: what can be seen on the photograph has been in front of the camera. Because of the indexicality of this medium, photography is often ascribed a status of mechanical objectivity, neutrally registering what has been in front of the lens, a realistic medium (Barthes [1964] 1977; Kracauer 1960; Daston/Galison 2007). Furthermore, in contrast to the abstracting or typifying graphics in comics, a photograph always presents a concrete individual and concrete object. For the comic as an otherwise clearly constructed, fictional and abstracted product, this insertion of bits of face-photographs produces a very disturbing yet unconscious effect. It brings the characters closer to us, they become human like us, as if they were our own undead in a photographic-indexical sense (cf. Fürst/Krautkrämer/Wiemer 2010).

This means that, in terms of the images, the comic dissolves the boundaries between the characters and the readers, the dystopian narrative world and the world in which we live, at the moment of reading. They 'have been there'—to invoke Roland Barthes's account of the photographic *"having-been-there"* (Barthes [1964] 1977: 44). Through the photographic layer, these image objects appear as emanation of a referent, as if they existed in our 'real' world. Not only the protagonists are shaped by these traces of humanity and individuality, but also the foils, the Gosiodo. This makes the aisthetic experience even more ambivalent: we cannot ban the antagonists as nonhuman, for they share the same traces of humanity even in their grotesque physical form. Again and again, a Gosiodo gazes out of the frame, looking directly into our eyes—they are us at the same time they are the Other, they are addressing us, calling for response and pulling us into their disturbing world.

With respect to the textual performance in comics, we can observe that the written text depends on the images and, at the same time, enforces a temporal flow in the panel. Yet the relationship between text and images in comics is far from trivial. Speech bubbles and commentary boxes frame much of the text, suggesting a particular relationship with the visuals that oscillate between immediacy and (narrative) mediation. Speech bubbles, like quotation marks in a novel, suggest the presence of voice and add not only temporal sequence but also an auditory layer to the image, highlighting the performative dimension of written text. Yet the text in commentary boxes, using past tense, serves to create a temporal distance between the moment of reading and the story world, the diegesis. In *Singularity 7*, written text is used in different ways to further emphasize this distance. The narrative begins with an embedded narrative related to text written in quotation marks in box commentaries. Text is also scribbled into the images themselves, usually providing seemingly redundant information—for example, an onomatopoetic "boom" creates a sound effect for the image, whose high-contrast composition already suggests a loud sound in a synesthetic manner (#1: 13, panel 7). While the images address the beholder directly in the present tense, the text here creates an effect of distance and absence through the use of past tense. Thus, while the narrative rests on the interplay between text and image, it is the written text that situates the narrative temporarily and marks its genre affiliation. In comics there is therefore always a tension between the temporal distance of the narrative world in the act of storytelling and its presence through the embeddedness in the images. The act of narration as presented in fiction also constitutes the make-believe or imagination of presence: the narrator and the reader conceived as embodied and engaged in the act of making meaning at the same time (Berns 2014). The act of narration is not only the performance of telling a story; it is also the performance of gender (cf. Lanser 1981)—alongside ethnicity, sexuality, and class.

The images in comics make the fictional world present and rely on the written text to create the sense of a performance with actors acting out the narrative on a stage. This is relevant when we look at graphic narratives as practices of speculation in a wider sense, since speculation always requires a point of reference. In other words, speculative fiction is fictional only in relation to an assumed actual world: the world in which the act of reading must take place. The assumed actual world affords to the fiction the condition of make-believe. In this way, in comics, speech bubbles signal performance and immediacy, yet the box commentary also serves to indicate the presence of mediating speech. *Singularity 7* at the beginning presents a character in the act of storytelling, whose speech is identified through quotation marks in the box commentary—highlighting the embeddedness of the narrator's words within the control of another narrative instance, but also signaling the physical presence of the narrator in the frame. The quotation marks suggest both temporal distance and immediate presence, allowing the comic as a whole to oscillate between narrative and performance, both pulling the story forward and producing a series of immediate effects between image and text.

Intertextuality/Interpictoriality

While the aisthetic experience in this comic breaches the boundaries between speculation and evident factuality, between this world and another, the images also have another agenda that connects them with other images. Just as narrative in *Singularity 7* draws from the traditions of storytelling in biblical apocalypse, science fiction, dystopia, and superhero fiction, so too do the images draw from the visual iconography of shared fear and hope. Visual intertextualities become relevant to the comic's entanglement or engagement with speculation; these intertextualities are quite transparent, but they do bring in another level of complexity to the speculative work these images perform.

As the story of genesis told in the embedded opening narration, a redemption narrative is set up and swiftly cut short without much fanfare. When the aliens finally arrive on earth to survey the terraforming work performed by their nanites, the Singularity greets them as "the Masters" in a pose that clearly references Christ on the cross (fig. 10.5).

The Christ imagery is far from subtle and thus tightens the irony of the moment. It also reinforces the religiously informed visual language used throughout the comic that references the visual history of the Bible without either creating a critique of Christianity or hailing religion as a solution to the technoscientific uncertainties that literally plague the narrative world.

Figure 10.5: Christ imagery when the Singularity greets the aliens as "the Masters." Singularity 7 *(Templesmith [2004] 2011, #4: 17).*

This imagery is reminiscent of German Renaissance artist Albrecht Dürer, who was instrumental in shaping Western religious iconography. His series of fifteen woodcuts on the Apocalypse, *Die heimlich offenbarung iohannis (Apocalipsis cum figuris)* (1498), still have a powerful presence in the visual tradition of the end of history. References to this tradition in *Singularity 7* anchor the comic's religious borrowings from an era before the advent of both modern fiction and probability calculation, that is, before the emergence of a contingent future in the modern world (cf. Esposito 2007: 7–12). These images contradict the idea of the future as subject to change based on events in the world rather than predestined by an external power. On one level, these visual references point to an idea of certainty that is lost by imagining the future as contingent upon what happens in the world. This memory of certainty is in tension with the radical uncertainty with which the comic is saturated, in terms of both its visual aesthetics and its narrative. In other words, the idea of certainty suggested by—in this case—the figure of Christ on the cross throws into relief the uncertainties in the comic.

In a less obvious way, a young woman who appears out of nowhere in issue #3 may also be seen as a related instance of visual intertextuality. She appears incongruously at a point in the narrative when the makeshift superhero-posse gets ready to face the threat of the Singularity. On a cinematic, three-panel page showing different iterations of light at the end of a tunnel, she emerges from the light apparently walking directly towards the viewer. The first panel is empty; the second panel shows her walking form indistinctly; and the third panel shows her gazing out of the center of the image pleadingly, holding an infant, awash in light from the tunnel: "Help me, please . . ." (Templesmith [2004] 2011, #3: 17). This image calls up representations of the Virgin Mary with the Christ child (including Dürer's), suggesting fragility, vulnerability, and invoking nostalgic notions of domestic bliss, reproduction, and procreation—as well as the question of who may be the father of the child. Ultimately, the woman turns out to be a bomb. She will become one in a series of terminal catastrophes in the comic, all of which are entirely contingent and follow no apparent logic other than that of destruction. The child will be the only remnant of humanity, its lone survival testament to the way in which the comic scoffs at teleological speculation.

A very different interpictorial strategy is invoked by the promotional group shot that announces the superhero narrative in the comic (fig. 10.6), another opportunity to frame a narrative of redemption.

Figure 10.6: Superhero group shot. Singularity 7 (Templesmith [2004] 2011, #1: 24).

The group shot invokes a particular subgenre of the superhero narrative that features bands of superheroes working together to counteract and manage the contingencies of the narrative world and restore a safe equilibrium. The classic superhero provides certainty in a contingent world. Like the references to Christ and Mary, the band of superheroes in this comic ultimately signify the opposite of what they visually suggest. Applying the weaponized nanites produced by the human scientists, they cause the complete dissolution of virtually everything in the narrative world, including the seemingly omnipotent aliens. Again, the intertextual reference introduces an additional layer of meaning to the image here, one that highlights the contradictions among the disturbing visual aesthetics, the iconography of certainty, and the ambiguous and paradoxically open-ended narrative.

These various references invoke the certainties of religion and classic superhero narratives neither nostalgically nor critically. These certainties simply hover in the background and intensify the effect of the comic's disturbing uncertainties. While it makes sense to *read* the images, to contextualize them culturally and historically, the images also create an affective response long before we start thinking about them, long before we historicize and categorize the images of Christ, Mary, superheroes, and science. Narrative embedding and layering, as well as a multiplicity of different layers in each individual image, become instrumental in engaging with uncertainty in this comic. Yet the comic adds yet another, crucial layer that comments on these acts of speculation; in this layer, the comic looks back at itself and reflects upon its status as a composite of images, written text, performance, and narration.

Reflexivities: Disrupting Boundaries between Text and Image

Taking a closer look at the opening page (fig. 10.1), which we discussed above in terms of narrative embedding, we see another layer of text in addition to the box commentary: the star constellations of the zodiac superimposed on the image of the night sky. Besides just presenting a world, this page also invites an intertextual reading, for it represents an astronomical map that spatially organizes the sky and gives it meaning. It references long-established scientific certainties, the periodic return of the same, marking the seasons, marking time. The image thus points to both the biblical story of origin and the beginnings of science, two historical paragons of absolute certainty.

Yet in addition to this graphic reference and the box commentary, the page features handwritten notes haphazardly scratched across the image, as if the image were just a draft and not a page in a carefully edited and published book. The note says "the light"—or perhaps "THE light"—turning the indefinite article of the narrator's speech ("a light") into a definite light, the light of the story, the light that always marks the beginning, that is, the clichéd light of all creation narratives, duplicating the light already seen in the image and also undermining it, as if imaging were insufficient to convey these meanings on its own. This note introduces another layer of uncertainty while simultaneously announcing the text's fictional status, as well as its perhaps ironic reference to myth. The handwritten note poses as a simple description of the light in the image, yet it remains entirely indeterminate. At the same time, it is not clear at all where this writing comes from or where it belongs. It is almost invisible. And what about all the other written text: the speech box, the astronomical terms? The use of three different typographies points to the visuality of written text, its notational iconicity (*Schriftbildlichkeit*) (Krämer 2003) and the relation between image and text: the visual appearance of the letters gives us hints for assigning them specific functions in the comic. Yet the layering of three different typographies on this first page of the comic appears to make script itself indeterminate. Is the scribbled phrase "the light" an image caption? Is it a performative speech act that makes the light appear? Or is itself an image of a written text (or act of writing)? This image play is reminiscent of René Magritte's many variations in his picture series *Ceci n'est pas une pipe* (1928–1966), which performs the differences between image and text, words and things, while at the same time blurring the relations between them (Foucault [1973] 1983; cf. Mersch 2002a: 294–305). The play between image and text is infinite. The indeterminacy of the written "the light" reflects the mediality of the comic medium itself—and, in doing so, frames this comic as self-reflexive of its own medium. The interplay between image and text, the visibility and iconicity of script, and the schematic and abstract graphics themselves become texts instead of images. Yet it is the visual dimension of the comic that produces this indeterminacy between text and image.

Rereading *Singularity 7* with awareness of this framing calls attention to multiple iterations of such scribblings. For example, the panel that presents the superhero posse of "specials"—human beings somewhat immune to the nanite invasion—also features multiple layers of script (fig. 10.6). On a narrative level, the specials are taunting the Gosiodo and getting ready to fight them. Yet the panel does not simply tell the story and ironically reference the superhero genre. The narrative flow is disrupted yet again by a haphazardly scribbled note in square brackets on top of the scene: "standard group shot." Very similar to "the light," this note offers a descriptive commentary that does not describe the scene in the narrative world, but instead categorizes the type of image as a clichéd shot showing a group of superheroes displaying their individual superpowers as well as their coherence as a group. There are many handwritten notes throughout the comic, but these two offer explicit metalevel commentary, outside not only the narrative world but the act of narration itself. They announce that the comic is embedded in cultural practices of speculating (envisioning) origins and destinations, pasts and futures. Since the two scribbled notes appear to be in different handwriting, they may also be notes from previous readers providing their critical reading of the comic.

Figure 10.7: Nanites dissolving a human. Singularity 7 *(Templesmith [2004] 2011, #1: 22).*

The way in which the images visualize catastrophe and dissolution creates another medial reflexivity. Figure 10.7, for instance, shows the physical dissolution of a living human subject in an experiment conducted by surviving scientists in a desperate attempt to stop the nanite infections: the body not only dies but vanishes as a whole. This decomposition is visually performed as a dissolution of the very material constituents of the comic itself. The texture of the face disappears, the graphic lines dissolve, and nothing but a green mist remains—without iconic contrasts anymore, as if the image itself vanishes or becomes an almost empty green plane—a non-image which appears more as a modern abstract painting.

In the final catastrophe this aesthetic strategy is much more radicalized (Templesmith [2004] 2011, #4: 24–25). The final destruction dissolves the Gosiodo and the Singularity again by dissolving the graphic lines and then infecting the whole page spread, erasing the frames and, in the end, dissolving the medium itself—everything becomes a whitish picture plane, nothing will be left over, and we are almost at the end of the comic. It would have been even more radical if these were the very last pages of the comic, but they are not.

Visually, the comic dissolves, but the reference to biblical apocalypse here also gives this page spread a narrative significance. Specifically, the image can be read as a reference to the book of Revelation in the Bible, which details the final judgment: "And whosoever was not found written in the book of life was cast into the lake of fire" (Rev. 20:15, King James Version). This line does not represent the end of revelation, as the next verse envisions "a new heaven and a new earth: for the first heaven and the first earth were passed away; and there was no more sea" (Rev. 20:16). In this context, the final words on this comic page, "this is the end of everything," correlate with the uncertainty, the guessing in the narrative world and in the act of reading, but also with the certainties of demise and resurrection, prophecy and revelation suggested in biblical apocalypse and superhero narrative alike. In *Singularity 7*, as in the biblical book of Revelation, the end is a new beginning, even if it remains entirely uncertain here. The certainties suggested by the evidentiary character of the images, by the biblical narrative and the superhero genre, throw into relief the fundamental uncertainties radically explored in this comic. And these are the catastrophic uncertainties emerging from the idea of accidental human disappearance, with no narrative left to imagine an alternative ending, except an improbable fresh start with a crying baby that may bring life or new death. Who knows?

References

Ambush Bug (2008): "AICN Comics News Shoot the Messenger: News! Q&@ With Ben Templesmith! & The Tournament Continues: Winners & Bracket 2!" In: *Ain't It Cool News*, April 7 (http://www.aintitcool.com/node/36308).
Austin, J. L. (1962): *How to Do Things with Words*. Oxford: Oxford University Press.
Baetens, Jan (2011): "Abstraction in Comics." In: *SubStance* 40, 94–113.
Barthes, Roland ([1964] 1977): "Rhetoric of the Image." In: Roland Barthes: *Image–Music–Text*. Stephen Heath (ed. and trans.). London: Fontana Press, 32–51.
Barthes, Roland ([1969] 1989): "The Reality Effect." In: Roland Barthes: *The Rustle of Language*. Richard Howard (trans.). Berkeley: University of California Press, 141–148.
Barthes, Roland ([1980] 1981): *Camera Lucida*. Richard Howard (trans.). New York: Hill and Wang.
Berns, Ute (2014): "Performativity." In: Peter Hühn/John Pier/Wolf Schmid/Jörg Schönert (eds.): *The Living Handbook of Narratology*. Hamburg: Hamburg University (http://www.lhn.uni-hamburg.de/article/performativity).
Boehm, Gottfried (2007): *Wie Bilder Sinn erzeugen: Die Macht des Zeigens*. Berlin: Berlin University Press.
Buckland, Warren (1999): "Between Science Fact and Science Fiction: Spielberg's Digital Dinosaurs, Possible Worlds, and the New Aesthetic Realism." In: *Screen* 40, 177–192.
Daston, Loraine, and Peter Galison (2007): *Objectivity*. Cambridge, MA: MIT Press.
Didi-Huberman, Georges (1992): *Ce que nous voyons, ce qui nous regarde*. Paris: Les Editions de Minuit.
Eisner, Will (1985): *Comics and Sequential Art*. Tamarac, FL: Poorhouse Press.
Esposito, Elena (2007): *Die Fiktion der wahrscheinlichen Realität*. Nicole Reinhardt (trans.). Frankfurt a. M.: Suhrkamp.

Foucault, Michel ([1973] 1983): *This Is Not a Pipe*. James Harkness (ed. and trans.). Berkeley: University of California Press.

Fürst, Michael/Krautkrämer, Florian/Wiemer, Serjoscha (eds.) (2010): *Untot: Zombie Film Theorie*. München: Belleville.

Groensteen, Thierry ([2011] 2013). *Comics and Narration*. Ann Miller (trans.). Jackson: University Press of Mississippi.

Kracauer, Siegfried (1960): *Theory of Film: The Redemption of Physical Reality*. New York: Oxford University Press.

Krämer, Sybille (2003): "Writing, Notational Iconicity, Calculus: On Writing as a Cultural Technique." Anita McChesney (trans.). In: *Modern Language Notes* 118, 518–537.

Kukkonen, Karin (2013): *Studying Comics and Graphic Novels*. Chichester: Wiley-Blackwell.

Lanser, Susan S. (1981): *The Narrative Act: Point of View in Prose Fiction*. Princeton, NJ: Princeton University Press.

McCloud, Scott ([1993] 1994): *Understanding Comics: The Invisible Art*. New York: HarperPerennial.

Mersch, Dieter (2002a): *Was sich zeigt: Materialität, Präsenz, Ereignis*. München: Fink.

Mersch, Dieter (2002b): "Wort, Bild, Ton, Zahl: Eine Einleitung in die Medienphilosophie." In: Dieter Mersch: *Kunst und Medium: Zwei Vorlesungen*. Kiel: Schriften der Muthesius Kunsthochschule, 131-253.

Mersch, Dieter (2005): "Das Bild als Argument." In: Christoph Wulf/Jörg Zirfas (eds.): *Ikonologien des Performativen*. München: Fink, 322–344.

Mersch, Dieter (2011): "Aspects of Visual Epistemology: On the 'Logic' of the Iconic." In: András Benedek/Kristóf Nyíri (eds.): *Images in Language: Metaphors and Metamorphoses*. Frankfurt a. M.: Peter Lang, 169–194.

Metz, Anneke M. (2008): "A Fantasy Made Real: The Evolution of the Subjunctive Documentary on US Cable Science Channels." In: *Television and New Media* 9, 333–348.

Mitchell, W. J. T. (1994): *Picture Theory: Essays on Verbal and Visual Representation*. Chicago: University of Chicago Press.

Saraceni, Mario (2003): *The Language of Comics*. London: Routledge.

Templesmith, Ben ([2004] 2011): *Singularity 7*. Issues #1–4. Digital Edition. San Diego: IDW Publishing (https://www.idwpublishing.com/product-category/singularity-7/).

uncertain commons (2013): *Speculate This!* Durham, NC: Duke University Press.

Varnum, Robin/Gibbons, Christina T. (eds.) (2001): *The Language of Comics: Word and Image*. Jackson: University Press of Mississippi.

Wiesing, Lambert ([2005] 2009): *Artificial Presence: Philosophical Studies in Image Theory*. Nils f. Schott (trans.). Stanford, CA: Stanford University Press.

Wolf, Mark J. P. (1999): "Subjunctive Documentary: Computer Imaging and Simulation." In: Jane M. Gaines/Michael Renov (eds.): *Collecting Visible Evidence*. Minneapolis: University of Minnesota Press, 274–291.

Chapter 11: This World Which Is Not One
Superhero Comics and Other Dimensions of Reference

Mark Jerng and Colin Milburn

In 1961, the Flash discovered the secret history of comic books—a history of alternate histories, multiple worlds, and retroactive continuities. The original Flash, a young scientist named Jay Garrick, first appeared in 1940 in the anthology series *Flash Comics*, published by All-American Publications. Created by Gardner Fox and Harry Lampert, the Flash was one of many comic-book superheroes invented after the breakout success of Superman in 1938. The Flash eventually got his own series, *All-Flash*, but as sales of superhero comics dwindled following the end of World War II, the adventures of the Flash—along with many other heroes from the so-called Golden Age of comics—were cancelled, consigned to the rubbish bin of history. By 1951, the Flash had disappeared from this world.

But in 1956, a completely new Flash character appeared in the DC comics anthology *Showcase #4*. Created by Robert Kanigher and Carmine Infantino, the new Flash—now a police scientist named Barry Allen—had similar attributes to the old Flash, including superfast speed and lightning-bolt motifs on his costume. But otherwise he was a totally distinct character, living in a world in which the old Flash, Jay Garrick, had never existed. The popular success of the new Flash led to the rebooting of many other superhero characters in the 1950s and 1960s, ushering in what has come to be known as the Silver Age of comics. Then something remarkable happened. In the 1961 story "Flash of Two Worlds" (*The Flash* #123), written by Gardner Fox and drawn by Carmine Infantino, Barry Allen discovered that he could alter the speed of his molecular vibrations in such a way that he could enter another dimension of spacetime, a parallel world: "The way I see it, I vibrated so fast—I tore a gap in the vibratory shields separating our worlds! As you know—two objects can occupy the same space and time—if they vibrate at different speeds!" (Fox/Infantino/Broome [1961] 2009: 15). As Barry explored this other universe, overlapping his own universe but separated by an impossible vibrational barrier, he suddenly came face to face with Jay Garrick. As it turns out, the old Flash did not cease to exist in 1951. On the contrary, he and his world had continued in their own fashion: an entirely separate timeline, a different Earth than the one inhabited by Barry Allen. This science-fiction conceit, allowing both the original Flash and the new Flash to have independent realities, each with its own historical events, characters, and thematic concerns, was to have a profound impact on the narrative logic of superhero comics.

It was not actually the first time that a superhero had met an alternate version of themselves in a different universe. Wonder Woman had already discovered a parallel Earth and a parallel Wonder Woman in the 1951 story "Wonder Woman's Invisible Twin," written by Robert Kanigher and drawn by H. G. Peter (*Wonder Woman #59*). But "The Flash of Two Worlds" definitively established that all previously published comics were equally canonical, and if there were any discontinuities—internal contradictions, discrepancies in characterization, or even entire franchises that seemed narratively incompatible with other franchises—there was now a rational explanation: these things happened in other worlds, parallel realities. For DC Comics, it inaugurated the concept of the "multiverse"—initially involving just two different storyworlds, Earth-1 and Earth-2, but eventually coming to involve a sprawling multitude of alternate dimensions and timelines. Over time, as more and more comics were published, the multiverse became an invaluable trope for managing the proliferating complexities of ongoing serial narratives, branching plots, intersecting titles, and the occasional franchise reboot. Marvel Comics, Milestone Comics, Image Comics, and other companies would likewise embrace some version of a multiverse as a core feature of the superhero genre.

But in thematizing the concept of alternate timelines, the "Flash of Two Worlds" story also made a bold claim for superhero comic books as speculative media, with unique capacities to reflect upon events past, present, and future, to examine the unactualized potentialities of history. Indeed, when Barry Allen meets Jay Garrick for the first time in the alternate universe, he realizes to his great surprise that he has actually met the old Flash before, in a fashion: "You were once well-known in my world—as a fictional character appearing in a magazine called Flash Comics! When I was a youngster—you were my favorite hero!" (Fox/Infantino/Broome [1961] 2009: 17). As it turns out, according to "Flash of Two Worlds," comic-book writers and artists in all worlds have a super power of their own: they are preternaturally sensitive to the "vibrations" of other universes, and they are able to render these divergent realities graphically visible, making them available for cultural delectation and deliberation in comic-book form. As Barry Allen tells Jay Garrick, "A writer named Gardner Fox wrote about your adventures—which he claimed came to him in dreams! Obviously when Fox was asleep, his mind was 'tuned in' to your vibratory Earth!" (17). In this metafictional twist, the comics writer Gardner Fox becomes a character in Barry Allen's world—an alternate Gardner Fox from the one in our world, apparently, where both Flashes are nothing more than fictional characters. But at the end of this story, Barry Allen decides that his discovery of a parallel world is such an outlandish notion that only comic-book fans would take it seriously: "The only ones who'd really believe it would be the readers of Flash Comics! That's why I'm going to look up Gardner Fox who wrote the original Flash stories and tell it to him! He can write the whole thing up—in a comic book!" (32). A recursive joke, a self-reflexive quip about the tendency of comics to present notions of radical difference both seriously and ironically at the same time, it nevertheless implies that superhero comic books even in our own mundane world may be peculiarly attuned to vibrations from a different history entirely—reworking the givens of the present by forging new, retroactive continuities.

In other words, "Flash of Two Worlds" represents the speculative affordances of the residual. According to the cultural theorist Raymond Williams, processes of cultural formation are characterized by dynamic interrelations of dominant, emergent, and residual elements. For Williams, "The residual, by definition, has been effectively formed in the past, but it is still active in the cultural process, not only and often not at all as an element of the past, but as an effective element of the present" (Williams 1977: 122). In this regard, "Flash of Two Worlds" literalized the residual as an active and effective force in superhero comics. Furthermore, it suggested that the residual is not merely a lingering cultural memory—for example, Barry Allen's recollection of reading about Jay Garrick's allegedly fictive adventures in his childhood. For the residual also describes unactualized alternatives to the present, the residue of potential histories that did not take place or become culturally dominant but remain available for other reconstructable futures: they are reminders of what could have been and what might yet still come.

The cultural theorist Stuart Hall has likewise emphasized the importance of the residual: "An adequate account of the whole culture of the modern world cannot be given without reference to the traces of residual ideas and practices which are appropriated into an enormous variety of social struggles. [...] The point is that these images from the past are recuperated into the present, where they work again. We work on and with them; we even build on bits of them in order to envisage what we cannot know, what we have no image for" (Hall 2016: 49–50; cf. Bardini 2011). To be sure, after the two Flashes meet one another, they initially decide to proceed independently, each fighting crime in their separate ways. But they soon realize that they are more effective when they team up: "Together, the new Flash and the old Flash streak out to take up the challenges of the super-criminals—uniting as a duo for the very first time" (Fox/Infantino/Broome [1961] 2009: 26). The present recuperates the past, and previously unimagined futures suddenly emerge: "Vibrating in unison, the scarlet speedsters catapult forward . . ." (28). Moreover, even after Barry Allen returns to his own Earth at the end of "Flash of Two Worlds," the knowledge that each Flash has of the other—that there is another Earth, another mode of existence—continues to inform their actions. They would go on to have many adventures together over the years, often intersecting at pivotal moments with dramatic implications for the fate of the multiverse.

Indeed, "Flash of Two Worlds" became a key reference point for subsequent developments in the vast narrative of DC Comics. In 1962, for example, when the Flashes reunited in "Double Danger on Earth" (*The Flash* #129), a discreet footnote reminded readers of previous events: "*Editor's note: See *The Flash* #123, 'Flash of Two Worlds'" (Fox/Infantino/Broome [1962] 2009: 37). Later multiverse stories, such as *Crisis on Infinite Earths* (1985–1986), *Final Crisis* (2008), *Flashpoint* (2011), *Convergence* (2015), and *DC Rebirth* (2016), likewise make references to "Flash of Two Worlds," whether in terms of specific plot callbacks, or visual allusions to the original artwork, or the characterization of Barry Allen as the only superhero capable of transporting himself between universes by controlling his molecular vibrations. Grant Morrison's *The Multiversity* (2014–2015) even returns to the metafictional conceit introduced in "Flash of Two Worlds" that superhero comic books are windows onto other actually existing worlds, running with the idea that comics writers possess a preternatural capacity to glimpse events from other timelines, other universes, and make them available for serious contemplation among comics readers.[1]

Yet even as references to the foundational meeting between the two Flashes have served to provide a sense of continuity over the decades, calling back and reanimating the residual across many radical changes to the internal narrative history of DC Comics, each point of retroactive continuity, each retcon, has actually drawn attention to the radical discontinuities, the dynamic multiplicities of the superhero multiverse.[2] To be sure, in *Convergence*, the entire multiverse turns out to have been merely one multiverse among other multiverses. Which is to say, the retroactive continuity references, situating each major event in the history of the multiverse by calling back to the 'origin' of the superhero multiverse concept, actually highlight how superhero comics embed references in ways that actively resist coherency or unification. Residual elements remain vibrant—vibrating with potential, available for reinterpretation—even after their assimilation by the conditions of the present. It is in this way that superhero comics reveal their secret capacity for transformative radical politics, despite the tendency of many superhero narratives to recapitulate conservative or reactionary themes (cf. Fawaz 2016).

---

[1] On the conventions of worldbuilding in comics series, see Bukatman (2016); Bainbridge (2009); and Friedenthal (2019).

[2] Kukkonen argues that comics require readers to hold onto a "multiworld model of reality" as an "ontological given" and contain a variety of visual and narrative strategies to help facilitate this (Kukkonen 2013: 156). For debates about whether superhero comics are organized around continuity or multiplicity or both and to what degree, see Klock (2002); Kaveney (2008); Ndalianis (2009); Jenkins (2009); Hyman (2017); and Singer (2018).

In other discursive contexts—for example, historical narratives, scientific reports, or realist novels—references are stabilizing elements, explanations for causality, shared history, and the uniform worldness of the world. Literally, references are supposed to create the conditions for a frame of reference, a world in common. But in superhero comics, references are rather more speculative, linking the present to more worlds than one and opening altered perspectives on the continuity of lived history, which proves to have never been continuous or singular at all. The endless recombination of referential elements, drawing together characters and events from diverse and perhaps incommensurable narratives into the same representational space, is less about apprehending a world of differences than about affirming the difference of worlds, opening up the present to multiple other futures. It suggests that, even within the confines of one world, inside the "vibratory shields" of our consensus reality, we might yet glimpse a flash of the otherwise—and vibrate to the tune of another timeline.

What's in a Reference?

Superhero comics are littered with references.[3] Historical persons are drawn directly into comic book pages. Current events become incorporated into the month-by-month developing storylines. A real-world global conflict is mentioned as background for a comic plot. In their everyday speech, characters make analogies to contemporaneous and past moments and invoke cultural references. From the longstanding comparisons and debates about Charles Xavier and Martin Luther King, to the way in which the Marvel "Civil War" story arc mirrored the post-9/11 passage of the Patriot Act, to the writing of Barack Obama's historic presidential inauguration into *The Amazing Spider-Man* #583, superhero comics have incorporated, responded to, reflected, and refracted their extra-diegetic contexts.[4]

At the same time, though, superhero comics reference persons, events, or discourses from their own diegetic worlds, whether the Marvel Universe, the DC Multiverse, the Valiant Universe, the Milestone Dakataverse, or other comics franchises. Precisely because of the serialized production of comics and the ongoing

---

3 Gardner analogizes the form of comics to the archive because of its "excess data—the remains of the everyday" (Gardner 2012: 177).

4 Coogan locates this convention with what he calls the "reconstructive stage" of superhero comics (Coogan 2006: 221). For essays that foreground the relationship between comic books and cultural history, see Pustz (2012). Wright draws out sweeping sets of correspondences between superhero comics, their evolution, and U.S. social and cultural politics (Wright 2001: 226–253). A great deal of scholarship working on superheroes in relation to their historical contexts focus on U.S. militarism and geopolitics. See Hassler-Forest (2012); and Chute (2017). On Captain America and other nationalist superheroes, see Dittmer (2013).

construction of continuities both within individual titles and across titles, references to previous issues, characters, and story arcs abound.[5] One of the earliest forms of this kind of reference-making is the footnote, usually marked by an asterisk. Such references help readers to configure a provisional continuity; gaps in the storyline, for example, can be patched up by footnotes advising readers to consult other issues in the series or other series. Footnotes can also explain narrative references to characters who are no longer part of the current action, as in this footnote for "The Viper" in *Captain America and the Falcon* #174: "That supervillain *sparked* all this in CA&F #163. —Roy" (Englehart/Friedrich/Buscema [1974] 2017: 115). In this case, the footnote produces a retroactive understanding of cause and continuity (indeed, some readers might not otherwise agree that the Viper "sparked all this"). Such references, then, may not simply allude to an already understood past. They may reconstruct, fill in the gaps, or draw out overlooked aspects in order to reframe the current action. While footnotes are the most explicit forms of intra-diegetic reference, other forms include how a character is drawn, the details of his or her costume, and references to characters' pasts.

The superhero comics page becomes a space of incongruous interaction among imaginary, intra-diegetic, and historical references (fig. 11.1). These references do not work harmoniously to stabilize the relation between fictional text and history. Rather, each reference—each cite—is a site of speculation where continuities across worlds are fashioned at the same instant they are proliferated, always opening up new and potentially other worlds that were, in effect, already there.

Because the reference does not belong to one world, it follows less a criterion of temporal progression than a process of articulation, what Hall describes as the "articulation of different, distinct elements which can be rearticulated in different ways because they have no necessary 'belongingness'" (Hall 2016: 142; cf. Hall 1986). What brings together elements that "have no necessary 'belongingness'" are the culturally defined ways in which we know and feel about these references. Discussing the communicative function of images in comic books, the cartoonist Will Eisner notes,

> Comprehension of an image requires a commonality of experience. This demands of the sequential artist an understanding of the reader's life experience if his message is to be understood. An interaction has to develop because the artist is evoking images stored in the minds of both parties. (Eisner [1985] 2008: 7)

---

5 On the range of comic books' allusions, see Pustz (1999: 143–156). On the role of allusions and intertextuality for self-reflexivity in comics and the emergence of revisionary superhero narratives, see Klock (2002).

Figure 11.1: Worlds collide in a blend of references: dinosaurs and pilgrims and spaceships, oh my! Crisis on Infinite Earths #5, "Worlds in Limbo" (Wolfman/Pérez [1985] 2000: 127).

This "commonality of experience" is itself a contested domain of collective apperceptions or apprehensions of particular references—for example, how a reference is commented on, talked about, and understood. After all, in order for a reference to be a reference, it must be commented on and used in an allusive, metaphorical, allegorical, metonymic, or indexical fashion. It must 'stand for' something. The interaction between the reader's and the sequential artist's minds foregrounds the relationship between our cultural consciousness of these shared images and the manner in which they are narrated and thematized. The reference, a shared bit of cultural lore, does not have to be from the past: it could be from a not-yet present or even far future, so long as it is part of a shared cultural consciousness that invokes the referent in a particular way.

As such, the strange phenomenon of the reference in superhero comics forces readers to question in what sense histories are 'shared' and in what sense worlds can be held in common. As sites of speculation, references draw worlds together—underscoring the processes through which continuities are forged. When superhero comics use references, then, they are simultaneously speculating on our cultural consciousness—how we as readers might feel or how we might understand any residual element—dramatizing the crisis of what world(s) we do or do not share. In this way, references in superhero comics always instantiate the logic of the multiverse, that is, the multiverse as an epistemic formation. For even when they serve to anchor the assumptions of a single world, forging continuities both prescriptively and retroactively, the referential operations of superhero comics require us to think multiple worlds simultaneously.

Reference and Retcon

Let us consider a salient example. Published from January 10, 1974 to June 10, 1975, Steve Englehart's "Secret Empire" and "Nomad" storylines of *Captain America and the Falcon* (issues #169–186) explicitly speculate on the cultural consciousness of particular events, symbols, and figures during the then-ongoing Watergate scandal in the United States and the resignation of President Nixon. These sequential storylines revolve around the question of reference, in the strict sense of what something 'stands for.' Englehart writes,

> [*Captain America*] was being considered for cancellation when I got it, because it had no reason for existence. [...] The problem across the board at Marvel was that this was the 70s—prime anti-war years—and here was a guy with a flag on his chest who was supposed to represent what most people distrusted. No one knew what to do with him. (Englehart 2002a)

Englehart further clarifies how the "Secret Empire" arc alludes to Watergate:

> I was writing a man [Captain America] who believed in America's highest ideals at a time when America's President was a crook. I could not ignore that. And so, in the Marvel Universe, which so closely resembled our own, Cap followed a criminal conspiracy into the White House and saw the President commit suicide. (Englehart 2002b)

The literary scholar Matthew Vernon summarizes Captain America's perpetual dilemma: "Captain America embodies the problem of being torn between two worlds while seeking a way to reconcile them" (Vernon 2016: 126). Vernon analyzes two worlds that are separated by time. In Englehart's stories, Captain America must navigate worlds separated by shared referents.

These storylines depict Steve Rogers's crisis of consciousness as he uncovers a "secret empire" conspiracy, which begins with a media campaign targeting Captain America as an enemy of the state. The conspiracy, as it turns out, goes all the way up to the president of the United States. Seeing that corruption and greed extend to the president, Steve Rogers retires as Captain America only to reemerge as a new superhero, Nomad. The inexplicable reappearance of his old nemesis, the Red Skull, and the killing of Roscoe (who had taken up Captain America's mantle in Rogers's stead) prompts Rogers to become Captain America once more, vowing: "I won't be blind again" (Englehart et al. [1975] 2006, #183: 135). This new Captain America will no longer have his nationalist blinkers on; instead, he will supposedly become deeply self-reflexive about what he stands for.

In issue #169, which begins the "Secret Empire" arc, Captain America is framed as a vigilante, an anti-American villain, by the Committee to Regain America's Principles. The accusation eventually leads Captain America and Falcon to defeat the secret empire plot, in which the leader (Number One) is a thinly disguised version of Richard Nixon. The Committee to Regain America's Principles (CRAP) references the Committee to Re-Elect the President (CREEP), the group whose illegal activities led to Watergate. Of course, it is not a simple presentist reference. The name of the committee, emphasizing a desire to "Regain America's Principles," already anticipates the ignominious downfall of American consciousness *following* the Watergate affair and prospectively imagines linking the concerns of illegal vigilantism with a questioning of who is the proper referent for "America." The committee's ad attacking Captain America questions whether or not he stands for "Your America?" (Englehart/Friedrich/Buscema [1974] 2017, #169: 11) (fig. 11.2). In issue #176, Captain America's crisis of consciousness in both himself and the nation is figured through the incompatibility between different "versions" of what America is: "In the land of the free, each of us is able to do what he wants to do—think what he wants to think. That's as it should be—But it makes for a great many different versions of what America is." The dilemma becomes clear: "So when people the world over look at me—which America am I supposed to symbolize?" (Englehart/Friedrich/Buscema [1974] 2017, #176: 157) (fig. 11.3). Here, in the cartoon panel, racial difference is drawn as a conflict between different exercises of freedom and attached to the crisis of consciousness regarding one's faith in the nation. Moreover, it is internalized for Steve Rogers as a problem of reference: "when people the world over look at me."

Figure 11.2: CREEP reimagined as CRAP. *Captain America and the Falcon* #169 (Englehart/Friedrich/Buscema [1974] 2017: 11).

Figure 11.3: Which America? Whose America? *Captain America and the Falcon* #176 (Englehart/Friedrich/Buscema [1974] 2017: 157).

These storylines do not resolve this question by reviving Captain America's old enemies from World War II. They do not restore to Captain America the symbol of America or reconcile a different version of America to Captain America in any nostalgic way. His renewed commitment that he "won't be blind again" is not a renewed attachment to an ideal, but rather a drive in the psychoanalytic sense of a "constant force" that will never be satisfied (Lacan [1973] 1998: 179). In other words, this question of reference is answered neither through shoring up national identity against oppositional, un-American threats, nor by identifying Rogers more firmly as a symbol of the American people.[6] Instead, it is answered through creating psychic and cultural drives for Captain America in and amongst alternative continuities. The reference, working on and through the residual, shapes these drives; it forges and reconfigures continuities on which the coherence of political imaginaries depends.

Rogers's crisis ("which America am I supposed to symbolize?") articulates a world in which crises of belief are brought to signification by invoking challenges to white nationalism. The historical Watergate scandal—a political blunder in which one political party did not play by the proper rules of politics—is inserted as the background assumption of a cultural consciousness having to do with the ongoing white resistance to black struggles for freedom. As we move from "Secret Empire" to "Nomad," the new antagonist becomes the Serpent Squad and its brand of anti-capitalist terrorism. The Serpent Squad is described as "crazy," "fanatic," and fighting for the "cause" of "nihilism" (Englehart et al. [1975] 2006, #183: 102). But the Serpent Squad's "cause" is quickly pictured through a mainstream popular consciousness of black street politics. The Serpent Squad's story finds a powerful site of dissemination in a crowd led by the stereotypical image of an 'angry black man' (fig. 11.4). Relying on the iconicity of the race riot and the consciousness that links it to the false understanding of black struggle as reactionary, the superhero comic produces a cultural background that becomes Nomad's understanding of historical forces. Seeing the crowd, Nomad (formerly Captain America) thinks to himself: "Good lord! It's already started—the very thing the Viper predicted—The building of a legend around her, to inspire others to the goals she pretended to espouse! And they're calling *me* a *vigilante*, just the way the *Committee to Regain America's Principles* did!" (Englehart et al. [1975] 2006, #183: 122). What bothers Nomad so much is the inversion of consequence and cause, where consequence becomes cause in the future. He draws a continuity between CRAP and the Serpent Squad, creating a peculiar consciousness of his own persecution.

---

6 Dittmer (2013) analyzes Captain America in relation to a U.S. nationalism that continually evolves and incorporates geopolitical questions of gender, race, body and territory. He briefly treats the "Secret Empire" run (Dittmer 2013: 119–121), using it as an example of the rigid nationalist politics of a process of renewal and regenerative identification of Captain America with the nation.

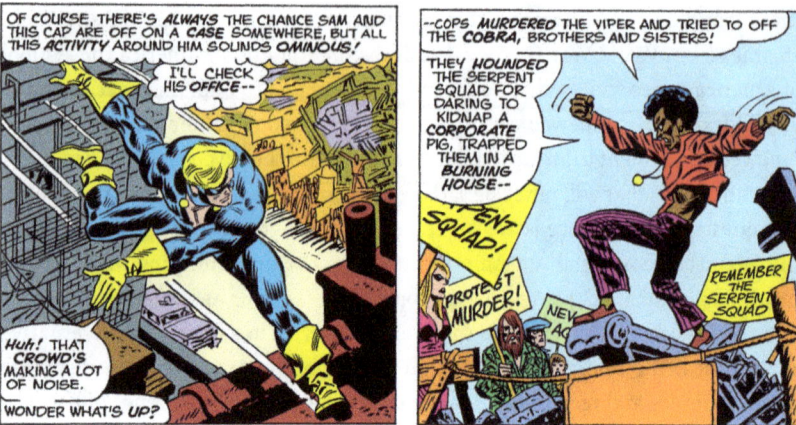

Figure 11.4: Serpent Squad drawn as racial unrest. Captain America and the Falcon #183 (Englehart et al. [1975] 2006: 122).

This technique of using residual elements of race riot images in order to forge white political consciousness mirrors the strategies used by Richard Nixon and Alabama Governor George Wallace before him. As Carol Anderson writes: "H. R. Haldeman, one of the Republican candidate's most trusted aides, later recalled, 'He [Nixon] emphasized that you have to face the fact that the whole problem is really the blacks. The key is to devise a system that recognizes this while not appearing to'" (Anderson 2016: 104). This recognition "while not appearing to" relies on race-neutral language and the strategic use of images to *picture* African Americans without referring to them. What distinguishes superhero comics' use of an otherwise familiar technique is that it creates continuities such that events are cognized in terms of historical drives.

Enter the retcon—that is, the technique of creating retroactive continuity in serial narratives and media franchises. The retcon, as Joshua Clover eloquently describes, "involves a kind of rearrangement of the already given facts into a new logically consistent constellation that can account for later, initially inconsistent developments" (Clover 2014: 15). Here, the retcon smooths over Nomad's drives by drawing from histories of racial affect. The retcon is used not so much to reproduce political identities as it is to form new drives.

Across a series in which the relationship between Captain America's identity as symbol of the United States and his drive to struggle for liberty are being questioned, it is the remaking of consciousness around juxtaposed residual elements of racial signification that creates a new continuity for this relationship. For example, after Rogers "abandon[s] the role of Captain America" because he is "deeply troubled by current political events," he remarks on the kind of freedom that he feels:

You know, Sharon, I don't think I've ever felt as free as I have these past weeks. I've had no master but myself, and no cause but my own. I don't mean that selfishly, now—Just that I've been able to live entirely as myself and not at all as a piece of public property! (Englehart et al. [1974] 2006, #179: 44–45)

It is a freedom, made clear by the comic itself through Rogers's rhetoric of "master," "cause," and "property," that is dependent on slavery and dependent on creating a distance between Steve Rogers and Falcon. It furthers the interests of capitalism because it creates a conceptual division that enables the creation of new understandings of what capitalist freedom looks like, one that is dependent on marking a distance from the appropriation of gendered labor, racialized labor, and other forms of devalued social standing (Singh 2017; Roediger 1999). Indeed, before becoming Nomad, Steve Rogers's freedom allows him to partake of the pleasures of heterosexual, romantic coupling with Sharon Carter. Previously, in issue #166, Rogers had been evicted and dispossessed from his apartment room, and Sam Wilson (Falcon) let him sleep in his social welfare office. After hearing Rogers complain about his dispossession, Wilson commented, "Easy, Steve! In Harlem, we been puttin' up with landlords like Trimble since forever" (Englehart/Buscema [1973] 2013: 16), bringing Rogers's relationship with labor and property close to his own. But in the passage from issue #179 above, Rogers is not worried about 'work' at all. Instead, this newfound freedom "banishes the specter of wageless life" (Singh 2017: 94). That this freedom is felt in relation to racial formations of territory and property is made clear in Rogers's offhand remark after an explosion that disturbs his taking a walk with Sharon: "Unless the American Indian Movement wants Manhattan back, somebody just tried to kill one of us!" (Englehart et al. [1974] 2006, #179: 46).

The reference as concretization of the residual takes center stage at a pivotal moment when Rogers tries to link his new superhero identity of Nomad to some new drive untainted by America's failures of democracy and the sign of Watergate. Early in the "Nomad" run, Nomad stands in front of the Lincoln Memorial. Rather than being a site for the unification of worlds of reference and thereby clarifying the single political horizon in which Captain America/Nomad will find meaning, the reference to the Lincoln Memorial becomes a site for speculation that refuses those totalizing logics. Words flood the page: first, a quotation from a speech that Lincoln gave at Independence Hall on February 22, 1861; and then, a second, longer quote from a speech given at Edwardsville, Illinois on September 11, 1858 (fig. 11.5). These quotations do not mirror the ones actually present on the Lincoln Memorial, which are instead drawn from the Gettysburg Address (November 19, 1863) and Lincoln's second inauguration speech (March 4, 1865). The panel emphasizes a non-correspondence with monumental history, a disjunction between possible worlds.

Figure 11.5: The Lincoln Memorial and its multiple continuities. Captain America and the Falcon #181 (*Englehart et al.* [1975] 2006: 82).

Lincoln's line begins the issue: "I have never had a feeling, politically, that did not spring from the sentiments embodied in the Declaration of Independence." The narration for the comic continues: "Abraham Lincoln said all that … but Steve Rogers—once called Captain America, now called Nomad—has often thought the same. He is thinking it now, here in Washington's Lincoln Memorial" (Englehart et al. [1975] 2006, #181: 82). Extracted from the rest of the speech, the quoted lines make an argument about resisting despotism and tyranny, not through strength of arms, but through inner spirit and inner love of liberty. The circuit defining Rogers's new drive forges a continuity with the Declaration of Independence.

In what sense is this a speculative retcon and not just a historical reference or revisionist history? It is not actually interested in revising our understanding of the past (revisionist history). Nor is it a historical reference that takes some event as given. Rather, it is a moment that rearranges the given facts in order to form a new continuity, a new way of orienting to the antagonisms of the contemporary era. This new continuity makes little mention of slavery, excising the original historical context. In the full speech from which these quotations are drawn, Lincoln directly addressed the Dred Scott decision. In U.S. Chief Justice Roger Taney's final majority opinion on the Dred Scott case, Taney admitted that it was difficult to reimagine public sentiment, whether at the time of the Declaration of Independence or at the time when the Constitution was adopted; but he nevertheless professed to do exactly that in bringing forward the hardened thought of "more than a century" in which "[the negro] had no rights which the white man was bound to respect" (Taney 1857: 407). Taney's speculations on historical consciousness became the basis for professing historical 'fact.' In *Captain America and the Falcon*, the blind spots in Taney's historical imagination of sentiment are reproduced through the comic's selective quotations from Lincoln that emphasize the transhistorical conduit of sentiment over other lines of thought.

Lincoln's argument in his 1858 speech was actually that the Dred Scott decision spuriously founded the "right of self-government" on the right to brutalize the "negro" (Lincoln [1858] 1953: 95). He stated that what Judge Stephen A. Douglas insisted on calling "popular sovereignty" really meant installing in the notion of "peoplehood" itself the right to treat black men and women with impunity (Lincoln [1858] 1953: 95). But Lincoln's rhetoric also aimed to rouse white sentiment and fear, compelling his audience to safeguard black interests with the idea that "you're next." Indeed, the lines immediately before the portion of Lincoln's speech quoted in the comic are:

> Now, when by all these means you have succeeded in dehumanizing the negro; when you have put him down, and made it forever impossible for him to be but as the beasts of the field; when you have extinguished his soul, and placed him where the ray of hope is blown out in darkness like that which broods over the spirits of

the damned; are you quite sure the demon which you have roused *will not turn and rend you*? (Lincoln [1858] 1953: 95)

The continuity that Steve Rogers derives from this partial reference involves both a severing of the concept of freedom from the history of slavery and a carrying forward of the sentiments of fear that white men, too, could become targets. Lincoln's own limited way of imagining U.S. anti-blackness only in terms of its potential threat to white men is carried forward into Rogers's cultural consciousness. The retroactive continuity making sense of Captain America's transformation into Nomad runs through the residual meanings actively formed in the sentiments of slavery and freedom.

But at the same time, this form of speculative history through which Captain America crafts his own consciousness is willfully blind. The sequence of panels displays this blindness. As Rogers stands in front of the Lincoln Memorial, lost in thought, an arrow points to a partially exposed arm with the line, "Which is why he's oblivious to … this!" The next panel repeats the blindness. Rogers thinks to himself, "Lincoln: Why did he sound so eloquent when everyone today sounds so forced? Why did our forefathers seem to understand America more clearly than we do now? We've been through so much, and yet—Eh? Someone behind me—!" (Englehart et al. [1974] 2006, #181: 83). He is suddenly interrupted by the Sub-Mariner, a figure whose fictional continuity with Captain America is crucial (after all, he is the character who discovered Captain America encased in ice). At this moment, Nomad is attempting to create a continuity with a retconned version of the historical past, one that brings forward the eloquence of Lincoln in order to align voice and body into a sentiment of freedom that has nothing to do with slavery and everything to do with the fear of tyranny. But the Sub-Mariner reintroduces another continuity: the problematic identity of Captain America.

This reintroduction unearths the multiple worlds drawn together in this scene. Here, the collisions of intra-diegetic references and extra-diegetic references open up multiple racialized histories that cannot be subsumed into a single line extending from the U.S. Civil War to the Civil Rights movement. While the story arc focuses on Captain America's crisis of consciousness linked to Watergate, the issue that introduces the entire "Secret Empire" arc actually begins with another ongoing storyline—one that centers on the Falcon's desire to get new powers so that he no longer feels inferior to Captain America. The Falcon storyline interpolates the Secret Empire plot into the longer-running narrative of Falcon's powers and his 'place' in relation to Captain America.[7] In the issue that begins the "Secret Empire" plot, Captain America saves the Falcon, again leading Falcon to ask for extra pow-

---

7 As a sidekick character whose position appears to mirror structural inequalities, Falcon has garnered less attention from scholars writing on the politics of race and comics. See Brown (2001);

ers. Captain America responds, "He has a right to better himself, of course. I only wish I believed that what he wants is *for* the better" (Englehart/Friedrich/Buscema [1974] 2017, #169: 10). Captain America here references longstanding discourses of black freedom struggle and white resistance to that freedom. It also references the deep hypocrisy of white superiority in the language of rights discourse. But more importantly, it situates the whole CRAP advertising campaign in relation to the spacetime of the Falcon's long discontent and his critique of Captain America: Falcon's history as a history of white retrenchment.

For the critical theorist and poet Fred Moten, interpolation can interrupt interpellation, the way in which we are recruited by ideologies and constituted as subjects. The insertion of new matter simultaneously disrupts continuities and creates new continuities (Moten 2017: 28–33). In issue #174 of "Secret Empire," Falcon learns from Professor Charles Xavier of the X-Men that he may be a mutant and have a "paranormal mind" (Englehart/Friedrich/Buscema [1974] 2017, #174: 114). This speculative retcon of Falcon's origins would explain his uncannily telepathic relationship with the falcon, Redwing. In this sense, the Falcon as superhero carries forward the residual—untapped potentialities, discarded alternatives. Captain America refuses to follow this alternate continuity. Early in the Nomad storyline when Falcon tries to get Steve Rogers to investigate with him whether he might in fact be a mutant, Rogers responds: "No, Sam—You have to find out! Captain America doesn't exist anymore! He's a legend of World War II—no longer living! And since he doesn't exist, he doesn't go on patrol!" (Englehart et al. [1974] 2006, #177: 10). Rogers registers his complete indifference to this possible retconned storyline. In fact, he disavows this possible continuity, diminishing Falcon's desired mission as simply going "on patrol." But Falcon's mission potentially revises his origin story by articulating a different set of reference points—namely, the X-Men—with the long struggle of black resistance to conceptions of freedom centered on white affect. Falcon is a fragment from another world, but one that anticipates the conditions of possibility by which he is made into a problem.

As a further manifestation of Falcon's interruptions, he continually points to Captain America's affective drives: "Cap was so intent on gettin' this trip started, he didn't even take time to switch to civvies! This thing is really eatin' at 'im!" And then, "Partner, you have got to lighten up! You nearly drove that dude into screamin' paranoia!" (Englehart/Friedrich/Buscema [1974] 2017, #172: 72). Falcon repeatedly notes how crazy and forgetful Captain America has become, making clear the reactionary nature of Captain America's actions. In the example above of Falcon's response to Rogers's eviction ("we been puttin' up with landlords like Trimble since forever"), Falcon's "since forever" inserts a different temporality, which

---

Howard/Jackson (2013); Gateward/Jennings (2015); carrington (2016); and Wanzo (2009) for analyses of black superheroes, masculinities, stereotypes, and genres.

interrupts Rogers's indignant focus on the immediate past and immediate future. Falcon puts the brakes on the reactionary emotions that drive Captain America forward and that structure his cultural and historical consciousness.

The manner in which the crossing of intra-diegetic and extra-diegetic references opens up sociopolitical horizons is further articulated through the referent of whiteness. When Steve Rogers as Captain America announces his retirement, various characters insert themselves into the vacated position. First, the famous baseball player Bob Russo takes his shot at being Captain America. Seven panels is all it takes to dispose this wannabe Captain America: Russo swings into a wall and breaks his arm. Second, a biker gang member, Scar Turpin, makes his move to take on the mantle: "I been kinda leary about trottin' my costumed bod down to the cops, to show 'em who they got workin' with 'em now—They might just put me away for disrespectin' the flag" (Englehart et al. [1974] 2006, #179: 56). These interpolations from different sectors of society (baseball and biker culture in San Rafael, California) display both the popular accessibility of the icon (people believe they can become Captain America) and the exceptional quality of the icon (they inevitably fail to do so). The third and most significant interpolation is Roscoe Simons, who trains with Falcon to be the new Captain America and whose death at the hands of the Red Skull actually propels Steve Rogers to resume his role as Captain America.

These failures are signaled precisely in their deviation from a specific alignment of whiteness in relation to labor and language. Scar Turpin imagines Captain America as someone who "works" and who affiliates with the "cops," neither of which apply to him. Roscoe's defining characteristic is his speech written in dialect: "Ain't dis a kick inna teet'? I bend da rules ta scam Mr. Rogers' address in da gym registry—and den he ain't home! But heck, if I lived inna welfare office, I'd travel a lot, too! I didn't know tings was so bad for 'im" (Englehart et al. [1974] 2006, #180: 74). This dialect places Roscoe Simons within a range of possible ethnic identities—Irish, Jewish—and the uses of 'dis' and 'dat' recall Bre'r Rabbit caricatures of blackness. The failures of these men to become Captain America—failures of interpolation—serve the construction of Steve Rogers as *generically* white, that is to say, both *general* and *genre-specific* within the discourse of superhero comics.

These multiple, alternative continuities appear as paradoxes on the cover of *Captain America and the Falcon* #181 (fig. 11.6). This cover image does not reproduce a scene from the narrative. Instead, it imagines an encounter between Nomad, Falcon, and the new Captain America (Roscoe Simon) that never actually happens. Falcon says, "Stay back, Nomad! You had your chance to be Captain America! Now it's his turn!" Nomad does not speak. This fictional non-encounter shows the alliance between Falcon and Roscoe as something that never fully matured, but whose

Figure 11.6: Drawing out the refused continuity. Captain America and the Falcon #181 (Englehart et al. [1975] 2006: 81).

residual possibility remains available for representation as an alternate history, a counterfactual world. A glimpse of their possible alliance does occur earlier in the narrative proper when Falcon overcomes Roscoe's racist language and Roscoe overcomes his own embarrassments and humiliations in being trained by Falcon.[8] Indeed, to understand this scene as something that actually happens is to interpolate a past in which Falcon's multiple interruptions—here manifested through his command to Rogers ("Stay back")—are given standing and in which Roscoe is Falcon's partner and not the other way around. It is also to form a linkage across blackness and a non-generic, non-generalizable whiteness that has historically been foreclosed by specific political formations that have traded on black images of inferiority and what W. E. B. Du Bois has called the "public and psychological wage" of whiteness, a construction of public space, institutions, and the economic value of white freedom as a public good (Du Bois [1935] 1998: 700).

The cover depicts an encounter that does not happen within the story's diegesis—and, in fact, it *could not happen*. For it is Roscoe's death that causes Steve Rogers's guilt. (He feels that he should have been the one to confront the Red Skull.) This guilt and mourning drive Steve Rogers to become Captain America once again. The pictured encounter on the cover thus replaces one set of affective potentialities (mourning, guilt) with another (astonishment, surprise, feelings of betrayal from Steve Rogers and refusal from Falcon). The cover image's non-event is necessary for the dominant storyline, insofar as it enables Steve Rogers's affective drive through the comic. In imaging what *could not happen*, the cover points to the reorganization of affective elements that would be necessary to form a continuity and thereby an alternative cultural consciousness.

Captain America's drive to resolve his crisis of consciousness requires revising the problem of being in the wrong history, the wrong timeline—or, as he puts it in issue #168, "the feeling that I'm a walking anachronism—a guy who looks like he's twenty … even though he was fighting Hitler's hordes some thirty years ago!" (Thomas/Isabella/Buscema [1973] 2013: 3). He expresses this crisis in terms of linking the idea and material reality of what he 'stands for.' This drive runs circles around and repeatedly avoids an alternative consciousness. It is a drive predicated on the refusal of Falcon's claims and activated through speculating on residual meanings of race and history, as in the Lincoln Memorial reference. The return of Rogers as Captain America with his statement "I won't be blind again" epitomizes the cultural consciousness and temporal continuity that the series repeats: a looking ahead that disavows alternate continuities in order to secure a drive for liberty. As we have seen, however, Captain America is often caught not looking behind him. Always looking in front of him instead of behind him, Captain Amer-

---

8 In *Captain America and the Falcon* #182, Falcon forgives Roscoe for calling him a "joik" and refashions the relationship as one where he watches out for Captain America, not the other way around.

ica's continuity relies on the retcon to smooth out inconsistencies at the same time that the proliferation of continuities body forth alternate modes of consciousness and reference-making. Falcon becomes important as a figure for and interruption of the intra-diegetic and historical continuities that weave Captain America and Falcon together. Falcon indicates the referential consciousness built around blackness that drives Captain America's blindness and also interrupts this drive with other affective possibilities—specifically, a refusal of given social relations.⁹

Beyond the One-World World

By drawing attention to contradictions, residual histories, and alternate timelines even while retconning them, superhero comics expose the coercive force of continuity as the condition of a unified world—the violence and repressions inherent to one-world ideologies and the desire for a "one-world world" (Law 2015; cf. de la Cadena 2015; de la Cadena/Blaser 2018; Escobar 2018; Reiter 2018). Superheroes themselves have often represented such one-world ideologies: forces of vigilante justice or homeland security determined to bring order, unity, and liberty to an unruly universe. Captain America looks ahead to universal freedom, even while overlooking the structural occlusions and injustices on which his own sense of freedom relies. But the system of references in superhero comics likewise indicates how the speculative drives that characterize one-world ideologies, aspiring to produce the conditions for one world to persist at the expense of another, ultimately threaten the continuity of any world whatsoever. This is, of course, the whole point of Alan Moore and Dave Gibbons's *Watchmen* (1986–1987).

A singular reference establishes *Watchmen* as an alternate history of our own world, marking the inflection point when it changed: the publication of *Action Comics* #1 in 1938, representing the first appearance of Superman. In *Watchmen*, the advent of superhero comic books inspired groups of people to become heroes themselves. The generation of the Minutemen (allegorizing the Golden Age of comics) was followed by the generation of the Crimebusters (allegorizing the Silver Age of comics). In these eras, the worlds of fiction and reality collided: "[T]he super-heroes had escaped from their four-color world and invaded the plain, factual black and white of the headlines" (Moore/Gibbons 1987, I: 32). Because these real costumed heroes dominated the news media, the comic book industry in *Watchmen* instead went in a different direction, prioritizing stories of pirates and swashbucklers. In *Watchmen*, the presidency of Richard Nixon in the U.S. never

---

9 Drawing on the work of the black studies scholars Saidiya Hartman and Hortense Spillers, Tiffany Lethabo King writes, "Blackness is a form of malleable potential and a state of change in the 'socio-political order' of the New World" (King 2019: 103).

ended because the Watergate scandal never came to light. (Indeed, it is implied that a superhero working on behalf of the U.S. government—perhaps the Comedian—murdered the reporters Bob Woodward and Carl Bernstein before they could expose the dirty tricks carried out by the Committee to Re-Elect the President.) In the context of this political history, costumed heroes have come to stand for a one-world world, stamping out petty crime as well as mobilizing against other forms of social deviance, including "promiscuity," "drugs," "campus subversion," "anti-war demos," and "black unrest" (II: 10–11). While some heroes such as the Comedian and Dr. Manhattan have aligned with the U.S. military to contain the spread of communism, others, such as Ozymandias, aim for a unification of the world's people into a common frame of reference, namely, globalized consumer capitalism. Ozymandias plots to achieve this goal—the end of global conflict and the overcoming of ideological differences, the creation of a neoliberal planet as the end of history as such (Hoberek [2014] 2017)—through an elaborate scheme, staging a fake alien invasion of New York. Ozymandias believes that only by providing the global superpowers—the U.S. and the Soviet Union, as well as the individual heroes that represent them—with a common enemy will a worldwide peace be achieved: "Unable to unite the world by conquest . . . I would trick it; frighten it towards salvation with history's greatest practical joke" (XI: 24).

The story of *Watchmen* is explicitly about the practice of interpreting references and the production of retroactive continuity. On the one hand, the main storyline follows the efforts of the masked heroes Rorschach and Night Owl to solve a series of murders and other mysterious events that suggest an extraordinary conspiracy to eradicate superheroes. Rorschach's own name, of course, references the famous psychological test that involves interpreting arbitrary inkblots as meaningful references. While putting together the pieces of the mystery, Night Owl remembers that "Ozymandias" was the ancient Greek name for the Egyptian pharaoh Rameses II, which turns out to be the secret password on Ozymandias's office computer. Night Owl thus discovers Ozymandias's role as the mastermind behind the conspiracy.

On the other hand, Ozymandias himself is figured as an expert interpreter of references (fig. 11.7). As the "smartest man in the world" (XI: 32), he has built his personal fortune by observing patterns in popular media and television advertising that guide his strategic business investments. Watching multiple television broadcasts simultaneously, reading across images and forging continuities among a multitude of references and allusions—analogous to the practice of reading across comic book panels, suturing words and images (see McLuhan [1964] 1994: 166–168; Milburn 2015: 135–172)—Ozymandias discerns patterns of cultural consciousness, the lineaments of a world: "These reference points established, an emergent *worldview* becomes gradually *discernible* amidst the media's white noise" (XI: 1). For Ozymandias, comprehending the ensemble of reference points is an exact practice of speculation, providing "subliminal hints of the future" and a model of things to come: "This jigsaw-fragment model of tomorrow aligns itself piece by piece" (XI: 1). His speculative synthesis of reference points from global media streams likewise convinces him that the incommensurable one-world ideologies of the twentieth century will never be reconciled:

> I saw *East* and *West*, locked into an escalating *arms spiral*, their mutual terror and suspicion mounting with the *missiles* [...] Both sides *realized* the suicidal *implications* of nuclear conflict, yet couldn't stop racing *towards* it lest their *opponents* should *overtake* them. [...] Simply given the *mathematics* of the situation, sooner or later *conflict would be inevitable*. (XI: 21)

Ozymandias determines that only a wild science-fiction scheme—revealing to the people of Earth that a multidimensional multiverse does exist—will make the Earth whole: "To frighten governments into *co-operation*, I would convince them that Earth faced imminent *attack* by beings from another *world*" (XI: 25).

Ozymandias commissions a team of scientists, artists, and science fiction writers to help him create the hoax (though Ozymandias has them all killed before they learn the full truth of his plan). Significantly, Ozymandias recruits Max Shea, the famous comics writer and novelist whose work on *Tales of the Black Freighter* expanded the artistic horizons of pirate comic books, tasking him to create horrifying scenes from the alien world.

Figure 11.7: Ozymandias reads across images, connecting points of reference. Watchmen *(Moore/Gibbons 1987, X: 8).*

Of course, Ozymandias was not the only one to have envisaged such a scenario. Around the same time as Moore and Gibbons were creating *Watchmen*, the former Hollywood actor and president of the United States Ronald Reagan was indulging similar speculative fantasies. During the 1985 Geneva Summit, Reagan and the Soviet Premier Mikhail Gorbachev took a private walk to a cabin in the vicinity. Years later, Gorbachev revealed what they had discussed on this walk:

> President Reagan suddenly said to me, "What would you do if the United States were suddenly attacked by someone from outer space? Would you help us?" I said, "No doubt about it." He said, "We too." So that's interesting. (Gorbachev 2009)

The idea of a world united by war against an extraterrestrial threat was often on Reagan's mind. For example, in his address to the 42nd Session of the United Nations General Assembly on September 21, 1987, Reagan once again waxed in a subjunctive mood, implicitly referencing any number of science fiction stories:

> In our obsession with antagonisms of the moment, we often forget how much unites all the members of humanity. Perhaps we need some outside, universal threat to make us recognize this common bond. I occasionally think how quickly our differences worldwide would vanish if we were facing an alien threat from outside this world. And yet, I ask you, is not an alien force already among us? What could be more alien to the universal aspirations of our peoples than war and the threat of war? (Reagan 1987)

Like Ozymandias's scheme, Reagan's wish for an alien invasion to end divisiveness on Earth only reveals the violence inherent to the one-world ideal: eradicating the "alien force already among us" requires a displacement of internal hostilities elsewhere, a unification made possible only through the expulsion of the alien in whatever form it may take. Tellingly, Ozymandias's plan to achieve peace actually demands the sacrifice of many thousands of innocent people: dropping a gigantic, bioengineered "alien" creature in the middle of Manhattan results in massive destruction, which Ozymandias believes is necessary to convince the people of Earth about the scale of risks still to come (cf. Cortiel/Oehme 2015). But more generally, Ozymandias's plan highlights the speculative orientation of a one-world vision, where the resolution of the various conflicts referenced in *Watchmen*—between the capitalist world and the communist world, the white nationalist world and the black unrest world, the straight world and the queer world, the world of ordinary people and the world of superheroes—becomes imaginable only through the projection of a new, alternative world to hate.

Watchmen ends with professions of peace between the Americans and Soviets, now committed to weaponizing the Earth together in preparation for transdimensional warfare. Enter the retcon, once more: like Captain America looking ahead, vowing never to be blind again, the people of Earth now look ahead to conflict with all the denizens of a vast multiverse, discovering retrospectively the continuities of their common humanity, as if the Earth had always been a world—"one world, one accord" (XII: 31)—all along. But the narrative of *Watchmen* has already indicated that this situation is doomed to failure, precisely because this new cohesion demands a condition of perpetual, forever war—and, of course, there really is no alien enemy to play the antagonist in perpetuity. Moreover, a globally unified, ever vigilant military-industrial complex, now looking ahead to an endless arms race with a phantom enemy of incalculable strength, still presents a significant threat to the planet Earth itself. Ozymandias had already noted that, during the Cold War, the anticipation of conflict alone had damaged the natural world thanks to nuclear waste and reactor leaks, deforestation, and other ecological problems: "War aside, atomic deadlock guided us downhill towards environmental ruin" (XI: 22). Ozymandias's drive to create a unified world thus leaves him willfully blind to the limitations of any détente achieved through the displacement of internal conflicts elsewhere (Paik 2010). Indeed, his entire plan has been based on a thoroughly fatal process of *misreading*.

Despite Ozymandias's self-fashioning as an expert reader of references, he has apparently overlooked a set of references highlighted in the narrative of *Watchmen* itself. For one thing, while Ozymandias intends his own superhero name to reference the figure of Rameses II/Ozymandias and his historical meaning in antiquity, the text makes several allusions to Percy Bysshe Shelley's poem "Ozymandias" (1818)—"Look on my works, ye mighty, and despair!" (XI: 28)—to suggest that Ozymandias has, curiously enough, misread the significance of his own name in the context of a post-Romantic world. The whole point of Shelley's poem is that, given world enough and time, even the mightiest empires will eventually crumble, becoming residues of other histories, remembered only by ruins. Dr. Manhattan, near the very end of *Watchmen*, does try to remind Ozymandias of the fact that there is no end of history: "Nothing ends, Adrian. Nothing *ever* ends" (XII: 27). But Ozymandias does not catch the reference: "Jon? *What!* What do you mean by . . ." (XII: 27).

Likewise, throughout the narrative of *Watchmen*, various films are playing at the Utopia cinema in New York: *This Island Earth* (1955), *Things to Come* (1936), *The Day the Earth Stood Still* (1951), *The Sacrifice* (1986), and *Nostalghia* (1983). These films each consider the hazards and pitfalls of the one-world ideal, whether explicitly depicting how the drive to secure a singular, homogenous world threatens to displace violence onto other worlds, or critiquing the delusions and obsessions of those who believe they might avert catastrophe by committing sacrificial violence. After Ozymandias's giant creature has exploded in Manhattan, the Utopia cinema is covered with alien gore, its entryway is littered with dead human bodies, and the marquee has fallen apart (fig. 11.8). While *The Day the Earth Stood Still* implies that a utopian future might be achieved by recognizing the existence of other worlds and relinquishing the internal conditions for conflict, Ozymandias's scheme has instead rendered any such "utopia" illegible.

In the denouement shortly after this climactic event, a television rebroadcast of "The Architects of Fear," a 1963 episode of *The Outer Limits* (1963–1965), makes the point even more starkly. "The Architects of Fear" is about a team of scientists who create a hoax alien invasion in order to produce global peace, precisely by offering the alien as a new enemy to fear. But the plan goes completely wrong and has no effect on geopolitical conditions at all. The narrator sums things up:

> Scarecrows and magic and other fatal fears do not bring people closer together. There is no magic substitute for soft caring and hard work, for self-respect and mutual love. If we can learn this from the mistake these frightened men made, then their mistake will not have been merely grotesque, it would at least have been a lesson. A lesson, at last, to be learned. ("Architects of Fear" [1963] 2008)

Ozymandias has misread the lesson, apparently, but *Watchmen* invites readers to connect the residual media and residual meanings excluded from Ozymandias's speculative scheme. Together, these references animate a set of other fictive worlds that critically reflect upon the drive for retroactive continuity—in comics or otherwise.

To be sure, in his sorting through the media streams of popular culture, it seems that Ozymandias has utterly overlooked the referential affordances of comic books themselves. Throughout the chapters of *Watchmen*, Bernie, a young man of color, is reading a story in *The Tales of the Black Freighter* comic: the notorious "Marooned" storyline written by Max Shea. The significance of this comic is signaled by its formal prominence in *Watchmen*. The main storyline is intersected repeatedly by resonant images, parallel phrases, and mirrored events from *Tales of the Black Freighter*. By the end, it becomes clear that the "Marooned" narrative is an allegory for Ozymandias's plan to save the world from itself. Awash in references to other works of literature, including Samuel Taylor Coleridge's "Rime of the Ancient Mariner" (1798) and William Blake's "The Tyger" (1794), "Marooned" depicts the formidable drive of a man who fights against overwhelming odds but ends up destroying the very things he loves in pursuit of phantasmatic enemies: the mariner protagonist accidentally murders his neighbors and his family while under the delusion of trying to save them from evil pirates. "Marooned" concludes with the mariner swimming toward the haunted Black Freighter, now fated to join its damned crew. Late—too late—in the story of *Watchmen*, Ozymandias has

Figure 11.8: Due to Ozymandias's shortsighted scheme, alternative references remain unseen and utopia becomes illegible (u-opia). Watchmen (Moore/Gibbons 1987, XII: 3).

a brief flash of insight, almost making a connection between his own actions and the plight of the mariner in the "Marooned" comic: "I dreamt about swimming toward . . . No, never mind" (XII: 27). The continuity fails to stick. For Ozymandias, these worlds remain isolated. For the reader, however, the reference is unmistakable. With *Tales of the Black Freighter*—a comic within a comic—*Watchmen* recapitulates the famous trope from "Flash of Two Worlds," showing how comic books present imaginative echoes or speculative diagrams that trace the alternate histories obscured by consensus reality.

As an indictment of one-world ideologies, then, *Watchmen* also affirms the capacities of comic books to help us see otherwise, to see multiple. Yes, comic-book superheroes have often contributed to power fantasies, military propaganda, and fascist notions of ethnic superiority—these aspects of cartoon history are objects of *Watchmen*'s self-referential critique of superpowers and the super as such (Wright 2001; Hughes 2006). But more importantly, it shows that comics can be read and misread in more than one way, precisely because every comic tells more than one story at the same time. Manifested in its system of references—both internal and external, intradiegetic and extradiegetic—the presumption of multiple universes is now intrinsic to the form of superhero comics. Superhero comics afford ways of engaging with residual pasts and potential futures through narratives of unactualized realities—and thus they present ways of living in this world which is not one.

References

Anderson, Carol (2016): *White Rage: The Unspoken Truth of Our Racial Divide*. New York: Bloomsbury.

"The Architects of Fear" ([1963] 2008). Byron Haskin (dir.). Meyer Dolinsky (writer). In: *The Outer Limits: The Complete Original Series*. Vol. 1. (DVD set, 3 vols.). MGM Home Entertainment.

Bainbridge, Jason (2009): "'Worlds Within Worlds': The Role of Superheroes in the Marvel and DC Universes." In: Angela Ndalianis (ed.): *The Contemporary Comic Book Superhero*. London: Routledge, 64–85.

Bardini, Thierry (2011): *Junkware*. Minneapolis: University of Minnesota Press.

Brown, Jeffrey A. (2001): *Black Superheroes, Milestone Comics, and Their Fans*. Jackson: University Press of Mississippi.

Bukatman, Scott (2016): *Hellboy's World: Comics and Monsters on the Margins*. Oakland: University of California Press.

carrington, andré m. (2016): *Speculative Blackness: The Future of Race in Science Fiction*. Minneapolis: University of Minnesota Press.

Chute, Hillary (2017): *Why Comics? From Underground to Everywhere*. New York: HarperCollins.

Clover, Joshua (2014): "Retcon: Value and Temporality in Poetics." In: *Representations* 126, 9–30.

Coogan, Peter (2006): *Superhero: The Secret Origin of a Genre*. Austin: Monkeybrain.

Cortiel, Jeanne/Oehme, Laura (2015): "The Dark Knight's Dystopian Vision: Batman, Risk, and American National Identity." In: *European Journal of American Studies* 10(2) (https://doi.org/10.4000/ejas.10916).

de la Cadena, Marisol (2015): *Earth Beings: Ecologies of Practice across Andean Worlds*. Durham, NC: Duke University Press.

de la Cadena, Marisol/Blaser, Mario (eds.) (2018): *A World of Many Worlds*. Durham, N.C.: Duke University Press.

Dittmer, Jason (2012): *Captain America and the Nationalist Superhero: Metaphors, Narratives, and Geopolitics*. Philadelphia: Temple University Press.

Du Bois, W. E. B. ([1935] 1998): *Black Reconstruction in America, 1860–1880*. New York: Free Press.

Eisner, Will ([1985] 2008): *Comics and Sequential Art: Principles and Practices from the Legendary Cartoonist*. Revised edition. New York: Norton.

Englehart, Steve (2002a): "Captain America I." In: *Steve Englehart Writes*, December (http://steveenglehart.com/Comics/Captain%20America%20153-167.html).

Englehart, Steve (2002b): "Captain America II." In: *Steve Englehart Writes*, December (http://steveenglehart.com/Comics/Captain%20America%20169-176.html).

Englehart, Steve/Buscema, Sal ([1973] 2013): *Captain America and the Falcon #166*. In: Marvel Unlimited, April 29 (https://www.marvel.com/comics/issue/7547/captain_america_1968_166).

Englehart, Steve/Friedrich, Mike/Buscema, Sal ([1974] 2017): *Captain America and the Falcon: Secret Empire*. Issues #169–176. New York: Marvel.

Englehart, Steve/Warner, John/Buscema, Sal/Robbins, Frank/Trimpe, Herb ([1974–1975] 2006): *Captain America and the Falcon: Nomad*. Issues #177–186. New York: Marvel.

Escobar, Arturo (2018): *Designs for the Pluriverse: Radical Interdependence, Autonomy, and the Making of Worlds*. Durham, NC: Duke University Press.

Fawaz, Ramzi (2016): *The New Mutants: Superheroes and the Radical Imagination of American Comics*. New York: New York University Press.

Fox, Gardner/Infantino, Carmine/Broome, John ([1961–1967] 2009): *DC Comics Classics Library: The Flash of Two Worlds*. New York: DC Comics.

Friedenthal, Andrew J. (2019): *The World of DC Comics*. New York: Routledge.

Gardner, Jared (2012): *Projections: Comics and the History of Twenty-First Century Storytelling*. Stanford: Stanford University Press.

Gateward, Francis/Jennings, John (eds.) (2015): *The Blacker the Ink: Constructions of Black Identity in Comics and Sequential Art*. New Brunswick: Rutgers University Press.

Gorbachev, Mikhail (2009): Interview in "Beyond the Pale: A Reunion Between President Mikhail Gorbachev and Secretary of State George Shultz." Charlie Rose (moderator). Emma Lazarus Statue of Liberty Award Luncheon at the Rainbow Room, March 26, 2009. In: American Jewish Historical Society, "American Jewish Historical Society Presents Beyond the Pale, pt. 2 of 3," YouTube, September 12, 2014 (https://www.youtube.com/watch?v=Arsb-DUcRto&t=219s).

Hall, Stuart (1986): "On Postmodernism and Articulation: An Interview with Stuart Hall." Lawrence Grossberg (ed.). *Journal of Communication Inquiry* 10(2), 45–60.

Hall, Stuart (2016): *Cultural Studies 1983: A Theoretical History*. Lawrence Grossberg/Jennifer Daryl Slack (eds.). Durham, N.C.: Duke University Press.

Hoberek, Andrew ([2014] 2017): *Considering Watchmen: Poetics, Property, Politics*. New edition. New Brunswick: Rutgers University Press.

Howard, Sheena C./Jackson, Ronald L., II (2013): *Black Comics: Politics of Race and Representation*. London: Bloomsbury.

Hughes, Jamie A. (2006): "'Who Watches the Watchmen?': Ideology and 'Real World' Superheroes." In: *Journal of Popular Culture* 39, 546–557.

Hyman, David (2017): *Revision and the Superhero Genre*. London: Palgrave.

Jenkins, Henry (2009): "Just Men in Tights: Rewriting Silver Age Comics in an Era of Multiplicity." In: Angela Ndalianis (ed.): *The Contemporary Comic Book Superhero*. London: Routledge, 16–43.

Kaveney, Roz (2008): *Superheroes! Capes and Crusaders in Comics and Films*. London: I.B. Tauris.

King, Tiffany Lethabo (2019): *The Black Shoals: Offshore Formations of Black and Native Studies*. Durham, NC: Duke University Press.

Klock, Geoff (2002): *How to Read Superhero Comics and Why*. New York: Continuum.

Kukkonen, Karin (2013): "Navigating Infinite Earths." In: Charles Hatfield/Jeet Heer/Kent Worcester (eds.): *The Superhero Reader*. Jackson: University Press of Mississippi, 155–170.

Lacan, Jacques ([1973] 1998): *The Seminar of Jacques Lacan, Book XI: The Four Fundamental Concepts of Psychoanalysis*. Jacques-Alain Miller (ed.). Alan Sheridan (trans.). New York: Norton.

Law, John (2015): "What's Wrong with a One-World World?" In: *Distinktion: Journal of Social Theory* 16, 126–139.

Lincoln, Abraham (1953): *The Collected Works of Abraham Lincoln*. Volume 3. Roy Basler (ed.). New Brunswick: Rutgers University Press.

McLuhan, Marshall ([1964] 1994): *Understanding Media: The Extensions of Man*. Cambridge, MA: MIT Press.

Milburn, Colin (2015): *Mondo Nano: Fun and Games in the World of Digital Matter*. Durham, NC: Duke University Press.

Moore, Alan/Gibbons, Dave (1987): *Watchmen*. New York: DC Comics.

Moten, Fred (2017): *Black and Blur*. Durham, NC: Duke University Press.

Ndalianis, Angela (2009): "Enter the Aleph: Superhero Worlds and Hypertime Realities." In: Angela Ndalianis (ed.): *The Contemporary Comic Book Superhero*. London: Routledge, 270–290.

Paik, Peter Y. (2010): *From Utopia to Apocalypse: Science Fiction and the Politics of Catastrophe*. Minneapolis: University of Minnesota Press.

Pustz, Matthew J. (1999): *Comic Book Culture: Fanboys and True Believers*. Jackson: University Press of Mississippi.

Pustz, Matthew J. (ed.) (2012): *Comic Books and American Cultural History: An Anthology*. New York: Continuum.

Reagan, Ronald (1987): "Address to the United Nations General Assembly, New York." In: Reagan Library, "President Reagan's Address to the United Nations in New York City, New York, September 21, 1987," YouTube, June 8, 2016 (https://www.youtube.com/watch?v=dJ-mf8agFP0).

Reiter, Bernd (ed.) (2018): *Constructing the Pluriverse: The Geopolitics of Knowledge*. Durham, NC: Duke University Press.

Roediger, David (1999): *The Wages of Whiteness: Race and the Making of the American Working Class*. London: Verso.

Singer, Mark (2018): *Breaking the Frames: Populism and Prestige in Comics Studies*. Austin: University of Texas Press.

Singh, Nikhil Pal (2017): *Race and America's Long War*. Oakland: University of California Press.

Taney, Roger Brooke (1857): *Dred Scott v. Sandford*, 60 U.S. (19 How.), Supreme Court of the United States (December 1856 term, decided March 5, 1857), 393–633. In: Library of Congress, *U.S. Reports*, March 13, 2018 (https://www.loc.gov/item/usrep060393a/).

Thomas, Roy/Isabella, Tony/Buscema, Sal ([1973] 2013): *Captain America and the Falcon* #168. In: Marvel Unlimited, April 29 (https://www.marvel.com/comics/issue/7549/captain_america_1968_168).

Vernon, Matthew (2016): "Subversive Nostalgia, or Captain America at the Museum." In: *Journal of Popular Culture* 49, 116–135.

Wanzo, Rebecca (2009): "Wearing Hero-Face: Black Citizens and Melancholic Patriotism in *Truth: Red, White, and Black*." In: *Journal of Popular Culture* 42, 339–362.

Williams, Raymond (1977): *Marxism and Literature*. Oxford: Oxford University Press.

Wolfman, Marv/Pérez, George ([1985] 2000): *Crisis on Infinite Earths*. New York: DC Comics.

Wright, Bradford M. (2001): *Comic Book Nation: The Transformation of Youth Culture in America*. Baltimore: Johns Hopkins University Press.

List of Figures

5.1: David Vetter featured in "First Grader in a Bubble," *Buddy's Weekly Reader*, January 1979

5.2: David Vetter with his parents, sister, and family dog. Photograph archived in the David Vetter Collection (1971–1986): Box 9 (David Vetter and Family, 1976–1983). Courtesy of Archives Center, National Museum of American History, Smithsonian Institution, Washington, DC

6.1: The incubated Sporometer

6.2: The completed protocol form

6.3 & 6.4: Exploring the old foundry's former archive. Photographs by Christoph Schemann

10.1: Mapping the night sky. *Singularity 7* (Templesmith [2004] 2011, #1: 3)

10.2: Moment-to-moment or aspect-to-aspect transition? *Singularity 7* (Templesmith [2004] 2011, #1: 6)

10.3: Looking straight at the beholder. *Singularity 7* (Templesmith [2004] 2011, #1: 6)

10.4: Layering with photographic images. *Singularity 7* (Templesmith [2004] 2011, #1: 9)

10.5: Christ imagery when the Singularity greets the aliens as "the Masters." *Singularity 7* (Templesmith [2004] 2011, #4: 17)

10.6: Superhero group shot. *Singularity 7* (Templesmith [2004] 2011, #1: 24)

10.7: Nanites dissolving a human. *Singularity 7* (Templesmith [2004] 2011, #1: 22)

11.1: Worlds collide in a blend of references: dinosaurs and pilgrims and spaceships, oh my! *Crisis on Infinite Earths* #5, "Worlds in Limbo" (Wolfman/Pérez [1985] 2000: 127)

11.2: CREEP reimagined as CRAP. *Captain America and the Falcon* #169 (Englehart/Friedrich/Buscema [1974] 2017: 11)

11.3: Which America? Whose America? *Captain America and the Falcon* #176 (Englehart/Friedrich/Buscema [1974] 2017: 157)

11.4: Serpent Squad drawn as racial unrest. *Captain America and the Falcon* #183 (Englehart et al. [1975] 2006: 122)

11.5: The Lincoln Memorial and its multiple continuities. *Captain America and the Falcon* #181 (Englehart et al. [1975] 2006: 82)

11.6: Drawing out the refused continuity. *Captain America and the Falcon* #181 (Englehart et al. [1975] 2006: 81)
11.7: Ozymandias reads across images, connecting points of reference. *Watchmen* (Moore/Gibbons 1987, X: 8)
11.8: Due to Ozymandias's shortsighted scheme, alternative references remain unseen and utopia becomes illegible (u-opia). *Watchmen* (Moore/Gibbons 1987, XII: 3)

Biographical Notes

Katherine Buse is a doctoral candidate in English with an emphasis in science and technology studies at the University of California, Davis. Her publication and research areas focus on the relationship between environmental science and speculative media. She is completing a dissertation on how the history of climate modeling has interacted with speculative world-building in science fiction literature, cinema, and videogames.

Jordan S. Carroll is Visiting Assistant Professor in English at the University of Puget Sound. His work has appeared in *American Literature, Twentieth-Century Literature,* and *Post45*.

Jeanne Cortiel is Professor of American Studies at the University of Bayreuth. She has published on feminist science fiction, feminist religious thought, and on race/ethnicity in nineteenth-century American literature. Currently, she is exploring technoscientific risk and catastrophe in contemporary dystopian/utopian speculative fiction, with a focus on film and comics.

Joseph Dumit is Professor of Science and Technology Studies and Anthropology and Chair of Performance Studies at the University of California, Davis. His research focuses on brain imaging, pharmaceutical clinical trials, drugs and life, fascia science and movement, contact improvisation, touchy subjects, art and neuroscience, data science, capitalism and gaming, passions and justice.

Wolf-Dieter Ernst is Professor of Theatre at the University of Bayreuth. His research topics include postdramatic theatre, media art, and the history and theory of acting. He is the review editor for the journal *Forum Modernes Theater,* and his most recent book is *Psyche-Technik-Darstellung: Beiträge zur Schauspieltheorie als Wissensgeschichte* (2015), co-edited with Anja Klöck and Meike Wagner.

Christine Hanke is Professor of Digital and Audiovisual Media at the University of Bayreuth and Principal Investigator in the Cluster of Excellence 2052 "Africa Multiple: Reconfiguring African Studies." Her teaching and research focusses on media theory, epistemologies of the image, science and technology studies, postcolonial studies, data politics, and media resistance.

Matthew Hannah holds the Chair in Cultural Geography at the University of Bayreuth. His research revolves around knowledge, power, and constructions and embodied experiences of spatiality.

Jan Simon Hutta is Assistant Professor in the cultural geography working group at the University of Bayreuth. His research focuses on urban politics and peripheralization in Brazil, as well as affect, citizenship, LGBTIQ+ politics, and relations of subjectivity, movement, and space. He is the founding editor of the critical urban research journal *sub\urban: Zeitschrift für kritische Stadtforschung*.

Mark Jerng is Professor of English at University of California, Davis. He is the author of two monographs, *Racial Worldmaking: The Power of Popular Fiction* (2018) and *Claiming Others: Transracial Adoption and National Belonging* (2010), as well as numerous articles on genre and critical race studies.

Susanne Lachenicht is Professor of Early Modern History at the University of Bayreuth. She works on Europe and the Atlantic world with a special focus on diasporas, religious migrations, knowledge transfer and transformation, as well as temporalities in the early modern world.

Sylvia Mayer is Professor of American Studies at the University of Bayreuth. Her major research areas are ecocriticism and African American studies. Her publications include monographs on Toni Morrison and the environmental ethics of New England regionalist writing. Currently, she focuses on environmental risk narratives, climate change fiction, and petrofiction.

Colin Milburn is Gary Snyder Chair in Science and the Humanities and Professor of Science and Technology Studies, English, and Cinema and Digital Media at the University of California, Davis. His books include *Nanovision: Engineering the Future* (2008), *Mondo Nano: Fun and Games in the World of Digital Matter* (2015), and *Respawn: Gamers, Hackers, and Technogenic Life* (2018).

Felix Raczkowski is Assistant Professor in the Department of Media Studies at the University of Bayreuth. His PhD thesis investigated the instrumentalization of digital games and play, focusing on the historical precursors of gamification and serious games. Among his research interests are game studies, media history, media aesthetics, media in working environments, fakes in digital environments, and motivational media.

Christoph Schemann is a research associate in the cultural geography working group at the University of Bayreuth. He studied sociology, cultural anthropology, and human geography in Frankfurt and Bayreuth, and he is chiefly concerned with topics of biopolitics, multispecies studies, and more-than-human geographies. He is currently continuing his research on socio-material spores of contamination in a PhD project.

Melissa Wills is a doctoral candidate in English at the University of California, Davis. Her research examines how conceptions of microbial life are changing in response to contemporary microbiome science, as evidenced in scientific discourse, science fiction, and popular science writing. Her work has appeared in *Games and Culture* and *Philosophy, Theory, and Practice in Biology*.

Cultural Studies

Elisa Ganivet
Border Wall Aesthetics
Artworks in Border Spaces

2019, 250 p., hardcover, ill.
79,99 € (DE), 978-3-8376-4777-8
E-Book: 79,99 € (DE), ISBN 978-3-8394-4777-2

Andreas Sudmann (ed.)
The Democratization of Artificial Intelligence
Net Politics in the Era of Learning Algorithms

2019, 334 p., pb., col. ill.
49,99 € (DE), 978-3-8376-4719-8
E-Book: free available, ISBN 978-3-8394-4719-2

Jocelyne Porcher, Jean Estebanez (eds.)
Animal Labor
A New Perspective on Human-Animal Relations

2019, 182 p., hardcover
99,99 € (DE), 978-3-8376-4364-0
E-Book: 99,99 € (DE), ISBN 978-3-8394-4364-4

All print, e-book and open access versions of the titles in our list are available in our online shop www.transcript-verlag.de/en!

Cultural Studies

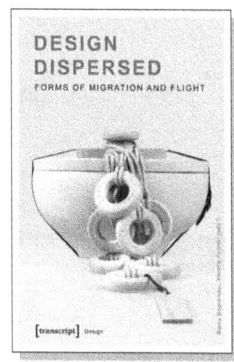

Burcu Dogramaci, Kerstin Pinther (eds.)
Design Dispersed
Forms of Migration and Flight

2019, 274 p., pb., col. ill.
34,99 € (DE), 978-3-8376-4705-1
E-Book: 34,99 € (DE), ISBN 978-3-8394-4705-5

Pál Kelemen, Nicolas Pethes (eds.)
Philology in the Making
Analog/Digital Cultures of Scholarly Writing and Reading

2019, 316 p., pb., ill.
34,99 € (DE), 978-3-8376-4770-9
E-Book: 34,99 € (DE), ISBN 978-3-8394-4770-3

Pablo Abend, Annika Richterich,
Mathias Fuchs, Ramón Reichert, Karin Wenz (eds.)
Digital Culture & Society (DCS)
Vol. 5, Issue 1/2019 –
Inequalities and Divides in Digital Cultures

2019, 212 p., pb., ill.
29,99 € (DE), 978-3-8376-4478-4
E-Book: 29,99 € (DE), ISBN 978-3-8394-4478-8

All print, e-book and open access versions of the titles in our list
are available in our online shop www.transcript-verlag.de/en!

GPSR Authorized Representative: Easy Access System Europe, Mustamäe tee
50, 10621 Tallinn, Estonia, gpsr.requests@easproject.com

www.ingramcontent.com/pod-product-compliance
Lightning Source LLC
Chambersburg PA
CBHW051531020426
42333CB00016B/1878